OXFORD
UNIVERSITY PRESS

fourth edition

English File

Advanced

Student's Book

WITH ONLINE PRACTICE

Christina Latham-Koenig
Clive Oxenden
Jerry Lambert
Kate Chomacki

Paul Seligson and Clive Oxenden
are the original co-authors of
English File 1 and *English File 2*

Contents

Course overview

English File

fourth edition

Welcome to **English File fourth edition**. This is how to use the Student's Book, Online Practice, and the Workbook in and out of class.

Student's Book

All the language and skills you need to improve your English, with Grammar, Vocabulary, Pronunciation, and skills work in every File. Also available as an eBook.

Use your Student's Book in class with your teacher.

Workbook

Grammar, Vocabulary, and Pronunciation practice for every lesson.

Use your Workbook for homework or for self-study to practise language and to check your progress.

Go to **englishfileonline.com** and use the code on your Access Card to log into the Online Practice.

ACTIVITIES AUDIO VIDEO RESOURCES

ONLINE

LOOK AGAIN

- Review the language from every lesson.
- Watch the videos and listen to all the class audio as many times as you like.

PRACTICE

- Improve your skills with extra Reading, Writing, Listening, and Speaking practice.
- Use the interactive video to practise Colloquial English.

CHECK YOUR PROGRESS

- Test yourself on the language from the File and get instant feedback.
- Try an extra Challenge.

SOUND BANK

- Use the Sound Bank videos to practise and improve your pronunciation of English sounds.

Online Practice

Look again at Student's Book language you want to review or that you missed in class, do extra *Practice* activities, and *Check your progress* on what you've learnt so far.

Use the Online Practice to learn outside the classroom and get instant feedback on your progress.

englishfileonline.com

Happy families are all alike; every unhappy family is unhappy in its own way.
From Anna Karenina by Leo Tolstoy, Russian author

G *have*: lexical and grammatical uses **V** personality **P** using a dictionary

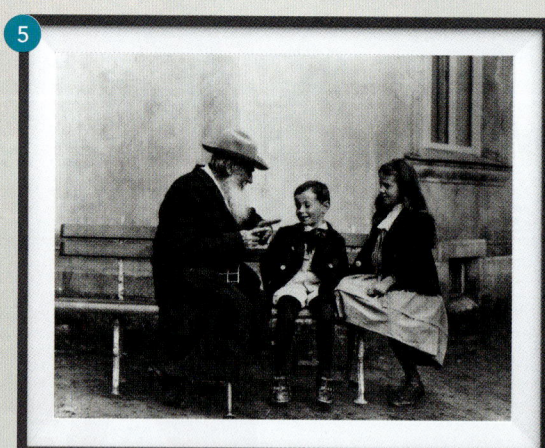

1 LISTENING

a Look at some photos of 19th- and 20th-century families from an exhibition. They show members of a royal family, two statesmen, a writer, a scientist, and an artist. Discuss the questions with a partner, giving your reasons.

1 Do you recognize or know anything about any of the people?
2 What family relationships do you think are shown?
3 Which do you think are the oldest and the most recent photos?

b 🔊 1.2 Listen to an audio guide from the exhibition. For each photo, write:

- the name and occupation of the most famous person in the photo.
- what relation to them the other people are.
- the year it was taken.

How many answers in **a** did you get right?

c Listen again and answer the questions with the name of one or more people in the photos.

Who...?

1 had a difficult relationship
2 had a very close relationship
3 died a violent death
4 is still alive today
5 was thought to be alive for many years after his / her death

d Look at some phrases from the audio guide. With a partner, say who they refer to and explain what the **bold** collocations mean.

1 the story of her survival was **conclusively disproved**
2 as so many of this **ill-fated family**
3 she wrote **a damning description** of him
4 their **shared beliefs** in national independence and education
5 she was **strongly opposed** to many of his views
6 he left home…**in the dead of night**
7 she **sought refuge** with her beloved brother

e Which photo draws you in the most? Why?

2 SPEAKING

a Work in small groups. Answer the questions.

- Do you have many old family photos? Are any of them framed or displayed? What's the oldest family photo that you've seen?
- Who is your oldest living relative? How much contact do you have with him / her?
- Who are you closest to in your family? Why do you get on well? Is there anyone you don't get on with?
- Who are you most like in your family? Are there any family traits (appearance or personality) that members of your family share?

b You're going to discuss the statements below. First, decide individually what you think about each one. Think of reasons and examples to support your opinion.

Parents should never try to be their children's friends.

People who are very dedicated to their work rarely manage to have a happy family life.

When children are young, it's better for one parent not to work and to look after them.

The only person who should be allowed to criticize your family is you, not your partner or friends.

Marrying very young almost inevitably ends badly.

You have to love your family, but you don't have to like them.

🔍 **Half-agreeing and politely disagreeing**
When you're sharing opinions, especially with people you don't know very well, and you don't entirely agree with them, it's more polite to use expressions of half-agreeing or politely disagreeing to introduce your point of view.

Half-agreeing	Politely disagreeing
I see what you mean, but…	*I'm not sure I agree with you.*
I agree up to a point, but…	*I don't really think that's right.*
I agree in theory, but…	

c 🔊 **1.3** Listen to five short conversations which include the expressions from the information box. Focus on the intonation in the expressions.

d 🔊 **1.4** Listen again and repeat the expressions, copying the intonation.

e Work in your groups and discuss the statements in **b**. If you half-agree or disagree, use expressions from the box.

3 GRAMMAR *have*: lexical and grammatical uses

a With a partner, look at all the sentences in groups 1–4. Answer the two questions for each group.

- Are all the options possible?
- Is there any difference in meaning or register?

1 **I haven't got**
  I don't have   any siblings.
  I haven't

2 **I've been making**
  I've made   loads of food for a family dinner tonight.

3 **Have** we **got to**
  Do we **have to**   dress up for the party, or is it just family?

4 **I've had** some lovely photos **taken**
  I've taken some lovely photos   of the children.

b 🅖 **p.142 Grammar Bank 1A**

c With a partner, say if each of the sentences below is true for you or not and why.

- I'm the most competitive person in my family. Whenever I play a sport or game, I always have to win.
- When someone in my family annoys me, I always keep quiet rather than having it out with them.
- I've been arguing a lot with my family recently.
- I don't mind having my photo taken, but I'd hate to have my portrait painted.
- I've got a lot of 'friends' on social media, but I only have a few close friends that I see regularly face-to-face.
- I've got to try to get out more. I spend too much time at home.
- I have a few possessions that are really important to me and that I would hate to lose.
- I've never wanted to leave home. I'm happy living with my parents.

4 VOCABULARY personality

a Look at the adjectives from the list that describe personality. Underline three that you think would make someone a good parent, and circle three that would make them a good partner.

affectionate ambitious assertive bossy
honest loyal mature moody open-minded
outgoing patient reliable sensitive stubborn

b Compare with a partner. Then decide together which adjectives might make someone a difficult parent or partner.

c **V** p.162 **Vocabulary Bank** Personality

5 PRONUNCIATION using a dictionary

> **determined** *adj*
>
> BrE /dɪˈtɜːmɪnd/ ◀); NAmE /dɪˈtɜːrmɪnd/ ◀)
>
> (of people) someone who, having made a decision, will not let anyone prevent them from carrying it out

a ◀ 1.8 Look at the dictionary entry for *determined*. Focus on the phonetics. Which syllable is stressed? What difference is there between the two pronunciations? Listen and check.

b Under<u>line</u> the stressed syllable in the words below.

1 con|sci|en|tious   5 spon|ta|ne|ous
2 re|source|ful   6 straight|for|ward
3 sar|cas|tic   7 stea|dy
4 tho|rough   8 self-su|ffi|cient

c What vowel sound do the stressed syllables have? Choose from the sound pictures below.

d ◀ 1.9 Listen and check.

e Look at the phonetics for some more adjectives of personality. With a partner, work out how they're pronounced, and say how they're spelled and what they mean. Then check with a dictionary.

1 /ˈæŋkʃəs/   3 /ˈnəʊzi/   5 /ˈstɪndʒi/
2 /ˈlaɪvli/   4 /ˈsəʊʃəbl/

f What features do you find most useful in the dictionary you use?

6 READING & SPEAKING

a To what extent do you think the following are good ways of predicting personality types?

- online quizzes
- personality tests
- your handwriting
- your star sign

b You're going to do a well-known personality test. Before you start, look at the painting for 30 seconds. Write what you see. You'll need this when you do the test.

c **Language in context** Look at the test *What's your personality?* Read the questions and possible answers. With a partner, try to work out the meaning of the highlighted phrasal verbs and idioms, but don't look them up yet.

d Now look them up in a dictionary and check your answers.

> 🔍 **Looking up phrasal verbs and idioms in a dictionary**
>
> **Phrasal verbs** PHR V
>
> Phrasal verbs are listed in alphabetical order after the entry for the verbs.
>
> For phrasal verbs with an object, the object (sb or sth) is shown **between** the two parts, e.g. *put* **sth** *off*. This means the phrasal verb is separable, and the object can go between the verb and the particle **or** after the particle. If the object is shown after the particle, e.g. *look for* **sth**, it means the verb and the particle cannot be separated.
>
> **Idioms** IDM
>
> You can usually find the definition of an idiom under one of its 'main' words (nouns, verbs, adverbs, or adjectives, but **NOT** prepositions and articles), e.g. the definition of *catch your eye* will be given under *catch* or *eye*.
>
> After some very common verbs, e.g. *be* and *get*, and adjectives, e.g. *good* and *bad*, the idioms are usually under the entries for the next 'main' word, e.g. *be a good sport* comes under *sport*.

e Do the test. For each question, decide which answer best describes you and circle a–d.

WHAT'S *your* PERSONALITY?

A PLANNER *or* SPONTANEOUS

1 **Are you…?**
   a a perfectionist who hates leaving things unfinished
   b someone who hates being under pressure and tends to overprepare
   c a bit disorganized and forgetful
   d someone who puts things off until the last minute

2 **Imagine you have bought a piece of furniture that requires assembly (e.g. a wardrobe or a cupboard). Which of these are you more likely to do?**
   a Check that you have all the items and the tools you need before you start.
   b Carefully read the instructions and follow them to the letter.
   c Quickly read through the instructions to get the basic idea of what you have to do.
   d Start assembling it right away. Check the instructions only if you get stuck.

3 **Before you go on holiday, which of these do you do?**
   a Plan every detail of your holiday.
   b Put together a rough itinerary, but make sure you leave yourself plenty of free time.
   c Get an idea of what kinds of things you can do, but not make a decision until you get there.
   d Book the holiday at the last minute and plan hardly anything in advance.

B FACTS *or* IDEAS

4 **Which option best describes what you wrote about the painting in b on page 8?**
   a It's basically a list of what appears in the painting.
   b It tells the story of what's happening in the painting.
   c It tries to explain what the painting means.
   d It's a lot of ideas that the painting made you think of.

5 **You need to give a friend directions to your house in the country. Do you…?**
   a write a list of detailed directions
   b give them the postcode and expect them to use a satnav
   c give rough directions
   d draw a simple map showing only the basic directions

6 **When you go shopping at the supermarket, do you…?**
   a always go down the same aisles in the same order
   b carefully check prices and compare products
   c buy whatever catches your eye
   d go round a different way each time, according to what you want to buy

C HEAD *or* HEART

7 **If an argument starts when you are with friends, do you…?**
   a face it head-on and say what you think
   b try to find a solution yourself
   c try to keep everyone happy
   d do anything to avoid hurting people's feelings

8 **Imagine you had the choice between two flats to rent. Would you…?**
   a write what your ideal flat would be like and then see which one was the most similar
   b make a list of the pros and cons of each one
   c just go with your gut feeling
   d consider carefully how each flat would suit the other people living with you

9 **Imagine a friend of yours started going out with someone new, and they asked you for your opinion. If you really didn't like the person, would you…?**
   a tell them exactly what you thought
   b be honest, but as tactful as possible
   c try to avoid answering the question directly
   d tell a white lie

D INTROVERT *or* EXTROVERT

10 **You are out with a group of friends. Do you…?**
   a say hardly anything
   b say a little less than most people
   c talk a lot
   d do nearly all the talking

11 **When you meet a new group of people, do you…?**
   a try to stay with people you already know
   b have to think hard about how to keep the conversation going
   c try to get to know as many people as possible
   d just enjoy yourself

12 **If your phone rings while you are in the middle of something, do you…?**
   a ignore it and carry on with what you're doing
   b answer it quickly, but say you'll call back
   c have a conversation, but make sure you keep it short
   d welcome the interruption and enjoy a nice long chat

Adapted from the BBC website

f Now find out which type you are for each section.

A more a and b = PLANNER	C more a and b = HEAD
more c and d = SPONTANEOUS	more c and d = HEART
B more a and b = FACTS	D more a and b = INTROVERT
more c and d = IDEAS	more c and d = EXTROVERT

g **Communication** What's your personality? p.106 Find out which personality you have and read the description. Compare with a partner. How accurate were the descriptions of your personalities?

Go online to review the lesson

> Whenever you are asked if you can do a job, tell 'em, 'Certainly I can'. Then get busy and find out how to do it.
> *Theodore Roosevelt, US President 1901–1909*

G discourse markers (1): linkers **V** work **P** the rhythm of English

1   VOCABULARY work

a Look at some adjectives which are often used to describe jobs. With a partner, brainstorm three jobs which could be described with each of the adjectives.

challenging   repetitive   rewarding

b **V** p.163 **Vocabulary Bank** Work

c What qualities and features are important to you in a job?

2   READING & LISTENING

a Look at the title of the article and the five photos of Emma Rosen. What job do you think she's doing in each photo?

b Read the article once and check your answers to **a**. Then answer the questions with a partner.

1 What qualification did Emma need for her job as a civil servant?
2 What did she see as the pros and cons of the job?
3 How did she prepare for her year trying out different jobs?
4 Did you want to do any of the jobs Emma mentions when you were growing up?

25 jobs before she was 25

Emma Rosen had one of the best, most sought-after graduate jobs in the country, in the civil service. 20,000 people apply, but fewer than 1,000 are offered jobs. But it turned out that she didn't like commuting and she didn't like sitting at a desk all day, and she struggled to see how what she was doing would make much difference to anything. 'I thought, 'Get over it, you're being a snowflake millennial,' she says. 'I had a job for life. I thought, 'I'm so lucky to be here, I can't believe I'm not enjoying it. What's wrong with me? Why am I so ungrateful and selfish?''

Emma could have gone to work every day and complained about her job until she reached retirement age. Instead, she decided to find out what made her happy, what her skills were, and what sort of career would use them. She wrote a bucket list of the jobs she had wanted to do since childhood and set about getting two-week placements in all of them, over the course of a year. She was 24 years old, and before her 25th birthday she

wanted to have tried out at least 25 different jobs. She spent the months before she resigned from the civil service saving up her salary to cover the cost of her year off, and spent all her free time setting up the different jobs.

'There was archaeology in Transylvania, property development for a company in London, alpaca farming in Cornwall, wedding photography, travel writing, interior design, journalism, landscape gardening, marketing, TV production, publishing – all things that I thought I might want to do.'

Glossary

snowflake /ˈsnəʊfleɪk/ (informal, disapproving) a person who is too sensitive to criticism and easily upset

millennial /mɪˈleniəl/ a person who became an adult in the early 21st century

bucket list /ˈbʌkɪt lɪst/ a list of things people want to do in their lifetime, e.g. places they'd like to travel to

Adapted from The Times

c 🔊 **1.13** You're going to listen to an interview with Emma. Which of the jobs she mentions in the last paragraph of the article do you think she liked the most / the least? Listen to Part 1 and check.

> **Glossary**
> **networking** trying to meet and talk to other people who may be useful to you in your work
> **cold-calling** telephoning somebody that you do not know, in order to sell them something or get them to do something for you
> **shear** /ʃɪə/ cut the wool off an animal, e.g. a sheep
> **typo** /ˈtaɪpəʊ/ a small mistake in a text

d With a partner, look at the points below and see if you can remember any of the information from Emma's answers. Then listen again and make notes about:

1 how she got the jobs.
2 what she could find out about a job in two weeks.
3 why it didn't matter that she didn't have qualifications for the jobs.
4 what the job she liked best involved.
5 what she didn't like about her least favourite job.

e 🔊 **1.14** Now listen to Part 2. Choose a, b, or c.

1 One thing Emma learned from the experience was that _____.
   a she enjoyed things that she was good at
   b she discovered what her ideal job was
   c she might end up doing many different jobs

2 She thinks that in the future _____.
   a young people will still be doing 9–5 jobs
   b people will no longer retire in their 60s
   c people will need many more technical skills

3 One thing she thinks young people need to learn is how to _____ that might help them in their career.
   a form relationships
   b choose subjects
   c get qualifications

4 At the moment Emma _____.
   a only works as a writer
   b teaches journalism in a public school
   c doesn't have one specific job

5 Emma believes that what jobs she does in the future may depend on _____.
   a where she decides to live
   b how old she is
   c how many children she has

f Imagine you have decided to do the same thing as Emma. Make a list of five jobs you would like to try. Then compare with a partner and explain why you chose the jobs. Do you both agree with Emma's view that a career for life no longer exists?

3 PRONUNCIATION & SPEAKING
the rhythm of English

> 🔍 **Fine-tuning your pronunciation: the rhythm of English**
> In spoken English, words with two or more syllables have one main stressed syllable. In sentences, some words have stronger stress and other words are weaker. This pattern of strong and weak stress gives English its rhythm. Stressed words in a sentence are usually **content words**, e.g. nouns, verbs, adjectives, and adverbs. Unstressed words tend to be **function words** and include auxiliary verbs, prepositions, conjunctions, determiners, and possessive adjectives.

a 🔊 **1.15** Listen to some extracts from Emma's interview in **2**. Then practise saying them, trying to copy the rhythm as exactly as possible.

1 It was just enough to get a flavour of it.
2 I wasn't expected to have qualifications or to lead my own work.
3 The first half of each day was traditional farming jobs…
4 Networking was a big part of it, too.
5 But what I found out was that that's not necessarily true at all.

b Choose two people you know: one who really likes their job and one who doesn't. Think about:

- what their job is and what it involves.
- what kind of company or organization they work for, or whether they are self-employed.
- how long they have been doing the job, and what they did before.
- how they feel about their job and why.

c In small groups, describe the people in **b**. Try to use natural rhythm.

d Of the jobs that you have all described in your group, each say if there is one that…

✓ you would quite like to try.

£ you might consider trying if you needed the money.

✗ you would never do under any circumstances.

4 READING

a *The Guardian* runs a weekly series called *What I'm really thinking*, where people in different jobs or situations reveal their true feelings. Look at the titles of the three articles. What do you think each person might like and dislike about their job?

b Read the articles and check your answers to **a**. Which person, A–C,…?

1. ☐ enjoys their job the most
2. ☐ enjoys their job the least
3. ☐ doesn't have a good relationship with some of their colleagues
4. ☐ trains others as part of their job
5. ☐ struggles with the lack of sleep
6. ☐ helps people in need

c Read the articles again. With a partner, say what you think the people mean by the following phrases or sentences.

1. …it's my structure and my sanity.
2. …I challenge someone's expectations a little bit…
3. …'night receptionist' is not a good thing to put on a CV.
4. Travelling against commuter traffic is great…
5. …have random weekdays off.
6. …with almost zero opportunities to develop broader interests…

d Look at the <mark>highlighted</mark> phrases in the articles and work out their meaning from the context. Then match them to definitions 1–7.

1. _____ = managed to arrive
2. _____ = not understood the most important fact
3. _____ = do things spontaneously, without reflecting
4. _____ = defend myself
5. _____ = continue working hard without respite
6. _____ = ended a long time ago
7. _____ = reasonable, acceptable

e Were you surprised by anything the three people said?

What I'm really

A The female boxing coach

Apparently, I don't look like a boxer. I get told that a lot. I've lost count of the number of times people have exclaimed, 'What about your nose?' and 'What if you mess up your face?' They've <mark>missed the point</mark>: I'm not a model, so what does it matter if my nose isn't straight? And anyway, boxing means more to me than that: it's my structure and my sanity. Cheaper than therapy, that's what we say. Injuries are part of the game, but I've been lucky so far.

As the only girl in my gym, I'm aware that I'm a novelty. I've always been a tomboy, though, so it doesn't bother me to train with the blokes. Some men don't like to box with a woman, and that's <mark>fair enough</mark>. But mostly they get used to it.

When I'm not in the mood and consider giving up, I think about the children I help teach. There are a couple of young girls coming up who are really good and I want to be an example. Every time I <mark>hold my own</mark> in the ring, I challenge someone's expectations a little bit, and I'm proud of myself for that.

B The night receptionist

People assume I get bored, but I enjoy the solitude. I like the hourly walks through the quiet corridors and listening to the patter of the rain on the windows while enjoying a cup of tea. I enjoy finishing a good book or watching the birds in the car park feeding on the muffins I put out yesterday.

The tiredness is the hardest. Sometimes I have a good routine and my sleep is not affected. Other times, I walk into doors, zombie-like, and occasionally I've been surprised to find that I've actually <mark>made it</mark> home. My husband tells me I should find a new job, and I have been applying for some since I began working here, but 'night receptionist' is not a good thing to put on a CV.

I'm good with people; I just don't like a lot of them. But though my job often perpetuates this dislike, I am compassionate towards those in need. I <mark>never think twice</mark> about letting someone in from the cold, or giving away a free room if it is a genuine cause. But if the intercom goes off at 2 a.m. and I see a couple who can hardly stand, I'll probably say the hotel is full, even when it isn't, especially if I've just made a tea.

thinking

C The orchestral musician

I have done this for so long, my mind is free to wander while I play. The thrill of this being a fresh challenge has long gone: I just want to get to the end of the concert and go home. Travelling against commuter traffic is great, but it's also a reminder that most people are on their way to relax and I'm only just getting started.

We're not all friends. The person on my right had an affair with the person on my left, and the ex sits close by. People fraternize exclusively according to the instrument they play, especially on tour.

Late nights and out-of-town work mean I often get home after midnight, but I sleep only around six hours or I'll miss the family in the only half-hour we have together. I work most weekends and holidays, then have random weekdays off. The freelance pay structure and low fees keep my nose to the grindstone, with almost zero opportunities to develop broader interests or a social life outside.

Adapted from The Guardian

5 GRAMMAR discourse markers (1): linkers

a Read some extracts from other *What I'm really thinking* articles. Match them to the jobs from the list. What point is each person making about their job?

☐ A&E doctor   ☐ dental hygienist   ☐ fashion stylist
☐ political advisor   ☐ university lecturer   ☐ 999 operator

1 Although it is not my place to judge, I get frustrated sometimes. The man who rang because his toothpaste was burning his mouth; the mother whose baby was afraid of a fly.

2 When you are really disengaged and disconnected, I see hands reach for phones in bags. Sometimes you even pass notes and giggle. Yet I also see you when you laugh at my jokes.

3 I'm exhausted. It is demoralizing to start a shift only to find that the department already has a four-hour wait to see someone. There are people lining the corridors, and there is nowhere to take new patients, and consequently the wait gets longer.

4 One supermodel arrived at a shoot three hours late, then spent another couple of hours looking at Twitter while everyone waited for her. Then she was a nightmare. She was a world-class bully, and said she had never met anyone as rude as me. However, I fought back and she was lovely after that – though she made me sign a non-disclosure agreement not to talk about the shoot.

5 I'm only here in order to help get you elected. But why you? Yes, I know, you won the party's nomination, but did they realize that, despite your firm handshake and boyish charm, you know as much about corporate tax policy as I know about astrophysics?

6 I know it's not the most pleasant experience, so I try to alleviate the worry…

b With a partner, write the highlighted linkers in the correct column.

result	reason	purpose	contrast
			Although

c 🄖 p.143 Grammar Bank 1B

d 🔊 1.16 Listen and write the first halves of eight sentences. Compare with a partner, and then decide together how you think the sentences might continue.

e 🔊 1.17 Now listen and complete the sentences from d. Are they similar to what you predicted?

6 WRITING

🄦 p.116 Writing A job application Analyse a model email applying for a job, and write a covering email.

Go online to review the lesson

Colloquial English
Talking about...work and family

1 ▶ THE INTERVIEW Part 1

a Read the biographical information about Eliza Carthy. Have you ever heard any English, Scottish, or Irish folk music?

> **Eliza Carthy** is an English folk musician known both for singing and playing the violin. She is the daughter of singer / guitarist Martin Carthy and singer Norma Waterson, who are also English folk musicians. In addition to her solo work, she has played and sung with several groups, including as lead vocalist with Blue Murder. She has been nominated twice for the Mercury Music Prize for UK album of the year, has won eight BBC Folk Awards, and has also been given an MBE for services to folk music. When she released an album of collaborations with her mother, entitled *Gift*, a BBC reviewer wrote: 'The gift in question here...is a handling of talent from generation to generation.'

b Watch Part 1 of the interview. What is Eliza's overwhelming memory of her childhood?

c Now watch again. What does Eliza say about...?

1 her father in the 50s and 60s
2 The Watersons
3 her mother's grandmother
4 her mother's uncle and father
5 *The Spinning Wheel*
6 the farm where she was brought up
7 her parents' friends

d Do you think Eliza's upbringing sounds like it was fun or quite hard? Why?

> **Glossary**
> **Bob Dylan** (b.1941) an American singer-songwriter, who has influenced popular music and culture for more than five decades
> **Paul Simon** (b.1941) an American singer-songwriter, at one time half of the duo Simon and Garfunkel
> **Hull** /hʌl/ a city in Yorkshire, England
> **travellers / gypsies** people who traditionally travel around and live in caravans
> **banjo** a musical instrument like a guitar, with a long neck, a round body, and four or more strings
> **The Spinning Wheel** an Irish ballad written in the mid-1800s

▶ Part 2

a Now watch Part 2. What do you think Eliza Carthy was like as a child? What do you find out about her as a mother?

b Watch again and answer the questions.

1 Did Eliza originally want to become a musician?
2 Why did her mother retire?
3 How old was she at her first public performance?
4 How much did she sing during the concert?
5 How has she reorganized her life because of having her own children?
6 What does she feel she's lacking at the moment?

c What do you think of Eliza's work-life balance?

> **Glossary**
> **the Fylde** /faɪld/ an area in western Lancashire, England
> **Fleetwood** a town in the Fylde
> **the Marine Hall** a venue in Fleetwood

▶ Part 3

a Now watch Part 3. How has Eliza Carthy's family influenced her approach to music?

b Watch again. Mark the sentences **T** (true) or **F** (false). Correct the **F** sentences.

1 Eliza thinks the reason she doesn't like working alone is because of being brought up surrounded by people.
2 At the moment she has a 30-piece band.
3 Her father understands that working with family members is different.
4 Her father was a blood relation in the group The Watersons.
5 Eliza's daughter Florence plays three musical instruments and also sings well.
6 She thinks there's a close link between foreign languages and singing.
7 Her younger daughter Isabella is not yet interested in music.
8 She would rather her children didn't become touring musicians.

c Did you ever want to have the same job as your parents? Would you like to work with any members of your family? Why (not)?

> **Glossary**
> **Twinkle, Twinkle** a well-known children's song (*Twinkle, twinkle, little star, How I wonder what you are...*)

2 ▶ LOOKING AT LANGUAGE

> 🔍 **Discourse markers**
> Eliza Carthy uses several discourse markers when
> she speaks, that is, adverbs (e.g. *so*, *anyway*) or
> adverbial expressions (e.g. *in fact*, *after all*) which
> connect and organize language, and help you to
> follow what she is saying.

a Watch some extracts from the interview and
complete the gaps with one or two words.

1 '…and they were also instrumental in the beginning
of the 60s folk revival, the formation of the folk
clubs, and the, the beginning of, _____, the
professional music scene that I work on now.'

2 **Interviewer** 'And were your parents both from
musical families?'
Eliza 'Um, _____, both sides of my family are
musical…'

3 'My mum retired in 1966–65 / 66 from professional
touring to raise me. _____ _____, the road
is a difficult place…'

4 'But yes, _____ I just – the first song they started
up singing, tugged on his leg…'

5 **Interviewer** 'Has having children yourself changed
your approach to your career?'
Eliza 'Er, yes, _____ a _____. Yes, _____
a _____, it has.'

6 '…The Watersons was a brother and two sisters, and
he joined that, and _____ _____ he was
married to my mum, but he wasn't related to her.'

7 'And Isabella, my youngest as well, she's really, she's
really showing interest in it and I love it when they do
that. _____ _____ whether or not I'd want
them to be touring musicians…'

8 'But, you know, I think the – I think the world is changing
_____, I don't know how many touring musicians
there are going to be in the world in 20 years…'

b How do the discourse markers affect the meaning
of what Eliza says in each extract?

3 ▶ THE CONVERSATION

a Watch the conversation. Who…?

1 worked for their family business
2 knows someone who worked for their family business
3 doesn't mention their own family

b Watch again. Which of these advantages and
disadvantages of working in a family business are
mentioned, and by whom?

1 ☐ If your parents run a business, it can be very
convenient to work for them.
2 ☐ It can be a problem to take a break from work.
3 ☐ If the business is successful, all the money stays in
the family.
4 ☐ It can be difficult to achieve a good work-life balance.
5 ☐ Sometimes family members can be taken
advantage of.
6 ☐ It's impossible to maintain good relations with
your family.
7 ☐ It makes you understand how difficult it is to run a
business.

c Do you think that on the whole it's a positive thing
to work for a family business?

d Watch an extract where Joanne talks at the same
time as Alice. Complete what Joanne says. What is
Joanne's intention?

> **Alice** …my parents would go off to work and I
> knew that was a place that they went off…
> **Joanne** [1]_____.
> **Alice** …to make money…but I didn't see it, so I –
> **Joanne** I think that's really [2]_____, to appreciate
> it. Yes, [3]_____.
> **Alice** It makes you appreciate it, it more and you
> see the hard work and the stresses…
> **Joanne** [4]_____.
> **Alice** …of running a business.
> **Joanne** So it could be an [5]_____…
> **Alice** Definitely.
> **Joanne** …one [6]_____, rather than an exploitative
> situation.

e Now have a conversation in groups of three.
Discuss the statements.

1 It's much easier for the children of successful parents
to be successful themselves.
2 It's not possible to both have a successful career and
be a successful parent.

⊙ **Go online** to watch the video, review the lesson, and check your progress

Do you remember…?

G the past: habitual events and specific incidents   **V** word building: abstract nouns   **P** word stress with suffixes

1 READING

a Imagine that you were going to write your autobiography. What periods or specific incidents from your childhood would you definitely include?

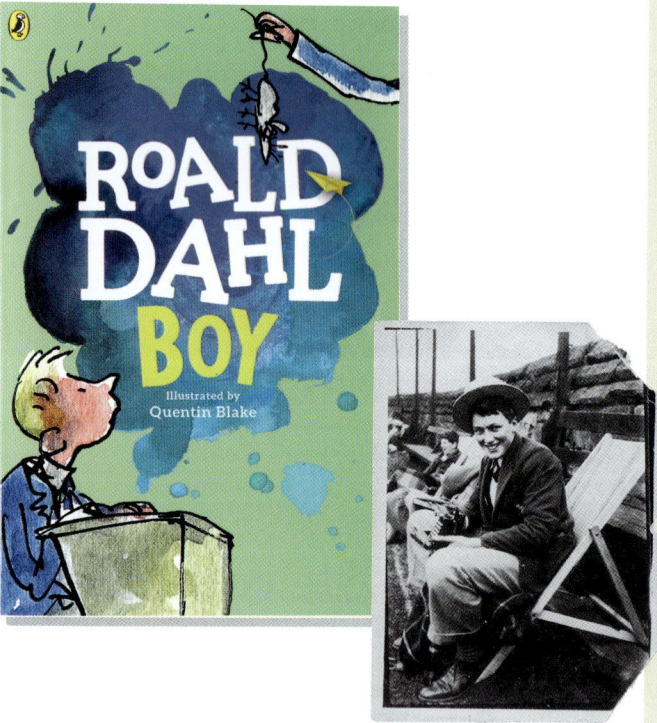

b Read Part 1 of an extract from *Boy*, the autobiography of author Roald Dahl. Answer the questions with a partner.

1 Why did the chocolate bars have numbers stamped underneath them?
2 What do you think was the point of the 'control' bar?
3 What exactly did the boys have to do?
4 Why was it clever of Cadbury's to use the boys?
5 How did the boys behave when they were sampling the products?

c Now do the same for Part 2.

1 How did Roald Dahl imagine the 'inventing room' to be?
2 What did he imagine himself doing in his recurring dream?
3 How did he imagine Mr Cadbury reacting to his invention?
4 How did the testing of the chocolate bars influence Dahl in his later life?

PART 1

Every now and again, a plain grey cardboard box was dished out to each boy in our House, and this, believe it or not, was a present from the great chocolate manufacturers, Cadbury. Inside the box there were twelve bars of chocolate, all of different shapes, all with different fillings, and all with numbers from one to twelve stamped on the chocolate underneath. Eleven of these bars were new inventions from the factory. The twelfth was the 'control' bar, one that we all knew well, usually a Cadbury's Coffee Cream bar. Also in the box was a sheet of paper with the numbers one to twelve on it as well as two blank columns, one for giving marks to each chocolate from nought to ten, and the other for comments.

All we were required to do in return for this splendid gift was to taste very carefully each bar of chocolate, give it marks, and make an intelligent comment on why we liked or disliked it.

It was a clever stunt. Cadbury's were using some of the greatest chocolate-bar experts in the world to test out their new inventions. We were of a sensible age, between thirteen and eighteen, and we knew intimately every chocolate bar in existence, from the Milk Flake to the Lemon Marshmallow. Quite obviously our opinions on anything new would be valuable. All of us entered into this game with great gusto, sitting in our studies and nibbling each bar with the air of connoisseurs, giving our marks and making our comments. 'Too subtle for the common palate' was one note that I remember writing down.

d 🔊 **2.1 Language in context** Roald Dahl achieves a more dramatic effect in Part 2 through his choice of language. Look at the dramatic verbs and listen to Part 2 as an extract from an audio book. Match the verbs to their synonyms 1–7.

picture	bubbling away	concocting	grab	rushing	leap	slap

1 _____ = jump
2 _____ = take quickly (in one's hand)
3 _____ = creating by mixing together
4 _____ = boiling continuously
5 _____ = running quickly
6 _____ = hit (with the hand)
7 _____ = imagine

PART 2

For me, the importance of all this was that I began to realize that the large chocolate companies actually did possess inventing rooms and they took their inventing very seriously. <mark>I used to picture</mark> a long white room like a laboratory with pots of chocolate and fudge and all sorts of other delicious fillings bubbling away on the stoves, while men and women in white coats moved between the bubbling pots, tasting and mixing and concocting their wonderful new inventions. <mark>I used to imagine</mark> myself working in one of these labs and suddenly <mark>I would come up with</mark> something so unbearably delicious that <mark>I would grab</mark> it in my hand and go rushing out of the lab and along the corridor and right into the offices of the great Mr Cadbury himself. 'I've got it, Sir' I would shout, putting the chocolate in front of him. 'It's fantastic! It's fabulous! It's marvellous! It's irresistible!'

Slowly, the great man would pick up my newly-invented chocolate and he would take a small bite. He would roll it round his mouth. Then all at once, he would leap up from his chair, crying, 'You've got it! You've done it! It's a miracle!' He would slap me on the back and shout, 'We'll sell it by the million! We'll sweep the world with this one! How on earth did you do it? Your salary is doubled.'

It was lovely dreaming those dreams, and I have no doubt at all that thirty-five years later, <mark>when I was looking for</mark> a plot for my second book for children, <mark>I remembered</mark> those little cardboard boxes and the newly invented chocolates inside them, and <mark>I began</mark> to write a book called *Charlie and the Chocolate Factory*.

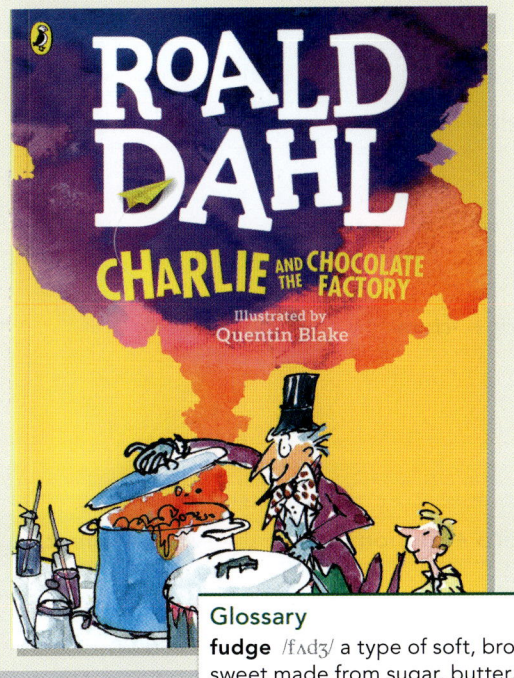

Abridged from Boy by Roald Dahl

> **Glossary**
> **fudge** /fʌdʒ/ a type of soft, brown sweet made from sugar, butter, and milk

e What kind of child do you get the impression that Roald Dahl was? When you were a child, what did you use to dream of doing?

2 GRAMMAR the past: habitual events and specific incidents

a Look at the <mark>highlighted</mark> verbs in Part 2 of the extract from *Boy*. Which ones describe…?

1 specific incidents in the past
2 repeated or habitual actions in the past

b What other verb forms do we use in these contexts?

c 🄖 p.144 Grammar Bank 2A

3 SPEAKING

a 🔊 2.2 Listen to six people starting to tell a story about their childhood. What different expressions do they use to say approximately how old they were at the time?

b With a partner, choose two of the topics below and talk about things you habitually did or felt in your childhood.

> (*When I was little, I used to be terrified of the dark, and I'd always sleep with the light on…*

things I used to be afraid of
my primary school
places we would go to for family holidays
food and drink I used to love (or hate)
Christmas or a special celebration
being ill
toys and games I used to love
birthdays
nightmares I used to have

c Now take turns to choose one of the topics and talk about a specific incident from your childhood.

> (*I remember the time when we went on our first family holiday abroad…*

4 WRITING

🄦 p.118 Writing An article Analyse an article about how children's lives have changed over the last 50 years, and write an article.

5 LISTENING & SPEAKING

a 🔊 **2.3** Listen to Part 1 of a radio programme about early childhood memories. Answer the questions for each speaker 1–3.

- How old was he / she?
- What event was his / her memory of?
- What emotion(s) did he / she feel?

b Look at some questions you're going to hear in Part 2 of the programme, an interview about research on first memories. Discuss them with a partner.

1 At what age do first memories generally occur?
2 Why can't we remember things before that age?
3 What are first memories normally about?
4 Why might some people's first memories be unreliable?

c 🔊 **2.4** Now listen to Part 2 and check your answers to **b**. Do you think the memories in **a** are reliable? Why?

d Listen again. Why does the presenter mention these things?

1 being in a pram or cot
2 seeing yourself in a mirror
3 using the past tense
4 fear and self-preservation
5 smells and sounds
6 your first word

e In Part 3 of the programme, you're going to listen to the first memory of Swiss psychologist Jean Piaget. Look at some words from the story. With a partner, try to predict what happened.

baby nanny **kidnap**
pram policeman
Champs-Elysées **reward**
run away fight a watch

f 🔊 **2.5** Now listen to Part 3. Was your prediction correct? What happened many years later?

g Tell a partner about your earliest memory. Answer the three questions in **a** about you. Having listened to the programme, how reliable do you think your first memory is?

6 VOCABULARY & PRONUNCIATION
word building: abstract nouns; word stress with suffixes

> 🔍 **Abstract nouns**
>
> An abstract noun is one that is used to express an idea, a concept, an experience, or a quality, rather than an object, e.g. *childhood* and *fear* are abstract nouns, whereas *a pram* and *a watch* aren't.
>
> Abstract nouns are formed:
>
> 1 by adding a suffix to nouns, adjectives, or verbs, e.g. *child – child**hood***. Commonly:
>   - nouns can add *-hood* or *-ship*
>   - adjectives can add *-ity*, *-ness*, or *-dom*
>   - verbs can add *-tion* or *-ment*
> 2 with a new word, e.g. *afraid – fear*.

a Make abstract nouns by adding a suffix to the words below and making any other changes necessary, and write them in the correct column.

achieve adult amaze aware bored celebrate curious disappoint excite free friend frustrate generous happy ill imagine improve kind member neighbour partner possible relation sad tempt wise

1 noun + *-hood*	2 noun + *-ship*

3 adj + *-ity*	4 adj + *-ness*

5 adj + *-dom*	

6 verb + *-(a)tion*	7 verb + *-ment*

b 🔊 **2.6** Listen and check.

c 🔊 **2.7** Underline the stressed syllable in these words. Listen and check. Which two endings often cause a change in stress?

1 a|dult   a|dult|hood
2 re|la|tion   re|la|tion|ship
3 free   free|dom
4 cu|ri|ous   cu|ri|o|si|ty
5 ha|ppy   ha|ppi|ness
6 ce|le|brate   ce|le|bra|tion
7 dis|a|ppoint   dis|a|ppoint|ment

d Now look at the abstract nouns and complete the adjective and verb columns.

Abstract noun	Adjective
1 anger	*angry*
2 shame	_____
3 death	_____
4 danger	_____

Abstract noun	Verb
5 belief	_____
6 hatred	_____
7 loss	_____
8 memory	_____

e 🔊 **2.8** Listen and check. Then cover the abstract nouns and try to remember them.

🔍 **Collocations**

Noticing and recording words that go together, e.g. *a remote possibility* not *a distant possibility*, will improve the accuracy and fluency of your speaking and writing.

---

f Complete the **bold** phrases with an abstract noun from **a** or **d** which collocates in the phrase.

1 I'm writing to express my sympathy for **your terrible _____**. John's death was a shock to us all…
2 **To my complete _____**, I realized I'd won first prize.
3 I've been seeing my girlfriend for about six months now. It's quite **a serious _____**.
4 There's **a strong _____** that I'll be offered the manager's job in the next few weeks.
5 I could smell gas in my kitchen, but the plumber decided there was **no immediate _____**.
6 When I heard I'd failed the exam, **it was a huge _____**. I'd been expecting to pass.
7 **Contrary to popular _____**, for many children, schooldays are not the happiest of times.
8 My eldest daughter has **a very vivid _____** – I think she'll end up becoming a writer.

---

7 SPEAKING

a 🔊 **2.9** Listen to someone describing a childhood memory. What is it about? What feelings does the speaker mention and why did he feel that way?

b Look at the feelings and events below. Choose one feeling and one event and prepare to talk about a childhood memory. Write the key words you'll need.

feelings: disappointment, excitement, happiness, sadness, amazement, embarrassment, shock, frustration, pain

events: a festival or celebration, the death of a pet, managing to do something for the first time, a day out, moving house, winning or losing something, the birth of a brother or sister, getting a wonderful or disappointing present

---

🔍 **Talking about memories**

When we're talking about a memory of the past, we use *remember / forget* (sb or sth) + verb + *-ing*:

I remember arriving, and it was dark…
I can remember feeling quite annoyed…
I'll never forget my mother shouting at me…

---

c In small groups, tell each other about your memories. Try to use expressions from the information box, and say exactly how you felt and why.

The feeling I'm going to talk about is embarrassment. I think I was about five and it was my first year at primary school. I remember…

 Go online to review the lesson

A synonym is a word you use when you can't spell the first word you thought of.
Burt Bacharach, US musician

G pronouns **V** lexical areas **P** sound–spelling relationships

1 READING & SPEAKING

a 🔊 2.10 A recent Oxford Dictionaries survey identified some of the most commonly misspelt English words. Listen and write the missing words. How many did you spell correctly? Why do you think the words are often misspelt?

1 The hotel can _____ 250 guests.
2 _____ do you prefer, coffee or tea?
3 We _____ a very warm welcome.
4 I won't leave _____ she gets here.
5 Something unexpected _____ on their journey.
6 I saw her on three _____ occasions.
7 The _____ is planning to raise taxes.
8 We'll _____ be there by 7.00.

b How much do you know about the English language? Answer the questions with a partner.

1 What two other languages have had the strongest influence on English?
2 How many letters are there in the English alphabet?
3 How many different sounds are there in English?
4 Which has changed more over the years, English pronunciation or English spelling?
5 Do children in English-speaking countries learn to read more quickly or more slowly than children elsewhere?

c Read the information from the website of the English Spelling Society. Check your answers to **b**. Then answer the questions.

1 What is the Society trying to do?
2 What's the knock-on effect on children's education if it takes them a long time to learn to read and write?
3 What does the website say is the best way to teach children to read and write in English?
4 What effect does low literacy have on adult offenders?

d Look at a quote from Masha Bell, of the English Spelling Society. Underline all the examples of simplified spelling. Do you find it easy to read?

> If u hav a por memory, yor chances of becumming a good speller ar lo. But wors stil, yor chances of lerning to read ar not good either, because of nonsens like 'cow–crow, dream–dreamt, friend–fiend' and hundreds mor like them.

e Do you agree that English spelling should be simplified? Do you think the English Spelling Society could ever succeed in its aim? Why (not)?

The English Spelling Society

Improving English Spelling

English spelling is broken. Let's fix it!

English spelling is broken. There are countless examples, such as *comb*, *bomb*, and *tomb*, or *height* and *weight*. The English Spelling Society exists to repair our broken spelling. The Society is working on a way to simplify current English spelling in order to improve access to literacy.

Why English spelling is exceptionally irregular

English as a language is relatively simple to learn. But its spelling system is possibly the most irregular of those based on an alphabet. Not only is it hard to predict the spelling from the pronunciation, but it is not always possible to predict the pronunciation from the spelling, for example, *thorough*.

English words derive mainly from old German and Norman French, and its alphabet of 26 letters makes it impossible to represent each of its 46 speech sounds with just one symbol. But that is not the only reason why many English spellings are irregular. In other languages, as pronunciation changed, the spelling changed too. However, in spite of the many ways in which English pronunciation has evolved over the centuries, words have often maintained their original spelling, which reflects the original pronunciation, but not how many words are pronounced today. For example, *blood* /blʌd/ used to be pronounced to rhyme with *good* /gʊd/.

The economic and social costs of English spelling

- Children in English-speaking countries take almost twice as long to learn to read and write compared to children in other countries. A longer time needed for learning to read and write means less time for other subjects.

- There has been much expensive research into how to teach reading and writing in Anglophone countries, but there is no standard method, and much disagreement, about how best to teach English literacy.

- Education is the proven best way to prevent criminals from reoffending. In countries where the literacy rates of prisoners are generally higher, improving their education while behind bars is also much easier. The poor literacy skills of many English-speaking offenders make this more difficult, and repeated returns to jail more likely.

Abridged from the English Spelling Society website

2 PRONUNCIATION
sound–spelling relationships

> 🔍 **Learning spelling rules or patterns**
> The English Spelling Society would like to simplify spelling by removing all the irregularities. However, estimates suggest that around 80% of English words are pronounced according to a rule or pattern, e.g. the letter *h* before a vowel is almost always pronounced /h/.

a With a partner, say each group of words aloud. How are the pink letters pronounced? Circle the different word in each group if there is one.

1 /h/	5 /dʒ/	9 /ɜː/
dishonest	enjoy	reporter
heart	jealous	work
herb	job	world
himself	journalist	worse
inherit	reject	worth
2 /əʊ/	**6 /tʃ/**	**10 /ɜː/**
allow	achieve	birth
borrow	catch	dirty
elbow	challenging	firm
overthrow	charge	third
shallow	chorus	T-shirt
3 /aɪ/	**7 /s/**	
compromise	seem	
despite	sense	
quite	sure	
river	sympathetic	
write	synonym	
4 /w/	**8 /ɔː/**	
whenever	awful	
where	drawback	
which	law	
whose	raw	
why	yawn	

b 🔊 **2.11** Listen and check. What's the pronunciation rule for each group? Can you think of any more exceptions?

c Look at the spelling patterns in **a**. Now decide how you think the words from the list below are pronounced. Check their pronunciation and meaning with your teacher or with a dictionary.

chime	howl	jaw	whirl	worm

3 GRAMMAR pronouns

a 🔊 **2.12** Listen and write three sentences. Which three words are pronounced exactly the same but spelt differently?

b 🌐 **p.145 Grammar Bank 2B**

4 LISTENING

> 🔍 **Understanding accents**
> Many English words can be pronounced in different ways, depending on where you come from. For example, *herb* is pronounced /hɜːb/ in British English, but /ɜːrb/ in American English; *bath* is pronounced /bæθ/ in northern England, but /bɑːθ/ in standard English, or RP (Received Pronunciation). RP is the accent used in dictionaries to indicate the pronunciation of a word. Listening to speakers with different accents will make a huge difference to your ability to communicate with English speakers.

1 Mairi 2 Diarmuid 3 Laura 4 Jerry
5 Andrea 6 Anita 7 Lily 8 Paul

a 🔊 **2.13** Listen to eight people talking about where they're from. Answer the questions.

1 Which person, 1–8, do you think speaks with RP?
2 Which two people do you think don't speak English as a first language?
3 Can you match any of the accents to the countries from the list?

Australia	England (RP)	Ireland	Lithuania
Scotland	South Africa	Spain	the USA

b 🔊 **2.14** Listen and check which countries the people are from. Who describes the place they're from as…?

A ☐ a city well-known for both its university and its industry
B ☐ a very multicultural city with fantastic facilities and beaches
C ☐ a village on the coast, friendly but a bit inward-looking
D ☐ a city of economic and cultural importance with several universities
E ☐ a small and welcoming country town
F ☐ a city with a big student and tourist population, where there is always something going on
G ☐ a city with beautiful old buildings and a mountain nearby
H ☐ an area where you can enjoy both nature and shopping

c Which people did you find easiest to understand? Was it because of their accent, or for some other reason?

5 VOCABULARY lexical areas

a Look at headings 1–4 in *Word Challenge*. With a partner, say what they mean.

b In pairs, do the exercises in *Word Challenge*. All the answers have come up in lessons **1A**, **1B**, and **2A**. How many did you get right?

Word Challenge

hard work

pick up a language

awful / terrible

on the tip of my tongue

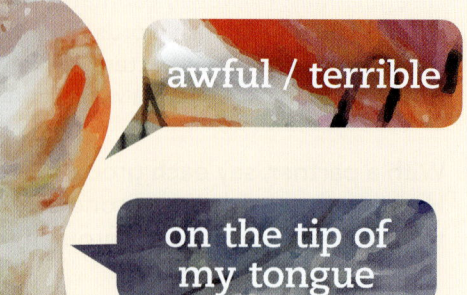

1 Collocations

(Circle) the correct word.

1 After her marriage broke up, she **looked for / sought** refuge with friends.
2 To our **full / complete** amazement, our daughter passed all her exams.
3 My grandfather has quite a **fast / quick** temper.
4 I spent a **pair / couple** of hours yesterday looking through old photos.
5 We've got **distant / far** relatives in Australia.
6 I don't think going freelance is a very good **job / career** move.
7 I'm sorry if I **hurt / damaged** your feelings.
8 I haven't really planned my trip yet, but I have **an approximate / a rough** itinerary.
9 We are **strongly / highly** opposed to the government's new policy.
10 I'm not very good in a crisis. I hate being **under / below** pressure. ☐ 10

2 Phrasal verbs

Complete the sentences with a verb from the list in the correct form.

> carry (x2) come dress get
> go lay make put turn

1 Look out for the Picasso drawings when you _____ **round** the exhibition.
2 We should _____ **off** the meeting till next week.
3 She was really ill and it took her a long time to _____ **over** it.
4 She finally _____ **up with** a brilliant solution to the problem.
5 Don't stop – _____ **on** with what you're doing.
6 He often _____ **up** excuses for why he's late.
7 The children love _____ **up** in their grandparents' clothes.
8 The book sounded fascinating, but it _____ **out** to be really dull.
9 A thousand workers were _____ **off** when the factory closed.
10 He's completely useless. He can't even _____ **out** simple instructions. ☐ 10

3 Synonyms and register

Match words or phrases 1–10 to synonyms A–J. Which word is more formal in each pair?

1 ☐ ill-fated
2 ☐ brothers and sisters
3 ☐ conversation
4 ☐ task
5 ☐ perk
6 ☐ against
7 ☐ quit
8 ☐ man
9 ☐ resemble
10 ☐ need

A job
B benefit
C resign
D siblings
E guy
F look like
G unfortunate
H require
I chat
J opposed to
☐ 10

4 Idioms

Complete the idioms.

1 I told a **wh_____ l_____** because I didn't want to upset him.
2 We tried to **c_____** the waiter's **e_____**, but he just ignored us.
3 I woke up suddenly in **the d_____** of **n_____** – there was a noise downstairs.
4 He's a really nice guy – very **d_____** to **e_____**.
5 This printer is such a **p_____** in the **n_____**; it never works.
6 **H_____** on **e_____** could you spend $2,000 on a watch?
7 I **followed** the instructions **to the l_____**, but I still couldn't get the wi-fi to work.
8 Let's not focus on the details. We need to see the **b_____ p_____**.
9 Jack's got his **n_____** to the **gr_____**, revising for his exams.
10 I've got a **g_____ f_____** that this meeting is going to go badly. ☐ 10

6 READING

a Read some extracts from an article about words which have changed their meaning. Which words do you think changed their meaning the most?

A *blockbuster* was originally a bomb

A blockbuster is literally a bomb large enough to destroy an entire block of buildings. The first blockbuster was dropped on the German city of Emden in March 1941. The wartime press was quick to pounce on the nickname 'blockbuster', and soon it was being used to describe anything that had an impressive or devastating effect. The military connotations gradually disappeared after the war, leaving us with the word we use today to describe bestselling films and books.

A *girl* originally referred to a girl or a boy

When the word 'girl' first appeared in the language, in the early 1300s, it was used to mean 'child', regardless of the gender of the child in question. That didn't begin to change until the early 15th century, when the word 'boy' – possibly borrowed from the French *embuie*, meaning a male servant – began to be used more generally for any young man. As a result, 'girl' was forced to change to mean a female child.

Alcohol originally meant eyeshadow

The ancient Egyptians made their distinctive jet-black eyeshadow out of the mineral stibnite, which was crushed and heated to produce a fine dust that could then be mixed with animal fat to make a cosmetic. The name of this was *al-kohl*, from an Arabic word meaning 'stain' or 'paint'. Alchemists and scientists of the European middle ages then picked up this term from their Arabic-origin textbooks, and began applying it to all kinds of other substances that could be produced in a similar way – which included wine and spirits, ultimately given the name 'alcohol'. This is now the most common meaning, though you can still buy kohl eyeliner pencils.

A *cupboard* used to mean a table

In the late 1300s, a cupboard was just a board on which to place your cups. Or put another way, a cupboard was originally a table. No one is entirely sure why, but in the early 16th century, that meaning suddenly disappeared from the language – a cupboard was no longer a tabletop on which to use one's crockery, but a piece of furniture in which to store it.

A *treadmill* was originally a prison punishment

The original treadmill was an enormous man-powered mill used for tasks such as crushing rocks and grinding grain. It was a wheel of steps encircling a cylinder attached to a millstone, on which prisoners could be employed for many hours a day; famously, the writer Oscar Wilde was made to work on the treadmill during his imprisonment in Pentonville Prison in 1895. Prison reform made the treadmill a thing of the past, but the term was resurrected in the 1950s, and was applied to a piece of gym equipment, a running machine comprised of a seemingly endless belt.

Adapted from The Guardian

b Read the extracts again. Which word…?

1 has a modern meaning which refers to the way something is made
2 has a modern meaning which refers to the same kind of activity
3 used to refer to two things, but changed to only one
4 changed its meaning as a result of its use by the media
5 changed its meaning for an unknown reason

c **Language in context** Look at the highlighted words in the extracts, which are all used metaphorically. What is their literal meaning?

d **G Communication** Changing meanings A p.107 B p.112 Read about two more words that have changed their meaning, then tell your partner.

7 ▶ VIDEO LISTENING

a You're going to watch a documentary on the history of English. With a partner, try to number the influences on English in chronological order.

```
[  ] America
[  ] the Anglo-Saxons
[  ] British colonies
[  ] Christian monks
[  ] the French
[ 1 ] the Romans
[  ] Shakespeare
[  ] technology
[  ] the Vikings
```

b Watch the documentary once and check.

c Watch again and mark the sentences **T** (true) or **F** (false). Correct the **F** sentences.

1 English has been changing for more than 1,000 years.
2 The Anglo-Saxons invented the alphabet.
3 The arrival of the Vikings gave English about 2,000 new words.
4 At first, the Normans didn't introduce many French words.
5 Shakespeare gave English as many new words as the Vikings.
6 In the 20th century, British English 'borrowed words' from American, but not vice versa.
7 Today, more people speak English as a first language than as a second language.

d What have been the main influences on the development of your language? Does it share any with English?

Go online to watch the video and review the lesson

GRAMMAR

a Complete the sentences with one word.

1 We need to _____ the broken window fixed soon, before it starts getting cold.
2 The Chinese economy is growing and _____ a result, the standard of living is rising.
3 We were very late _____ of an accident on the motorway.
4 Everybody seemed to enjoy the barbecue even _____ the weather wasn't very good.
5 She wants to take six months' unpaid leave _____ she can travel round the world.
6 When I was young, my family _____ spend every summer holiday at the seaside.
7 This street looks different from when I was a child. Didn't _____ use to be a sweet shop on the corner?
8 Will the person who left _____ boarding pass at security please go back and collect it?
9 If we lived closer to _____ another, we'd probably spend more time together.
10 Joe is quite reserved – he never talks about _____.

b Complete the sentences using the **bold** word(s).

1 I need to pick my mum up from the station. **got**
I _____.
2 If we buy a dishwasher, it won't be necessary to do the washing-up. **have**
If we buy a dishwasher, _____.
3 The last time I saw him was in 2010. **seen**
I _____ 2010.
4 They managed to get here even though the traffic was heavy. **despite**
They managed to get here _____.
5 It was snowing, so the train was cancelled. **due**
The train _____.
6 She wore dark glasses so that she wouldn't be recognized. **so as**
She wore dark glasses _____.
7 My aunt always used to bake biscuits for us. **was**
My aunt _____ for us.
8 If you learn a bit of the language, the local people really appreciate it. **one**
_____, the local people really appreciate it.
9 Jane sees Martha once a month. **each**
Jane and Martha _____ once a month.
10 The children wrapped the present on their own. **by**
The children wrapped the present _____.

VOCABULARY

a Complete the missing words.

1 He sometimes co_____ ac_____ as quite sarcastic, but he doesn't mean it.
2 They suddenly got married on holiday in Las Vegas – they're very sp_____.
3 She never asks for anyone's help. She's completely se_____-su_____.
4 Alexa can always find a way of solving problems – she's very re_____.
5 My brother wasn't very sy_____ when I failed my driving test – in fact, he just laughed!
6 He was de_____ to be a musician, even as a boy.
7 She's always open and honest – she's just really st_____ to work with.
8 On the surface he seems tough, but de_____ do_____ he's quite sensitive.

b Complete the idioms with one word.

1 My kids can be **a real _____ in the neck** when we eat out – they're so fussy!
2 My grandmother has always had **a quick _____**. We were quite scared of her when we were young.
3 He can be a bit bad-tempered, but he's got **a _____ of gold**.
4 My boss is very **down to _____**; you can talk to her about anything.
5 When you're doing your tax return, you have to follow the instructions **to the _____**.
6 You've been here loads of times! **How on _____** did you get lost?
7 Don't worry about every little detail – try to focus on **the big _____**.

c Circle the correct word or phrase.

1 She's been *off / out of* work for three days with the flu.
2 I won't get that job; I don't have the *qualifications / benefits*.
3 He resigned before they could *quit / sack* him.
4 I'm hoping to get *promoted / a rise* to a more senior post.
5 I don't earn much, but it's a very *rewarding / high-powered* job.
6 *Job-searching / Job-hunting* can be really demoralizing.
7 Factory work is often a bit *monotonous / motivating*.
8 The manager is in charge of 400 *staff / workforce*.

d Complete the sentences with the correct form of the **bold** word.

1 I wish there were more good restaurants in our _____. **neighbour**
2 We have been able to build a new library thanks to the _____ of the local community. **generous**
3 Please don't let this misunderstanding get in the way of our _____. **friend**
4 The _____ of his job affected him very badly. **lose**
5 _____ of speech is a basic human right. **free**
6 The news of their engagement caused great _____. **excite**
7 My _____ is getting worse as I get older. **remember**

CAN YOU understand this text?

a Read the article once and complete the headings.

b Read the article again and mark the sentences **T** (true) or **F** (false). Correct the **F** sentences.

1 Babies can distinguish between different voices before they are born.
2 Newborn babies can recognize languages other than their own.
3 The first kinds of words a toddler learns are words describing coloured objects.
4 Children watch adults carefully when trying to learn new words.
5 Until they are two years old, children can only name people or objects.
6 Small children all learn and say single words before they learn and say groups of words.
7 Children tend to learn regular verb forms before irregular ones.
8 Making mistakes is an effective way to learn language.
9 Children pick up grammar rules without being taught.

▶ CAN YOU understand these people?

🔊 **2.15** Watch or listen and choose a, b, or c.

1 **Alison**'s brother is ____.
  a older than her
  b younger than her
  c the same age as her
2 **Roslinn** has worked in ____ different fields.
  a two b three c four
3 **Rabia** had problems at her French-speaking school because ____.
  a French wasn't spoken in the place where she was born
  b the teacher spoke a different dialect from the French she had learned
  c French wasn't her parents' first language
4 **Margaret** has a problem spelling ____.
  a less common English words
  b all English words
  c a lot of French words

How children learn language

There are five things that every parent should know about how children learn language.

1 It begins e_____
Children don't even wait until they are born to start listening to language. Speech can be heard in the womb clearly enough to identify the basic rhythm and certain features of the speaker's voice. At birth, babies prefer their mother's voice to other female voices, the language of their parents over other languages, and they are able to recognize that an English sentence does not sound the same as a French sentence.

2 It happens f_____
Between age two and six, children average ten new words a day. By age six, they have a vocabulary of about 14,000 words, and over the next few years, they learn as many as twenty new words per day. At the beginning, they rely on simple strategies. One is to assume that new words refer to objects, rather than to colour, or texture, or activities. If a father points to a sheep and says *sheep*, his eighteen-month-old daughter assumes that 'sheep' refers to the animal itself, not to the fact that it's white, or woolly, or munching on grass. Perhaps the most important strategy involves noticing subtle clues in the behaviour of adults. For example, realizing that adults tend to look at the thing they are talking about makes it a lot easier to understand the meaning of what is said.

3 No two children are the s_____
Some children are initially better than others at identifying individual words and at pronouncing them clearly. By eighteen months, they can name people (*Daddy, Mummy*) and objects (*cat, car*), and they use simple words like *up, hot*, and *hungry* to describe how they feel and what they want. Other children memorize and produce relatively large chunks of speech, even though they are often poorly articulated: *whatsat* (What's that?), *dunno* (I don't know), *awgone* (It's all gone), and it's unlikely that children know what the component parts are.

4 Errors are g_____
Children make many mistakes when they learn language, such as 'goed' for *went* or 'eated' for *ate*. Mistakes mean that children are discovering the rules of English – adding *-ed* to a verb is the basic way to form the past tense in English. It may take several hundred exposures to the right past tense form of a verb before all the errors are eliminated, but mistakes are a normal part of the language acquisition process, and they disappear as a normal part of that same process.

5 It's w_____ you say
Children most need to hear language being used to talk about things they can see and feel, what they have just experienced or are about to experience. This provides the raw material they need to figure out what words mean, where a subject or a direct object fits into a sentence, how to ask a question, and all the other things that make up language. So, talk to children about what matters to them. They will take care of the rest.

Abridged from an academic website

🔄 **Go online** to watch the video, review Files 1 & 2, and check your progress

3A A love-hate relationship

Dating has become a sport, and not about finding the person you love.
Rashida Jones, US film-maker

G *get* **V** phrases with *get* **P** identifying attitudes

1 READING & SPEAKING

a What makes a relationship work? Tick (✓) the three things you think are most important, and cross (✗) any you think don't matter.

LIKING

the same music
the same sorts of clothes
the same sorts of food and drink
each other's families
each other's friends
the same football team
the same cultural activities
the same free-time activities
the same TV programmes and films
the same politicians

b Compare your ideas with a partner. Are there any other things you think it's important for both people to have in common?

c Read about a dating app called Hater. Does it sound like a good idea to you? Why (not)?

hater

How does the Hater app work?

It presents you with various topics (from loud chewing to cargo shorts to guacamole) that you must swipe right to hate or swipe left to love. Your answers are collated and you are then shown matches who hated the same things that you did.

d Read two articles about the Hater app, and match a title to each (there is one title you don't need). Who likes Hater and who doesn't?

Share the hate, ruin the date

Hate them or date them

If you want to be a good lover, be a great hater

Giles Coren

A new app offers to help single people find a partner by uniting them not with others who like the same things, such as opera, vegan sausages and pedigree cats, but with people who share their dislikes.

It's called Hater and strikes me as quite brilliant. 'Likes' tell you nothing about anyone. 'Good food, great music, and lively conversation…'. 'Laughter, red wine, and French movies…'. Ugh. The idea that a romantic life together is about sharing your stupid hobbies is deluded and childish. Love is about making something completely new out of two separate individuals, not finding activities those two individuals can do together to take their minds off how boring and unsexy the other one is.

My wife and I have absolutely no interests in common. None. But we do love hating things together. From the moment she looked in my eyes, she could sense that I was revolted by theatre, motorcyclists, tall people, and entertaining at home. Just as I knew from the first kiss that this was a woman who had no time for sandals on men, skiing, supermarket own-brand loo paper, or poached fish. Indeed, it later turned out that the main thing she liked about me was that I laughed when she was rude about our friends, whereas all her previous boyfriends had said, 'Why can't you just be nice?'

But being nice is meaningless. Liking things is weak. Our natural human hatred of things should be indulged every day. Hating is natural and fine and people want to do it. Celebrate the things you dislike every day and you'll feel much better – and probably find love.

Adapted from The Times

Victoria Coren Mitchell

Hater promises to **bond** potential lovers over things they **loathe**. Overturning the traditional cheery positives, Hater allows **eager singletons** to form relationships based on their mutual **aversions** instead. **Boy**, let's really get that negativity out there! More openly expressed hatred in the world – just what we need!

Nevertheless, like most apps, it would pass the time happily enough at a bus stop. If someone else at the same bus stop were also on the app, simultaneously swiping their own dislike of cat calendars or people who walk too slowly in the street, that would make a decent start for flirtation.

And yet, *and yet*. One of the key dangers of the internet is that it encourages us to give everything an immediate verdict, a thumbs up or down (and usually down). It's easy for our first thoughts on anything to be negative, and we forget to be kind.

The search for love has always motivated us to make an effort; on first dates, we are usually our best selves. Our hair is at its cleanest, our interest its sharpest, our smiles their readiest. That's why dating questionnaires traditionally list the things we enjoy: it's a shop window for the happy life we are offering a prospective partner. And surely, the longer you keep trying to be your best and most cheerful self, the happier life will be? It can't be wise to start complaining before you've even had your first date. When it comes to finding a partner, discovering the things you both love is a far healthier start.

Adapted from The Guardian

e Read the articles again. Tick (✓) the reasons each person gives for his / her opinion.

Giles

1 ☐ You don't get to know a person by finding out what they like.
2 ☐ If you hate the same things, you will probably like the same things, too.
3 ☐ More people hate the same things than like the same things.
4 ☐ He and his wife are united by things they hate.

Victoria

5 ☐ The Hater app is harder to use than a normal dating app.
6 ☐ The internet makes us want to judge things too much.
7 ☐ Focusing on things you like shows a new partner how you might enjoy life together.
8 ☐ It is easier to find a match through likes than through hates.

f With a partner, discuss the tone of the two articles. Answer the questions with **G** (Giles) or **V** (Victoria). Give examples to explain your answers.

Which writer do you think…?
1 ☐ is trying to make a serious point about modern life
2 ☐ is trying mainly to entertain
3 ☐ has mixed feelings about the Hater app
4 ☐ uses sarcasm in the opening paragraph
5 ☐ exaggerates for comic effect
6 ☐ is more provocative

g **Language in context** Both writers use a very wide vocabulary. Look at the highlighted words in the first paragraph of Victoria's article and match them to these synonyms.

1 enthusiastic   3 dislikes (*noun*)   5 unite
2 hey   4 hate (*verb*)   6 single people

h Cover the synonyms above and read out the paragraph using the synonyms instead of the highlighted words.

i Do you agree more with Giles or Victoria? Why?

2 PRONUNCIATION identifying attitudes

a 🔊 3.1 Listen to two sentences from the articles. Which sounds sarcastic? Which sounds genuinely enthusiastic?

1 It's called Hater and strikes me as quite brilliant.

2 **More openly expressed hatred in the world – just what we need!**

> 🔍 **Fine-tuning your pronunciation: identifying enthusiasm and sarcasm**
> It's important to be able to tell if someone is being enthusiastic about something or if they're being sarcastic. A lot of the clues are not in the words they use, or what they say, but <u>how they say it</u>, and this is to do with the pitch (= how high or low the voice is) and intonation (= the way the voice rises and falls).

b 🔊 3.2 Listen to the conversations. For each response, a and b, write **E** (enthusiastic) or **S** (sarcastic).

1 Oh great! Your mum's such a wonderful cook.   a ☐ b ☐
2 Good idea – it's only two miles.   a ☐ b ☐
3 Five pounds? Yes, thanks, that'll really help!   a ☐ b ☐
4 Oh good, I love vegetarian food.   a ☐ b ☐
5 Cool. I was dying to see some!   a ☐ b ☐
6 Thanks, that's just what I needed.   a ☐ b ☐
7 Oh great, well done.   a ☐ b ☐
8 That'll be fun!   a ☐ b ☐

c 🔊 3.3 Listen and repeat the enthusiastic responses in **b**.

3 LISTENING & SPEAKING

a Look at four possible ways of meeting a new partner. Which ones do you think would be the most / least successful?

1 going up to a stranger and starting a conversation
2 trying a new activity, e.g. a sport or hobby
3 going to a social event for single people
4 going on a blind date set up by a friend

b Read the beginning of an article. How does Anna feel about trying to meet someone IRL? Why did she decide to try it out?

c 🔊 3.4 Listen to Anna talking about what happened when she tried out the four ways, and answer the questions for each challenge. Does she agree with your opinion in **a**?

1 Where did each challenge take place?
2 Did she manage to chat successfully with anyone? If yes, who with? If no, why not?
3 How does she sum up the experience? What mark out of 5 does she give?

d Listen again. In which challenge, 1–4, did Anna feel...?

A ☐ optimistic, then embarrassed, awkward, and a bit depressed
B ☐ scared and rather uncomfortable
C ☐ very nervous, then relaxed and happy
D ☐ a bit nervous at first, then more confident and quite positive

e 🔊 3.5 **Language in context** Listen and complete the phrases.

1 The dating coaches suggested_____ four ways of meeting someone new.
2 James suggested _____ to guys in bookshops.
3 Hayley suggested _____ conventional chat-up lines.

I swapped apps for dating IRL – this is what happened
Anna Johnstone

I downloaded *Tinder* in 2014, during my final year of university. Back then, the dating app world felt new and exciting. Using our phones to swipe our way to (potential) love? That was game-changing. Now, aged 26, I'm on seven dating apps, and the thought of meeting someone IN REAL LIFE brings me out in a cold sweat.

But despite the growing popularity of dating apps, one recent study says that 50% of people would prefer to meet someone in real life. I know it's not impossible (for example, I have a friend who fell down some stairs and then got together with the paramedic). But first, I needed a plan. I spoke to two dating coaches, Hayley Quinn and James Preece, and they suggested trying four different ways of meeting someone new. Here's what happened...

f Read the information box. How could you say these sentences in the three different ways using *suggest*?

1 She advised me to go to the doctor.
2 I recommended that they visit the museum.
3 He said to me, 'Why don't you talk to her?'

g 🔊 **3.6** Listen to Anna's verdict on dating in real life. Answer the questions.

1 What did she learn from the experience?
2 What does she think are the advantages of the two ways of meeting people?
3 What is she planning to do in the future?

h Imagine you were looking for a new partner. Do you think you would use an app, or try to meet someone in real life?

4 GRAMMAR & VOCABULARY *get*

a Look at some sentences from the listening in **3**. In which sentence, 1–4, does *get / got* mean…?

arrived	became	persuade	obtain

1 If **I get a match** on an app, we already have things in common…
2 …**I got way more nervous** than before any other first date I'd been on.
3 So, as soon as **I got there**, I had two glasses of wine.
4 …I finally managed to **get a friend to organize** a date for me.

b 🅖 **p.146 Grammar Bank 3A**

c Complete the expressions to do with dating and relationships with phrases with *get*.

1 We **get** _____ very well most of the time. (= have a good relationship)
2 We **got** _____ when we were at university. (= started a relationship)
3 It's much easier to **get** _____ _____ somebody in real life than online. (= find out what somebody is like)
4 We're having so many family problems at the moment, it's really **getting** _____ _____. (= depressing me)

d 🅥 **p.164 Vocabulary Bank** Phrases with *get*

5 SPEAKING

Work in pairs. Read the *get* questionnaire and tick (✓) eight questions you'd like to ask your partner. Then ask and answer the questions. Explain your answers.

get questionnaire

☐ Are you the kind of person who regularly **gets rid of** clothes you don't wear any more, or do you tend to keep things forever?

☐ Did you use to **get into trouble** a lot when you were a child?

☐ Do you consider yourself a person who usually **gets their own way**? Why (not)?

☐ Do you tend to keep up to date with your work or studies, or do you often **get behind**?

☐ Do you think young drivers **get stopped** by the police more than older drivers? Do you think this is fair?

☐ Have you ever **got caught** cheating in an exam? Have you ever cheated in an exam and **got away with it**?

☐ Do you think going on holiday together is a good way to really **get to know** people?

☐ How often and where do you usually **get your hair cut**?

☐ If an electrical appliance doesn't work, do you try to sort it out yourself or do you immediately **get somebody to come** and fix it?

☐ If you were able to **get** just **one room in your house redecorated**, which would it be and why?

☐ Do you think women are better than men at **getting presents** for people?

☐ If you were invited to a karaoke evening, would you try to **get out of** going?

☐ If you were supposed to **get a flight** the day after a serious plane crash, would you cancel it?

☐ Is there anyone in your family or group of friends who really **gets on your nerves**?

☐ What kinds of things do / did your parents **get you to do** around the house?

☐ Is there a band or singer you've recently **got into**?

☐ What kind of weather tends to **get you down**?

> History never really says goodbye.
> History says, 'See you later'.
> *Eduardo Galeano, Uruguayan writer*

1 VOCABULARY conflict and warfare

a Look at the quiz questions with a partner and work out the meaning of the highlighted words. Then circle the correct answer.

HOW'S YOUR HISTORY?

1 Who was **executed** in London in 1606, after trying to **blow up** the Houses of Parliament?
   Oliver Cromwell   Guy Fawkes   Walter Raleigh
2 Who was US President during the American **Civil War**?
   Abraham Lincoln   George Washington   Thomas Jefferson
3 In which country was the Velvet **Revolution** in 1989?
   Poland   Hungary   Czechoslovakia
4 Which country has the most **troops**?
   the USA   India   China
5 Who **captured** and **looted** Rome in 410 AD?
   the Greeks   the Visigoths   the Vikings
6 Where was the **treaty** that ended World War I signed?
   Paris   Versailles   Vienna
7 In which war were there more civilian **casualties**?
   World War I   World War II   they were both the same
8 In which country was President Allende **overthrown** in a **coup** in 1973?
   Brazil   Chile   Argentina

b **V** p.165 **Vocabulary Bank** Conflict and warfare

2 PRONUNCIATION stress in word families

> 🔍 **Changing stress in word families**
> It's useful to learn words in 'families', e.g. *capture* (noun) – *a captive* (person), *revolutionary* (adjective) – *to revolt* (verb), etc. However, you should check whether the stressed syllable changes within the 'family'.

a Complete the chart. Then under<u>line</u> the stressed syllable in all the multi-syllable words.

noun	person	adjective	verb
cap|ture	cap|tive / cap|tor	cap|tive	_____
co|mmand	_____	co|mman|ding	co|mmand
ex|e|cu|tion	_____	_____	_____
_____	his|to|ri|an	his|to|ric / _____	_____
loo|ting	loo|ter	_____	_____
_____	_____	re|bell|ious	_____
_____	_____	re|vo|lu|tion|ary	re|volt
siege	_____	be|sieged	_____
sur|vi|val	_____	sur|vi|ving	_____
_____	_____	vic|to|ri|ous	_____

b 🔊 3.13 Listen and check.

3 READING

a Look at the stills from two films on p.31. What historical period do you think they're set in? Have you seen either of them?

b Read the descriptions of two memorable scenes. What information does each description give? Tick (✓) the boxes.

1	prizes the film won	A ⬜	B ⬜
2	where and when the film is set	A ⬜	B ⬜
3	who the main characters are played by	A ⬜	B ⬜
4	who directed the film	A ⬜	B ⬜
5	how the scene makes the audience feel	A ⬜	B ⬜
6	whether the scene is historically accurate	A ⬜	B ⬜
7	what probably happens at the end of the film	A ⬜	B ⬜

c **Language in context** Look at the highlighted words in sentences 1–5 and, with a partner, say what they mean.

1 I'm not sure they will **succeed** in reaching an agreement.
2 My nephew is studying **engineering** at university.
3 'Please don't go,' he said, **gripping** her arm.
4 Cook the sauce, **stirring** frequently, until it has thickened.
5 In the 19th century, most middle-class households had at least one **servant**.

d Now find the same words in text **A**. Are they the same part of speech? What is their meaning in this context?

e Which of the two descriptions created the most vivid image of the scene in your mind?

History brought to life

Two film critics choose memorable moments from historical films

'I will have my vengeance in this life, or the next.'

'You, the British people, what is your mood?'

A *Gladiator*, which won five Oscars, tells the story of a Roman general, Maximus Decimus Meridius, a favourite of Marcus Aurelius, Emperor in the second century AD. The Emperor wants Maximus (Russell Crowe at his best) to succeed him, but Commodus, the Emperor's weak and treacherous son (wonderfully played by Joaquin Phoenix), has other plans. Commodus kills his father and becomes Emperor himself, and arranges for Maximus and his wife and child to be executed. Maximus escapes, but cannot save his family. He is captured and sold as a gladiator, and eventually makes his way to the Colosseum in Rome, where he becomes a hero by engineering a spectacular victory against overwhelming odds. In this gripping scene, Emperor Commodus descends to the arena to congratulate him – not knowing his true identity. Maximus confronts the Emperor in one of the most stirring speeches in modern cinema: 'My name is Maximus Decimus Meridius, commander of the armies of the north, general of the Felix Legions, loyal servant to the true Emperor, Marcus Aurelius, father to a murdered son, husband to a murdered wife, and I will have my vengeance in this life, or the next.' And somehow, we just know he's going to get it!

B *The Darkest Hour* is set in May 1940, early in World War II. German forces are winning the battle for Europe, and British soldiers are trapped in northern France. Winston Churchill, the new Prime Minister, is faced with a desperate decision – to continue the fight against Hitler and the Nazis, or to negotiate a peace treaty. Unable to decide what to do, and under pressure from Parliament to negotiate, Churchill decides that he needs to find out what the people want. For the first time in his life, he travels on the London Underground, where he asks his startled fellow passengers two questions. First, he asks, 'What would you do if the enemy invaded?' and they answer 'Fight!' Then he asks them, 'Should I negotiate with Hitler?' and their answer is a very clear 'Never!' Churchill is inspired by their certainty, and goes on to use their words in one of his most famous speeches: 'We shall fight on the beaches, we shall fight on the landing grounds, we shall fight in the fields and in the streets, we shall fight in the hills; we shall *never* surrender.'

This is the key scene in the whole film, but unlike almost all the rest of the film, it has been criticized for its historical inaccuracy – Churchill's ride on the Tube never happened. The director, Joe Wright, has defended the scene as 'a fictionalization of an emotional truth'. Does it matter? Not to the awards committees, who gave the film two Oscars and numerous other awards.

4 SPEAKING & WRITING

> 🔍 **Describing a scene from a film**
> Churchill **decides** that he **needs** to find out what the people want. For the first time in his life, he **travels** on the London Underground, where he **asks** his startled fellow passengers two questions.
>
> We normally use the present simple ('the dramatic present') when we describe a scene from a film, or the plot.

a Think of a film or TV series you really enjoyed that was set in a historical period or based on a real event. Look at the prompts and think about this information for your film or TV series.

> • Where and when is it set? What is it about?
> • Who are the main characters and who are they played by?
> • Why did you enjoy it?
> • Is there a memorable scene that you remember? What happens?

b Work in small groups. Describe the film or TV series and the scene to others in the group. Do those who have seen it agree with you?

c Now write a paragraph describing the film or TV series and the scene, using the prompts in **a** and the two descriptions in **3** as models.

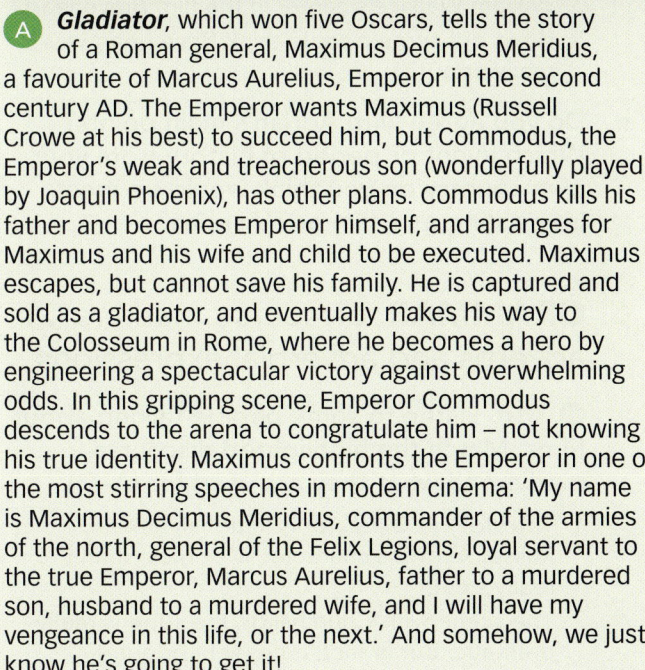

5 LISTENING

a 🔊 **3.14** Listen to Part 1 of an interview with Adrian Hodges, who has written screenplays for several historical films and TV series. Choose the best summary of his opinion.

1 Adrian thinks historical details don't matter as long as they're things that most people wouldn't notice.
2 Adrian thinks historical details don't matter as long as a drama is honest about whether it is history or fiction.
3 Adrian thinks historical details don't matter at all.

> **Glossary**
> **Macbeth** /mək'beθ/ a play by Shakespeare about a king of Scotland
> **William the Conqueror, Charles II, Victoria** English monarchs from the 11th, 17th, and 19th centuries
> **to play fast and loose with** IDM (*old-fashioned*) to treat sth or sb in a way that shows you feel no responsibility or respect for it / them

b Listen again and tick (✓) the points Adrian makes.

1 ☐ It isn't a problem that Shakespeare's plays are not historically accurate.
2 ☐ Writers can change historical details if the drama requires it.
3 ☐ Most people never notice historical inaccuracies.
4 ☐ Nobody is certain how people spoke in ancient Rome.
5 ☐ Historical inaccuracies with costume are worse than with dialogue.
6 ☐ You need to be more careful about being accurate when you are writing about recent history.
7 ☐ Writers should feel responsible for the history people might believe from a film.
8 ☐ Julius Caesar is not a good subject for drama because we know so much about him.

Mel Gibson in *Braveheart*

c 🔊 **3.15** Now listen to Part 2. In general, is Adrian positive or negative about *Spartacus* and *Braveheart*?

> **Glossary**
> **Spartacus** a 1960 film about a gladiator who led a slave rebellion against the Romans in the first century BC
> **Braveheart** a 1995 film about William Wallace, one of the leaders in the late 13th- and early 14th-century Wars of Scottish Independence

d Listen again and answer the questions.

1 What does Adrian mean when he talks about the danger of a film becoming the 'received version of the truth'?
2 What famous scene in the film *Spartacus* is an example of this?
3 What facts do we actually know about Spartacus?
4 What does Adrian say about the portrayal of William Wallace's career in the film *Braveheart*?
5 What did some people think *Braveheart* was really about?

e Do you agree with Adrian's main points? Which event or period of history from your own country do you think would be most interesting as a film or TV series?

6 GRAMMAR discourse markers (2): adverbs and adverbial expressions

a 🔊 **3.16** Listen to some people talking about films. Match the highlighted discourse markers to what they are used for (A–D).

1 The story in *Gladiator* is fictional; **I mean**, Russell Crowe's character, Maximus, didn't really exist.
2 The scene with Churchill on the Tube is really dramatic, but **in fact**, it never happened.
3 A Do you want to watch *Spartacus* tonight?
  B Not really. It's three hours long, and **besides**, I don't like old films.
4 A I really loved Mel Gibson in *Braveheart*.
  B **Talking of** Mel Gibson, have you seen the news today?

A ☐ to introduce surprising or unexpected information
B ☐ to change the direction of a conversation
C ☐ to make things clearer, or give more details
D ☐ to introduce an additional point

b 🄖 **p.147 Grammar Bank 3B**

c Complete the sentences in your own words. Then compare with a partner and see if you completed any in the same way.

1 A lot of people think the film is a true story, but as a matter of fact,…
2 The script was terrible; the acting was awful; the story was dull. In other words,…
3 The cinema was really crowded and hot, but at least…
4 I don't feel like going to the cinema tonight, and besides,…
5 I don't know how people can watch films on their phone. I mean,…
6 There were a few little things the film-makers invented, but on the whole,…
7 We weren't expecting to enjoy the film, but actually,…
8 You should book tickets for most cinemas nowadays, otherwise…

7 SPEAKING

a Look at the four images from films and TV series about British queens and read the captions. Try to match them to the centuries in which they are set.

16th century		18th century	
19th century		20th century	

b Two of the things mentioned in the captions are facts and two are fiction. With a partner, say which you think are which.

c ⓒ **Communication** Historical inaccuracies **A p.107 B p.113** Find out what is fact and what is fiction, and tell your partner.

d Answer the questions in pairs.

- Do you ever check whether a film or TV series was accurate, either during or after seeing it?
- If a film or TV series is historically inaccurate, does it bother you? Why (not)?
- Which historical films or TV series that you've seen taught you something about the period or event?

A In *The Favourite*, Queen Anne has 17 pet rabbits which represent the 17 children she lost.

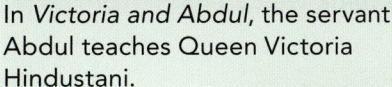

In *Victoria and Abdul*, the servant Abdul teaches Queen Victoria Hindustani.

In *Mary Queen of Scots*, there is a dramatic meeting between Mary and Queen Elizabeth I.

In *The Crown*, Jackie Kennedy, the US President's wife, criticizes the Queen after a dinner at Buckingham Palace.

Go online to review the lesson

1 ▶ THE INTERVIEW Part 1

a Read the biographical information about Mary Beard. What do you think 'Classics' and 'classicist' refer to?

Mary Beard is Professor of Classics at the University of Cambridge and a fellow of Newnham College. She is author of many books about ancient history, and writes a popular blog called *A Don's Life*. In 2010, she presented the BBC historical documentary, *Pompeii: Life and Death in a Roman Town*, which showed a snapshot of the residents' lives before the eruption of Mount Vesuvius in 79 AD. In 2012, she wrote and presented the three-part television series *Meet the Romans*, about 'the world's first global metropolis'. She also wrote and presented *Caligula with Mary Beard* in 2013, where she attempts to sort the truth from the myth. In 2018, she presented *Julius Caesar Revealed* for the BBC and also became a Dame for services to the study of classical civilisations. Her frequent media appearances and sometimes-controversial public statements have led to her being described as 'Britain's best-known classicist'.

Glossary

Julius Caesar /ˈdʒuːlɪəs siːzə/ a Roman general (100–44 BC) who played a critical role in the fall of the Roman Republic and the rise of the Roman Empire. He was assassinated by a group of senators led by his former friend, Brutus.

b Watch Part 1 of the interview. What does Mary Beard think is the right (and the wrong) way to get people interested in ancient history? What does she think we can learn from history?

c Now watch again. Complete sentences 1–5.

1 If a place name ends with -*chester* or -*caster*, it means that it…
2 London is the capital of Britain because…
3 In 63 BC, there was a terrorist plot in Rome to…
4 When Cicero discovered the plot, he decided to…
5 Mary Beard compares this situation with…

d What periods and places in history did you study at school? Did you enjoy history as a subject?

Glossary

torch (*verb*) set fire to
Marcus Tullius Cicero /ˈsɪsərəʊ/ a Roman politician and lawyer, one of Rome's greatest orators
the Senate a political institution in ancient Rome
be exiled be sent to another country for political reasons or as a punishment
Guantanamo Bay a US military prison, where many suspected terrorists have been held

▶ Part 2

a Now watch Part 2. Mark the sentences **T** (true) or **F** (false).

1 Mary Beard would not like to go back in time to any historical period.
2 She thinks that women have a better life now than at any time in the past.
3 She doesn't think that men would suffer from going back in time.
4 In her programme *Meet the Romans*, she decided to focus on the celebrities of the ancient world.
5 She thinks that most history textbooks don't answer questions about how people dealt with practical issues in the past.
6 She thinks that questions about practical issues are just as interesting as why Julius Caesar was assassinated.
7 She doesn't think we can learn much from studying the assassination of Caesar.

b Watch again. Say why the **F** sentences are false.

c How do you think a teacher can get students interested in history?

▶ Part 3

a Now watch Part 3. Answer the questions.

1 How important does Mary Beard think accuracy is in historical films?
2 What historical film did she really enjoy and why?
3 How does she feel about the fact that there are so many historical films nowadays?

b Watch again. What do you think the highlighted informal words and phrases mean?

1 'I think that, that, um, film and television, um, programme makers can be a bit, can be a bit sort of nerdish about accuracy.'

2 '…if we're going to have a dog in the film, should it be an Alsatian or, you know, a Dachshund or whatever?'

3 '…look, these guys are getting the whole of Roman history…utterly wrong…'

4 '…never mind its horribly schmaltzy plot…'

5 '…there's no such good story as a true story – and that's what history's got going for it…'

6 '…non-fiction in a, in a kind of way is always a better yarn than fiction is.'

c Do you think you have learnt more about history from school or from books and films?

> **Glossary**
> **Alsatian, Dachshund** /æl'seɪʃn, 'dæksnd/ breeds of dog

2 ▶ LOOKING AT LANGUAGE

> 🔍 **Collocations**
> Many of the expressions Mary Beard uses are typical collocations. Try to learn these expressions as phrases. Incorporating them into your active language will help you both to understand spoken English more easily and to sound more fluent in your own speech.

Watch some extracts from the interview and complete the collocating words in the highlighted phrases.

1 '…an _____ lot of our culture and our geography and our place names and so on are actually formed by the Romans…'

2 '…one _____ example of that is a famous incident in Roman history in 63 BC where there's a terrorist _____ in, in the city of Rome…'

3 'Now, in many ways that's the kind of problem we're still _____…'

4 'I mean, what – how far does, how far should homeland security be more important than _____ rights…'

5 'And in part we've learnt from how they debated those rights and _____.'

6 '…if it, if it was a small antidote to modern _____ culture, I'm extremely pleased.'

7 '…look, these guys are getting the whole of Roman history in, in the big _____ utterly wrong…'

8 'But I think also, I mean, it shows that you don't always have to be deadly _____ about history.'

3 ▶ THE CONVERSATION

Joanne Sean Emma

a Watch the conversation. Match the period they'd like to go back to to the reason why.

1 ☐ Joanne would like to go back to the 1920s to…
2 ☐ Sean would like to go back to the 1960s to…
3 ☐ Emma would like to go back to Tudor times to…

A find out more about the politics of the time
B learn more about daily life during that period
C experience the cultural influences of the period

> **Glossary**
> **the Cavern Club** a music venue in Liverpool, England, where The Beatles played
> **the Tudors** the English kings and queens who ruled from 1485–1603, e.g. Henry VIII, Elizabeth I

b Watch again. Answer the questions.

1 What aspects of her grandmother's life does Joanne mention? What does she think these would tell her about her grandmother?

2 What two things would Sean be especially interested in experiencing?

3 Which historical figure is Emma particularly interested in? Why does she say she'd like to see things happening 'from a safe platform'?

c Which period of history would you like to go back to? What positive and negative things would you expect to find?

d Watch some extracts in which the speakers respond to what the previous person says, in order to keep the conversation going. In which one(s) does the speaker…?

A ☐ suggest something the person could do
B ☐ ask for more detail
C ☐☐ agree enthusiastically
D ☐ refer to a sensible comment the person has made
E ☐ extend the range of the conversation

e Now have a conversation in groups of three. Discuss the statements.

1 Historical films and novels are popular mainly because they tell exciting and dramatic stories.

2 Modern politicians can learn important lessons from history.

🔵 **Go online** to watch the video, review the lesson, and check your progress

4A An open book

> There's no such thing as a happy ending.
> *Stephen King, US author*

G adding emphasis (1): inversion **V** describing books and films **P** foreign words

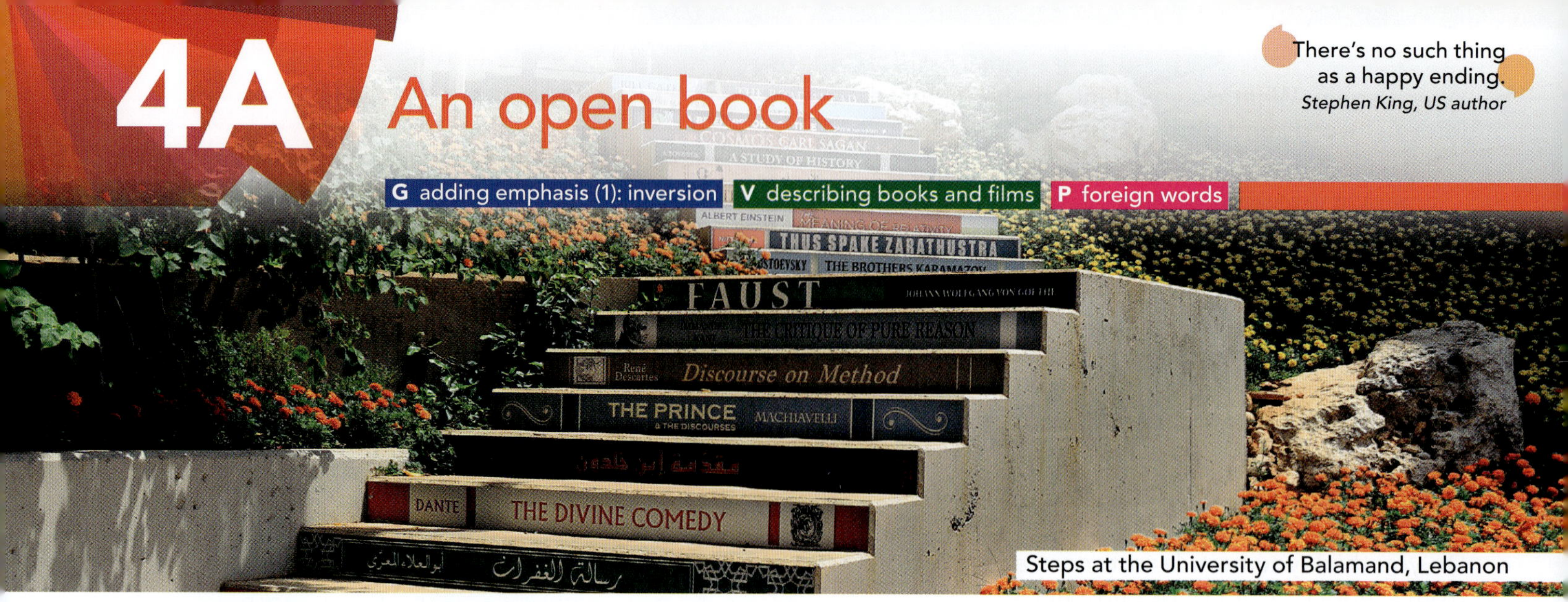

Steps at the University of Balamand, Lebanon

1 LISTENING & SPEAKING

a Look at the six book titles. Have you heard of or read any of them?

CATCH 22 *Carbonel* **Big Little Lies** The Silmarillion **The War of the Worlds** To Kill a Mockingbird

b 4.1 Listen to six people talking about the books in **a**. Match the speaker, A–F, to the topic they're talking about.

1 ☐ a book you started but couldn't finish
2 ☐ a book you think would make a good film
3 ☐ a book you feel you ought to have read, but haven't
4 ☐ a book you decided to read after seeing the film or series
5 ☐ a book you couldn't put down
6 ☐ a book you were forced to read at school and didn't enjoy

c Listen again. Which speaker says that...?

1 ☐ the characters and events in the book are easy to imagine
2 ☐ they read the book when they were abroad
3 ☐ the language of the book was too challenging
4 ☐ they mainly read to relax
5 ☐ they also enjoyed a series of books for older teenagers
6 ☐ the book has a lot of detailed background information in it

d 4.2 Listen to six extracts from the listening and complete the missing words.

1 ...I just sat under a tree in the shade and read the whole thing from __________ to __________.
2 ...I think it's a __________ __________.
3 So that was __________ __________ a TV series on HBO, I think...
4 ...it's sort of more information about the world that *The Lord of the Rings* __________ happens in.
5 ...I really was __________ science fiction as a kid, and, and the __________ looked, you know, like, really exciting.
6 ...for me, reading is a way of __________ off, so I don't really want to read anything that's quite a __________.

e Look at topics 1–6 in **b** and choose three that you can talk about. Then tell a partner.

2 READING

a Would you ever look at the last page of a book before reading it, or ask someone about the ending of a film or TV series you were planning to watch?

b Read the text from the back covers of two stories. Which one would you most like to read?

1 ***The Adventure of the Speckled Band***
Arthur Conan Doyle

Helen and Julia Stoner live with their violent stepfather, Dr Grimesby Roylott. Just before Julia is due to marry, for several nights she hears a strange, low whistle from outside her bedroom. Shortly afterwards, she dies in her room one night in terrible pain, crying out the words: 'It was the band! The speckled band'. No cause of death is found and no one could have entered her room, as she always locked herself in at night. Two years later, Helen becomes engaged to be married, but she is terrified one night to hear a strange, low whistle outside her bedroom. She asks Sherlock Holmes to investigate.

2 ***Lamb to the Slaughter***
Roald Dahl

One night, detective Patrick Maloney comes home and announces his intention to leave his pregnant wife, Mary. Devastated, Mary hits Patrick over the head with the frozen leg of lamb she intends to cook for dinner, killing him instantly. Mary knows that, if she gets caught, she will be executed for murder, so she concocts a plan to fool the police.

c **Communication** What happens in the end? **A** p.108 **B** p.112 Read extracts from the end of the stories in **b** and tell each other what happens.

d Now read the title and the first paragraph of the article. What is a 'spoiler'?

Spoilers actually enhance your enjoyment

I am one of those people who can't read a book without flicking to the end to check what's going to happen. It turns out that, actually, I am very wise. Psychologists at the University of California in San Diego gave students 12 short stories, by authors including Agatha Christie and Roald Dahl. Some stories were in their original form and others had spoiler paragraphs added at the beginning. And do you know what? The readers of 'spoiled' stories actually had more fun.

According to the psychologists who carried out the research, 'students significantly preferred the spoiled versions of the stories. For instance, knowing in advance in an Agatha Christie story that Poirot will discover that the 'victim' of the attempted murder is, in fact, the real murderer, not only didn't hurt the enjoyment of the story, but actually improved it.'

As a huge reader of crime and thrillers, this definitely rings true for me. When I'm reading horror novels, I need to check the hero or heroine is still alive at the end of the book. And I usually take a sneaky look at the end of a romantic novel, just to make sure who is going to end up with whom. 'It could be,' says psychologist Jonathan Leavitt, 'that once you know how the story turns out, you're more comfortable processing the information and can focus on a deeper understanding of the story.'

I will also admit that, even when I know full well what is going to happen in a book, either because I've read it a million times before, or because I've read the end, I often find myself hoping that, this time, it's going to be different, that the sad ending will turn into a happy one!

Adapted from The Guardian

e Read the rest of the article and underline…

1 an example of a spoiler.
2 two reasons the writer looks at the ending of a book.
3 a possible explanation for why we get more enjoyment out of a story when we know the ending.
4 something the writer knows will never happen.

f Talk to a partner.

- Do you agree with the article that knowing how a story ends makes you enjoy it more?
- Are there any books or films that you enjoyed more the second time because you knew how they were going to end?
- Has anyone ever spoiled a film, a book, a sports match, or anything else for you by telling you how it ended?

3 VOCABULARY describing books and films

a Complete the short reviews about books and films with an adjective from the list.

creepy   fast-moving   gripping   ~~haunting~~   heart-warming
heavy going   implausible   intriguing   moving
thought-provoking

1 A _haunting_ film which stayed with me long after I left the cinema. ✪✪✪✪✪
2 A wonderful story. So _____ I cried! ✪✪✪✪✪
3 Such a _____ plot. I was on the edge of my seat all the way through. ✪✪✪✪✪
4 It was a _____ story which restored my faith in human nature. ✪✪✪✪
5 A _____ story which jumps from past to present and back again at breakneck speed. ✪✪✪✪
6 The plot was _____. I really couldn't predict how it would end. ✪✪✪✪
7 A _____ documentary that raised many interesting questions. ✪✪✪
8 A ghostly atmosphere and strange goings-on. This film was just too _____ for me. ✪✪✪
9 Rather _____. I really had to make an effort to finish it. ✪✪
10 The characters were totally _____. I couldn't take any of them seriously. ✪

b 🔊 4.3 Listen and check.

4 GRAMMAR adding emphasis (1): inversion

a Complete the extracts from book reviews 1–5 with endings A–E. How does the word order change when you put the adverbial expression (*Not only…, Never…,* etc.) at the beginning of the sentence?

1 ☐ **Not only** is this an entertaining book for children,…
2 ☐ **Never** have I read…
3 ☐ **Not until** the very last page…
4 ☐ **No sooner** had I finished this gripping novel…
5 ☐ **Only when** she leaves…

A did I guess who the murderer was.
B such a well-written novel by a first-time author.
C than I wanted to read it all over again.
D but parents will also find it intriguing.
E does he realize that he is in love with her.

b 🄖 p.148 Grammar Bank 4A

c Complete the sentences in your own words, using inversion to make them as dramatic as possible.

1 Only when we arrived at the airport…
2 No sooner…than I realized…
3 Never in all my life…
4 Not until it was too late…
5 Not only…, but…

5 LISTENING

a Discuss in small groups.

1 How often do you read books which have been translated into your language? What languages have they been translated from?
2 Do you prefer reading English books in translation to reading them in English? Have you ever read a book which you felt was probably badly translated?
3 Have you ever used an app, e.g. Google Translate, to translate something into your language? How well did you think it worked?
4 Do you tend to watch foreign films dubbed or with subtitles? What do you think are the advantages and disadvantages of the two options?

b 🔊 **4.4** Listen to the first part of an interview with Beverly Johnson, a professional translator. From what she says, do you think you would enjoy working as a translator?

c Listen again and choose the correct answer(s).

1 One of the reasons Beverly decided to become a translator was that…
   a she thought teaching English was boring.
   b she really enjoyed the postgraduate course that she took.
   c she wanted to be self-employed.
2 Which two of these things does Beverly mention as drawbacks of being a freelance translator?
   a working alone   b earning a low salary   c time pressure
3 Which two of these things does she say are good about her job?
   a the freedom to charge what you like
   b flexibility about where you work
   c managing your own time
4 One piece of advice she gives to would-be translators is to…
   a specialize.   b study abroad.   c take a translation course.

d Look at some of the kinds of texts translators work on. Which ones do you think might be especially difficult to translate?

▨ novels   ▨ advertising slogans   ▨ film titles
▨ poetry   ▨ legal documents   ▨ film dialogue (for subtitles)
                  ▨ technical manuals

e 🔊 **4.5** Now listen to the rest of the interview. Tick (✓) the kinds of texts in **d** that Beverly talks about.

f Listen again and answer the questions.

What does Beverly say…?
1 you need to be if you specialize in translating novels
2 is good about translating an author who is still alive
3 would sound odd in English

What is the most difficult thing about translating…?
4 the title of a film into other languages
5 film subtitles
6 humour in films
7 slang and swear words

g Can you think of any films where the title in your language was completely different from the English version? Why do you think it was changed?

6 READING & SPEAKING

sobremesa

a Look at the two words and photos above. Do you know what languages the words are from? Can you work out from the photos what they might mean?

b Read the extracts and check your ideas from **a**. What does each word tell you about the culture of the country?

sobremesa /sobreˈmesa/ is the time when Spanish people sit around tables inside a restaurant, or out on the terrace, relaxing after lunch. It is a pleasant time, a recognition that there is more to life than working long hours, and that few activities are nicer than sharing a table and chatting for what remains of the day. The world may not have been put completely to rights by the end of the *sobremesa*, but it will seem a calmer, kinder place.

ta'arof /taˈaːrɒf/ is a Persian word that specifically refers to correct or polite behaviour in Iranian society. It means 'both people denying what they want in order to please the other person'. 'You go first,' says Mr A when he meets Mr B at the door, as they try to enter a building. 'No, absolutely not, you go first,' Mr B insists. They then both wait for a couple of unnecessary minutes before one steps forward to enter. It is seen almost in all aspects of life, from hosts insisting on guests taking more food, to buying something in a shop.

Adapted from The Guardian

ta'arof

c Look at some more words that have no equivalent in English. Do you have equivalent words in your language?

1 **gigil**
(Filipino) the urge to pinch or squeeze something that is unbearably cute, like a baby's cheeks

2 **age-otori**
(Japanese) to look worse after a haircut

3 **cavoli riscaldati**
(Italian) literally *reheated cabbage*, an attempt to revive an old romantic relationship

4 **seigneur-terrasse**
(French) a person who spends a lot of time but very little money in a café

5 **Drachenfutter**
(German) the presents that guilty husbands give their wives

6 **vranyo**
(Russian) lying when everybody knows that's what you're doing

7 **neko-neko**
(Indonesian) a creative idea which only makes things worse

8 **skuffuskald**
(Icelandic) a person who puts their poems in a drawer rather than publishing them

d Can you think of any English words for which there is no exact translation in your language?

7 PRONUNCIATION
foreign words

> 🔍 **Saying foreign words in English**
> There are some foreign words and phrases which are commonly used in English because we don't have another word for them, e.g. *coup* /kuː/ (French), *angst* /æŋst/ (German). They're usually said in a way that is close to their original pronunciation, so they don't necessarily follow normal English pronunciation patterns.

a <u>Underline</u> the foreign word or phrase in each sentence below. What do you think they mean? Which languages are they from?

1 I made a real faux pas when I mentioned to our boss that Sam had been asked to leave his previous job.
2 When we were introduced, I had a sense of déjà vu, even though I knew we had never met before.
3 It might be a bit of a cliché, but I think it's actually true that 'opposites attract'.
4 Their business venture ended in a complete debacle and the manager resigned.
5 She's a real aficionado of Italian opera – she knows a lot about it and goes whenever she can.
6 Don't overcook the pasta – just until it's al dente.
7 I'm afraid I felt a certain schadenfreude when my ex-husband told me his girlfriend had left him.
8 After the earthquake, there was a tsunami warning, but luckily, it didn't happen.

b 🔊 **4.6** Listen and focus on how the foreign words or phrases in **a** are pronounced. Then practise saying the sentences.

c Do you use any untranslated words from other languages, e.g. English, in your language? Why do you think they are used? Do you pronounce them as in the original language?

8 WRITING

Ⓦ **p.120 Writing A review** Analyse a book review, and write a review of a book or film.

🔍 **Go online** to review the lesson

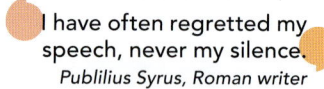

I have often regretted my speech, never my silence.
Publilius Syrus, Roman writer

G speculation and deduction   **V** sounds and the human voice   **P** consonant clusters

1 VOCABULARY sounds and the human voice

a Try to sit in silence for one minute, listening carefully to the sounds around you. Write everything you hear. Then compare with a partner. Did you hear the same things?

b **V** p.166 **Vocabulary Bank** Sounds and the human voice

c **4.10** Listen to twelve sounds and say the word for what you hear.

2 PRONUNCIATION consonant clusters

> 🔍 **Fine-tuning your pronunciation: consonant clusters**
> Combinations of two or three consonant sounds, e.g. *crunch*, *splash*, can be difficult to pronounce, especially if the combination of sounds is not common in your language.
> Three-consonant clusters at the beginning of words always begin with *s*, e.g. *scream*.
> Three-consonant clusters at the end of words are often either plurals (*months*), third person singular verbs (*wants*), or regular past tenses (*asked*).

a **4.11** Listen to the words in the chart. Then practise saying them.

At the beginning of a word		
two sounds		**three sounds**
click	drip	screech
slam	snore	scream
crash	stammer	splash
slurp		

At the end of a word		
two sounds		**three sounds**
shouts	yelled	crunched · crisps
sniffs	hummed	mumble · rattled

b **4.12** Listen and repeat the sentences.
1 She screamed when her friend splashed her in the swimming pool.
2 The brakes screeched and then there was a tremendous crash.
3 I hate the crunching of someone eating crisps.

c Write three sentences of your own, using two words from **a** in each sentence. Give them to your partner to say.

3 LISTENING & SPEAKING

a You're going to hear a list of people's best and worst sounds. Look at the sounds below. Tick (✓) the ones you think are 'best sounds', and cross (✗) the ones you think are 'worst sounds'.

The best and worst

☐ the tap of the keys on a mobile phone when someone hasn't turned off the keyboard sound

☐ the crunch of walking on a fresh layer of snow

☐ the roar of a revving motorbike

☐ the patter of rain on the roof while you're in bed

☐ the crackling noise of an open fire

☐ the whine of a dentist's drill

☐ the strange hum in your house that you can't locate

☐ the sound of a golf ball dropping into the hole

☐ the popping noise when you squeeze bubble wrap

b 🔊 **4.13** Listen and check. Do you agree?

c 🔊 **4.14** Now listen to eight people talking about sounds they love or hate. Answer the questions.

1 What sound does each person describe?

2 Do they love it or hate it?

sounds...

- someone eating popcorn at the cinema
- people laughing at one of your jokes
- the 'ding' sound when a plane has landed and switched off the engines
- the sound of someone filing their nails
- the crashing of waves on a beach
- someone sniffing
- birds singing very early in the morning
- people slurping their food
- someone else's child crying

Adapted from the British press

d Listen again and answer the questions.

Speaker 1	What kinds of things does the dog bark at?
Speaker 2	Why does she make her daughter buy a little box?
Speaker 3	Why does she enjoy hearing that her children are asleep?
Speaker 4	What app has he got on his phone?
Speaker 5	In what circumstance is the sound particularly annoying?
Speaker 6	Where did she hear this sound recently?
Speaker 7	What kind of music does he not want to hear at all?
Speaker 8	How does she need to sit when travelling?

e Talk in small groups.

- Are there any sounds that you really love? Why do you love them? What do they make you think of, or how do they make you feel?
- What about sounds that you hate? How often are you affected by them in your daily life? Is there anything you can do to avoid them?

4 GRAMMAR speculation and deduction

a 🔊 **4.15** Listen to three groups of sounds which tell stories. What do you think is happening? Write three sentences for each story using the phrases below.

Story 1 must be, might be, can't have
Story 2 could have, might have, unlikely that
Story 3 probably, could be, must have

b 🔊 **4.16** Compare with a partner. Then listen to the ending and say what actually happened in each story.

c Ⓖ **p.149 Grammar Bank 4B**

d Look at the photo above and, with a partner, make speculations and deductions.

- When and where could the photo have been taken?
- Who might the man be? What do you think he might be doing and why?
- What might have just happened?
- How might the man and the chimp be feeling?

e Ⓖ **Communication** What's going on? **A p.108 B p.113** Look at some more photos and make speculations and deductions.

5 READING

a In these situations, do you prefer background music or silence? Why? If you prefer music, what kind? Compare with a partner.

When you're…
- working or studying.
- relaxing at home.
- cooking.
- in the gym.
- in a bar or restaurant.
- shopping for clothes.
- put on hold on the phone.
- taking off in a plane, or landing.
- driving or in a car.

b Read the introduction to an article about the growing popularity of 'silent events'. What does the writer suggest may be the new and different thing about this trend?

c Read the rest of the article. Which of the **bold** events, 1–4, do the summaries describe?

A ▢ It helps people to understand what others are really like and encourages the use of body language.

B ▢ It is not usually held in a city and helps people feel better in mind and body.

C ▢ It discourages people from using their phones and allows them not to worry about social rules.

D ▢ It has only recently become popular in Britain and allows people to get away from the noise of their daily life.

d Find the following phrases in the article, and with a partner, explain what they mean in your own words.

1. something quite radical (*l.04*)
2. show up, shut up, and read (*l.08*)
3. escape the hubbub (*l.14*)
4. break the ice (*l.20*)
5. uninterrupted eye contact (*l.22*)
6. the age-old connections (*l.31*)
7. strips away (*l.32*)
8. hadn't been able to deal with (*l.37*)
9. cherish rare moments of peace and quiet (*l.46*)
10. muster up the self-restraint (*l.48*)

e If you had to do one of the four silent activities in the article, which would you choose? Why?

How being quiet can change your life

Silence is on the rise. Whole businesses have sprung up to meet a rising demand for quiet time, from silent weekends away to silent dining, silent reading parties, and even silent dating. We usually only spend silent time with those closest to us, so there is something quite radical
05 **about the recent trend for enjoying silence with strangers.**

The concept of [1] **silent reading** began in Seattle, USA. Devised as a literary meeting place for people who don't like book discussion groups, the idea was simple: show up, shut up, and read. Then the trend spread to the UK. Mariel Symeonidou started a regular silent reading party in Dundee,
10 Scotland, just under a year ago. Readers bring their books and meet in a bar, where they read together in silence for an hour or two, then put the books away to chat and have a drink. 'When the reading starts, everything goes quiet,' says Symeonidou. 'There is something special about sharing silence with others. An event like this gives people the opportunity to escape the
15 hubbub of their lives for a while.'

London's [2] **silent speed dating** event organizers, Shhh!, say that we are 'instinctively better at choosing the right partner when we have the chance to put aside words and see each other as we really are'. Shhh! hosts regular singles events which are very popular with creative professionals in their
20 20s and 30s. The sessions begin with games to break the ice. Then you are paired off for a limited time, when you are allowed to communicate only with gestures, before engaging in 60 seconds of uninterrupted eye contact. Afterwards, you are given the contact details of people who are interested in you. A second date might be something like a silent dinner date or a mute
25 trip to the pictures.

Honi Ryan, from Berlin, began hosting [3] **silent dinners** over ten years ago. The rules of the dinner are: no talking, no using your voice, no reading or writing, try to make as little noise as possible, do not interact with technology, and stay for at least two hours. So far, Ryan has hosted silent
30 dinners in Mexico, the USA, Australia, Lebanon, and China. 'It's evident that the age-old connections we make over food do not depend on the words around it,' she says. 'Silence strips away our rehearsed social behaviours.'

Perhaps the most well-known event is the [4] **silent retreat**. These often have a religious or spiritual element. They can last anywhere between a couple of
35 days to a few weeks, and are usually held in remote locations. Peter Cadney first discovered the power of silence on a ten-day silent meditation course. 'There had been a number of events in my life that I hadn't been able to deal with very well – relationship break-ups and the death of a close friend. Also, I'd spent years working at a computer and was feeling the effects of muscle
40 tension, anxiety, and stress.' Cadney says silent meditation has helped to improve both his mental and physical health. 'When I first sat down in silence, it felt very peaceful. I started noticing just how many thoughts were coming and going in my mind. It was as if there had been no space for silence.'

Silence is taking on a new meaning in an era in which we are consuming
45 information and engaging in conversation with each other endlessly on social media, without ever opening our mouths. However, while we might cherish rare moments of peace and quiet, when it comes to embracing silence and stillness, the real question is, can we actually muster up the self-restraint?

Adapted from The Guardian

6 SPEAKING

a Look at the sign on a British train. Do you think it's a good idea? Why (not)? Do you have these signs on trains in your country?

Quiet zone....Shh...!
Please show consideration for other passengers by not using mobile phones, headphones or personal stereos etc., in this peaceful area

b Read an online thread about quiet carriages. How many people think it works well?

> **Tony** 52m ago **Original poster**
>
> What IS the point of the quiet carriage? I was sat in one the other day and people were playing music that I could hear through their headphones, and talking loudly for ages on their phones.

> **Sheila** 48m ago **#2**
>
> I asked someone to stop using his phone once, and he just ignored me. ¹ As far as I'm concerned, the sign is completely pointless.

> **Cathy** 45m ago **#3**
>
> Even in the quiet carriage, there's bound to be some noise, and they're still quieter than normal carriages. ² My feeling is that it's best to live and let live, unless someone is being really obnoxious.

> **Jennifer** 39m ago **#4**
>
> The staff should ask passengers not to use mobile phones, and keep their music down. ³ In my view, that's their job, but they don't often do it.

> **Harry** 33m ago **#5**
>
> ⁴ If you ask me, they're never going to work. They can't stop people talking altogether. It really annoys me that people ignore the sign, but I would never dare challenge anyone about it.

> **Anna** 27m ago **#6**
>
> It's the quiet coach, not the silent coach. ⁵ Personally, I think that normal conversation is acceptable. I find them relatively restful.

> **Thomas** 18m ago **#7**
>
> ⁶ I'd say the only way round it is to buy yourself a set of noise-cancelling headphones.

c 🔊 4.17 Look at the highlighted phrases in **b** for giving opinions. Underline the word with the strongest stress in each phrase. Then listen and check.

d Read about some noise regulations from different countries. Then discuss them in small groups. Do you think they're a good idea? How would you adapt them for your country? Try to use the phrases in **b** to give your opinions.

1 In Germany, you aren't allowed to do loud DIY jobs on Sundays.
2 In Petrolia, Canada, you can't shout, whistle, or sing in the streets at any time.
3 On the island of Capri, Italy, you aren't allowed to wear noisy footwear, including flip-flops.
4 In some Swiss blocks of flats, it isn't permitted to flush the toilet after 10 p.m.
5 In Sydney, Australia, you aren't allowed to play a musical instrument between 10 p.m. and 8 a.m.

7 ▶ VIDEO LISTENING

a Watch a documentary about the British percussionist Evelyn Glennie. Tick (✓) the things that are mentioned.

- ☐ Evelyn's early life
- ☐ the repertoire for solo percussion
- ☐ problems associated with her deafness
- ☐ the different kinds of performances she gives
- ☐ musicians she's performed with
- ☐ her most memorable performance
- ☐ her instrument collection
- ☐ her own compositions
- ☐ her advice for beginner percussionists
- ☐ her favourite kind of music
- ☐ significant moments in her career
- ☐ why she thinks listening is important

b Watch again. Why does Evelyn Glennie mention these things?

1 targeting composers
2 playing at the front of the orchestra
3 dancers, visual artists, storytellers, sound designers
4 a favourite child
5 films, radio, television
6 being close to neighbours
7 playing to a group of five-year-olds
8 glue
9 dementia

c What do you think is the most impressive thing about Evelyn Glennie's career? Which do you think is more important in being a good communicator, being able to express yourself or being able to listen? Why?

Go online to watch the video and review the lesson

GRAMMAR

a Complete the sentences with the correct word or phrase.

1 It's 2.30 now – what time do you think we'll get _____ London?
2 Unfortunately, Allie got _____ cheating in her final exam.
3 The windows are absolutely filthy. Shall we get someone _____ them?
4 I don't think Keith will ever get _____ to doing his own laundry – his parents always did it for him.
5 My visa expires quite soon, so I really need to get it _____.

b Right (✓) or wrong (✗)? Correct any mistakes in the highlighted phrases.

1 Basic, I think he still hasn't got over the break-up of their marriage.
2 We've finished the interviews and all of all we think Joe Young is the most suitable candidate.
3 Not only we saw the sights, we managed to do some shopping as well.
4 Only when the main character dies does her husband realize how much he needed her.
5 Dave's really late, isn't he? I think he might get lost.
6 The waiter didn't probably notice that they had left without paying.
7 I think it's unlikely that I'll be given a work permit.
8 What a wonderful smell! Somebody must bake some bread.
9 You definitely won't pass your driving test if you drive that fast!
10 I called you yesterday. You should have got a message on your voicemail.

c Complete the sentences with the correct form of the verb in brackets.

1 No sooner _____ married than James lost his job. (they / get)
2 Never _____ such a wonderful view. It completely took my breath away. (I / see)
3 The traffic is quite bad – she's unlikely _____ before 7.00. (arrive)
4 Maria is bound _____ the news – everybody was talking about it yesterday. (hear)
5 My neighbour can't _____ very long hours. He's always home by early afternoon. (work)

VOCABULARY

a Complete the missing words.

1 She's quite shy, but you'll soon get to _____ her.
2 When did your son and his girlfriend first get _____?
3 I've been trying to get _____ of Danny, but he's not answering his phone.
4 My boss is always phoning me at home – it really gets on my _____.
5 I hope I get _____ this cold by the weekend; I'm supposed to be going to a wedding.
6 His parents let him do whatever he wants, so he's used to getting his own _____.
7 When I was a student, I had to get _____ on less than £50 a week.
8 I hope I get the _____ to talk to him before he goes home.

b Circle the correct word.

1 The government has *declared / executed* a state of emergency.
2 After days of fighting, both sides agreed to a *retreat / ceasefire*.
3 The city finally fell after a three-month *siege / coup*.
4 During the civil war, thousands of *refugees / allies* crossed the border to safety.
5 It was a fierce battle and *civilians / casualties* were heavy on both sides.
6 The rebels *broke out / blew up* the railway lines.
7 Even though they were surrounded, the troops refused to *surrender / defeat*.
8 The president has refused to *overthrow / release* any information about his tax returns.

c Complete the sentences with a verb from the list in the past simple.

buzz   creak   rattle   screech   sigh   slam
whisper   whistle

1 Mabel _____ the door and walked off angrily.
2 'Thanks, darling', she _____ softly in his ear.
3 He _____ a happy tune as he walked down the street.
4 'I wish he was here – I really miss him', she _____.
5 The wind was so strong that the windows _____.
6 The car's brakes _____ as it came to a stop.
7 A bee flew in through the window and _____ round the room.
8 The door of the old library _____ open slowly, but there was nobody there!

d Write the adjectives for the definitions.

1 th_____-pr_____ = making you think seriously about a particular subject or issue
2 h_____-w_____ = making you feel happy
3 in_____ = very interesting because of being unusual or not having an obvious answer or ending
4 gr_____ = exciting or interesting in a way that keeps your attention
5 m_____ = causing you to have deep feelings of sadness or sympathy
6 im_____ = not seeming reasonable or likely to be true

CAN YOU understand this text?

a Read the article once. How good was Branko's English when he first met Faith? How good is it now?

b Read the article again and choose the best words to complete the gaps.

1 a journey b trip c travel d voyage
2 a therefore b so c because d but
3 a translate b talk c understand d interfere
4 a off b down c on d over
5 a met up b made up c broken up d got together
6 a already b now c ever d still
7 a go back to b remember c imagine d go up to
8 a often b rarely c frequently d sometimes
9 a during b when c as d while
10 a watch out b look out c find out d turn out

▶ CAN YOU understand these people?

◀》4.18 Watch or listen and choose a, b, or c.

1 **Sophie** first met her partner ____.
a through mutual friends
b on Facebook
c when they were young

2 **Sarah** learned a lot about ____ in the TV series *Victoria*.
a relationships within the royal family
b the introduction of the railway in Britain
c an affair between an aristocrat and a servant

3 **James** enjoys reading ____.
a historical novels
b books about classical composers
c books set in imaginary worlds

4 A sound **Amy** finds irritating is one she hears ____.
a in the autumn
b when she wants to work
c when she's outside

We fell in love without speaking

▲ Faith and Branko Ristic: 'It felt unreal, like magic.'

I'll never forget the first moment I saw Branko. It was 2009, and I was 25, working as a musical director for a circus in the UK. I'd travelled alone to the village of Gornja Grabovica in Serbia, on a mission to learn Roma-style accordion. A week or so into my two-month [1]____, a friend called Dusan took me to meet his cousin Branko, who he said was one of the country's best violinists.

When we arrived, Branko came out of the house wearing a white vest and jeans. I don't remember thinking he was attractive, [2]____ for some reason I took a photo of him that I still have today. We all sat around a table in the garden. I didn't speak a word of Serbian and Branko knew no English, so Dusan tried to [3]____. Branko was shy; it wasn't every day an English woman turned up at his house. The following day I went back, and we played music together late into the night. We did this several more times, quickly developing a strong connection. It was totally platonic, however; nothing else entered my head, partly because he had a girlfriend.

After two months, I returned to Britain and for the next couple of years I was busy touring with my work. Then, in July 2011, I had a few weeks [4]____, and went back to Serbia. As soon as Branko heard I was back in Gornja Grabovica, he came straight to see me. With Dusan translating again, he told me he'd thought about me every day since I had left. He had [5]____ with his girlfriend months earlier. It felt unreal, like magic. It was exciting to acknowledge our connection, but unusual to feel something for each other without being able to communicate fully.

That night we went to an *igranke*, a dance. I just enjoyed being near Branko. His body language was so open, and he was so kind and loving. The next day we played music together for hours, creating new compositions. He [6]____ couldn't say a word in English, and I'd only picked up basic things in Serbian, but it just felt right. We could usually work out instinctively what the other was trying to say, and if we couldn't, we'd just laugh. It was so romantic. If I could rewind time, I'd [7]____ that moment.

Branko and I planned to go to Britain together for a while, to earn money and introduce him to my life; but he had [8]____ travelled even in his own country, and his tourist visa was refused twice. It was difficult to go back alone. When I returned to Serbia, we decided to get married, and we had a simple but chaotic wedding. We built a house on the exact spot we first met, in Branko's grandmother's garden. Today my Serbian is pretty good, and [9]____ Branko still doesn't speak fluent English, he understands a lot. They say music is the language of the soul. We took a leap to [10]____ if that is true, and music has held us together ever since.

Abridged from The Guardian

🔗 **Go online** to watch the video, review Files 3 & 4, and check your progress

It is not enough to be busy. So are the ants.
The question is: What are we busy about?
Henry David Thoreau, US philosopher

G distancing **V** expressions with *time* **P** linking in short phrases

1 SPEAKING

a Think about the last time you were very busy. What things did you have to do?

b Do the quiz.

Am I too busy?

Circle *Yes* or *No* for each statement.

1 I often commit to things and then regret it. Yes No

2 I never feel like I've accomplished enough at the end of the day. Yes No

3 When I do have a day off, I fill it with activities. Yes No

4 I have difficulty saying no. Yes No

5 I often miscalculate how long certain activities will take. Yes No

6 I find myself constantly wishing I had more time. Yes No

7 I rarely have time to do the things I really love. Yes No

8 I feel powerless over my time and commitments. Yes No

9 I rarely, if ever, schedule downtime in my calendar. Yes No

10 Others complain that my schedule doesn't allow enough time for them. Yes No

c **☺ Communication** Am I too busy? **p.111** Find out what your score means.

d Compare your score with a partner and discuss the reasons for your answers. How similar are you?

2 READING

a Look at the two nouns below. How are they pronounced? What do they mean?

business   busyness

b Read the first paragraphs of two articles about busyness. In pairs, try to complete the missing word in both titles. Which article is positive and which is negative about being busy?

c Now read the rest of the two articles and answer the questions.

Article 1

Why…? 1 does social media cause FOMO
2 might people who have recently split up try to keep busy
3 might being busy improve somebody's social status
4 might somebody feel guilty or ashamed

Article 2

Why…? 5 is it becoming harder to live a life of leisure
6 might busy people sleep better
7 might it be a bad idea to retire early
8 is it beneficial for older people to do voluntary work

d **Language in context** Look at some verb phrases from the articles. Complete the gaps with a particle. Then, in pairs, decide what they mean. Use the context to help you.

1 get _____ to sb (*Text 1, l.01*)
2 be _____ the go (*Text 1, l.02*)
3 stand _____ sth (*Text 1, l.08*)
4 keep your mind _____ sth (*Text 1, l.18*)
5 keep sth _____ bay (*Text 2, l.07*)
6 ward _____ sth (*Text 2, l.27*)

e Talk to a partner.

- For you, is being busy a good or a bad thing?
- Do you ever feel guilty if you aren't busy?
- Do you ever have a problem relaxing?
- Do you ever feel that you have too much free time?
- What do you do to help yourself feel less stressed?

1 Are you a _____ to being busy?

'Let me check my diary and get back to you', is a phrase we've all uttered. We are constantly on the go, trying to squeeze friends and family, work, and fitness into our increasingly demanding lifestyles.
05 And while we have all struggled with a jam-packed week at some stage, it's possible some people have developed an actual addiction to 'busyness'.

Many busy people suffer from FOMO, which stands for 'fear of missing out', and is defined as anxiety, often
10 caused by social media, that an exciting or interesting event is happening somewhere which they are not part of. Others pack their schedules in order to avoid dealing with other things in their lives. 'When our mind isn't occupied with a task, we are left with our thoughts and
15 our emotions,' says psychologist Jaimie Bloch. 'This makes many people feel uncomfortable and anxious. For example, those who have recently left relationships might use excessive activity as a way to keep their minds off the break-up. Others may have a fear of being unproductive,
20 so busyness feels like a way to achieve success. When these people aren't busy, it's a form of failure.' Ms Bloch also says that in a society obsessed with productivity and achievement, being busy can be a way to elevate your social status. 'Being busy creates a sense of importance
25 and value. The idea of relaxing, not doing anything, is linked to emotions such as guilt and shame.'

2 What keeps you h_____ is being busy, busy, busy!

We all dream of leading a life of leisure. Often that dream just keeps receding from our grasp. Pension ages are going up, and smartphones and social media mean we're never really 'switched
05 off'. But now, emerging medical research suggests that staying busy helps us to live longer, keeps us strong, and could even keep dementia at bay.

Recently, American researchers revealed that we sleep better when we have lots of reasons to jump out of bed
10 in the morning. Neurologists in Chicago reported that people who are busily purposeful – in particular, having a packed agenda of future plans – are less troubled by insomnia. And psychologists at the University of Texas reported that the busier people are, the stronger their
15 mental powers, regardless of age or education.

It appears that keeping busy as we age is particularly beneficial – even if it means working beyond retirement age. Italian neuroscientists have warned that people aged over 50 who retire early are more likely to lose
20 muscle strength and become ill. Last year, another report found that people who retired later were significantly less likely to develop cognitive difficulties like loss of memory. Voluntary work has a similar effect. Professor Yannick Griep, a psychologist at Canada's
25 University of Calgary, says that seniors who volunteer are more physically, mentally, and socially active, which helps to ward off dementia.

Adapted from The Daily Mail

3 LISTENING

a Mindfulness is a technique which many busy people use to help them focus on the present and stop worrying about the future. You're going to do a well-known mindfulness exercise called *The Chocolate Meditation*. Before you listen, with a partner, say what you think these verbs mean.

unwrap   inhale   pop (sth) into   melt   chew   swallow

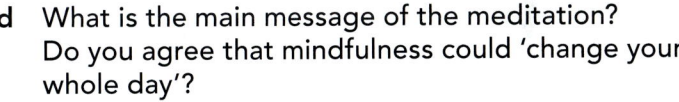

b 🔊 5.1 Close your eyes and listen. Imagine doing all the stages.

c Listen again. What does the speaker say about…?
1 the type of chocolate to choose
2 what to do before you unwrap it
3 what to notice as you unwrap it
4 what to do before you eat it
5 what to notice and do as you put it in your mouth
6 when to swallow it

d What is the main message of the meditation? Do you agree that mindfulness could 'change your whole day'?

4 GRAMMAR distancing

a Read three sentences about mindfulness and focus on the highlighted phrases. What effect would it have on the meaning if they were left out?
1 Jon Kabat-Zinn is considered to be the 'father' of mindfulness.
2 He claims to help people cope with stress.
3 It appears that mindfulness helps to reduce anxiety.

b 🅖 p.150 Grammar Bank 5A

c You're a journalist. You've been asked to write three breaking news stories for a website. However, the facts haven't been confirmed yet. Write two or three sentences for each headline, using the prompts and appropriate distancing expressions.

Politician's wife seeks divorce

Which politician? After how many years of marriage? What do people say is the reason?

Footballer linked to match-fixing scandal

Which footballer? What did he do? What is his club planning to do about it?

Sugar: the new health benefits

What are the benefits? How much sugar do you need to eat? When / In what form should you eat it?

5 LISTENING

a Look at a survey by the watch manufacturer Timex. Which two things would make you the most impatient?

How long are we prepared to wait before we freak out?

How long do you think the average person will wait for something before getting annoyed and trying to do something about it? Here are the answers, according to a survey by Timex.

When you're waiting...	Average time before getting annoyed
1 for a car in front of you to start moving when the light turns green.	
2 for people to stop talking during a film at the cinema.	
3 for a child to stop crying before you give their parents an angry look.	
4 to see the doctor.	
5 for your partner to get ready to go out.	
6 in a queue at a coffee shop.	
7 for a blind date to arrive.	
8 for someone to stop talking loudly on their phone before you tell them to keep their voice down.	

b With a partner, try to complete the survey with the times from the list.

32 minutes
26 minutes
21 minutes
7 minutes

2 minutes 41 seconds
2 minutes 25 seconds
1 minute 52 seconds
50 seconds

c ◆) 5.2 Now listen to an American journalist, Sam Greenspan, talking about the Timex survey. Check your answers to **b**.

d Listen again. Does Sam agree or disagree with each survey answer? Is he more or less patient than the average person?

e **Language in context** Look at some American English expressions that Sam uses. What is the usual British English word or phrase?

1 a movie theater
2 it doesn't really bug me
3 get mad
4 waiting in line
5 a takeout
6 a server

f Work with a partner. Look at the survey in **a** again. Would you wait a longer or shorter time than average in these situations? In what other circumstances do you hate having to wait?

6 VOCABULARY expressions with *time*

a ◆) 5.3 Listen to three people talking about waiting for things. What situations do they complain about? Do you agree with them?

b Listen again and complete each extract with four words.

1 ...but more often they'll say it _____ from 7 a.m. to 7 p.m...
2 It doesn't really happen so much nowadays, but _____, I'll be somewhere where there's, like, really bad internet connection...
3 ...I always _____ – in fact, usually at least five minutes early...

c **V** p.167 **Vocabulary Bank** Expressions with *time*

d Complete the sentences so that they are true for you or reflect what you think. Then compare with a partner.

1 By the time I'm..., I'll be...
2 Everyone should...from time to time.
3 It's only a matter of time before...
4 I had the time of my life when I...
5 I waste a lot of time...
6 It's going to take me a long time to...
7 It's about time I...
8 I find...very time-consuming.
9 If I had more time off, I'd...

7 PRONUNCIATION linking in short phrases

a 🔊 **5.7** Listen to sentences 1–10. Why are the words linked? Read the information box and check.

1 We need‿to make‿up for lost‿time.
2 He gave me a really hard‿time.
3 We're going to run‿out‿of time.
4 Could‿I have some time‿off next week?
5 At‿times‿I feel‿like giving‿up completely.
6 Time's‿up. Please‿stop writing.
7 Let's not waste‿time‿on that.
8 It's‿only a matter‿of time before they break‿up.
9 Did you have‿a good‿time last night?
10 It's‿about‿time you learned‿to cook!

> 🔍 **Linking in fast speech**
>
> When people speak quickly, they tend to link two or more words together so they sound like one word. This could be because:
>
> 1 a consonant sound at the end of a word is linked to a vowel sound at the beginning of the next, e.g. *I met him‿a long time‿ago.*
>
> 2 a word ending with a consonant sound is followed by a word beginning with the same consonant sound, e.g. *I need‿some‿more time.* This also applies to two very similar sounds, like /d/ and /t/, e.g. *Have a good‿time!*, and /z/ and /s/, e.g. *Please‿sit down.*
>
> 3 a word ending with a silent *r* or *re*, e.g. *quarter, spare*, is followed by a word beginning with a vowel sound. In this case, the words are linked and a /r/ sound is added, e.g. *a quarter‿of an‿hour.*

b 🔊 **5.8** Listen to some three-word phrases which are often heard as one word. First, you'll hear the phrase on its own, and then you'll hear it in context. Write the phrases.

1 _____ _____ _____
2 _____ _____ _____
3 _____ _____ _____
4 _____ _____ _____
5 _____ _____ _____

c Practise saying the sentences and phrases in **a** and **b**, trying to link the words.

8 SPEAKING

a Complete the questions in *Time and you*.

Time and you

1 Do you have any apps that you think really s_____ you time? Which ones?
2 When you do an exam or test, do you tend to have **time l_____** at the end, or do you usually r_____ o_____ of time?
3 When you were younger, did your parents g_____ you a h_____ **time** if you came home late? Where had you usually been?
4 On a typical weekday morning, are you usually **sh_____ of time?** Why?
5 What do you usually do to k_____ **time** while you're waiting at an airport or a station?
6 When you go shopping, do you like to buy things as quickly as possible, or do you prefer to t_____ **your time?**
7 Is there anything or anybody who is t_____ u_____ a l_____ **of your time** at the moment? How do you feel about it?
8 Are you usually o_____ **time** when you meet friends? Does it bother you when other people are late?
9 Do you usually get to the airport or station w_____ **time to** sp_____ or at the last minute?
10 What do you most enjoy doing when you have some **m_____ time?**

b Now ask and answer the questions in small groups. Give examples.

(*My banking app definitely saves me time – I can…*

🔵 **Go online** to review the lesson

G unreal uses of past tenses · **V** money · **P** silent consonants

1 VOCABULARY money

a Look at eight pictures which represent idioms related to money. With a partner, explain what you think they mean. Do you have a similar expression in your language?

1 Money doesn't grow on trees.

2 He's really tight-fisted.

3 It must have cost an arm and a leg.

4 I can't make ends meet.

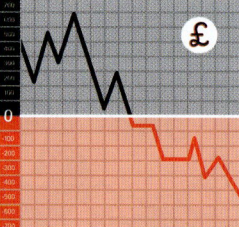

5 We're in the red. (opp *in the black*)

6 It's a rip-off!

7 We're going to have to tighten our belts.

8 My sister's definitely living beyond her means!

b **V** p.168 **Vocabulary Bank** Money

c Circle the correct word according to meaning, collocation, or register.

1 Mum, can you lend me some money? I'm *broke / penniless*.
2 I'm trying to get a *mortgage / loan* from the bank to buy a car.
3 We're going to have to be careful this month if we don't want to end up *in the red / in the black*.
4 He took part of his pension as a *lump sum / deposit*.
5 One of my cousins is absolutely *affluent / loaded* – she inherited a fortune from her parents.
6 The *currency / exchange* rate is terrible! £1 is only $1.20.
7 We like living here because we have a much better *cost / standard* of living.
8 A Is breakfast included in the price of the room?
   B No, sir. It's 12 *pounds / quid* extra.

d Look at the questions below. Think of two or three people you know and tell a partner about them.

> **Do you know anybody who...?**
> - is a bit tight-fisted
> - lives beyond their means
> - buys and sells shares on the stock market
> - charges very high fees for what they do
> - was given a grant to study abroad
> - often gives donations to charity
> - has difficulty making ends meet

2 PRONUNCIATION silent consonants

a Look at these words related to money and say them aloud. Cross out the consonants that are not pronounced.

debt   mortgage   dishonest

b 🔊 5.13 Listen to ten sentences and write the last word in each. Then cross out the silent consonant.

3 READING & SPEAKING

a With a partner, choose the correct definition of *capitalism*.

> **capitalism**
> /ˈkæpɪtəlɪzəm/ 🔊
> an economic system in which businesses and industry are...

1 controlled and run for profit by private owners.
2 controlled and run for profit by the government.
3 controlled by the government, but non-profit-making.

b Read the introduction to the article, and look at the ten headings. Do you already do any of these 'small things'?

10 small ways to lead an anti-capitalist life

When I asked readers recently for examples of 'everyday things that represent non-capitalist living', I received a [1] deluge of replies. One reader said: 'Living in our consumer society, I am frequently filled with despair at the way things are going in the world at the moment, and doing this small thing at least makes me feel as though I'm doing something positive,' which really [2] gets to the heart of the idea.

1 Freecycle as much as possible When you're [3] lumbered with something you either don't want or don't need, you can connect via the internet with someone for whom it might have a use. Scores of readers recommended the Freecycle network and the UK group Freegle. You can get anything, from beds, pianos, and bikes, to a 'bag of make-up and toiletries, opened but still usable'.

2 Leave stuff outside for your neighbours Chris Everitt lives in Berlin. 'We have a little covered alleyway just off our high street where people leave things all the time: books, furniture, clothes, [4] knick-knacks, even food. When you have something that no longer serves you in your life, you can place it there. Within a few hours, it will be part of someone else's life.'

3 Make your own clothes 'I no longer buy clothes,' says Clea Whitley, 33, from London. 'I make them myself. I do have to buy fabric and clothing patterns, but I only buy what I need. It's not that I can't afford high-street clothes. But hopefully, with mine, no child labour, toxic chemicals, or animal cruelty are involved.'

4 Forget the gym A 23-year-old graduate writes, 'I once had a gym membership: £25 a month to be breathing in warm air [5] laced with sweat, and listening to extremely loud pop music promoting a glamorous and affluent lifestyle. I now enjoy jogging in the park, where I can enjoy nature while exercising in a much healthier way. There are no mirrors to show you how 'good' or 'bad' you look, so no reasons to make yourself feel bad or [6] pump up your ego.

5 Make your own spreadable butter A small contribution, perhaps, but ingenious. You just have to mix butter with oil, preferably something without too strong a taste. 'It's easier to spread, and reduces the amount of butter we use,' advises a reader from London. 'It's an alternative to spreads in plastic tubs, and those that use palm oil. I don't contribute to the destruction of the habitat of orangutans.'

6 Stop buying cleaning products Not so long ago, one respondent had a look around her kitchen and bathroom and had a [7] watershed moment. 'Most of my household cleaning products have been replaced with a homemade mix of white vinegar and water, 1:3 parts. Bicarbonate of soda works, too.'

7 Go online, then visit the library 'Search for books on Amazon, read the reviews and then go to the public library,' advises Kath, from Oxford.

8 Get an allotment 'Keep fit by growing vegetables,' offers a retired teacher. 'We give the excess produce to people as we walk home after harvesting. In summer, we are self-sufficient as far as vegetables are concerned, and in winter we have enough potatoes, squash, and onions to use until March.'

9 Don't drive 'I have never driven a car,' says Sara Gaynor. 'I decided from 1988, after living in Copenhagen, that I would never be part of car culture and all that goes with it – petrol, pollution, traffic jams, the oil and advertising industries. I cycle every day to work. I do my shopping using my bike, and my kids were brought up travelling around by bike and public transport.'

10 Use your TV remote And finally, someone got in touch with this [8] pearl of wisdom: 'If you watch any TV at all, you can't avoid the adverts to buy this, buy that… Just turn the sound down when the adverts are on.'

Adapted from The Guardian

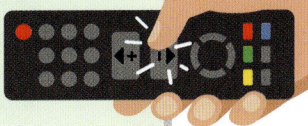

---

c Read the whole article and put activities 1–10 into the correct category. Some activities go in more than one category.

Which readers are...?	
doing things that are free instead of paying for them	
giving things away that they don't need	
creating or producing things instead of buying them	
doing something that doesn't pollute and is healthier	
doing something to avoid the temptation to spend	

d Look at the highlighted words and phrases in the article and match them to meanings A–H.

A ☐ left with sth that you don't want and can't get rid of
B ☐ small, decorative objects
C ☐ a turning point, after which things will never be the same
D ☐ (*literally*, a flood) a large number of things that happen or arrive at the same time
E ☐ (*metaphor*) a wise remark
F ☐ mixed together with
G ☐ (*metaphor*) focuses on the most important part of sth
H ☐ (*metaphor*) to increase your sense of your own value or importance

e Talk in small groups.

1 Which of the suggestions in the article do you think are a good idea? Which ones might you try? Do you think any are a bit ridiculous?

2 Do you agree that making small changes to your lifestyle can make a significant difference to the world?

3 Have you bought anything in the last week that you wanted but didn't really need?

4 Do you ever buy things for yourself that are second-hand, e.g. vintage clothes? Would you ever give somebody something second-hand as a present, or give a home-made present?

4 GRAMMAR unreal uses of past tenses

1 When we got married, we were penniless but happy!

2 If we bought bikes, we'd be able to sell the car.

3 It's time Jon stopped spending so much on stuff we don't really need.

4 If only I could work part-time and get an allotment.

5 I wish we'd been able to save more when we were younger.

6 I can't believe that Sarah didn't accept that promotion!

7 If she borrowed some money from her parents, we could afford a new car.

8 I'd rather the kids went to a private school.

a Look at the couple in the photo and read what they're thinking. Who is more 'anti-capitalist'?

b Look at the highlighted verbs and answer the questions with a partner.
   - Which verbs refer to things that really happened in the past?
   - What do the others have in common?

c Ⓖ p.151 Grammar Bank 5B

d Ask and answer the questions in small groups. Do you ever wish…?
   - you'd chosen to study different subjects at school or university
   - you could have a year off to travel
   - you could learn a new skill
   - you had more free time for your hobbies and interests
   - you lived in another town or city
   - you could come up with a great idea for a business

5 LISTENING

a Read a website extract about small businesses. Do you agree with the six reasons? How often do you buy from a small business? What do you buy?

Six reasons to shop small and local

Last Saturday, the annual celebration of Small Business Saturday was a great day for small businesses in the UK. An estimated £748 million was spent across the country with small businesses in 24 hours. But Small Business Saturday is not a one-day-a-year publicity drive. It aims to change mindsets all year round.

So why should we be buying from small businesses?

1 Small businesses create jobs.
2 Spending money with a small business keeps more money in your local economy.
3 Small businesses add colour and variety to our towns.
4 Small business owners are at the forefront of innovation.
5 Small businesses care about their reputation.
6 Small food businesses are often more environmentally friendly.

b Look at an extract from the website of a small food business. Do you think the business is a good idea? Would you order from them? Why (not)?

WHAT IS PASTA EVANGELISTS?

We deliver what we think is the best pasta in the UK to homes across the country. You can then prepare a 5-star pasta dish in just five minutes, impressing friends and delighting family.

Our little team is passionate about its mission. Our pasta and sauces are made exclusively in London, usually by Italian hands, and prepared with the best ingredients from across Italy. No additives, no bad stuff. We deliver in insulated packaging, meaning it's not a problem if you're not home for delivery: your food will stay cool and fresh until you're back. *Buon appetito.*

'Really delicious and simple to cook.'
William Sitwell, *MasterChef* judge and food critic

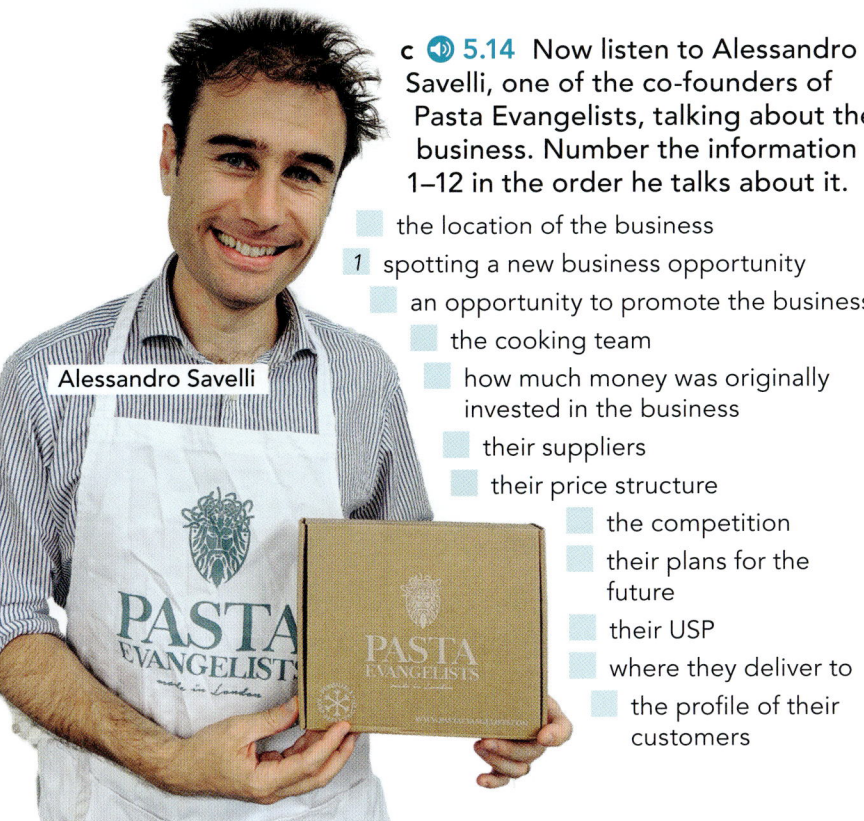

Alessandro Savelli

c 🔊 **5.14** Now listen to Alessandro Savelli, one of the co-founders of Pasta Evangelists, talking about the business. Number the information 1–12 in the order he talks about it.

- ☐ the location of the business
- 1 spotting a new business opportunity
- ☐ an opportunity to promote the business
- ☐ the cooking team
- ☐ how much money was originally invested in the business
- ☐ their suppliers
- ☐ their price structure
- ☐ the competition
- ☐ their plans for the future
- ☐ their USP
- ☐ where they deliver to
- ☐ the profile of their customers

Glossary

Dragons' Den a TV programme where people pitch ideas for new businesses to a panel of judges, who decide whether or not to invest money

Deliveroo an online company that delivers food from restaurants to customers' houses

d Listen again. Why does Alessandro mention the following?

1 selling gnocchi
2 Harrods
3 *sfoglini*
4 Sicily and Piemonte
5 £2,000
6 two million individuals
7 restaurants and takeaways
8 £12.00
9 small villages
10 'We've just scratched the surface.'

e Do you think Pasta Evangelists would be a success in your country? Why (not)?

6 SPEAKING

a Read about a scheme to encourage small businesses.

> The local town council is looking for people with fresh new ideas for small food-related businesses, and is prepared to offer a loan. It is interested in the following areas:
> - a small café or restaurant
> - a food delivery service
> - a shop specializing in one type of food or drink
> - a new local product, e.g. cheese, olive oil, etc.
>
> If interested, please submit your business proposal via our website.

b Work in small groups. You're going to put in a proposal. Decide together:
- what your business is going to be.
- whether it will be online or a physical café, shop, etc.
- what businesses currently exist in this area.
- what your USP will be.
- who your customers are likely to be.
- how many people you will employ.
- what your price structure will be.
- how you will promote your business.
- why you think it will be a success.

c Now present your proposal to the class. Have a class vote on who should get the loan.

7 WRITING

Ⓦ **p.122 Writing** A proposal Analyse a proposal for increasing student numbers at a language school, and write a proposal.

1 ▶ THE INTERVIEW Part 1

a Read the biographical information about Jordan Friedman. Would you be interested in participating in one of his stress reduction programmes?

Jordan Friedman, also known as 'The Stress Coach', lives in New York City and is a specialist in the field of stress and stress reduction. He has been developing stress management programmes and resources for individuals, companies, and universities worldwide for over 20 years, and his client list includes Harvard University, the Massachusetts Institute of Technology, and the New York City Department of Education. He is the author of *The Stress Manager's Manual*, and his work has been featured by *The New York Times*, *The Wall Street Journal*, and *The Today Show*. Jordan is an expert on student stress, and has developed a programme called Stressbusters, which helps nearly 250,000 university students and staff.

b Watch Part 1 of the interview. Why does Jordan Friedman think it's important to reduce stress?

c Now watch again. Complete sentences 1–5.

1 The biggest causes of stress are…
2 Compared with 20 years ago, life today is more stressful because…
3 Nowadays, we don't have time to…
4 If our immune systems are weakened by stress,…
5 If we don't sleep well,…

d To what extent are you currently affected by stress? What impact is it having on you?

> **Glossary**
> **stressor** (*technical*) something that causes stress
> **the immune system** the system in your body that fights infection and disease
> **punching bag** (*AmE*) a heavy leather bag on a rope, used by boxers when they train (*BrE* **punchbag**)
> **stroke** a sudden serious illness when a blood vessel in the brain bursts or is blocked, which can cause death or the loss of the ability to move or to speak clearly

▶ Part 2

a Now watch Part 2. Mark the sentences **T** (true) or **F** (false).

1 Different people should choose different ways of dealing with stress.
2 The stress management techniques Jordan Friedman mentions all take a minute or less.
3 The most important thing about stress management techniques is to make them a habit.
4 Friedman worked with a student who felt very stressed when he had to drive.
5 The student's classmates suggested that he should travel at a different time of day.
6 The solution to the student's problem was difficult for him to see for himself.

b Watch again. Say why the **F** sentences are false.

c What kinds of situations make you feel stressed? What do you do to try to reduce the stress?

> **Glossary**
> **salad bar** a counter in a restaurant where customers can serve themselves from a variety of salad ingredients
> **walk around the block** go for a quick walk near where you live or work in a town or city
> **subway car** a carriage on an underground train

▶ Part 3

a Now watch Part 3. Do students in your country suffer from similar stress?

b Watch again and answer the questions.

1 At what age do people tend to be most stressed?
2 What main reasons does Jordan Friedman give for student stress?
3 How does stress affect memory? How might this affect students?
4 What two things does the Stressbusters programme give students?
5 What feedback have students given about Stressbusters?

c Do you ever have back rubs or massages when you feel stressed? Do they help you?

> **Glossary**
> **back rub** a short back massage
> **campus** the buildings of a university and the land around them
> **wellness resources** facilities for helping people to stay healthy

2 ▶ LOOKING AT LANGUAGE

> 🔍 **Compound nouns**
> Jordan Friedman frequently uses compound nouns, e.g. *stress response*, etc. Remember that when you hear new compound nouns, the first noun usually describes the second one – this will help you to work out the meaning.

a Try to complete the highlighted compound nouns in these extracts from the interview.

1 '…when you have emails coming in and t_____ messages left and right…'
2 'Stress is really important, and, in fact, it can be a l_____ saver…'
3 'Er, stress contributes to high bl_____ pressure, which contributes to h_____ problems and stroke.'
4 'So these are all reasons to really pay attention to our st_____ levels and to take action to reduce the stress.'
5 'The great thing about stress m_____ is that it's like a salad bar.'
6 'We can do one-minute br_____ exercises, we can, er, exercise, we can take a ten-minute walk around the block…'
7 'Stress is a very democratic occurrence, so older people are stressed, c_____ students are stressed, babies get stressed…'
8 '…there's a greater need to get help for, er, them while in school, but if you're not with your usual s_____ network, it's even more challenging sometimes to do so.'

b Watch and check.

3 ▶ THE CONVERSATION

Ida | John | Josie

a Watch the conversation. Circle the correct option to sum up each speaker's response to the question.

Josie It's *frustrating* / *motivating* to be able to compare yourself easily with other people.
Ida The slower pace of life in the past was stressful in *the same* / *a different* way.
John People nowadays have less *ambition* / *patience* than in the past.

b Watch again. What do the speakers mean when they say…?

1 '…you're pitted against everyone else in your career field…'
2 '…that was a different kind of stress.'
3 '…there was nothing you could do in between…'
4 '…you're expected to be reachable at all times…'
5 'There's no hiding place…'
6 '…nowadays it's like 'Now. I want it now.''

c Do you agree with the speakers that life is more stressful than it used to be? Why? Is your life getting more stressful?

d Watch some extracts in which the speakers refer back to something mentioned earlier. What do the **bold** words in each phrase refer back to?

1 …I think a big part of **that** is…
2 …because **it, it** sort of highlights the fact that…
3 And I think **you're absolutely right**,…
4 …I imagine **you do as well**…
5 …**that's** the problem…

e Now have a conversation in groups of three. Discuss the statements.

1 Being stressed can have positive as well as negative effects.
2 A 'slower pace of life' is always better.

> You know how advice is. You only want it if it agrees with what you wanted to do anyway.
> *John Steinbeck, US author*

G verb + object + infinitive or gerund **V** compound adjectives **P** main and secondary stress

1 READING & SPEAKING

a Look at problems 1–5 below. Where would you go to get advice for each problem? Would you…?

- ask a friend, colleague, or family member
- look online
- read a self-help book
- phone a helpline or contact a professional

> 1 Your wi-fi isn't working.
> 2 You're worried about some symptoms you have.
> 3 You want to know the best way to invest a sum of money you've inherited.
> 4 Your two-year-old child wakes up a lot at night.
> 5 You're having relationship problems because your partner travels a lot and you hardly ever see them.

b Read an online forum giving advice. Try to imagine yourself in this situation, and choose the three tips you think give the best advice.

c Read the forum again and choose the best word or phrase for each gap.

1 a effect b affect c spoil
2 a avoid b plan c cope with
3 a cooling b chilling c warming
4 a through b over c round
5 a pre-arranged b pre-booked c pre-ordered
6 a in and out b up and down c on and off
7 a remember b remind c recall
8 a exciting b common c mundane
9 a without b beside c beyond
10 a do b don't c won't

d Do you know anyone who is in a long-distance relationship? What problems do you think they have? Are there any advantages to their situation?

10 tips for long-distance relationships

We asked our online community to send us their top tips for surviving long-distance relationships. Here are some of their responses.

There may be people who don't believe your relationship will work, and that's OK, but you mustn't let what other people think ¹____ you, because you're the ones who are actually in the relationship. As long as you love each other and trust each other, and you think you can make the relationship work, then that's the only thing that matters. *Eileen*

I've been in a happy long-distance relationship for nearly two years. I find that it helps to think of it in the same way as trying to ²____ a break-up: I focus on my work, I rely a lot on my friends, and keep myself busy in the evenings and at weekends, to try to avoid ever feeling lonely. *Bruce*

Don't try to do too many different things when you do meet up. Make time for just ³____ and doing nothing. *Marshall*

Sometimes being apart really gets you down, and the only person who could make you feel better is a million miles away. It's OK to get emotional, it's OK to cry or get angry – just do whatever you need to do. It's so important not to keep your feelings inside. Your partner is the only person who really understands what you're going ⁴____, so never, never hide what you're feeling from them. *Sarah*

Don't forget to say good morning and goodnight to each other, every day without fail, even if you just send a quick text with a smiley face. We also have a regular ⁵____ time to Skype every day, which we can both look forward to. *Andy*

We played online games ⁶____ throughout the day, like Dominoes and Scrabble. It really helped to do something together even when we couldn't talk to each other. You can also get an app that lets you watch shows on Netflix at exactly the same time, which made it feel more like we were together. *Sandra*

My husband gave me one of his sweatshirts to wear, and I gave him a ring of mine on a leather necklace that he could wear all the time to ⁷____ him of me. It's really comforting to have a physical thing that belongs to them. *Shawna*

e Look at the titles of two articles giving advice from different points of view. Think of one piece of advice for each situation.

How to survive…
living with your parents
If you are among the quarter of young adults still living at home with Mum and Dad, read on!

The secret to…living with adult children
If you are one of the many parents whose adult children have returned to the nest, read on!

f **⊙ Communication** I need some help **A** p.109 **B** p.114 Read the articles and tell each other about the tips.

g Which do you think is better for getting advice, a forum or an article? Why? What are the advantages of each?

Talk to each other as often as you can, about everything, little things and big things. When you do have the chance to meet up, try to do ⁸____ things together, like doing the food shopping, as well as exciting things like concerts or expensive meals out. Try to keep your lives as normal as possible. *Jane*

Try not to get into situations where you're in some kind of competition about who cares less or more, or who's happier or unhappier. If you're apart, you need to learn to live ⁹____ each other. But you also need to appreciate how much happier you feel when you're together. If you find that you don't just need each other, you also want each other, that'll make your relationship stronger. *Alan*

Make sure you send your partner lots of photos of you. Maybe you think it's a bit self-centred, or maybe you really hate taking selfies, but they ¹⁰____ want to look at your face! *Owen*

2 GRAMMAR verb + object + infinitive or gerund

a Right (✓) or wrong (✗)? With a partner, correct any mistakes in the highlighted phrases.
1 If your partner can only call at a certain time, try not to keep them waiting.
2 I want that my boyfriend comes on holiday with me.
3 I recommend that you try to see each other once a month.
4 When I lived with my parents, I was always made load the dishwasher.
5 I hate my parents talk to me as if I was five years old.
6 Mum, could you let me borrow the car tonight?
7 I don't mind you not tidy your room, but at least make your bed!
8 Living at home may involve you paying around 50% of the market-rate rent.
9 Can you help me do the washing-up?

b **G** p.152 Grammar Bank 6A

c Answer the questions with a partner.
1 When you were a child, were you ever **made to eat** something you really disliked? Why do you think your parents tried to **make you eat** it?
2 Do you ever **need to spend time catching** up on things you haven't done, or do you always **try to keep** on top of things?
3 Can you **imagine yourself living** in another country? How far from, and how different from, your country would you **prefer it to be**?
4 What kinds of things do you **dislike people helping you to do**? Why would you rather do them yourself?
5 Is there anything you **would prefer people not to do** when they are invited to your house? What kinds of things do you **expect them to do**?

3 WRITING

a Look at four topics from an advice website. Think of a good piece of advice for each situation.

How to survive…**a visit from difficult relatives**

How to survive…**a trip to the dentist's**

How to survive…**exam stress**

How to survive…**a family holiday**

b Compare your advice with a partner. Then, together, choose one topic and write headings for at least four tips. Plan what information to give under the headings, e.g. reasons for the tip, examples, etc.

c Tell your tips to another pair. See what they think of them, and if they have anything to add.

d Using all these ideas, write a short paragraph for each tip.

4 LISTENING

a Read about The School of Life. Why do you think it's been successful? Would you like to do one of their courses?

b 🔊 6.1 Listen to a School of Life presentation called *Why small pleasures are a big deal*. Number the slides in the order the presenter mentions them, 1–9. Which things from the slides does he suggest are 'small pleasures'?

c Why does the presenter mention…?
1 pineapples and caviar
2 a well-known violinist
3 marriage, career, and travel
4 a Caribbean island, the Uffizi Gallery, and a hang-gliding lesson
5 fancy holidays
6 having a bath, talking to a grandparent

d In pairs, complete the summary of the central message of the presentation. Then compare with another pair. Are your summaries similar?

> We expect to get most pleasure from things which are…
> However,…

CALM

LEISURE

RELATIONSHIPS

THE SCHOOL OF LIFE is an educational company that offers advice on life issues. It was founded in London in 2008 and now has branches around the world, including Berlin, Istanbul, São Paulo, Seoul, and Sydney. The school offers a variety of programmes, courses, videos, and presentations covering finding fulfilling work, mastering relationships, achieving calm, and enjoying leisure time.

SELF-KNOWLEDGE

SOCIABILITY

WORK

A

B

C

D

E

F

G

H

I

Glossary
the Uffizi Gallery an important art museum in Florence, Italy
lobster thermidor a rich French dish made with lobster, egg yolks, and brandy

lily of the valley

5 SPEAKING

a Look at the statements below. Choose one of them to talk about, and make notes under the following headings:

- Whether you agree with the statement or not and why
- Examples from your personal experience
- Any arguments on the other side
- Advice for your audience

❛Everyday life is full of small pleasures.❜

❛The best things in life are free.❜

❛Travelling abroad is more enjoyable than travelling in your own country.❜

❛A weekend at home is better than a weekend away.❜

b Read the tips for giving a presentation. Then, in small groups, give a short presentation about your statement. Listen to other people's presentations and ask questions.

PRESENTATION TIPS

1 Organize your presentation logically, so you can remember what you're going to say.

2 Don't read your notes – use your own words.

3 Speak slowly and pause between important points.

4 Make eye contact with the people you're talking to.

5 If the audience ask you questions, answer them clearly and concisely.

6 VOCABULARY & PRONUNCIATION
compound adjectives; main and secondary stress

🔍 Compound adjectives

A **well-known** violinist once donned scruffy clothes and busked at a street corner.

Small-scale pleasures can be anything but small.

A compound adjective is an adjective made up of two parts. It's usually written with a hyphen.

a Combine words from each list to make ten compound adjectives and use them to complete questions 1–10.

air	narrow
high	second
home	self
last	well
old	worn

fashioned	made
hand	conditioned
minute	behaved
risk	minded
out	conscious

1 Have you ever bought a _____-_____ car or motorbike? Did you have any problems with it?

2 What boys' or girls' names are considered _____-_____ in your country?

3 Do you usually do a lot of _____-_____ revision the night before a test?

4 Do you normally feel _____-_____ when you're having your photo taken? What do you do to try to be more natural?

5 Do you have any old clothes that you still like wearing even though they're a bit _____-_____?

6 Do you prefer _____-_____ food to restaurant meals?

7 In the summer, do you spend much time in _____-_____ buildings or cars? Do you consider it a necessity or a luxury?

8 Do you do any _____-_____ sports, e.g. white-water rafting? What attracts you to them?

9 Do you think as people get older, they tend to get more _____-_____ and intolerant?

10 Do you think children should be asked to leave restaurants if they aren't reasonably _____-_____?

b 🔊 6.2 Listen and check.

🔍 Fine-tuning your pronunciation: main and secondary stress

Some words, especially compounds or words with suffixes and prefixes, have both main stress and secondary stress. Secondary stress is shown by ˌ in a dictionary, e.g. /ˌself-ˈkɒnʃəs/.

c Listen again. Which word usually has the main stress in compound adjectives? Then ask and answer questions 1–10 in **a** with a partner and give examples.

d Use these compound adjectives to complete some high-frequency collocations.

dead-end	eco-friendly	extra-curricular
feel-good	groundbreaking	high-heeled
high-pitched	labour-saving	life-changing	low-cost

1 _____ airline
2 _____ activity
3 _____ job
4 _____ movie
5 _____ research
6 _____ voice
7 _____ device
8 _____ shoes
9 _____ detergent
10 _____ experience

e 🔊 6.3 Listen and check.

f Use three compound adjectives from **a** or **d** to write questions. Then ask and answer the questions with a partner.

❛Do you ever fly with low-cost airlines?❜

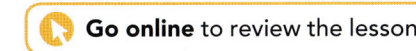 🔄 **Go online** to review the lesson

59

Technology is a good servant but a bad master.
Gretchen Rubin, US author, blogger, and speaker

G conditional sentences | **V** phones and technology, adjectives + prepositions | **P** /æ/ and /ʌ/

1 VOCABULARY phones and technology

Talk to a partner. How would you explain the difference between…?

1 a **screen** and a **touch screen**
2 a **keypad** and a **keyboard**
3 a **password** and a **passcode**
4 your **contacts** and your **settings**
5 **broadband** and **wi-fi**
6 an **update** and a **pop-up**
7 **coverage** and **signal**
8 to **download** and to **stream**
9 to **scroll** and to **swipe**
10 to **hang up** and to **top up** (your phone)
11 to **put sb through** and to **get through to sb**
12 to **switch off** and to **unplug**

2 PRONUNCIATION /æ/ and /ʌ/

> 🔍 **Fine-tuning your pronunciation: /æ/ and /ʌ/**
>
> The sounds /æ/ and /ʌ/ are quite similar and it can be difficult to hear and produce the difference. The /æ/ sound is always spelt with the letter *a*, e.g. *contact*, and the /ʌ/ sound is usually spelt with the letter *u*, though it can also be *o*, e.g. *coverage*, or *ou*, e.g. *touch*.

a 🔊 **6.4** Listen to five pairs of words. Focus on the difference between the two vowel sounds.

	a		b
1	a	hang up	b	hung up
2	a	app	b	up
3	a	crashed	b	crushed
4	a	ran out	b	run out
5	a	rang	b	rung

b 🔊 **6.5** Listen. Which word or phrase in **a** did you hear?

c Practise saying the sentences.

1 WhatsApp is currently one of the most popular messaging services in the country.
2 Jack was cut off, so he hung up.
3 I ran out of credit, so I had to top up my phone.
4 I updated the software on my Mac and now it keeps crashing.

3 READING & LISTENING

a Approximately how many hours a day do you think you spend using your phone? Are you happy with this, or would you like to cut down?

b Read the beginning of the article and complete the verbs in the *Rules* and *Challenges* sections.

A beginner's guide to divorcing your phone

What's the first thing you do when you wake up? Read the news? Check your emails? Scroll through social media? Now, imagine your phone's not in the room. If that makes you feel uncomfortable, it may be time for a digital detox.

Tanya Goodin, a digital detox specialist, has devised a seven-day detox. She recommends first downloading a tracking app which measures how much time you spend looking at your screen and how many times a day you pick up your phone, so then you can compare your normal phone use with the end results.

Rules for a digital detox

- [1] D_____ all social media apps from your phone; check these only from a desktop computer.
- [2] T_____ off all banner-style / pop-up / sound notifications from all other apps.
- [3] L_____ your phone in your pocket or somewhere where you can't see it for meetings / get-togethers / conversations / meals involving other people.
- [4] K_____ your phone out of sight during your commute.
- [5] Don't t_____ your phone with you into the bathroom or toilet.

Challenges

Day 1 Leave your phone outside your bedroom overnight; get an alarm clock or [6] t_____ up the volume on your phone, so you can hear its alarm easily from your bed through the door. Continue this all week.

Day 2 Put your phone in a central place when you return home and go to the location of the phone (rather than carrying it around with you) if you need to [7] ch_____ it.

Day 3 [8] T_____ your work email account off your phone (notify everyone in advance that you're doing this).

Day 4 Go out to dinner, lunch, or to an evening event / gym session and [9] l_____ your phone behind.

Day 5 [10] K_____ your phone on airplane mode as default all day; take it off this mode only when you need to use it.

Days 6 and 7 Your complete digital detox: [11] sw_____ off your phone and put it away from 7.00 p.m. Friday to 8.00 a.m. Monday.

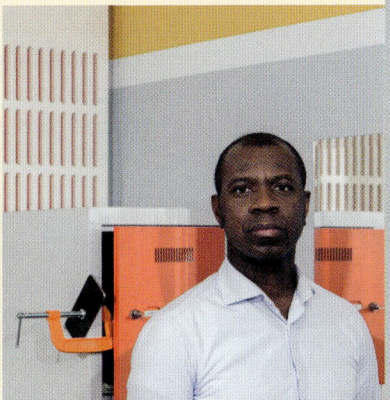

Anisah Osman Britton, 24, is the founder of 23 Code Street, a coding school for women. She has lived on a boat for the last five years with her dog.

Before detox
Daily phone screen time:
3 hours 50 minutes
Number of pick-ups a day: 88

Clive Myrie, 53, has worked for the BBC as a news presenter and foreign correspondent for more than 30 years. He lives with his wife in London.

Before detox
Daily phone screen time:
45 minutes
Number of pick-ups a day: 11

Anisah

I rely on my phone for everything; I leave my laptop at work, as there is no wi-fi on the boat. My top four apps are WhatsApp, Telegram, Instagram, and Twitter, and when it comes to deleting them, I think, 'I can do this!' I substitute Instagram with reading books and finish two by the end of the week, [1] which makes me **cringe** at how much time I must waste on my phone.

I struggle with insomnia and often wake up at 4.00 a.m. and scroll through my phone. I'm amazed that, [2] without it **to hand**, I simply go back to sleep. I set the alarm on my old-fashioned Casio watch now, and stay asleep a lot longer.

By day three, I'm feeling left out of my family's WhatsApp group, but I welcome taking work emails off my phone. [3] Things **take a turn for the worse** on day four, when I'm sick and have to stay home. I decide there is no way I'm doing it without my phone – I need it in bed with me – and I go back to checking work emails, WhatsApp-ing my family and watching dog videos on YouTube.

I'm not worried about switching my phone off at the weekend. I tell my family, and my business partner, Tom, that I'll speak to them on Monday. By Saturday lunchtime, [4] I **have a meltdown**. It's so dead and quiet; I can't even listen to music, as my only source is my phone. I don't see a single person until my neighbour knocks on my door on Sunday morning with some chocolate. I almost cry. Later, I walk to the supermarket, just so I can speak to someone. This is the worst weekend of my life.

After the detox...

*I couldn't cope with...*not being able to take photos. I missed that so much.

I can now do without...[5] **flicking through** social media in bed before getting up. I've given myself an extra hour in the morning.

After detox
Daily phone screen time: 3 hours | Number of pick-ups a day: 70

c Look at the photos and read the information about Anisah and Clive, who did the detox. With a partner, discuss who you think might have found it more difficult and why.

d Now read about Anisah's experience of the detox. Underline all the positive effects of the challenges, and circle the negative ones.

e With a partner, look at the highlighted expressions in the article and choose the exact meaning of the **bold** words or phrases, a–c.

1 **a** feel angry **b** feel embarrassed **c** feel sad
2 **a** in my hand **b** to hold **c** near me
3 **a** suddenly get worse
   b change from bad to worse
   c start to improve
4 **a** calm down **b** break down **c** slow down
5 **a** looking carefully at
   b looking slowly at
   c looking quickly at

f 🔊 6.6 Now listen to an interview with Clive about his experience of the detox. Answer the questions.

1 Do you think he found the experience more or less stressful than Anisah? Why?
2 What did he learn about his phone use?
3 Why were his results surprising?

g Listen again. What does he say about...?

1 being a 'techie'
2 deleting apps
3 using phones at dinner
4 checking the football
5 preparing for *News at Ten*
6 the Queen
7 not being kept in the loop on WhatsApp
8 being a journalist

h Answer the questions with a partner.

1 How would you score for 'daily phone screen time' and 'number of pick-ups a day'? How dependent is your work or social life on having a phone?
2 Have you ever spent a long time without your phone, either as a detox, or because of circumstances? How did you feel?
3 Which of the detox rules and challenges would you find the most difficult?

4 WRITING

Ⓦ p.124 Writing A discursive essay (1): A balanced argument Analyse a model essay about smartphone use, and write a discursive essay.

5 GRAMMAR conditional sentences

a Match the halves of the conditional sentences.

1. ☐ If I'd had my phone with me,
2. ☐ If my laptop wasn't so new,
3. ☐ If he wasn't always on social media,
4. ☐ If I didn't have fast broadband,
5. ☐ If they bring out a new version of the game,
6. ☐ If you hadn't sent me a message,

a I wouldn't have known where you were.
b I wouldn't be able to work from home.
c I'd have texted to say I was going to be late.
d I might actually be able to have a conversation with him.
e I'm definitely going to buy it.
f I wouldn't have bothered to get it repaired.

b Which sentences refer to present or future situations and which ones refer to the past? What is different about sentence 2?

c **G** p.153 **Grammar Bank 6B**

d Complete the sentences so that they are true for you. Then compare with a partner.

1. I could manage for a week without the internet, provided that…
2. I would only lend someone my car on condition that…
3. Even if I had all the money in the world, I would never…
4. Had I not decided to learn English, I…
5. I'd be prepared to move abroad as long as…

6 LISTENING & SPEAKING

a Look carefully at a photograph which was shortlisted in a Sony photography competition asking students to illustrate millennials' obsession with technology. Why do you think the judges liked it? Do you know any people who are obsessed with technology?

Adam Zadlo, from Poland, said millennials are 'the generation with technology in their hands'

b 🔊 6.7 You're going to listen to five people talking about someone they know with an obsession. First, listen to some extracts and try to guess what the obsession is.

c 🔊 6.8 Now listen to the people and check your answers to **b**.

d Listen again. Which speaker, A–E, mentions someone who…?

1. ☐ doesn't enjoy the results of their obsession
2. ☐ likes to discuss their obsession with friends
3. ☐ has a space problem as a result of their obsession
4. ☐ missed a fun activity because of their obsession
5. ☐ has to do something daily because of their obsession

e 🔊 6.9 **Language in context** Listen to some extracts from the listening and complete the highlighted phrases related to obsessions.

1. …she's really _____ baking.
2. I think she's got every _____ cookery book, baking book, that's in print…
3. He's _____ talking about how he feels…
4. …and going _____ and _____ about his health problems.
5. …has a _____ of an obsession with cats.
6. …she does have a _____ about cats.
7. Right now it's getting a bit out of _____, because she doesn't have a very big flat…

f Talk in small groups. Use some of the highlighted phrases in **e**.

> **Do you know anyone who is (a bit) obsessed with…?**
> - a kind of game or toy
> - a hobby or free-time activity
> - their health
> - an animal or pet
> - a particular film or type of film
> - keeping fit
> - cleaning or being tidy
> - a celebrity
> - a sportsperson or team
> - a particular object, e.g. their car, their phone, etc.
> - anything else

7 VOCABULARY adjectives + prepositions

> 🔍 **Adjectives + prepositions**
>
> Some adjectives need a certain preposition when they're followed by a noun or gerund, e.g. *obsessed with*. It's important to learn these prepositions with the adjectives.
>
> See p.173 for more information on prepositions.

a Complete the **Prepositions** column.

		Prepositions
1	Nowadays, a lot of people are **obsessed** celebrities and their lifestyles.	*with*
2	A lot of young people are **addicted** social media.	_____
3	Many young people are **hooked** video games.	_____
4	Lots of teenage boys are **mad** football.	_____
5	Many 30-year-olds are still **dependent** their parents.	_____
6	Some people are **fed up** the amount of sport on TV.	_____
7	Older people aren't always as **open** new ideas as younger people are.	_____
8	People are **sick** being bombarded with depressing news.	_____
9	Most parents nowadays are **aware** the negative effect of too much screen time.	_____
10	Couples are not as **keen** getting married as they used to be.	_____
11	If TV programmes are **unsuitable** children, they have to be shown after 9 p.m.	_____
12	People are becoming more **suspicious** technology companies.	_____
13	Far too many people are **dissatisfied** their mobile phone network.	_____
14	People are getting so **accustomed** fake news that they can't tell what's true and what isn't.	_____
15	It's going to be difficult to reduce emissions as long as people are so **attached** their cars.	_____

b 🔊 **6.10** Listen and check.

c Cover the **Prepositions** column and say the sentences with the correct preposition.

d With a partner, say to what extent sentences 1–15 are true for your country, giving examples.

8  VIDEO LISTENING

a You're going to watch a documentary about addiction to technology. Before you watch, decide with a partner which sentences you think are true.

1. More than half the world's population uses the internet.
2. Social media and video games are deliberately designed to be addictive.
3. Children under the age of ten don't suffer from technology addiction.
4. The best way to deal with addiction is to stop using technology altogether.
5. Sleep patterns are very affected by technology use.
6. Technology is the best way to really connect with other people.

b Watch the documentary once and check your answers to **a**.

c Watch again and answer the questions.

1. What examples of behavioural addictions are mentioned?
2. How many people in the world use social media?
3. How much is the global video game industry worth?
4. What examples does Dr Graham give of 'rewards' within games?
5. Who is the youngest person that Dr Graham has treated face to face? What problems did he have?
6. What difference is there between a technology addict and an enthusiastic user?
7. Why aren't digital detoxes a practical treatment?
8. What does Dr Graham say technology can't do?

d Are you optimistic about our future relationship with technology? At what age do you think children should be introduced to social media or other types of entertainment technology?

🔴 **Go online** to watch the video and review the lesson

GRAMMAR

a Circle a, b, or c.

1 It _____ that the king is to abdicate next month.
   a has announced   **b** announced it
   c has been announced

2 Excuse me. _____ to be a problem with this seat – I can't change its position.
   a It seems   **b** There seems   **c** It appears

3 _____ to a recent article, eating a lot of salt may not cause long-term health problems.
   a According   **b** Apparently   **c** Considering

4 _____ that the murderer is being concealed by friends.
   a There is thought   **b** It is thought   **c** It thought

5 My flat looks a mess – if only I _____ so untidy!
   a 'm not   **b** weren't   **c** was

6 I'd _____ you didn't come in with your muddy shoes on.
   a rather   **b** prefer it   **c** wish

7 I really wish we _____ that white sofa – it gets dirty much too easily.
   a haven't bought   **b** hadn't bought   **c** don't buy

8 I'd like _____ it in the morning, if that's possible.
   a that they deliver   **b** them delivering
   c them to deliver

9 If we hadn't had to work late, _____ the match now.
   a I'd be watching   **b** I'd have watched   **c** I'll watch

10 I'll pay for your English classes _____ you promise not to miss any.
   a supposing   **b** unless   **c** providing

b Complete the sentences with the correct form of the verb in brackets.

1 The president is believed _____ his holiday in the Caribbean this week. (spend)

2 It's time you _____ to think about what subjects you want to study next year. (start)

3 My parents always encouraged me _____ foreign languages. (learn)

4 My new job involves me _____ to Canada two or three times a year. (travel)

5 They're incredibly generous people and they wouldn't let me _____ for anything. (pay)

6 Daniel can stay the night as long as he doesn't mind _____ on the sofa. (sleep)

7 Supposing Ajax lost their last two matches, _____ they still _____ the league? (win)

8 Marcus might have hurt his head if he _____ a helmet when he fell off his bike. (not wear)

9 If you _____ me earlier that you were coming, I would have taken the day off. (tell)

10 If I hadn't inherited a lot of money, we _____ in a house like this now. (not live)

VOCABULARY

a Complete the sentences with a preposition.

1 We arrived _____ time to spare.

2 Don't tell me you're still listening to CDs! You're really _____ the times.

3 Let's set off early. There's so much to see, and I don't want to run _____ of time.

4 We've decided to stay here _____ the time being.

5 We missed the bus, so _____ the time we got to the cinema the film had started.

6 The table's booked for 8.30, so please make an effort to be _____ time.

7 He met Lara in Moscow, where he was working _____ the time.

8 It's _____ time you started revising.

b Circle the correct word or phrase.

1 The *standard / cost* of living is higher in Edinburgh than in any other Scottish city, with the highest rents.

2 Liz spent a fortune on her new bag! She must be *loaded / affluent*.

3 *Fares / Fines* on the London Underground aren't that expensive – about £3.00 to £5.00 depending where you're going.

4 **A** This hat cost $20.
   B Twenty *bucks / quid*? You're kidding!

5 They wanted to buy a flat, but the bank wouldn't give them *an instalment / a mortgage*.

6 The top rate of *income / inflation* tax in the UK is currently 45%.

7 We've only got a holiday *budget / grant* of £1,000, so we won't be able to go to Australia.

8 Would you like to make a *donation / deposit*? It's for UNICEF.

c Complete the compound adjectives.

1 My father is rather intolerant and **narrow-**_____.

2 Don't say anything about her new hairstyle. She's feeling very _____**-conscious**.

3 Emma gets her vintage clothes from **second-**_____ shops.

4 You shouldn't have gone to the interview in those _____**-out** jeans.

5 Their kids are really **well-**_____. They always do what they're told.

6 Our trip to Uganda was a _____**-changing** experience.

7 We only use **eco-**_____ cleaning products.

d Complete the sentences with one word.

1 Can I _____ your charger? I need the socket for mine.
2 I tried to call you at work but I couldn't _____ through, I just got a buzzing noise.
3 If you _____ down the homepage, you'll find the contact details at the bottom.
4 I'm really _____ up with his constant excuses for not doing his job properly.
5 My sister is totally _____ on that new reality show on TV.
6 I'm completely _____ to crisps. I buy a packet almost every day.
7 My wife isn't very _____ on flying, so we're going to take the train to Rome.

CAN YOU understand this text?

a Read the article once. Have you heard of or used any of these apps?

b Read the article again and complete it with phrases A–I. There is one phrase you don't need.

A and after that, subscription starts at £7.99
B to put your critical thinking to the test
C depending on how much you choose to spend
D to focus on achieving this goal in five minutes
E it might as well be useful
F and stress is known to be bad for your well-being
G so you can find one that works for any situation
H and do something to improve them
I and encourage and challenge each other

▶ CAN YOU understand these people?

🔊 **6.11** Watch or listen and choose a, b, or c.

1 **Adina** thinks her impatience is ____.
 a unfortunate
 b hereditary
 c obvious
2 **Guy**'s family make an effort ____.
 a not to use plastic
 b not to waste water
 c to use public transport
3 A simple thing that makes **Vicky** happy is ____.
 a having her cat sleeping on her bed
 b playing with one of her relatives
 c feeling refreshed in the morning
4 **Hywel** thinks mobile phones have advantages so long as we ____.
 a use them wisely
 b all have one
 c use them to speak to people, not just to send messages

Seven self-care apps that will reduce your stress levels

When it comes to self-care, we are often advised to put our phones away. It makes sense, since phones come with so many distractions. But thanks to the many apps focused on self-care, your phone can actually be a useful tool when it comes to taking some time out and recharging. We have rounded up some of the best apps that help you to look after yourself, because if you're going to have your phone with you at all times, [1]____.

Happify
The main aim of the Happify app is to make you a little happier. It works by letting you set mental health and well-being goals, like 'building confidence' and 'reducing stress'. Once you have set these targets, it gives you quick activities that will help you to reach your goals. It's a small, but useful way to help you become aware of your feelings, [2]____.

Headspace
Headspace consistently gets rave reviews and ratings. It's a meditation app that aims to help you get more from your day, through mindfulness. It has a range of meditation themes, from falling asleep to fundamental techniques of meditation. The first ten sessions on the app are free, [3]____.

Talkspace
The Talkspace app is basically therapy on your phone. Through a free consultation, it matches you with licensed therapists and gives you 24/7 access. The app comes with a range of affordable plans to choose from and you can text, voice message, or video chat with your therapist once or twice a day, [4]____.

MyFitnessPal
MyFitnessPal allows you to log your weight, workouts, food, and fitness goals. It works as a social network app, so you can connect with friends, [5]____.

Lumosity
Lumosity is all about your brain health. It aims to improve your memory and problem-solving skills through a bunch of brain teasers and mind-training games, designed [6]____.

Breathing Zone
The Breathing Zone app is mainly for defusing stress. It's a simple app that helps you slow your breathing rhythm when you need to calm down and relax. You set the target number of breaths per minute you want to reach (eight is the default) and the app helps to reduce your breathing rate to that number. The app helps you [7]____.

Sleepfulness
As the name suggests, this app helps you to sleep better. It's free, with options to pay for upgrades, and provides tracks to encourage you to be more mindful of your sleeping habits. You can choose tracks to listen to before you sleep, to start your day, and for during your day. The tracks range from 5 to 20 minutes, [8]____.

Adapted from a lifestyle website

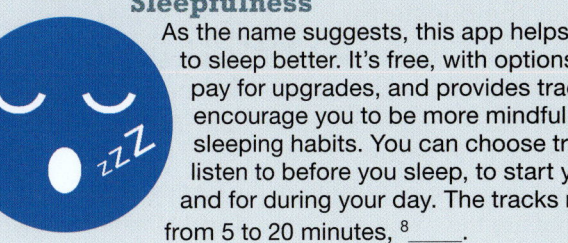

🔵 **Go online** to watch the video, review Files 5 & 6, and check your progress

> If you obey all the rules, you miss all the fun.
> *Katharine Hepburn, US actress*

G permission, obligation, and necessity | **V** word formation: prefixes | **P** intonation and linking in exclamations

Everything you think you know is probably wrong...

The natural world
1 What kind of bears cause the most fatal injuries?
2 Of all the dog breeds, which is the most genetically similar to wolves?

Science
3 What colour is the Sun?
4 Is ice cream a solid, a liquid, or a gas?

History
5 When was the last time elephants were used in wartime?
6 Where is the oldest known boomerang from?

Geography
7 Which is the wettest – London, Rome, or Barcelona?
8 Where is the highest mountain on British soil?

Sport
9 What was the first sport to have a World Championship?
10 At the first modern Olympics, what were the medals for winners made of?

Miscellaneous
11 Who designed the Eiffel Tower?
12 In what job are people most likely to suffer injuries at work?

1 LISTENING & SPEAKING

a Look at the questions from a book based on a popular TV quiz show called *QI*. In pairs, try to agree on answers to questions 1–12.

b **C Communication** *QI* quiz A p.109 B p.114 Read the answers to the questions and explain them to each other.

c 7.1 Listen to Part 1 of a programme about *QI* and answer the questions.

1 Why was the show called *QI*?
2 What is the basic principle behind the show and its books?
3 What two examples are given from *The QI Book of General Ignorance*?
4 What does the popularity of the books prove?
5 What are the two reasons Lloyd and Mitchinson give for why children often do badly in school?

d 7.2 Now listen to Part 2. Complete the five suggestions Lloyd and Mitchinson make about education.

1 Education should be more _____.
2 The best people to control what children learn are _____.
3 Children should be in control of _____
   _____.
4 There should never be _____.
5 There's no reason why school has to _____
   _____.

e Listen again and make notes about the reason for each suggestion.

f In small groups, discuss suggestions 1–5 in **d**. Do you think they are good ideas?

2 PRONUNCIATION intonation and linking in exclamations

a 🔊 **7.3** Listen to two conversations and complete the exclamations.

> 1 **A** Lloyd and Mitchinson think that school shouldn't be compulsory.
> **B** _____! If it wasn't compulsory, no one would ever go.
>
> 2 **A** Did you know that at the time of the French Revolution, only half the population spoke French?
> **B** _____! So what language did the other half speak?

b Listen again and answer the questions with a partner.

1 Which word has extra stress in each exclamation?
  What happens to the intonation?
2 Why do you think a /w/ sound is added between *How* and the adjective?

c Practise saying some more exclamations with *What* and *How*.

What a great idea!   What an amazing coincidence!   What a pain!
What a terrible experience!   How annoying!   How embarrassing!
How weird!

d Ⓒ **Communication** What a ridiculous idea! **A** p.111 **B** p.112
Respond to what your partner says with an exclamation.

3 VOCABULARY word formation: prefixes

a Look at ten more *QI* facts. Which do you find the most surprising?

b Look at the **bold** prefixes in the highlighted words. Answer the questions with a partner.

1 Which three are negative prefixes and make the word mean the opposite?
2 What meaning do the other prefixes add to a word?

c Ⓥ **p.169 Vocabulary Bank** Prefixes

d Add a prefix to the **bold** words and make any other necessary changes to complete the sentences.

1 I completely _____ Alan. I thought he was self-centred, but I see I was wrong. **judge**
2 This paragraph in your essay is rather unclear. I advise you to _____ it. **write**
3 I can't read my doctor's handwriting. It's completely _____. **legible**
4 Having to take care of my sister's dogs while she's on holiday is terribly _____. **convenient**
5 The police have promised to tackle _____ behaviour in city centres. **social**
6 The expedition failed because they were _____. **equip**
7 It's going to be an _____ struggle to motivate the team after last week's defeat. **hill**
8 Food poisoning from _____ meat can be very serious. **cook**
9 We're not going back to that restaurant – they _____ us last time we went. **charge**
10 The hotel has an _____ swimming pool that's only open from June to September. **door**

...and everything is interesting

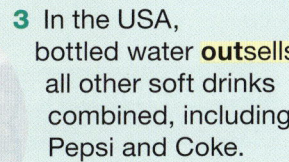

1 Snow fleas survive the cold because their bodies contain natural **anti**freeze.
2 You are more likely to order dessert in a restaurant if the waiter is **over**weight.
3 In the USA, bottled water **out**sells all other soft drinks combined, including Pepsi and Coke.
4 In Honolulu, it's **il**legal to cross the street using a mobile phone.
5 Tea leaves **un**curl when hot water is poured on them, a process known as 'the agony of the leaves'.

6 Starfish can **re**grow a whole new body from a single arm.
7 The most common time for people to **mis**spell Facebook as 'Facbook' is 3.08 a.m.
8 The word *anomia* means 'the **in**ability to remember names'.
9 You could listen to a radio on the moon, but it's virtually impossible on a **sub**marine. Radio waves travel much more easily through space than through water.

10 Seven per cent of the **micro**plastic in the sea comes from the paint used for road markings.

4 READING

a Talk to a partner.

> **Have you ever...?**
> - been told to turn your phone off in a public place
> - had something taken away from you at airport security
> - been told to stop taking photographs in a public place
>
> Did you think you were being treated reasonably?

b Read three questions on the back cover of a book called *In the Interests of Safety*, which exposes the truth behind some of the rules which govern our lives. How would you answer the questions?

> **Can a mobile phone cause a major explosion at a petrol station?**
>
> **What would happen if the no-liquids rule at airports was abolished?**
>
> **And are all the child protection measures really making children safer?**

c Now read three extracts from the book. In which extract do the authors say that...?

- ☐ the rule is based on something which is possible in theory, but not in practice
- ☐ no rule actually exists, only advice
- ☐ the rule is based on an outdated rumour

d Read the extracts again and complete them with phrases A–J. There is one phrase you don't need.

- A a theoretical possibility
- B a very bad idea
- C actively encouraged
- D personal and private use only
- E going along with
- F nothing to that effect
- G always criticized
- H popularly supposed
- I to improve security
- J under any circumstances

e What are the authors' answers to the three questions in **b**? Are you convinced by their arguments?

1 Have you ever wondered why, if it is so dangerous to make a mobile phone call at a petrol station, you are even allowed to carry one in a car?

In fact, the chance of a spark from a mobile phone detonating petrol or diesel is effectively zero, because both these fuels are far less flammable than is ^{1}___. Even dropped cigarettes don't ignite petrol. There has not been a single case of a phone igniting petrol. So what is the source of the phone myth? In the early days of mobile phones, manufacturers thought phone ignition was ^{2}___, and included a warning about not using them near fuel, which led to the warnings at service stations. By the 1990s, this warning changed – now users were simply instructed to obey any signs telling them to switch their phones off. Meanwhile, petrol pump attendants recounted stories about pumps which had blown up because of a phone, even saying that they had seen footage on YouTube. However, no footage exists. It is true that using a phone might distract people while refuelling. So, rather than ^{3}___ stories about lethal mobile phones, shouldn't the authorities make it clear that this is the only real problem?

2 Scientist Richard Dawkins was queuing up recently at London Heathrow Airport's security when he saw a mother growing agitated because she was not allowed to take her young daughter's eczema cream on board. Dawkins wrote later, 'No sane person, witnessing that scene, seriously feared that this woman was planning to blow herself up on a plane.'

To passengers around the world, the 100 millilitre rule means one thing: airport security officials are stopping anyone from boarding with enough liquid to blow up the aircraft. But is liquid all you need to make up an explosive device? When we started asking experts, they confirmed that the explosive that most worried airlines was triacetone triperoxide (TATP). However, making TATP before boarding would be ^{4}___, as it is likely to detonate without warning, just as a result of physical movement. And mixing the ingredients on the plane would be even more complicated, as TATP must be prepared at a temperature of around 50 degrees Fahrenheit. You would also need a lot of scientific equipment, and making the liquid would take several hours. Even if no one knocked on the toilet door during the hours you were in there, you would then have to wait several more hours for the liquid to dry to a powder. No wonder the chemists we interviewed expressed disbelief about the whole idea. The only real justification for the liquids rule appears to be that giving people, especially nervous flyers, the idea that you are doing something ^{5}___ is a good thing. The irony is that passengers are not only allowed, but ^{6}___, to carry bottles of highly flammable alcohol onto airplanes.

5 GRAMMAR permission, obligation, and necessity

a Look at the pairs of sentences. With a partner, say if they are the same or different in meaning. In which pair of sentences is there a difference in register?

1 **It is not permitted to** use your phone here.
 You aren't allowed to use your phone here.
2 **You'd better** finish your water before we go through security.
 You ought to finish your water before we go through security.
3 **We aren't supposed to** take photos here.
 We mustn't take photos here.
4 **You don't have to** fill in the form now. You can do it later.
 You needn't fill in the form now. You can do it later.
5 **We should have** left home early.
 We had to leave home early.

b ⓖ p.154 Grammar Bank 7A

---

③ Ken Paine was watching his son, Jake, play in a local under-sixteens' football match. When Ken tried to take a photo, the referee came over to him and told him he couldn't take photos, as it was against the Child Protection Act.

This was not an isolated incident. Many schools in the USA and Britain now have a policy that no parent may photograph any child, even their own, ⁷____, on school property. One school in the UK told parents they could no longer take pictures during the Christmas school play or the sports day, and then employed an official photographer to record these events. The photos were then offered for sale to the parents. The referee who told Paine to put his camera away cited the Football Association and the Child Protection Act as responsible for the ban on photography. We decided to take Ken's case up with these two authorities.

The Football Association replied that they had no problem with parents taking still or video images of football matches involving children, so long as they were for ⁸____, and were not posted on the internet. We then looked into the situation with the Child Protection Act. First, we approached the Local Government Association, which is responsible for many schools and sports facilities. They said they had no policy on photographing children, and referred us to the Association of Directors of Children's Services (ADCS). The ADCS said, 'We offer no sort of guidance of this type. Each school makes their own decision.' Furthermore, we could find ⁹____ in the text of the Child Protection Act. The only guideline which does exist (and remember this is not a law, or even a rule) boils down to: Be careful about sharing images of other people's children on the internet.

Adapted from In the Interests of Safety by Tracey Brown and Michael Hanlon

6 SPEAKING

a Talk in small groups. Imagine the following laws or regulations have been proposed for your country. Would you be in favour of them or not? Say why.

On the road

People over 85 **should not be allowed to** drive.

It should be against the law for pedestrians to cross the street while wearing earphones.

Cyclists **ought to be made to** pass a test to get a cycling licence before they are allowed on the road.

At home

It should be compulsory to turn off all electrical appliances at night and not leave them on standby.

It ought to be illegal to leave children under 12 alone in the house.

It should be against the law for parents to give fast food to obese children.

Public health

Smoking in the street **should be banned**.

Restaurants and bars **ought not to be allowed to** serve more than two alcoholic drinks per person.

People who abuse their health **should be made to** contribute to expensive medical treatment.

Society

It should be compulsory for people to vote in elections.

All advertising aimed at children under the age of 12 **ought to be banned**.

Couples **should have to** attend three months of marriage counselling before they are allowed to get divorced.

b In your groups, come up with a new law or regulation that you would like to see introduced for two of the categories above.

c Appoint a spokesperson to present your laws or regulations to the rest of the class and give reasons. Then have a class vote to choose the best one to introduce.

Creativity is allowing yourself to make mistakes. Art is knowing which ones to keep.
Scott Adams, US comic artist

G perception and sensation **V** art, colour idioms **P** -ure

A

B

C

1 LISTENING

a Look at three works of public art. What might they have in common?

b 🔊 7.6 Listen to the first part of a documentary and check your answer to **a**. Answer the questions with a partner.

1 What was the fourth plinth originally built for?
2 Why did it remain empty for over 150 years?
3 What possibilities were discussed for its use?
4 Why might they have been rejected?

c 🔊 7.7 Listen to the rest of the documentary about the fourth plinth, where the presenter talks about the three works of art in **a**. Complete the information boxes and match them to photos A–C.

1
TITLE	*Nelson's* _____
BY	_____ artist **Yinka Shonibare**
Displayed from	_____ to _____

2
TITLE	_____, *Fig. 101*
BY	_____ artists **Michael Elmgreen** and **Ingar Dragset**
Displayed from	_____ to _____

3
TITLE	*The* _____ *should not exist*
BY	_____-_____ artist **Michael Rakowitz**
Displayed from	_____ to _____

Glossary
date (**syrup**) a sweet sticky brown fruit that grows on a date palm tree

d Listen again and answer the questions about each work of art.

1 a What ship is inside the bottle?
  b What does the sculpture symbolize?
  c What happened to the sculpture after it was removed from the fourth plinth?
2 a What kind of horse is the boy riding?
  b What did previous statues of men on horseback tend to celebrate?
  c What are the artists celebrating with this statue, and what is their hope for the future?
3 a What project did Michael Rakowitz start in 2006?
  b What exactly is the *Lamassu*, and where was the original?
  c What was it made of and why?

e Talk to a partner.

• Which of the works of art in **a** do you like best? Why?
• Imagine there was an empty plinth in the main square in your town, and a sculpture was going to be placed on it.
  – What would you like it to be of?
  – Is there anything you would like it to commemorate?

2 GRAMMAR perception and sensation

a Complete some comments made about Rakowitz's *Lamassu* sculpture with the correct form of a verb or verb phrase from the list.

look look as if look at look like see seem

1 'It really _____ the original statue.'
2 'You can only _____ what it's made of when you _____ it really closely.'
3 'From a distance, it _____ it's made of gold and precious metals.'
4 'The artist _____ to be trying not to replicate the lost statue, but to make something which _____ similar but is more connected with modern life.'

b ◉ 7.8 Listen and check.

c Answer the questions with a partner.

1 What's the grammatical difference between *look as if* and *look like*, and in meaning between *look at* and *see*, and between *look* and *seem*?
2 *Sight* is one of the five senses. What are the other four?

d ⓖ p.155 **Grammar Bank 7B**

e Ask and answer the questions with a partner.

- Are there any sculptures, paintings, or pictures that you like or dislike **looking at** because of how they make you **feel**?
- Who do you **look like** most in your family? Do you resemble them in any other way?
- In your opinion, which foreign language **sounds** a) the most attractive, b) the most similar to your language?
- Are there any sounds or kinds of music that you don't like **hearing** because they make you **feel** uncomfortable?
- Are there any foods you dislike because of their **smell** or their **texture**, rather than their **taste**?
- What kinds of perfume or cologne do you really like or dislike the **smell** of on yourself or on other people? Why?
- Are there certain materials you love to wear, or never wear, because of the way they **feel**?
- Look at the list of creatures below. Are there any that you don't like to **look at**, even in a photo? Would you be prepared to **touch** any of them in a zoo? Why (not)?

| a lion   a lizard   a parrot   a rat |
| a snake   a tarantula |

3 PRONUNCIATION *-ure*

a Write the words in the correct group according to the pronunciation of *-ure*.

sculpture picture allure architecture capture creature culture endure feature furniture future immature impure leisure measure nature obscure pleasure secure signature structure sure temperature texture treasure

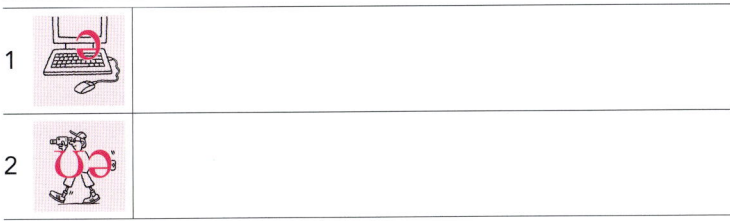

1	
2	

b ◉ 7.9 Listen and check.

c Look at the words in the two groups above. Answer the questions.

1 In group 1, where is the stress in all the words?
2 What sounds do the *t* and the *s* make before *-ure*?
3 In group 2, which syllable is stressed?

d Practise saying the sentences.

1 In this pic**t**u**re**, the artist cap**t**u**re**s the all**ure** of na**t**u**re**.
2 The Minister of Cul**t**u**re** takes no plea**s**u**re** in sculp**t**u**re**.
3 He has a trea**s**u**re**d collection of old furni**t**u**re**.
4 Are you su**re** the new struc**t**u**re** is secu**re**?
5 The architec**t**u**re** has some unusual fea**t**u**re**s.

4 VOCABULARY & SPEAKING art

a Talk to a partner. What's the difference between...?

1 a **sculpture** and an **installation**
2 a **statue** and a **monument**
3 **abstract** art and **figurative** art
4 a **landscape** and a **still life**
5 a **portrait** and a **self-portrait**
6 a **drawing** and an **illustration**
7 a **poster** and a **painting**
8 a **canvas** and a **frame**

b Talk in small groups.

- What public art is there in your town / city? Are there any pieces that you particularly like or dislike?
- What famous statues, sculptures, or monuments have you seen, either in your country or abroad? Are there any that you really like or dislike?
- Do you ever go to museums or art galleries in your hometown, or when you are on holiday? Which ones do you remember and why?
- What art do you have in your daily life, for example...?
  - on the walls of your bedroom or living room
  - as the screen saver on your computer or phone

5 READING & LISTENING

a Read the first paragraph of an article about a TV programme. Explain why each programme might end in joy or disappointment.

b Read the rest of the article. Then work with a partner and cover the text. **A** say what you can remember about Lucian Freud. **B** say what you can remember about Jon Turner and why he contacted the programme.

[FAKE OR FORTUNE?]

For every known masterpiece, there may be another, still waiting to be discovered. *Fake or Fortune* is the art series where presenter Fiona Bruce and art expert Philip Mould try to prove whether works of art owned by viewers are fakes, or are genuine lost works by great artists and therefore worth a fortune. The investigation can end in joy or in bitter disappointment. In one episode, the team try to discover whether a portrait is a lost work by one of the twentieth century's most important painters, Lucian Freud.

Philip Mould and Fiona Bruce

Lucian Freud, grandson of the famous psychoanalyst Sigmund Freud, was born in Germany in 1922, but his family emigrated to London in 1933 to escape the rise of Nazism. From 1939 to 1942, he studied at the East Anglian School of Painting and Drawing, where he was considered a very promising student. Freud had a magnetic personality – he could move effortlessly between low and high society, and even painted the Queen. But he was known for being ill-tempered and was often at the centre of controversy and feuds. His work obsessed him; each painting could take thousands of hours, as he created intensely observed portraits – sometimes beautiful, sometimes disturbing. At his death in 2011, he left an estate worth almost £100 million.

In 1997, London-based designer Jon Turner was given a painting of a man in a black cravat, which he was told was an early work by Lucian Freud. Jon wanted to be sure that the painting really was by Freud – if it was, it would be worth a fortune. However, he knew that there were some doubts about the painting's authenticity. Firstly, it was unsigned. But there was a second and more serious issue. In 1985, Christie's, the famous London auction house, had examined the painting, and had agreed that it was an authentic work. However, Christie's then sent a photo of the painting to Lucian Freud himself, and to their shock and surprise, he replied, saying that the painting was not by him! Jon didn't know what to believe. Was the picture a fake, then, or perhaps just painted by someone else? And if it really was by Freud, why did he deny it? After unsuccessful investigations, as a last resort, Jon contacted *Fake or Fortune*, who agreed to investigate.

Jon Turner with *The Man in the Black Cravat*

c ⏵ **7.10** Now listen to a documentary about the painting, including an interview with Jon Turner. Number the events 1–8.

- ☐ The painting was examined by an expert, who found a long hair embedded in it.
- ☐ The programme discovered that Freud had admitted to his lawyer that he <u>had</u> started the painting.
- ☐ The programme found letters which confirmed the identity of *The Man in the Black Cravat*.
- ☐ Scientific analysis proved that the portrait had been painted by only one person.
- ☐ DNA analysis proved that the hair did not belong to Lucian Freud.
- ☐ *1* The programme investigated how Denis had got hold of the painting.
- ☐ The programme showed the evidence they had uncovered to three Freud experts.
- ☐ The programme investigated who the subject of the painting was.

> **Glossary**
> **Denis Wirth-Miller** an artist who studied with Freud at the East Anglian School of Painting and Drawing
> **John Jameson** a member of the Jameson family, who were Irish whiskey distillers
> **Libby Sheldon** an expert in the scientific analysis of paintings, specialist in painters' use of pigments and their brushstrokes
> **Diana Rawstron** Lucian Freud's solicitor (a kind of lawyer)

d Listen again and check your order of events in **c**. How likely do you think it is that experts will say that the painting is genuine?

e ⏵ **7.11** Listen to the end of the documentary and answer the questions.

1 What did the experts decide?
2 Why does Jon think that Freud denied the painting was his?
3 How does Jon feel about the painting and why?
4 Have his feelings changed during the process of authentication? Why (not)?
5 What is he going to do with the painting?

f ⏵ **7.12** Listen to five extracts from the documentary and complete some idiomatic expressions that Jon uses. With a partner, say what you think they mean from the context.

1 I was absolutely _____.
2 …I got _____ _____ with adrenalin and excitement…
3 So we were all _____ our _____ at this moment…
4 I could have _____ _____ _____.
5 …it just _____ straight away with me that it was so like Freud's early drawings.

g What do you think of the painting? If you had been in Jon's situation, what would you have done with the painting?

6 SPEAKING

a ⓒ **Communication** Which is the fake? **A** p.110 **B** p.115 Describe the paintings to each other and decide which one is genuine and which is a fake.

b Look at the items from the list and then answer the questions in small groups.

---
bags   clothes and shoes   sports equipment
sunglasses   watches
---

1 Have you ever bought or been given something that was a fake? Did you know it was a fake when you got it? How do you feel about it? Do you think you would like it more if it was the real thing?
2 Are the fakes as good as the originals? If they are worse, in what way?
3 Do you think it should be illegal to sell fakes?
4 Are many pirate versions of books, films, or music sold or downloaded in your country? Are they good quality? Do you think it's acceptable to use pirate copies?

7 VOCABULARY colour idioms

a Complete the **bold** idioms with a colour from the list.

---
black (x2)   **blue**   **grey**   **red** (x2)   white (x3)
---

1 John Singer Sargent's lost great flamenco picture, *El Jaleo*, turned up **out of the** _____, and amazingly, it was absolutely genuine.
2 It's very difficult for thieves to sell famous paintings, even on **the** _____ **market**.
3 We tried to organize an exhibition tour, but there was so much _____ **tape** to deal with that we had to cancel.
4 When you said how nice her dress was, were you telling **a** _____ **lie**? I thought it was awful.
5 The impact of social media on today's society isn't a _____ **and** _____ issue – there are upsides and downsides.
6 That huge clock my sister-in-law gave me is **a** _____ **elephant**. It doesn't fit anywhere and it's taking up space in the spare room.
7 There are lots of rules about copyright for printed text, but online copyright is still a bit of **a** _____ **area**. Nobody is quite sure who owns what.
8 The anonymous letter was **a** _____ **herring** – it was nothing to do with the murder at all.

b With a partner, say what you think the idioms mean.

c Write true sentences about you or your country using four of the colour idioms, and compare with a partner.

1 ▶ THE INTERVIEW Part 1

a Read the biographical information about Quentin Blake. Have you ever read any books illustrated by him? What else has he done apart from book illustrations?

> **Quentin Blake** is probably the best-known British illustrator of children's books. Apart from his illustrations of stories by other authors, for example, his famous drawings for Roald Dahl's books, he has also both written and illustrated many stories of his own. In recent years, his work has increasingly appeared in public places such as galleries and museums, and he has produced work for the walls of several hospitals and mental health centres in both the UK and France. He has also illustrated adult books, such as Cervantes' *Don Quixote*. He is a trustee of the House of Illustration, a centre in London for exhibitions and other activities, and was the subject of the first exhibition held there in 2014.

b Watch Part 1 of the interview. What does Quentin Blake think is the most important thing for someone who wants to become an illustrator?

c Now watch again. Complete sentences 1–5.
1 Quentin Blake describes himself as…
2 When he was in his early 20s, he…
3 In 1960, he and John Yeoman…
4 He finds it touching when…
5 A lot of young people say they want to become illustrators because…

d Did you use to draw a lot when you were a child? Do you ever draw nowadays?

> **Glossary**
> **ceramic** (*adj.*) (objects, e.g. pots) made of clay that has been permanently made hard by heat
> **John Yeoman** author of *A Drink of Water*, the first children's book illustrated by Quentin Blake

▶ Part 2

a Now watch Part 2. Mark the sentences **T** (true) or **F** (false).
1 Quentin Blake says that authors and illustrators usually need to have a lot of conversations.
2 The most important thing is the relationship between the illustrator and the words in the book.
3 Quentin Blake never drew any of Roald Dahl's characters without first talking to him about them.
4 He thinks conversations with Dahl helped him to get into the mood of the books.
5 Roald Dahl sometimes changed his text if an illustration wasn't working.
6 The BFG was originally described as wearing a leather apron.
7 The apron was found to make the BFG look too old.
8 The shoes the BFG wears were based on a pair of Quentin Blake's own shoes.

b Watch again. Say why the **F** sentences are false.

c Do you think illustrations help to make a story come alive? Is there an age at which illustrations are no longer needed?

> **Glossary**
> **The BFG** a book by Roald Dahl published in 1982; BFG stands for Big Friendly Giant

▶ Part 3

a Now watch Part 3. What does Quentin Blake say about…?

1 his relationship with the characters he creates in an illustration
2 his attitude to children
3 drawing from life
4 digital drawing
5 the advantage of quills, nibs, and reed pens
6 Ronald Searle and André François
7 his exhibition in Paris

b Watch again. Can you add any more details?

c Can you remember a book you loved because of the illustrations? What did you like about them? Do you remember any you disliked or were scared of?

> **Glossary**
> quill  nib
> **reed pen** a pen made from a tall plant that grows in or near water
> **Ronald Searle** British artist and satirical cartoonist
> **André François** Hungarian-born French cartoonist

2 ▶ LOOKING AT LANGUAGE

> 🔍 **get**
>
> *get* is one of most common verbs in English; it is frequently used by Quentin Blake in this interview. Learning expressions with *get*, and thoroughly assimilating the variety of meanings of this important verb, will help you to understand native speakers better.

a Watch some extracts from the interview and complete the missing words in the highlighted phrases.

1 '…but we got _____ _____. And I thought, 'Well, I'll, I'll try – keep – I'll try and keep on with this until I'm 30…''
2 'Um, and I got _____ _____, but I passed 30 and I didn't notice!'
3 'But, um, er, we talked quite a lot, again, some of it was about the, about the technicalities of the book, getting it _____ _____ better…'
4 '…but I think, to get, to get _____ the _____ of the book, which is a terribly important thing…'
5 'So he – after a bit he said, 'This apron's getting _____ the _____, isn't it?''
6 '…if you have a quill, or a nib, or a reed pen, you get a _____ _____ of scratch…'
7 'When I was a young man, I got _____ _____ and went to see him.'

b With a partner, say what the phrases mean, using a synonym for *get* where possible.

3 ▶ THE CONVERSATION

Debbie   Christian   Lucy

a Watch the conversation. Who says that illustrations…?

1 are what attracts a child to a book
2 are more important for very young children
3 can spoil a book for some people

b Watch again. Answer the questions.

1 What did Lucy love reading when she was younger? Why does she say the graphic novel she read was a disappointment?
2 Why did Christian have a problem with reading when he was younger? How did he manage to enjoy books as a small child?
3 According to Debbie, how do pictures help children to understand stories? Why was she so impressed by the Harry Potter films?

c Do / Did you like comics or graphic novels? Which do you think is more important, the story or the illustrations?

d Watch some extracts and complete the adverbs or adverbial phrases. Why do the speakers use them?

1 …I _____ love books, um, _____ classic novels…
2 I grew up reading *The Hobbit* _____ _____ _____ _____…
3 …and I didn't enjoy it _____ _____…
4 …which I think is _____, _____ important…
5 …I think pictures are _____ important…

e Now have a conversation in groups of three. Discuss the statements.

1 Lots of adult books would benefit from being illustrated.
2 The cover of a book heavily influences whether people choose to read it.

🖱 **Go online** to watch the video, review the lesson, and check your progress

G advanced gerunds and infinitives   **V** health and medicine, similes   **P** /ə/

1 VOCABULARY health and medicine

Work in small groups and do the quiz.

How good a doctor are you?

1 Why might someone have...?
  a a bruise
  b a rash
  c a blister
  d side-effects

2 What treatment might you be given for...?
  a a small cut
  b a deep cut
  c a throat infection
  d a sprained ankle
  e a broken arm

3 What are the symptoms of...?
  a a cold
  b the flu
  c food poisoning
  d a heart attack
  e a stroke

4 What might happen to you if you...?
  a had to stand for a long time in a hot, crowded room
  b were stung on your hand by a bee
  c spent the night outdoors in the cold

5 In what circumstances might somebody need to see...?
  a their GP
  b a specialist
  c a surgeon
  d a psychiatrist

2 READING

a With a partner, look at the list below. Which things do you think doctors might <u>not</u> do themselves and why?

smoke   have a full health check   see a counsellor
drink alcohol   use alternative medicine
follow a low-carb diet   vaccinate their children against childhood illnesses, like measles
take vitamin supplements   have cosmetic surgery
go to the doctor with a long list of symptoms   take anti-malaria pills when visiting a country where it is common
sunbathe   take sleeping tablets

b Read the article on p.77 once and complete headings A–G with a treatment or behaviour from **a**.

c Read the article again. Why wouldn't the doctors do these things? Match reasons 1–7 to paragraphs A–G.

1 ☐ Because it might be difficult later to stop doing this.
2 ☐ Because the doctor may take you less seriously.
3 ☐ Because the short-term benefit may be outweighed by long-term problems.
4 ☐ Because you may develop another illness as a result of unnecessary treatment.
5 ☐ Because you may end up having unnecessary tests or medication.
6 ☐ Because you may not necessarily be treated by a professional.
7 ☐ Because you are doing something that is deliberately damaging.

d **Language in context** Look at the highlighted phrases in the article and focus on the **bold** verbs. With a partner, decide what they mean.

e Discuss in small groups.

- Do any of the doctors' opinions surprise you?
- Might their opinions affect the way you behave? Why (not)?
- Is there anything connected with medicine or health that you would never do?

What doctors won't do…

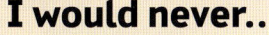

Doctors reveal the treatments or behaviours they would avoid

I would never…

I would never take up the regularly advertised offers by private medical companies. Why? Well, if you have symptoms, you go to your GP and they listen to your history, examine you, request investigations, and reach a decision. This process is known as 'diagnosis'. A full check when you feel totally well is not diagnosis, it is 'screening'. There are few screening tests where [1] the advantages **outweigh** the disadvantages, and they could lead you to have potentially harmful investigations, or indeed treatment, that you may not have needed. One hears anecdotes about the advantages of health checks. One hears anecdotes about people who have fallen out of sixth-floor windows and lived, but I wouldn't try it myself.   *Mike Smith, GP*

Patients often think this helps, but [2] it makes the doctor's heart **sink**. They're not going to be able to deal with everything in one go, and most importantly of all, it makes them think you haven't got one particular problem, you've got multiple problems, which is a sure sign of a hypochondriac.   *Carol Cooper, GP*

[3] People **underestimate** the risk. They think, 'My skin looks all right; how can it be damaged?' Even if your skin doesn't look aged, you can end up with skin damage that sets you up for potential cancers in the future. Sunbathing in your teens and early 20s is a very strong risk factor. We are now seeing cancers in the under-40s that we used to see only on the faces of old, weather-beaten guys who had spent a lifetime outdoors. I would go out in the sun, but I would never lie in it with the purpose of getting a tan.   *Carol Cooper, GP*

I have come across many patients who have been taking them for decades. They are addictive and [4] it can be very difficult for people to **wean themselves off** them; the side-effects can include falls, confusion, sleepiness in the daytime, and the feeling that increasingly high doses are needed to achieve the same effects. I can't imagine any situation in which I would start using them.   *Helen Drew, GP*

Why? Because although you will probably lose weight, it may kill you. Don't take my word for it – read about the 43,396 Swedish women followed for an average of 15 years. [5] Those who **stuck to** low carbs and high protein had a rising risk of dying from heart attacks and strokes. There was a staggering 62% higher risk of such illnesses among the women eating the strictest diet over those who ate normally. Eating is for enjoyment; these diets turn food into medicine and it's the wrong medicine.   *Tom Smith, GP*

The reason for my reluctance? Nothing to do with anaesthetics (safe these days), but entirely to do with surgery, which [6] should never **be undertaken** for what you might call 'soft' reasons. It's not that surgery is so dangerous that I would worry about death. Mainly it's the worry of an infection, which can be very unpleasant.   *Mark Patrick, consultant anaesthetist*

G

I'd never go to one if I was having mental health problems. This is an entirely unregulated area and absolutely anyone can claim to be one. As a result, [7] quality **varies** hugely. I have seen too many patients who have been further psychologically damaged by seeing poorly-qualified practitioners.
Max Pemberton, psychiatrist

Abridged from The Guardian

---

3 LISTENING & SPEAKING

a Look at the types of alternative medicine below. Do you know what any of them involve? Do you know of any other kinds of alternative treatment?

> acupuncture   aromatherapy   chiropractic   herbal medicine   homeopathy   hypnotherapy   osteopathy

b 🔊 **8.1** Listen to five people talking about alternative medicine. Answer the questions for each speaker.

Did they have any treatment?
Yes What treatment did they have? What for? Was it successful?
No Why not?

Glossary

placebo /pləˈsiːbəʊ/ a substance that has no physical effects, given to patients who do not need medicine but think that they do, or used when testing new drugs

---

c Listen again. Which speaker, 1–5,…?

A ☐ was rather discouraged by the cost and the process of the treatment
B ☐ thinks that they didn't have the treatment at the right time
C ☐ was amazed that they were able to have the treatment more than once
D ☐ thinks that research shows that the treatment works
E ☐ thinks that using alternative treatments can have serious consequences

d 🔊 **8.2** Listen and complete some expressions the speakers used.

1 …although I was very sceptical about it, I really do think it _____ _____ _____…

2 You only ever hear _____ _____ that it's worked for individual people…

3 …so I thought, 'Why not _____ _____ _____ _____?'

4 Sadly, it _____ _____ _____ on me whatsoever.

e Discuss in small groups.

- Have you ever tried any forms of alternative medicine, or do you know anyone who has? Was the experience positive or negative?
- Do you, or does anyone you know, feel strongly either that alternative medicine really works or that it's 'a waste of time and money'?

4 GRAMMAR advanced gerunds and infinitives

a Complete the sentences with the correct form of the verb in brackets. Then say if they are true for you.

1 I'm really bad at remembering _____ medicine. (take)
2 I have never enjoyed _____ to the dentist's. (go)
3 My parents never used to make me _____ suncream when I was a child. (put on)

b Write the verbs or verb phrases in the correct column.

afford   agree   avoid   be worth   can't help   can't stand
deny   had better   happen   imagine   involve
look forward to   manage   miss   needn't   practise
pretend   refuse   regret   risk   suggest   tend   threaten
would rather

+ to + infinitive	+ gerund	+ infinitive without *to*

c 🔊 8.3 Listen and check.

d ⓖ p.156 **Grammar Bank 8A**

e ⓒ **Communication** Guess the sentence **A** p.110 **B** p.115 Try to guess the missing phrases.

5 LISTENING & SPEAKING

a With a partner, look at the photos of leisure activities and think of one physical or mental health benefit of doing each activity.

b Read the extract from a news article. What is 'social prescribing'?

c 🔊 8.4 Now listen to a radio interview with a research scientist about 'social prescribing'. Match activities 1–7 in **a** to health benefits A–G.

A ▢ improves the body's defences against disease
B ▢ slows the heart down
C ▢ makes you feel less anxious
D ▢ lowers blood pressure
E ▢ reduces the likelihood of cancer
F ▢ stops the brain ageing as quickly
G ▢ reduces allergies

> **Glossary**
> **thymus** /ˈθaɪməs/ an organ in the neck that produces cells to fight infections
> **diabetes** /ˌdaɪəˈbiːtiːz/ a medical condition that causes a person's blood sugar to become too high

Forget the pills – dancing and gardening are better for your health

Many people find hobbies rewarding. However, they may also be more effective than medicine at keeping us healthy. The government is now asking GPs to move away from automatically prescribing drugs and to encourage patients to become more sociable and active, through taking up hobbies such as gardening, yoga, book clubs, and cookery classes. Research suggests that what is known as 'social prescribing' could cut A&E visits by a quarter, reduce GP appointments, help improve long-term health, and delay cognitive decline.

Adapted from The Times

d Listen again. What does the scientist say about the following things? Note as much information as you can.

1 what dancing does to your brain
2 how cycling affects the thymus
3 how yoga makes a difference to your health
4 what impact golf has on chronic diseases
5 how long people need to spend looking after plants to feel the benefit and the impact this has
6 what effect stroking a dog has
7 how knitting improved the lives of a group of women

e 🔊 **8.5 Language in context** Listen to some extracts from the interview and complete the highlighted phrases. With a partner, say what they mean.

1 …to reduce _____ _____ prescription drugs…
2 …patients who _____ _____ social activities…
3 …that _____ an important _____ _____ memory and learning.
4 …can _____ blood pressure _____ as much as 10%.
5 …help to offset the _____ _____ getting diabetes…
6 …less likely to _____ _____ depression.
7 …are less _____ _____ developing allergies…
8 …has a beneficial _____ _____ your health.

f Talk to a partner.

- How would you feel if your doctor refused to prescribe you medicine and suggested golf or gardening instead?
- Do you do any of the activities mentioned in the interview? Do you do them alone, or with other people? What other leisure activities do you think might also have health benefits?
- Does the government in your country give advice about a healthy lifestyle? Do you think people take it seriously? Do you think advice like this is helpful, or should people be left to make their own lifestyle decisions?

6 VOCABULARY & PRONUNCIATION similes; /ə/

a Talk to a partner. Do you know anyone who…?

- eats anything they like, but is really skinny
- can't see anything if they aren't wearing their glasses
- drinks too much
- can't hear very well, but won't use their hearing aid
- is in great physical shape
- is elderly, but never seems to get ill
- always sleeps really well at night
- refuses to do something even though you keep telling them
- has incredibly well-behaved children

b Read the information box. Then, with a partner, try to complete sentences 1–10 with a word from the list.

> 🔍 **Similes for comparisons**
> A simile is a fixed expression of comparison using *as* or *like*, which adds emphasis to an adjective, adverb, or verb, e.g.
>
> *Are you OK? You look **as white as a sheet**!*
> *When I called her, the nurse came **as quick as a flash**.*
> *My new medication **works like a dream**.*

blind deaf drinks eats fit good sleeps stubborn thin tough

1 He's as _____ as a mule.
2 She's as _____ as a post.
3 He's as _____ as a bat.
4 She's as _____ as a fiddle.
5 He's as _____ as a rake.
6 He _____ like a horse.
7 She's as _____ as gold.
8 She's as _____ as old boots.
9 He _____ like a log.
10 She _____ like a fish.

c Now use similes 1–10 to describe the people in **a**.

My brother eats like a horse, but he's still as thin as a rake.

d Look at the sentence below and answer the questions.

> He **refuses** to **go** to the **doctor** about his **bad back** – he's as **stubborn** as a **mule**.

1 Which unstressed words contain the /ə/ sound? Circle them.
2 Which two stressed words also contain the /ə/ sound? Is it on a stressed syllable or an unstressed syllable?

e 🔊 **8.6** Listen and check. Practise saying the sentence.

f 🔊 **8.7** Now listen and write five sentences. Then match them to five of the similes in **b**. Practise saying both parts.

🔵 **Go online** to review the lesson

G expressing future plans and arrangements **V** travel and tourism **P** homophones

1 READING

a Look at the photos of six famous tourist attractions and read the captions. Do you know where they are? Do you know anything else about them?

The Empire State Building
Once the world's tallest building, the elegant skyscraper is now a revered American icon.

The Little Mermaid
A much-loved work of art by the harbour, of a mermaid becoming human, from a fairy tale by Hans Christian Andersen.

Machu Picchu
A magnificent 15th-century Inca citadel, perched on a mountain ridge.

Waikiki
Perhaps the world's most famous and most filmed beach, a surfing paradise.

Mount Rushmore An imposing granite sculpture hewn into the mountainside, depicting the heads of four US presidents.

Isla del Sol
A gorgeous island on Lake Titicaca, the largest high-altitude lake in the world.

b Read an article about the places in **a**. Match the visitors' comments A–F to photos 1–6.

'Is that it?'

Have you ever visited a famous tourist attraction and been distinctly [1] underwhelmed? Here are some accounts by visitors to some of the world's most well-known tourist sights.

A 'The location is breathtaking, and the fact they got the stones up there without wheels is [2] jaw-dropping. However, it is essentially a pile of rubble, just a load of big stones. The idea is far more amazing than the remnants. The hill behind was beautiful though.' ***Derek, 43***

B 'You always have this image of [3] sheer perfection, yet I will always remember the massive sense of disappointment. The place was barren, soulless, and empty. The sand wasn't white, the hotels were tacky, and there was nothing there that captured my imagination. If somebody hadn't told me it was the famous one, I'd probably never have known I'd been there. It was [4] so average, not the Hawaiian dream you picture.' ***Craig, 31***

C 'After joining a queue that stretched around the block, we thought we might be waiting to get in for 20 minutes or so. As we got closer and closer to the front, we got more and more excited…until we got inside and saw that the queue snaked back and forth and we were miles away from the front. We eventually got to the lift and went up – but not to the top. You have to join another queue that takes you up to the observation deck. Then, when you get to the top, it dawns on you that you don't actually get the classic view at all, the one with the iconic building in it, because you're on top of it.' ***Matt, 33***

D 'We booked a tour, as some people had told us how beautiful and remote it was. It turns out you can see it from the shore of the lake. When you land, there are a few run-down restaurants, and some locals who charge you the entrance fee, and others who clearly don't want tourists hanging around. A big [5] let-down.' ***Silvia, 34***

E 'This is widely agreed to be the Mona Lisa of statues. But to see it requires a long detour out of the city centre. It is usually surrounded by tourists queuing for photos, and it is, by its own admission, 'unimposing'. It's a bit like when you order something on Amazon and forget to read the actual dimensions, and it arrives the same size as the thumbnail on your screen. I thought it was [6] vastly overrated. Prepare to hear lots of confused people asking, 'Is that it?'' ***Miranda, 23***

F 'Pictures and video do not convey the awe of the Grand Canyon at sunset, nor the serene calm of the sunrise over the Great Barrier Reef. However, pictures do convey the boringness of these carved faces. You look at it from one angle, then another, then you say, 'OK, cool. Gift shop, then car?' Or you can hike to the top and see the great expanse of…flatness covered by trees. I've never been so disappointed.' ***Rob, 29***

c Read the article again. What was disappointing about each place? Did anyone say anything positive?

d **Language in context** Match the highlighted expressions 1–6 in the article to meanings A–F.

A ▢ very ordinary indeed
B ▢ a disappointment
C ▢ far less good than everyone says
D ▢ unimpressed
E ▢ as good as it could possibly be
F ▢ almost unbelievable

e Read some more comments from disappointed tourists and complete them with the places or things in the photos.

comments Sign in to join the discussion.

👤 12 Feb

1 [_____]

It's much smaller than I expected, and is so damaged that the face is almost gone.

👤 12 Feb

2 [_____]

About the size of a piece of printer paper, and you already know what it looks like. And you can't even get close to it because there's always a huge mob of people.

👤 13 Feb

3 [_____]

It looks much less grand in real life. I just pulled off to the side of the road and had a quick look. It feels like something a bored farmer might have put up to attract some tourists.

👤 13 Feb

4 [_____]

Heat and snakes, and if something goes wrong, you WILL die. You might even die without anything going wrong.

👤 14 Feb

5 [_____]

You can barely move for hours and there's nowhere to go to the bathroom.

the Australian Outback

The Mona Lisa

Times Square on New Year's Eve

the Sphinx

Stonehenge

f Have you been to any of the places mentioned in the article or the comments? Did you agree with the visitors' opinions? Which one(s) would you still like to see, despite the comments?

2 VOCABULARY travel and tourism

a Look at two sentences from **1**. What does *imposing* mean?

> An **imposing** granite sculpture hewn into the mountainside... (Mount Rushmore)

> ...and it is, by its own admission, '**unimposing**'. (*The Little Mermaid*)

b Look at some more adjectives from the article in **1**. Are they positive or negative? What might you describe with each one?

> breathtaking   iconic   run-down   soulless   tacky

c ⓥ p.170 **Vocabulary Bank** Travel and tourism

3 SPEAKING

Talk to a partner.

- Is there a place you've been to that...?
  1 was very disappointing and you felt was overrated
  2 was absolutely wonderful and much better than you expected
- Where was it?
- When did you go, and who with?
- What was your reaction when you first got there?
- What was it like?
- What did you do while you were there?

- Is there a world-famous tourist attraction that you would really like to visit? Is there anything you think might disappoint you about it? Do you know anyone who's been there? What did they think of it?

- What sights in your area do tourists always visit? Do you think they're ever disappointed? Why?

- Are there any sights in your area which are rarely visited by tourists, but which you think are really worth visiting?

4 LISTENING & SPEAKING

a You're going to listen to Clive telling a story about a terrible journey. Look at the words and guess what happens in the first part of the story.

Spain the UK
wife children
Christmas flight
message **brother**
weather Gatwick Airport
storm winds

b 🔊 **8.10** Listen to the first part of Clive's story and check your ideas from **a**. What do you think is going to happen next?

c Now listen to the rest of the story. After each part, answer the questions with a partner.

🔊 **8.11**

1 What did the pilot warn them about?
2 What happened when the plane started circling?
3 What could they see out of the window?
4 What did everyone think was going to happen?
5 What happened at the very last moment?
6 What did the pilot tell the passengers at the end?
What do you think is going to happen next?

🔊 **8.12**

7 Where did Clive think they might land?
8 Where did the plane end up going?
9 Why did the pilot think they would be able to land there?
10 What did the passengers do after they landed?
11 What were the passengers then told? Why?
12 What choice were they given?
What do you think is going to happen next?

🔊 **8.13**

13 Why did some of the passengers stay on the plane?
14 What did Clive and his family do?
15 How did they get to London?
16 When did they eventually arrive?

> **Glossary**
> **gale-force winds** extremely strong winds
> **bumpy** with a lot of sudden movements

d If you were Clive, do you think you would have made the same decisions about how to get to the UK?

e Work in small groups. Tell each other about a bad journey you've had, e.g. when you were on holiday, or on your way to work or school. Say…

- when it happened.
- what happened during the journey, and how you felt.
- how you felt in the end.

5 GRAMMAR expressing future plans and arrangements

a 🔊 **8.14** Listen and complete some extracts from Clive's story with the correct form of the verb in brackets.

1 …are you nearly ready? We _____ for the airport in 15 minutes. (leave)
2 …the flight _____ at 10.15. Don't worry, we've got plenty of time. (leave)
3 Anyway, we're about _____. (take off)
4 …we're _____ to land at Amsterdam… (try)
5 We're due _____ at Schiphol in approximately one hour. (land)
6 Good evening, everyone. We _____ shortly at Schiphol Airport. (land)

b With a partner, discuss whether there are any other forms you could use in each sentence in **a**.

c 🇬 p.157 **Grammar Bank 8B**

6 PRONUNCIATION homophones

> 🔍 **Homophones**
>
> The **weather** in Spain was really good…
> He's asking **whether** the flight's been cancelled.
>
> *Weather* and *whether* are homophones. They're spelt differently and have different meanings, but are pronounced exactly the same.

a 🔊 **8.15** Look at the phonetics and listen to the pairs of sentences. Then, with a partner, complete each pair with the correct spelling of the homophones.

1 /weɪt/   a We've got a three-hour _____ before the flight leaves.
  b What's the maximum _____ for hand luggage on this flight?

2 /bɔːd/   a Flight EZ472 is now ready to _____. Will passengers please proceed to Gate 10.
  b We're _____! We don't want to visit any more museums!

3 /piːs/   a Where's the _____ of paper with the address of the hotel?
  b We're going off the beaten track for a bit of _____ and quiet.

4 /kɔːt/   a There was terrible traffic on the way to the airport and we only just _____ the flight.
  b It's a four-star hotel and it's even got a tennis _____.

5 /breɪk/   a The airport bus had to _____ suddenly when a lorry pulled out.
  b We're going to _____ the journey in Milan.

6 /feə/   a My ticket cost twice as much as yours. It's not _____!
  b How much is the air_____ to Peru?

7 /pleɪn/   a The pilot landed the _____ very smoothly, and everyone clapped.
  b The cabin crew uniform is a dark blue suit with a _____ white shirt.

8 /θruː/   a When we arrived in the States, it took us ages to get _____ immigration.
  b They _____ away my perfume at security because it was 200 ml.

9 /saɪt/   a We visited an archaeological _____ on the banks of the Nile.
  b My first _____ of the Pyramids completely took my breath away.

10 /swiːt/   a The hotel gave us the honeymoon _____ – it was the only room available!
  b I don't like the local white wine. It's too _____ for me.

b Test your partner. **A** say one of the homophones, **B** give the two spellings and meanings. Then swap.

c 🔊 **8.16** Listen to ten sentences using the homophones in **a**. Say whether the homophone you hear is a or b.

7 ▶ VIDEO LISTENING

a Read the definition of 'screen tourism' and answer the questions.

screen tourism
a kind of tourism where large numbers of people visit a place because it has appeared in a TV series or film

1 Can you think of anywhere in your country where this happens?
2 Have you ever visited somewhere because it appeared in a TV series or film? If so, where was it? If not, is there a place you'd like to visit?

b Watch a documentary about screen tourism. What is the connection between these things?

Cornwall
1 Porthcurno Beach – the TV drama *Poldark*
2 the '*Poldark* Effect' – tourist numbers in Cornwall
3 the National Trust – Porthcurno Beach
4 the Cornish economy – the tourism industry
5 Charlestown – 500,000 people
6 high visitor numbers – local infrastructure

Northern Ireland
7 Northern Ireland – *Game of Thrones*
8 political violence – tourism in Northern Ireland
9 £65 million – £9 million
10 *Outlander* – *Downton Abbey*

c Watch again and answer the questions.

1 How do these people feel about screen tourism?

Simon Hocking	Ian Lay
Tania Plowright	Bridgeen Barbour

2 Do you think screen tourism has been generally good or bad for Cornwall and Northern Ireland? Why?

d Do you agree that if you live somewhere beautiful, you have to put up with the problems caused by tourism?

8 WRITING

Ⓦ **p.126 Writing** A discursive essay (2): Taking sides   Analyse a model essay about tourism, and write a discursive essay.

> 🖱️ **Go online** to watch the video and review the lesson

GRAMMAR

a Complete the sentences with the correct form of the verb in brackets.

1 Do you think I ought _____ to Mario yesterday? (apologize)
2 You'd better _____ to the doctor about that cough. (go)
3 You're not supposed _____ your phone at work, but everyone does. (use)
4 Alex seems _____ a lot at the moment. Do you think he's studying enough? (go out)
5 Isn't there anywhere _____ here? (sit down)
6 Rick hates _____ by his boss. (criticize)
7 I would love _____ the installation, but it finished the day before we arrived. (see)
8 There's no point _____ him. He always has his phone turned off while he's driving. (call)
9 It's important for celebrities _____ at all the right parties. (see)
10 Let's go and have a coffee. The meeting isn't due _____ until 10.30. (start)

b Circle the correct phrase. Tick (✓) if both are possible.

1 It is *not allowed / not permitted* to wear jewellery at school.
2 *You should have listened / You should listen* to my advice, but it's too late now.
3 The flight was at midday, so we *needn't have got up / didn't need to get up* early. In fact, we got up at 9.30.
4 You *look / seem* a bit down today. Is everything OK?
5 It smells *as if / as though* someone has burned the toast.
6 Is that your father upstairs? *I can hear / I'm hearing* his voice.
7 This coffee *tastes like / tastes of* tea. It's undrinkable!
8 *I'll be working / I'm working* at home this afternoon, so you can call me there.
9 You'd better get on the train now. It's *on the point of / about to* leave.
10 The princess is *to / due to* open the new hospital early next month.

VOCABULARY

a Complete the sentences with the correct form of the **bold** word and a prefix.

1 Sorry, but you've _____ my name. It's K-A-T-Y, not K-A-T-I-E. **spell**
2 I get very _____ when I feel that I'm not making any progress. **motivate**
3 Nowadays in Venice, local residents are completely _____ by tourists. **number**
4 The film isn't as good as everyone says it is. I think it's very _____. **rate**
5 Look, I think they've _____ us. The bill should be £80, not £60. **charge**
6 I'm afraid this style of jeans has been _____ – we won't be receiving any more. **continue**
7 The staff meeting has been postponed and will be _____ for a later date. **schedule**
8 Trying to improve people's lives by imposing all kinds of new laws on them is _____. **logical**

b Complete the expressions or idioms for the definitions.

1 a _____ life (*noun*) = a painting or drawing of arrangements of objects such as flowers, fruit, etc.
2 a self-_____ (*noun*) = a painting or drawing that an artist does of him / herself
3 a red _____ IDM = an unimportant fact or idea that takes people's attention away from the important things
4 a white _____ IDM = a thing that is useless even though it may have cost a lot of money
5 the black _____ IDM = an illegal form of trade in which goods that are difficult to obtain are bought and sold
6 red _____ IDM = bureaucracy

c Circle the correct word.

1 I wore my new shoes to work today and now I've got a *blister / sprain* on my toe.
2 He had a *sting / stroke* last year and he still finds it difficult to walk.
3 Do you know which *surgeon / GP* will be operating on you?
4 I've got a strange *bruise / rash* on my hands. I think it might be an allergy to detergent.
5 My husband is as stubborn as a *horse / mule*.
6 Grandad never hears the doorbell. He's as deaf as a *bat / post*.
7 I was so tired I slept like a *fish / log* last night.
8 Now that my laptop's been mended it works like a *dream / flash*.

d Complete the missing words.

1 It's a very quiet place, completely off the b_____ track.
2 We s_____ off at 7.00 and we were there by 11.00.
3 As soon as we get there, let's h_____ the shops!
4 It used to be an unspoilt village, but now it's really t_____ – there are at least ten hotels.
5 Our daughter isn't very well, so we've had to p_____ our holiday till next month.
6 It's been such a stressful couple of months. I need a break to r_____ my batteries.
7 Our room had a br_____ view of the mountains.
8 On the first day we decided to go to the market and s_____ the local street food.

CAN YOU understand this text?

a Read the article once. What advice does it give?

b Read the article again and choose the correct meaning for the highlighted words.

1 a cure   b limit   c protect against
2 a forget   b include   c remove
3 a the intestine   b the heart   c the liver
4 a an attack   b an infestation   c a mass
5 a improve   b alleviate   c cancel
6 a covered in   b soaked in   c wrapped in
7 a manage   b follow   c control
8 a tiredness   b severe pain   c irritation

▶ CAN YOU understand these people?

◉ 8.17 Watch or listen and choose a, b, or c.

1 **Sean** _____.
   a always uses the same password
   b doesn't like thinking of new passwords
   c never includes a number in his password
2 **Claire** _____.
   a often used to visit the Tate Gallery when she was a child
   b enjoyed family outings to two particular museums / galleries
   c preferred visiting museums when her children were younger
3 Neither **Helen** nor **Simon** _____.
   a really believe that alternative medicine works
   b have tried alternative medicine
   c think that there is a place for alternative therapies
4 When **Rob** visited the Pyramids, he _____.
   a had an awful experience there
   b thought the place was really overrated
   c was upset by how untidy it was

Why you always get ill on holiday

More than a third of us suffer from some sort of holiday health problem. One theory is that during our daily grind, our body is constantly producing stress hormones, which can help to [1] ward off infection. But once we relax, these levels drop and make us susceptible to illness. Philip Calder, from Southampton University, says, 'On top of this, when you visit foreign countries, your body encounters a whole new set of bacteria and viruses, starting with those of the passengers you sit with on the plane. [2] Throw in sunburn, drinking too much alcohol, and eating unhealthy food, and you have a recipe for getting sick.' But there's plenty you can do to prevent it.

Tummy trouble

Why? 'Most of our immune system is located in [3] the gut', explains Professor Glenn Gibson, of Reading University. 'We change our diet and lifestyle on holiday, which has an effect on our digestion and immunity.' We are also faced with [4] an onslaught of foreign bugs. Local street food and tap water can be a problem, but hotel food isn't always safer. In fact, tourists staying in all-inclusive resorts, where food and drink are provided, were found by research to be twice as likely to become sick as those with 'room only'. This is largely down to buffet meals – food left standing around in the heat can quickly attract a host of bugs.

Beat it Professor Gibson recommends trying foods such as probiotics, to prevent and [5] ease stomach problems. These encourage levels of good bacteria, effectively crowding out bad bacteria so they can't take hold, and unlike diarrhoea medication, they have no side-effects.

Colds and flu

Why? Colds are more than 100 times more likely to be transmitted on a plane than in normal daily life, according to the Journal of Environmental Health Research. Air-conditioning on planes and in hotels extracts moisture from the air, causing it to dry out, along with the lining of the nose, which is [6] coated with a layer of mucus to protect against infection. Cooler air may help viruses establish themselves.

Beat it 'Wash your hands frequently and thoroughly while travelling', advises GP Dr Sarah Brewer. 'I'd also take a good multi-vitamin and mineral and Omega-3 fish oils to boost your immune system before you go.'

Travel sickness

Why? Travel or motion sickness often happens on holiday, when people use modes of transport they don't take in their daily life, such as planes, boats, or coaches. Sickness strikes when the brain receives conflicting signals about the body's movement and balance. The brain finds it hard to [7] track the body's position, and this creates symptoms of nausea and dizziness.

Beat it 'Ask to sit in the middle of the plane or boat, or in the front seat of a coach or bus, as these areas tend to experience the least motion', suggests pharmacist Angela Chalmers. 'Help your body to manage symptoms by closing your eyes or fixing them on the horizon and distracting yourself by listening to music.'

Insect bites

Why? A mosquito bite can be quite nasty and causes the skin to redden and swell very quickly. And in some countries, mosquitoes can also carry some very serious diseases, including malaria, yellow fever, and dengue fever, which can be fatal. Other insects, such as ants, bees, hornets, and wasps can also give nasty bites and stings that will cause swelling, redness, and [8] itching. Factors that make mozzies more likely to bite include being hot and sweaty, drinking alcohol, and being pregnant.

Beat it Your best bet is to invest in a good insect repellent. Angela Chalmers says, 'The repellent disorientates the insect, preventing it from landing on you and causing it to fly away, keeping you bite-free.' It's also sensible to wear clothing to cover legs, ankles, and arms.

Adapted from Mirror news

◉ **Go online** to watch the video, review Files 7 & 8, and check your progress

> A rattlesnake loose in the living room tends to end all discussion of animal rights.
> *Lance Morrow, US writer*

1 READING

a Would you describe yourself as an animal-lover? Have you ever had a pet? How attached to it are / were you?

b Look at the title of the article. Does it imply that the writer likes animals or dislikes them?

c Now read the article once. Match each paragraph 1–7 to its topic.

- [ ] his attitude to dogs
- [ ] his current feelings about kittens
- [ ] people's preference for animals over children
- [ ] his general attitude to cats
- [ ] future plans about pets in his household
- [ ] his childhood experience of pets
- [ ] his children's attitude to animals

In defence of not liking animals

1 Our household at the moment is infested – sorry, blessed – with cats. Six of them. Having got rid of one, Dylan, last year – may he rest in peace – leaving only his infirm and senile brother, Floss, behind, my wife accepted a kitten. This kitten has just given birth to four of her own fluffy balls. I have to admit that the expression 'cute as a kitten' does not seem to be an arbitrary one. They are extraordinarily loveable. They meow and play and generally make the world a fluffier place. I like them.

2 But I doubt that it will last. I am a lifelong pet sceptic. Confronted with the kittens, it briefly slipped my mind why I was sceptical. I am now beginning to remember. The house is starting to smell. Cats come on to the bed in the morning at 6.00 a.m., sit on your head and wake you up. They drink the water in your bedside glass. If you close the door, they wait outside complaining until you open it, so they can sit on your head, etc. Their lovability is more than offset by their extraordinary flair in the art of being annoying.

3 My prejudice is not confined to cats – to dogs I am positively averse. They are needy, time-consuming, easy to trip over, and frequently smell bad. Also, they have been known to bite people – certainly a lot of dogs in my neighbourhood appear to have evolved specifically for this purpose.

4 There are people – 'animal-lovers' is the term – who find people like me, people who care very little about other species, barely human. If I were feeling apologetic, I would only say that I grew up in a house without pets, and so have never quite become acclimatized to them. My only pet was a stickleback I caught in the canal, which died after six hours in my mother's household bucket. And a tortoise, whose shell I found mysteriously empty one day.

5 But I'm not feeling apologetic. Should I feel sorry because I can stare at my children awestruck by love, but not feel the same way about another species? I cannot accept that people who don't much care for animals are emotionally defective. If anything, the reverse is true. Anybody who leaves their inheritance to a donkey sanctuary rather than research for, say, children's cancer, strikes me as profoundly cynical about the human race.

6 Human beings are difficult to love – they are complex, contrary, and they often let you down. Animals are simple and easy to love. But it's a soft option. My children appear to adore animals, but in a highly partial way. They ooh and aah when they see lambs frolicking in the fields, but then sit down and eat their Sunday lunch with mint sauce without a second thought. This is sentimentality rather than genuine love.

7 But for the moment, cynic or not, I am content to have the gorgeous balls of fluff around the house. Three are being given away, we're keeping one, and Floss can't be for this earthly realm much longer. That will leave us with two. I can live with that, just about, as long as no one asks me, ever, to clean out the litter tray.

By Tim Lott in The Guardian

Glossary

stickleback a small, freshwater fish with sharp points on its back
tortoise

mint sauce a sauce traditionally eaten in the UK with roast lamb
litter tray a shallow box full of a dry substance used by cats as an indoor toilet

d Read the article again. Then look at extracts 1–7 below which summarize the main idea of each paragraph. (Circle) the **bold** phrase which explains what each extract means.

1 I have to admit that the expression 'cute as a kitten' does not seem to be an arbitrary one.

= There are **good reasons / no good reasons** for thinking that kittens are cute.

2 Their lovability is more than offset by their extraordinary flair in the art of being annoying.

= Cats are **more loveable than annoying / more annoying than loveable**.

3 My prejudice is not confined to cats – to dogs I am positively averse.

= I dislike **cats even more than dogs / dogs even more than cats**.

4 I would only say that I grew up in a house without pets, and so have never quite become acclimatized to them.

= Because I never had pets when I was young, **I'm not used to / I don't like** living with them.

5 I cannot accept that people who don't much care for animals are emotionally defective.

= I believe that it's **completely normal / quite strange** for people not to like animals.

6 My children appear to adore animals, but in a highly partial way.

= My children have a very **consistent / inconsistent** attitude to animals.

7 I can live with that, just about, as long as no one asks me, ever, to clean out the litter tray.

= I'm **happy to have / prepared to tolerate having** pets in my house.

e Talk to a partner.

1 Is the tone of the article…?
   a humorous   b neutral
   c serious
2 Do you think the writer's attitude to animals is…?
   a realistic   b sentimental   c hard-hearted
3 What is your attitude to animals: 2a, b, or c? Explain why.

2 VOCABULARY & SPEAKING animal matters

a Write the names of the first three animals that come into your head. Compare your list with a partner. Then go to **Communication** Three animals **p.108** and find out what your animals represent.

b **V** p.171 **Vocabulary Bank** Animal matters Do Part 1.

c Choose five topics. Tell your partner about a person you know who…

- prefers animals to people.
- has an unusual pet.
- doesn't eat meat or fish because of their principles.
- is allergic to bee or wasp stings.
- is afraid of certain animals or insects.
- doesn't look after an animal properly.
- has a really annoying pet.
- has had an infestation of insects or animals in their house / garden.
- is obsessed with their pet, or with a particular kind of animal.
- would like a pet, but can't have one.
- can't eat shellfish.
- has been attacked or bitten by an animal.

d Read the sentences and definitions and choose the correct word from the list to complete the **bold** idioms.

bark   birds   chickens   donkey   duck   fish   horse   lion   rat   tail

1 I **did all the _____ work** on this project, so I hope I'm going to get the credit for it.   = did the hard, boring part
2 I told him what I thought of him, but **it's like water off a _____'s back**.   = criticism doesn't affect him
3 He moved from a village to London, but he **was like a _____ out of water**.   = felt uncomfortable or awkward in unfamiliar surroundings
4 You think you've passed the exam, but **don't count your _____ before they hatch**.   = don't be too confident that you will be successful
5 I think James was married before, but I'm not sure. He's a bit of **a dark _____**.   = a person who doesn't tell others much about their life (but sometimes surprises them)
6 When they divorced, Nick's wife got **the _____'s share** of everything they owned.   = the main part
7 The company says they're not going to make anyone redundant in the restructuring, but I **smell a _____**.   = think that sth is wrong or that sb is trying to deceive you
8 If the meeting is in Manchester, I can go and visit my mother at the same time – it'll **kill two _____ with one stone**.   = achieve two things by doing one action
9 My boss can seem quite scary, but in fact, **her _____ is worse than her bite**.   = her words are worse than her actions
10 After playing so badly, he walked off **with his _____ between his legs**.   = feeling ashamed, embarrassed, or unhappy after having been defeated or punished

e Which idioms are similar in your language? Which are different?

3 GRAMMAR ellipsis

a 🔊 9.5 Read a conversation and complete the gaps with one word. Listen and check. What is the function of the missing words?

> **A** Have you ever had a pet?
> **B** Sadly not. I've always wanted [1] *to*, but I've never been able [2]_____ because I'm allergic to cats and dogs.
> **A** Are you? I'm not, but my sister [3]_____, which is why we never had them either. But my kids really want a puppy, and so [4]_____ my husband.
> **B** I think you probably [5]_____, then. What's stopping you? You ought to go to a rescue centre for abandoned dogs.
> **A** I already [6]_____.
> **B** So, you really are going to get one, then?
> **A** I suppose [7]_____. I'm not 100% convinced, but the children [8]_____.

b 🄶 p.158 Grammar Bank 9A

4 PRONUNCIATION auxiliary verbs and *to*

a 🔊 9.6 Read the conversations and <u>underline</u> the auxiliary verbs or *to* when you think they are stressed. Listen and check. Then practise the conversations.

> **1 A** Do you like dogs?
> **B** No, I don't, but my husband does.
> **A** So does mine. We have three Alsatians.
> **2 A** I went to Kenya last summer.
> **B** Lucky you. I'd love to go there. Did you go on safari?
> **A** No. I wanted to, but it was a business trip and I didn't have time.
> **3 A** Allie doesn't eat meat or fish, does she?
> **B** She does eat fish sometimes. She loves shellfish.
> **A** Ugh. I don't like shellfish.
> **B** Neither do I. It's so difficult to eat.

b 🄲 **Communication** Match the sentences **A p.111 B p.113** Read sentences and choose responses.

5 LISTENING

a Look at the words from the list. With a partner, say what each of these people eats or doesn't eat.

| an omnivore | a flexitarian | a pescatarian | a vegetarian | a vegan |

b Look at the introduction to a radio discussion about veganism. With a partner, try to guess the correct statistics.

> Well over [1] *1 million / 500,000 / 250,000* people in the UK now describe themselves as vegan, an increase of over [2] *500% / 200% / 100%* in ten years, and [3] *30% / 20% / 10%* of people under the age of 35 have tried a vegan diet.

c 🔊 9.7 Listen and check. Do you think the statistics would be similar in your country? How easy is it for vegetarians and vegans to eat out where you live?

d 🔊 9.8 Now listen to the discussion between Jimmy, a vegan restaurant owner, and Simone, a dietician. Write **J** (Jimmy) and **S** (Simone) next to 1–6 in the chart according to whether they **agree**, **partly agree**, or **disagree**.

	agrees	partly agrees	disagrees
1 Eating meat is immoral.			
2 Veganism is good for the environment.			
3 Vegans have to be careful with their diet.			
4 Being vegan is a healthy choice.			
5 Vegans have problems eating out.			
6 Vegans make difficult dinner guests.			

> **Glossary**
> **quinoa** /ˈkiːnwɑː/ a South American plant grown for its edible seeds
> **soya bean** /ˈsɔɪə biːn/ a bean that can be used in cooking instead of animal protein

e Listen again and make notes about the reasons for each speaker's opinion. Then compare with a partner and explain the reasons. Whose side are you on for each argument, Jimmy's or Simone's?

f ◑ **9.9 Language in context** Look at some extracts from the discussion and complete the collocations with a word from the list. Then listen and check.

| deficiency | diet | footprint | impact | position | rights | risk |

1 The most obvious reason for veganism is to do with **animal** _____…
2 And the second big reason is that it reduces your **carbon** _____.
3 …the point about your **moral** _____, I do think that's a very personal decision…
4 And there's a significant **environmental** _____ associated with bringing those foods to Britain…
5 We hear a lot about **vitamin** _____ and so on…
6 …it's harder to maintain a **balanced** _____ if you're vegan…
7 …and that may present a serious **health** _____, especially for children and teenagers…

g Have you tried adopting a vegan diet or would you ever consider it? Why (not)? Do you think veganism is the future?

6 VOCABULARY & SPEAKING

a ⓥ **p.171 Vocabulary Bank** Animal matters Do Part 2.

b ◑ **9.11** Listen to some short extracts of people talking about the pros and cons of zoos and complete the expressions from the information box with an adverb.

> 🔍 **Common adverb collocations**
> 1 *It's something I feel _____ _____ about.*
> 2 *Well, I don't feel _____ _____ about it either way.*
> 3 *I have to say, I am _____ against zoos nowadays.*
> 4 *I don't _____ agree with you.*
> 5 *Well, I'm _____ convinced that the animal does not want to be there.*
> 6 *I'm _____ sure that kids could get the same amount of pleasure from seeing animals in the wild.*

c Work in small groups. You're going to discuss some of the tweets opposite. Each person in the group should choose a different tweet, for which they will start the discussion. Decide whether you agree or disagree with the statement and make notes with reasons and examples.

d Hold your discussions. Try to use the expressions from the information box.

e In your group, on which topic do you most strongly a) agree, b) disagree?

In today's society, there is no place for circuses or other entertainment that exploits animals. #animalissues

Animal rights activists are wrong to object to animals being used in experiments. #animalissues

Dogs and cats are fine, but nobody should keep a bird in a cage, or a fish in a tank. #animalissues

People should not be allowed to keep very aggressive breeds of dog, such as pit bulls, as pets. #animalissues

Hunting for food is acceptable; hunting for fun is not. #animalissues

People shouldn't wear anything made from animal skins, e.g. fur or leather. #animalissues

You shouldn't eat an animal that you wouldn't be willing to kill yourself. #animalissues

We spend too much time and money trying to save a few endangered species and not enough on general conservation. #animalissues

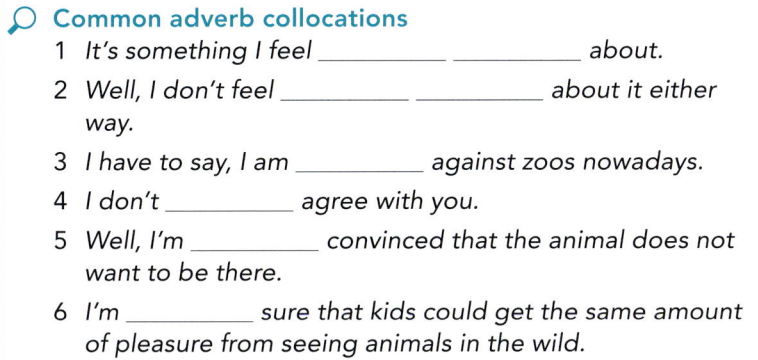

🔘 **Go online** to review the lesson

A first-rate soup is more creative than a second-rate painting.
Abraham Maslow, US psychologist

G nouns: compound and possessive forms   **V** preparing food   **P** words with silent syllables

1 VOCABULARY preparing food

a In pairs, in two minutes, try to think of as many different ways as possible of cooking the foods below.

chicken eggs
fish potatoes
rice

b Compare your answers with the class. Which pair got the most different ways?

c **V** p.172 **Vocabulary Bank** Preparing food

d Think of a popular dish from your region or country. Do you know how to say all the ingredients in English? How is the dish prepared?

2 PRONUNCIATION words with silent syllables

a Read these two sentences aloud. Which has more syllables? How many syllables do they each have?

1 Vegetable recipes can be interesting.
2 Everybody I know loves chocolate.

b 🔊 9.14 Listen to ten sentences. For each one, write the last word.

> 🔍 **Fine-tuning your pronunciation: silent syllables**
> Some common multi-syllable words in English have vowels that are often not pronounced, e.g. the middle *e* in *literature* and the *o* in *history*. When this happens, the word loses an unstressed syllable. If you pronounce these vowels, you'll still be understood, but leaving them out will make your speech sound more natural, and being aware of them will help you to understand these words in rapid speech.

c ~~Cross out~~ the vowels that are <u>not</u> pronounced in the words you wrote in **b**.

d Listen again and check. Practise saying the words.

3 READING & SPEAKING

a Talk in small groups. When you are making hard-boiled eggs, should you…?

• put the eggs in cold water or boiling water
• add anything to the water
• cook them on high or low heat
• cook them for over or under ten minutes

b Look at the cover of *The Food Lab* and read the extract from a review of the book. What do you think makes it different from most cookery books?

THE FOOD LAB
J. KENJI LÓPEZ-ALT
Better Home Cooking Through Science

❝ López-Alt's twin specialties are using the scientific method to figure out a better way to prepare a particular dish, and telling you why it works. ❞
New York Times

c Read the extract from *The Food Lab* on p.91 and complete it with verbs from the list. What makes hard-boiled eggs difficult to cook well?

add   bring   drop   heat   ~~lower~~   peel   remove   stick

d Now read López-Alt's recipe for hard-boiled eggs. How does it differ from what your group said in **a**? Would you be prepared to give it a go?

BOILED EGGS

Boiled eggs are about the simplest recipe in any cook's repertoire, right? But how often do you get truly *perfect* boiled eggs? Hard-boiled eggs should have a fully set, but not rubbery, white, and yolks that are cooked through, but still bright yellow and creamy. There's more to boiling an egg than meets the eye. Much more.

Nearly every basic cookbook offers a different technique for how it should be done: start the egg in cold water, or gently ¹*lower* it into boiling water; ²_____ vinegar to the water, or baking soda; cover the pan, or don't cover it; use old eggs, or new eggs; and on and on. But very few offer evidence as to why any one of these techniques should work any better than another. Apparently, boiling eggs is not…ahem…an *eggs*act science. Let's try and change that.

If we ³_____ the eggs directly into boiling water, the white will ⁴_____ up much faster than the yolk, so that by the time the very centre of the yolk is cooked, the white is hopelessly overcooked. You might put the eggs in cold water and ⁵_____ them to the boil gradually. This method works, but there's a problem: it causes the white to ⁶_____ to the shell when you try to peel the eggs.

So, cooking hard-boiled eggs slowly gives you good results, but cooking them fast makes it easier to ⁷_____ the shell. What I needed was a technique that combined both of these.

It took a few dozen tries to get the exact technique, but guess what? *It works.* You consistently get eggs that are both perfectly cooked through *and* easy to ⁸_____.

FOOLPROOF HARD-BOILED EGGS

2 litres water
1 to 6 large eggs
12 ice cubes

Pour the water into a lidded 3-litre saucepan and bring to the boil over a high heat.

Carefully lower the egg(s) into the water and cook for 30 seconds.

Add the ice cubes and allow the water to return to the boil, then reduce to a low simmer, about 85°C.

Cook for 11 minutes.

Drain the egg(s) and peel under cool running water.

Abridged from The Food Lab by J. Kenji López-Alt

---

e Read two more extracts from the book. Which is about *fried eggs* and which is about *scrambled eggs*? How do you know?

1 For a long time, I was happy with how I made _____, but then I saw a technique in Spain that made me rethink the way I did it. There, it's common to cook them not in a thin layer of oil, but in a shallow pool of it. Cooks would fill the pan with a half inch or so of olive oil and heat it up, then tilt it so the oil collected on one side, drop in the eggs, and spoon the hot oil over the whites as they cooked. The eggs cooked quite rapidly from all sides, the whites quickly setting around the still-liquid yolks.

2 There's a big divide between those who like _____ to be rich, dense, and creamy (that's me), and those who like them light, relatively dry, and fluffy (that's my wife). I decided that it was only right that I figured out how to make both types, so that we could both enjoy our breakfast.

f **ⓒ Communication** Cooking eggs **A p.107 B p.111** Explain a recipe for your partner to take notes.

g **Language in context** Look at the sentences from the extracts. What do the highlighted adjectives mean? Which three have a positive meaning? Which one is negative?

1 Hard-boiled eggs should have a fully set, but not rubbery, white, and yolks that are cooked through, but still bright yellow and creamy.

2 …and those who like them light, relatively dry, and fluffy…

3 Continue doing this until the egg whites are completely set and crispy on the bottom.

> 🔍 **Describing texture**
> A lot of words to describe the texture of food are made with a noun or a verb + -y, for example, *crunchy, greasy, juicy, lumpy, slimy, sticky, watery.*

h Which of the adjectives in **g** might you use to describe…?

an apple   chips   honey   an omelette   an oyster   a sauce   squid

4 GRAMMAR nouns: compound and possessive forms

a (Circle) the correct phrase in each pair. If you think both are possible, explain the difference between them, if any.

1 a recipe book / a recipe's book
2 a salad of tuna / a tuna salad
3 children's portions / children portions
4 a coffee cup / a cup of coffee
5 a chef hat / a chef's hat
6 a tin opener / a tins opener
7 James' kitchen / James's kitchen
8 a John's friend / a friend of John's

b **G** p.159 **Grammar Bank 9B**

5 LISTENING

a Look at the photos of some dishes on a restaurant website. Use compound nouns to say what you think they are.

b Now look at the menu on the website. Study it for a couple of minutes and choose what to have.

c Compare your choices with a partner. Was it easy to choose? Is there anything on the menu you'd never order? Is there anything you'd want to ask the waiter about?

Henry's

LUNCH MENU
2 courses £19.45   3 courses £24.95

Starters

Grilled squid with raw vegetable salad and chilli dressing G N

Tofu kebabs with red and green pepper, Indian spices, and cucumber yogurt N V

Avocado, tomato, and onion salad with lime dressing G N VV

Steamed duck egg with grilled asparagus and hollandaise sauce G N

Mains

New York strip steak with rosemary fries and onion rings N

Baked sweet potatoes with spicy Thai peanut sauce and jasmine rice G VV

Pan-fried salmon with lentils and roast cauliflower G N

Grilled lamb chops with mashed potato and paprika butter G N

Desserts

Warm chocolate and almond tart with mango custard V

Crème brûlée with stewed apricots G N

Orange and strawberry sorbet G N VV

Selection of British cheeses with grapes and walnuts

Extras

Handmade sourdough bread with herb butter N V
£2.95

Olives with balsamic vinegar and feta G N V
£2.95

G Gluten-free   N Nut-free   V Vegetarian   VV Vegan

If you have any allergies, please inform / ask a member of the waiting staff, who will advise on all ingredients used.

d You're going to listen to extracts from a book called *How to Eat Out*, by restaurant critic Giles Coren, giving advice about how to get the best out of restaurant meals. Before you listen, with a partner, decide what you think the missing word is in each tip.

1 Always order the _____.
2 Never eat the _____.
3 Have the vegetarian option – but not in a _____ restaurant.
4 Never sit at a table _____.
5 Insist on _____ water.
6 How to _____ – and get a result.
7 Be nice to the _____.

e 🔊 **9.15** Listen once and complete the tips. Did you guess any of them correctly? What two things on the *Henry's* menu would Giles Coren never order?

f Listen again. What reasons does Giles give for each of his tips in **d**?

g 🔊 **9.16** **Language in context** Listen and try to complete the missing words in these extracts. What do you think they mean?

1 It's often _____ _____ _____ and very smelly to cook.
2 So, whenever we meet for dinner, she is _____ _____ and _____ _____ the entire bread basket and three pats of butter without pausing for breath.
3 I don't know why they give you _____ _____ _____.
4 But in an expensive place with a TV chef and a whole range of exciting things to _____ _____ for the next couple of hours…
5 …personally, I would much rather restaurants focused on doing one or two things brilliantly than offered a _____ _____ _____ _____ that was just about OK.
6 …so don't order mineral water! Ask for a _____ _____ _____.
7 'I'm awfully sorry to _____ _____ _____,' you might say, 'but this fish really isn't as fresh as I'd hoped.'

6 SPEAKING

In small groups, discuss the questions.

1 Do you agree with Giles Coren's tips? Are they relevant in your country?

2 Are there any tips that you could give visitors to your country that would help them to get the most out of local food and restaurants?

3 In general, do you think that eating out is good value in your country? Why (not)?

4 Where would you recommend eating out…?
 • for a weekday lunch
 • to celebrate a friend's birthday
 • with a wealthy relative

5 Think of a good meal out you've had recently. Where was it? Who were you with? Can you remember what you had to eat and drink?

6 Have you had a meal out recently where something went wrong? What happened?

7 WRITING

Ⓦ **p.128 Writing** A formal email Analyse a formal email to a restaurant, and write a formal email.

🔵 **Go online** to review the lesson

1 ▶ THE INTERVIEW Part 1

a Read the biographical information about George McGavin and look at the photos of insects on these pages. How many of them have you seen?

> **George McGavin** is a well-known British entomologist, academic, author, explorer, and TV presenter. He is Research Associate at the Department of Zoology of Oxford University. He studied zoology at the University of Edinburgh before completing a PhD at the Natural History Museum and Imperial College London. He is a Fellow of the Linnean Society and the Royal Geographical Society, and has several insect species named in his honour. He has presented TV programmes for the BBC, including *Expedition Borneo*, *The Dark: Nature's Nighttime World*, and *Monkey Planet*, as well as for the Discovery Channel and Channel 4. He enjoys eating insects, which he describes as 'flying prawns'.

a wasp
/wɒsp/

b Watch Part 1 of the interview. What is an arthropod and why does George McGavin think they are so important?

c Now watch again. Answer the questions.

1 What examples does George McGavin give of animals with a spine and why does he think they are less important than arthropods?
2 When did he first decide to focus on arthropods? What insect caught his attention?
3 What usually influences how new species are named? How many does he have named after him?
4 What currently makes him sad about arthropods?

d Were you interested in animals when you were young? What kind(s)?

> **Glossary**
> **crustacea** /krʌˈsteɪʃʌ/ creatures with a soft body and a hard outer shell, usually aquatic, e.g. crabs, prawns
> **mammal** /ˈmæml/ an animal that gives birth to live babies (not eggs) and feeds its young on milk, e.g. a cow
> **amphibian** /æmˈfɪbiən/ an animal that can live on land and in water, e.g. a frog
> **badger** /ˈbædʒə/ a nocturnal animal with grey fur and wide black and white lines on its head
> **Borneo** /ˈbɔːniəʊ/ a large tropical island in south-east Asia

▶ Part 2

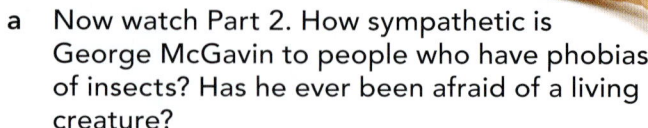
a mealworm /ˈmiːlwɜːm/

a Now watch Part 2. How sympathetic is George McGavin to people who have phobias of insects? Has he ever been afraid of a living creature?

b Watch again. Mark the sentences **T** (true) or **F** (false). Correct the **F** sentences.

1 People say they have a phobia of insects because of the way insects look and move.
2 George McGavin thinks children develop phobias as a result of adults' fears.
3 He thinks a fear of spiders is never justifiable.
4 In the UK, there are spiders whose bite can make you seriously ill.
5 He thinks curing people of phobias always takes a long time.
6 His first reaction when he saw the snake in the Amazon was excitement.
7 The snake didn't like the clothes McGavin was wearing.
8 When he realized how dangerous the snake was, he dropped it and ran away.

a shield bug
/ʃiːld bʌɡ/

c Do you have a phobia of any animals or insects? How does it affect your life?

> **Glossary**
> **tarantula** a large hairy spider
> **fer-de-lance** a poisonous snake native to South America and the Caribbean

▶ Part 3

a Now watch Part 3. What does George McGavin say about...?

1 killing insects at work
2 killing insects at home
3 'optimal foraging theory'
4 harvesting insects in cold and hot countries
5 a mealworm in a snack
6 cooking crickets for children in Oxford
7 one boy's mother

an ant /ænt/

a bee /biː/

b Compare with a partner. Then watch again. Can you add any more details?

a cricket /ˈkrɪkɪt/

a plant hopper /plɑːnt ˈhɒpə/

a cockroach /ˈkɒkrəʊtʃ/

c Have you ever eaten insects? Would you be prepared to? Do you think we will be doing this more in the future?

a moth /mɒθ/

> **Glossary**
> **a flash in the pan** IDM a sudden success which lasts only a short time and is not likely to be repeated
> **ecology** the relation of plants and living creatures to each other and to their environment
> **swarm** (verb) (of insects) move around together in a large group, looking for a place to live
> **harvest** (verb) cut and gather a crop; catch a number of animals or fish to eat
> **snail** a small soft creature with a hard round shell on its back, that moves very slowly and often eats garden plants

a flea /fliː/

2 ▶ LOOKING AT LANGUAGE

> 🔍 **Informal and vague language**
> George McGavin uses a lot of informal expressions, as well as vague language, which is common in colloquial English when we don't want to be too specific or precise. Vague language makes us sound more informal and chatty.

a Watch some extracts from the interview and complete the missing words in the highlighted phrases.

1 'And the sad truth is that although we are _____ sure there are eight million species of arthropods _____ there unknown,…'
2 '…and I think adults sometimes pass their fears on by, by _____, 'Oh, what's that? Oh, it's a spider…''
3 '…but, but still there are _____ like seven million people in the United Kingdom who are terrified of spiders, and, and moths.'
4 '…however, if you have a cat and you don't control the fleas, are a _____ of a pest…'
5 'No, it, it isn't a flash in the pan, um, we will have to, to address this quite seriously in the next, you know, hundred or _____ years.'
6 '…lots of people say it's because insects are dirty or they look funny or _____.'
7 '…and the kids went wild! They, they ate the _____ lot.'
8 'I _____, 'Yeah, and your point is?' She was _____, 'At home he doesn't even eat broccoli.''

b With a partner, say how you could express the highlighted phrases in more formal or neutral language.

3 ▶ THE CONVERSATION

Joanne   Sean   Emma

a Watch the conversation. Tick (✓) the correct option to sum up their main conclusion.

Wildlife programmes are popular because…
☐ all children are interested in animals.
☐ the programmes are of such a high quality now.
☐ David Attenborough is such a good presenter.

b Watch again. Complete the sentences.

1 Sean compares watching wildlife programmes to…
2 Joanne particularly enjoys finding out…
3 Joanne's younger child enjoys wildlife programmes because…
4 Although Emma recognizes wildlife programmes are popular, she…
5 Programmes filmed under the sea and in the jungle are examples Emma gives of…

c Do you ever watch wildlife programmes on TV? Why do you think they are so popular?

d Watch some extracts. Complete the missing words and phrases. What two functions do these have in the conversation?

1 **Emma** Takes ages, _____ _____?
2 **Joanne** ….learning something and reconnecting us with nature, _____?
3 **Joanne** …and he has this great way of just putting things across to us, _____ _____, in a way that we can all relate to, _____?
4 **Emma** And they're almost becoming more extreme, as well, _____ _____,…
5 **Emma** …there's so much variety, _____ _____?

e Now have a conversation in groups of three. Discuss the statements.

1 People are only interested in protecting appealing, fluffy animals and don't feel strongly about conserving species such as insects or reptiles.
2 It is justifiable to allow a few people to pay a lot of money to kill wild animals for sport as long as the money is used to support conservation.

> Apart from education, you need good health, and for that you need to play sports.
> *Kapil Dev, Indian cricketer*

G relative clauses **V** word building: adjectives, nouns, and verbs **P** homographs

1 SPEAKING

a Read the choices below and choose the option you'd rather do – you have to choose one!

WOULD YOU RATHER...?

go for a run in the rain for 20 minutes	OR	run on the treadmill in the gym for an hour
go on a yoga retreat	OR	go on an extreme fitness course
do 30 minutes of exercise before breakfast	OR	do 30 minutes of exercise after dinner
go for a long walk in 35 degrees	OR	go for a long walk in -5 degrees
swim in the sea	OR	do lengths in a pool
work out every day and be super-fit	OR	work out once a week and be fairly fit
learn to do ballroom dancing	OR	learn to box
play well in a match and lose	OR	play badly in a match and win
be the number 1 table tennis player in the world	OR	be the number 100 tennis player

b Work in small groups and explain your choices. Which things did you disagree about? Why?

I wouldn't like to do either, but if I had to choose,...

Actually, I would quite enjoy both of them, but...

Battle of the workouts

WEIGHTS OR CIRCUITS? YOGA OR PILATES? Making the decision to get fit is the easy part – choosing how to go about it is more difficult. We answer four key questions to help you decide for yourself.

1. How quickly will it make a difference?
2. How many calories does it burn?
3. Will it keep me motivated?
4. What are the benefits?

2 READING

a Read the introduction to the article and look at the three headings. Do you know what all the activities are? Do you do any of them, or have you ever done them?

b Look through the article quickly. For which activity are these statements true?

1 Once you start, you won't want to stop.
2 It's probably the least interesting of the six activities.
3 It takes the longest time to show any benefits.
4 Having professional guidance will make it more varied.
5 It will make some difference straight away.
6 Some gyms have equipment which can make it less dull.

c Read the article carefully. For each pair of activities, which do you think was the winner? Why? Compare with a partner.

d **Language in context** In pairs, find these nouns related to exercise and the body in the article.

1 tr_____ = the process of improving your fitness by doing exercises
2 fl_____ = the ability to bend
3 str_____ = the act of making your muscles longer
4 pr_____-_____ = an exercise in which you lie on your stomach and raise your body off the ground with your hands until your arms are straight
5 s_____-_____ = an exercise for making your stomach muscles strong, in which you lie on the floor on your back and raise the top part of your body
6 tr_____ = the main part of the body apart from the head, arms, and legs
7 sk_____ _____ = a piece of cord with a handle at each end that you turn over your head and then jump over
8 sp_____ = the bones down the middle of the back

e Think of a sport or physical activity which you have done, or know something about. In small groups, say as much as you can about it, answering some of the questions in the article.

Weights vs Circuits

1 After the first session, your muscles will feel more toned, but significant changes will take three to four weeks.

2 136–340 per hour, depending on weight lifted and the recovery time between repetitions.

3 If improved body tone is your goal, then yes.

4 Great for strengthening your muscles and improving overall bone density. Weight training speeds up the rate at which calories are burned, resulting in quicker weight loss.

1 After two weeks of twice-weekly circuits.

2 476 per hour.

3 You are unlikely to get bored, as circuits can constantly change their content and order.

4 Circuits address every element of fitness – aerobic, strength, balance, and flexibility. A good instructor should introduce new tools, like skipping ropes and weights, to make sure you are always developing new skills.

WINNER _____

Yoga vs Pilates

1 After eight weeks of thrice-weekly sessions.

2 102 per hour for a class based on stretching. Power yoga burns 245 per hour.

3 Yoga is about attaining a sense of unity between body and mind, rather than achieving personal targets. However, you will feel a sense of accomplishment as you master the poses and there are lots of different types to try.

4 The American Council on Exercise found that people who did yoga for eight weeks experienced a 13% improvement in flexibility. They were also able to perform six more press-ups and 14 more sit-ups at the end of the study.

1 After five to six weeks of thrice-weekly sessions.

2 170–237 an hour.

3 Once you start noticing positive changes in the way you move and hold your body, Pilates is hard to give up.

4 Widely used by dancers and top athletes, Pilates improves your posture and strength. It develops the abdominal muscles which support the trunk.

WINNER _____

Spinning vs Step

1 After two to three weeks of twice-weekly sessions.

2 408–646 an hour.

3 Although it's a group session, you can increase the workload as you get fitter. Avoid boredom by looking out for classes with video screens that take you on a virtual ride through pleasant scenery.

4 Pedalling works most of the muscles in the legs and buttocks, so you will get an unbelievably toned lower body. But your heart and lungs are the biggest beneficiaries.

1 After four weeks of twice-weekly classes.

2 510–612 per hour (depending on height of step).

3 You will notice changes in your body shape fairly quickly, but there are only so many times you can step on to a platform before utter boredom takes hold.

4 A study carried out in California showed that people who did step for six months experienced a 3.3% increase in the bone density of their spines, and hip and leg bones. It has good aerobic benefits as well as toning muscles in the bottom and legs.

WINNER _____

Adapted from The Guardian

---

3 **VOCABULARY** word building: adjectives, nouns, and verbs

a Without looking back at the article, complete the sentences with a word made from the adjective *strong*.

1 Widely used by dancers and top athletes, Pilates improves your posture and _____.
2 Great for _____ your muscles and improving overall bone density.

b Complete the chart.

adjective	noun	verb
strong		
long		
deep		
wide		
high		*heighten**
weak		
short		
thick		
flat		

* Note that *heighten* (verb) doesn't mean *make higher*; it means *intensify*, e.g. *Exercise can heighten your sense of well-being.*

c Complete the sentences with a word from **b** in the correct form.

1 I often have to _____ new trousers because they're usually too long for me.
2 Can you measure the _____ and _____ of the living room? I want to order a new carpet.
3 I'm more or less the same _____ as my sister, but my brother is much taller than us.
4 People's muscles tend to _____ as they get older.
5 **A** What's the _____ of the water here?
   B About ten metres, I think.
6 If you want to _____ the sauce, add flour.
7 The building was completely _____ in the explosion.
8 He's almost unbeatable. He doesn't have any real _____.
9 This road needs to be _____. It's too narrow.
10 The manager has _____ the team by buying several new players.
11 **A** I love this coat, but the sleeves are a bit short.
    B You could always get them _____.
12 You've been very ill. You need to build up your _____ again.

4 LISTENING & SPEAKING

a 🔊 **10.1** Listen to extracts 1–6 from sports commentaries and match them to six of the Olympic sports in the photos.

b Match phrases A–L from the commentaries to sports 1–6 in **a**. There are two phrases from each. Then listen again and check.

A ▢ a sprint finish
B ▢ great elevation on both jumps
C ▢ have lost their rhythm
D ▢ a little bit of a stumble
E ▢ make a long putt
F ▢ has got the arm lock
G ▢ getting into her stride
H ▢ are safely through
I ▢ go in for a birdie
J ▢ keep his elbow turned
K ▢ chase her down
L ▢ the gap is opening

c 🔊 **10.2** Listen to an interview with Olly Hogben, a sports commentator. Tick (✓) the things he talks about.

▢ his family background
▢ why he became a sports commentator
▢ how many different sports he commentates on
▢ how commentary should interact with pictures
▢ technology in sport
▢ a sport that he's an expert in
▢ cheating in football
▢ the value of good commentary
▢ the worst thing about his job
▢ his most memorable sporting occasion

d Listen again and mark the sentences **T** (true) or **F** (false). Correct the **F** sentences.

1 As a child, Olly enjoyed playing sport much more than watching it.
2 He's a talented sportsman himself.
3 He used to commentate when he was at school.
4 His love of words came before his love of sport.
5 He thinks you have to really understand a sport in order to commentate on it.
6 He thinks it's important to always keep talking.
7 He never disagrees with officials when he's commentating.
8 He finds it difficult to tell whether a sportsperson is cheating or not.
9 He thinks commentary should be functional, not ornamental.
10 He remembers his first Olympics because the stadium was incredible.

e **10.3** Listen to Olly telling the story of the Norwegian wrestler Stig-André Berge. Number the events in the correct order 1–5.

  ☐ He went to the Rio Olympics.
  ☐ He saw his mother for the last time.
  ☐ He won the bronze medal.
  1 He went to a tournament to qualify for the Rio Olympics.
  ☐ He found out that his mother was seriously ill.

f Answer the questions in small groups.

  - Do you know any feel-good sports stories like that of Stig-André Berge?
  - What do you think are the qualities of a good sports commentator?
  - Do you think you'd be a good sports commentator? Why (not)? Which sport(s) could you commentate on?
  - Olly says that most sportspeople 'are very honest people'. Do you agree?
  - Do you think athletes who have been banned for taking drugs should be allowed to return to sport?

5 GRAMMAR relative clauses

a Look at the options in sentences 1–7 and cross out any which are not correct.

  1 John McEnroe, *that / who / whom* won Wimbledon in the 1980s, now works as a sports commentator.
  2 He ran the marathon in 2 hours 22 minutes, *that / what / which* was a new course record.
  3 I feel really sorry for the players *that / who / (–)* lost.
  4 The captain, *that / who / whose* brother also plays in the team, is from Holland.
  5 The coach got on well with the players *that / who / (–)* she trained.
  6 New trainers! Thanks, they're just *that / what / which* I wanted.
  7 Those are the gloves *that / which / (–)* Muhammad Ali wore when he beat Joe Frazier in 1975.

b **G** p.160 Grammar Bank 10A

> 🔍 **Defining relative clauses in spoken English**
> In informal spoken English, we tend to use *that* rather than *who* or *which*, and almost always leave out the relative pronoun when the subject of the clause changes, e.g. *She's the player* (*that*) *John told us about.*

c Choose five new words from this lesson and define them for a partner to identify. Use *that* instead of *who / which* and leave out the relative pronoun where appropriate.

It's a kind of exercise class that involves lots of different, short activities. — *Circuits*

6 PRONUNCIATION homographs

> 🔍 **Homographs**
> Homographs are words that are spelt the same but have different meanings. Most are pronounced the same, e.g. *a football fan*, *an electric fan*, but some are pronounced differently, e.g.
> **bow** /baʊ/ = move your head or the top half of your body forwards and downwards, as a sign of respect
> **bow** /bəʊ/ = 1 a weapon used in archery for shooting arrows; 2 a hair decoration made of ribbon

a Look at the groups of sentences which contain homographs. Match the homographs to pronunciation a or b.

  lead a /led/ b /liːd/
  1 ☐ González is coming into the final straight; she's in the lead with 100 metres to go.
  2 ☐ Scuba divers attach lead weights to their belts to help them dive.
  row a /rəʊ/ b /raʊ/
  3 ☐ We were sitting in the front row, so we could almost touch the players.
  4 ☐ The coach had a row with the owner of the team.
  5 ☐ People who row tend to have very well-developed biceps.
  putting a /ˈpʌtɪŋ/ b /ˈpʊtɪŋ/
  6 ☐ He was still putting on his boots when the match started.
  7 ☐ She's been putting beautifully and is now six under par.
  tear a /teə/ b /ˈtɪə/
  8 ☐ If you tear a muscle or a ligament, you may not be able to train for six months.
  9 ☐ As she listened to the national anthem, a tear rolled down her cheek.
  content a /ˈkɒntent/ b /kənˈtent/
  10 ☐ Some footballers never seem content with their contracts. They're always trying to negotiate better terms.
  11 ☐ Sports drinks often have a high sugar content.
  wound a /wuːnd/ b /waʊnd/
  12 ☐ He wound the tape tightly around his ankle to prevent a sprain.
  13 ☐ You could see his head wound bleeding as he was taken off the pitch.
  use a /juːz/ b /juːs/
  14 ☐ If you use a high-tech swimsuit, you'll be able to swim much faster.
  15 ☐ It's no use complaining – the umpire's decision is final.

b **10.4** Listen and check. Practise saying the sentences.

🔵 **Go online** to review the lesson

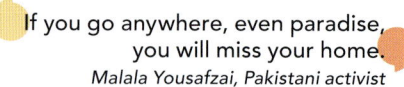

> If you go anywhere, even paradise, you will miss your home.
> *Malala Yousafzai, Pakistani activist*

G adding emphasis (2): cleft sentences   **V** words that are often confused   **P** intonation in cleft sentences

1 LISTENING & SPEAKING

Las Chimeneas

Accommodation, activities, and **discovery** in the Alpujarra mountains of Granada, Southern Spain

Las Chimeneas is a ¹ *dramatic* set of converted village houses which have been welcoming guests to the Alpujarra since 1998. There are nine ² _____ rooms, each with fabulous views across the hills to the sea in the ³ _____ distance. We provide very comfortable accommodation, with lots of antiques and books and hidden nooks and crannies, together with a delightful little restaurant that will surprise you by the quality of its freshly made ⁴ _____ produce.

We have an ⁵ _____ knowledge of the area and are anxious to share our enthusiasm for this place which has been our home for so long. We offer all kinds of holidays, including trekking, birdwatching, cycling, painting, cookery, and yoga.

Above all, what we supply is peace and relaxation, and a genuinely ⁶ _____ welcome. This represents a ⁷ _____ combination. Perhaps it is this that led *The Times* to number us amongst their top ten of Europe's best mountain hideaways.   *David and Emma Illsley*

a Can you think of some reasons why people decide to go and live in another country, or move to another city in their country?

b Read an extract from the website of Las Chimeneas and complete it with an adjective from the list. What would attract you to go there, and what might you do there?

~~dramatic~~   far   intimate   lovely
seasonal   warm   winning

c 🔊 10.5 You're going to listen to an interview with David and Emma Illsley, who run Las Chimeneas. Read questions 1–8 and then listen to Part 1 of the interview. Answer the questions with **D** (David), **E** (Emma), or **B** (both).

Who…?
1 ▢ first got a job in Spain
2 ▢ studied at Warwick University
3 ▢ taught English
4 ▢ fell in love with Mairena
5 ▢ taught in Granada for a year
6 ▢ worked in local government
7 ▢ thinks having children helped them to integrate
8 ▢ employs local people

d Listen again and answer the questions.
1 What does Emma say 'seduced' her about David's lifestyle in Majorca?
2 What does David say they did on their year off?
3 How does David describe his experience as Deputy Mayor?
4 How does David think having a business has helped them to integrate?

e 🔊 10.6 Now read questions 1–5 and the three options for each. Then listen to Part 2 and choose a, b, or c.

1 What Emma likes most about living in Mairena is ___.
  a being able to farm the land   b the size of the village
  c the amazing weather
2 What she likes least is the fact that ___.
  a there is so much bureaucracy
  b the local shops aren't very good
  c they have to use their car more than they would like
3 Apart from family and friends, David misses ___.
  a features of UK culture and behaviour
  b some types of entertainment in the UK
  c the varieties of beer in the UK
4 When Emma goes back to the UK, she enjoys ___.
  a the nightlife in London
  b being able to use public transport and not having to drive
  c mixing with different kinds of people
5 They think it ___ that they will go back to live in the UK.
  a is quite probable   b is highly unlikely   c is very likely

f ◉ **10.7 Language in context**
Listen to some extracts from the interview and complete the idioms and phrasal verbs. With a partner, say what you think they mean.

1 …he'd agreed to, to let us rent this house for, for _____ to _____…

2 …we wandered around and cycled around and finally _____ _____ this little village of Mairena, where we live now…

3 …we were _____ a _____ and enjoying it too much, really, to, to want to go back…

4 …as long as I can remember, I always _____ a _____ – I really wanted to live in a very small community…

5 …on the one hand, it's great being away from shops – it's like a kind of a, real kind of _____ _____…

6 …so we, we've never really _____ it _____. It would be tricky, I think, to come back, largely for economic or financial reasons.

7 To take them back to the UK, I think now, that would be perhaps a, a _____ _____.

8 …I think once you've spent 15 years building up a business, then also that's something you don't want to, to easily _____ your _____ on.

g Talk to a partner. Do you (or friends of yours) have any experience of going to live in another country?

Yes
- Where did you move from or to?
- Why did you move?
- What are / were the pros and cons?
- How integrated do / did you feel?
- What do / did you miss?
- Did / Might you go back home?

No
- What do you think are the pros and cons of…?
  – living in a country which is not your own
  – living in a city in your country which is not your own
- Would you like to move to another country or city yourself?

2 GRAMMAR adding emphasis (2): cleft sentences

a Sentences 1–4 convey ideas David and Emma expressed in **1**, but they phrased them in a slightly different way. Can you remember what they actually said?

1 David convinced me it was a good idea.
'It was _____.'

2 When we had children, it really made a difference.
'The thing _____.'

3 I really like that sense of cultural diversity in the UK.
'What I _____.'

4 I definitely can't see us going back, because of Dan and Tom…
'The main reason _____.'

b ◉ **10.8** Listen and check. What's the difference between the pairs of sentences?

c ⓖ **p.161 Grammar Bank 10B**

3 PRONUNCIATION & SPEAKING intonation in cleft sentences

> 🔍 **Fine-tuning your pronunciation: intonation in cleft sentences**
>
> Cleft sentences beginning with *What…* or *The person / place / thing*, etc. typically have a fall-rise-fall tone in the *What…* or *The person…* clause.
> *What I hate about my job* is having to get up early.
> *The reason why I went to France* was that I wanted to learn the language.
>
> Cleft sentences beginning with *It…* typically have a fall tone in the *It…* clause.
> *It was her mother* who really broke up our marriage.
> *It's the commuting* that I find so tiring.

a ◉ **10.9** Read the information box. Then look at the highlighted phrases and listen to each example sentence.

b ◉ **10.10** Listen and repeat the sentences, copying the intonation.
1 What I don't understand is why she didn't call me.
2 The thing that impresses me most about Jack is his enthusiasm.
3 The reason why I left early was that I had an important meeting.
4 The place where I would most like to live is Ireland.
5 It was the neighbours that made our lives so difficult.
6 It was then that I realized I'd left my keys behind.

c Complete the sentences in your own words. Then use them to start conversations with a partner.
- What I would find most difficult about living abroad is…
- What I love about living here is…
- What I like least about living here is…
- The person I get on with best in my family is…
- The place where I can relax the most is…
- The reason I decided to carry on learning English was…

4 READING & SPEAKING

a Read the title and the first two paragraphs of the article. Why did Michał decide to walk from Wales to Poland? What do you think he might have learned from his walk? Why do you think he is holding a bird's nest in one of the photos?

b Now read about Michał's walk and number paragraphs A–G in the correct order, 1–7.

'Go home, Polish' graffiti prompts photographer's 1,200-mile walk

When photographer **Michał Iwanowski**, 41, came across some graffiti in Cardiff that said, 'Go home, Polish', he decided to take it literally. Here, in his own words, he tells how and why he embarked on the 1,200-mile walk from Wales back to his country of birth.

I still remember seeing the graffiti. It was only small, but I was taken aback: 'Go home, Polish'. I had lived in Cardiff for many years and considered Wales my home. But I was also Polish, so I began to question whether I was at home or not, and where, in fact, home was. I had never felt any negativity towards me in Wales. I found the people warm and welcoming. But after the Brexit referendum, I felt a change in mood – not towards me, but towards immigrants in general. I felt some people were dehumanizing 'the other' and the concept began to terrify me. How could people turn on each other like this?

A ___ From there I walked through Belgium, Holland, Germany, and the Czech Republic before reaching Poland. Along the way, I told people what I was doing and why, to see what reaction I would get. It was almost always positive. People shared their own stories, their own hopes and fears, their worries about their lives and situations. Only once was I shouted at, when I wandered onto an allotment in Germany to ask a man for directions. I began to realize that on an individual level, we have so much in common.

B ___ I ended up low on energy and electrolytes. At one point, I remember throwing my backpack in the bushes and just wanting to give up, which is unusual for me, as I am an upbeat person. In the end, I sat there for about two hours, then got up again and continued the walk.

C ___ In total, it took me 105 days to arrive in my home village of Mokrzeszów, in western Poland. By the end, I was in survival mode. I was reclusive and refused company. I walked up my home street and, as I did, a group of my relatives slowly walked out to meet me carrying a 'Welcome home' banner. It felt like a funeral procession. It was very surreal.

D ___ Back in the UK, there is still anti-Polish and anti-immigrant graffiti, of course – much worse than what I saw – and I deplore it every time I see it. We must never tolerate racist language. But I need to put away my cynicism, and remember – as my walk showed me – that most people are generous and most people are good.

E ___ It was then I began planning my journey, setting off on 27th April 2018 with a rough route map and a 15 kg backpack. Carrying British and Polish passports, I often wore a T-shirt bearing the word 'Polska', so people would know I was Polish. I walked over the bridge from Wales into England, then took the ferry to France.

F ___ Of course, it didn't feel like an achievement at the time. Plenty of people walk long distances. But, looking back, it feels like I have achieved something. The walk helped me to solidify my views on 'home'. I felt utterly at home walking across the breadth of Europe's landscape. I don't need to be told by a person or government where my home is and isn't. I belong to the ground beneath my feet, not to any country where I happen to have a passport.

G ___ Much of the walking was enjoyable, whether it was through Brussels or Cologne, or through the bushes and wild forests of Germany. I would stay in Airbnbs, wild camp or sometimes stay with strangers, who would often offer me food. But, as I was walking in the summer, I was hit by the Europe-wide heatwave, and began to find my mission unbearable.

> **Glossary**
> **electrolytes** salts and minerals in your body that you lose when you sweat

Abridged from the BBC website

c Read the whole article again (in the correct order). Then, with a partner, describe in your own words how Michał felt / feels…

1 when he first saw the 'Go home, Polish' graffiti.
2 when he spoke to people along the way.
3 when the heatwave struck Europe.
4 when he almost gave up.
5 when he arrived in his home village.
6 when he looks back at what he did.
7 when he sees anti-immigrant graffiti now.

d Look at two of the things that Michał said. Do you agree with them? Why (not)?

> 'I belong to the ground beneath my feet, not to any country where I happen to have a passport.'

> '…most people are generous and most people are good.'

5 VOCABULARY words that are often confused

a Look at some groups of words that are often confused. With a partner, try to explain the difference between the three words in each group.

1 foreigner   stranger   outsider
2 emigrant   immigrant   migrant
3 journey   trip   voyage
4 walk   stroll   wander
5 reclusive   reserved   shy
6 achieve   succeed   reach
7 ground   floor   soil
8 deplore   deny   decline

b Now complete the sentences with the best word from each group in **a** in the correct form.

1 When I arrived at work, there was a complete _____ sitting at my desk.
2 The farm usually employs _____ workers in the fruit-picking season.
3 The *Titanic*'s first _____ was also its last.
4 Mark _____ at such a fast pace that I couldn't keep up.
5 The English have the reputation of being _____ – it's never easy to know what they're really thinking or feeling.
6 When we finally _____ our destination, we breathed a sigh of relief.
7 You can only grow these plants in acidic _____.
8 Most governments _____ the use of violence to control protesters.

6 ▶ VIDEO LISTENING

a Watch a documentary about Ellis Island. Why are these names mentioned?

Bursorsky
Annie Moore
Isaac Asimov, Max Factor, and Elia Kazan

b Watch again and complete the sentences with a number.

1 Ellis Island's first immigration point opened on 1st January _____.
2 From 1892 to 1954, _____ people passed through Ellis Island.
3 About _____% of America's population today have ancestors who came through Ellis Island.
4 The _____- and _____-class passengers were allowed to disembark in Manhattan.
5 The Great Hall was used as the Registry Room from 1900 to _____. On some days, _____ people waited there.
6 Each person had first to undergo a _____-second medical exam.
7 They then had to wait in the Great Hall for about _____ to _____ hours to be interviewed.
8 In the interview, they were asked another _____ questions.
9 About _____% of passengers failed the tests and were sent back home. Of those that were allowed to stay, a _____ stayed in the New York area.
10 The era of mass-immigration ended with the Immigration Act of _____.

c Do you think it is easier or harder to be an immigrant to the USA today than in the days of Ellis Island?

Go online to watch the video and review the lesson

GRAMMAR

a Right (✓) or wrong (✗)? Correct any mistakes in the highlighted phrases.

1 She's never been to the UK, but her son has.
2 She was shocked to receive his letter because had never expected to hear from him again.
3 **A** Do you think it's cold outside? **B** I hope no.
4 Do you have a tins opener?
5 **A** I'd love a wine glass. **B** Sure. Red or white?
6 Jim hasn't called back, that is a bit strange.
7 This is the café I used to work in.

b Circle the correct word or phrase. Tick (✓) if both are possible.

1 **A** Can I come with you?
  B I suppose so / yes, but hurry up.
2 **A** You must see her latest film.
  B I already am / have.
3 Look, I found an old photo album / album of photos in the attic!
4 Come over at 9.00. We'll be at Alex's / Alex's house.
5 I can't find my car's key / car key. Have you seen it?
6 She has two sisters, both of whom are at university / who are both at university.
7 I got exactly that / what I wanted for my birthday – a new iPad.
8 Her aunt, who / that never normally said a word, suddenly burst out laughing.

c Complete the sentences using the **bold** word.

1 I didn't bring sunscreen because the weather forecast said rain. **reason**
  The _____
  because the weather forecast said rain.
2 I spoke to the head of Customer Services. **person**
  The _____
  the head of Customer Services.
3 I don't like the way he blames other people for his mistakes. **what**
  _____
  the way he blames other people for his mistakes.
4 I only said that I thought she was making a big mistake marrying him. **all**
  _____ I thought that she was making a big mistake marrying him.
5 A girl from my school was chosen to carry the Olympic torch. **it**
  _____
  was chosen to carry the Olympic torch.

VOCABULARY

a Write the words for the definitions.

1 _____ (noun) = a young cow
2 _____ (noun) = a small shelter for a dog to sleep in
3 _____ (verb) = (of a horse) to make a long, high sound
4 _____ (noun pl) = the sharp curved nails on the end of an animal or a bird's foot
5 _____ (noun) = a group into which animals, plants, etc. of the same type are divided
6 _____ (verb) = to chase wild animals or birds in order to catch or kill them for food or sport
7 _____ (noun) = the hard pointed outer part of a bird's mouth
8 _____ (noun) = a thing you use to cut vegetables on
9 _____ (verb) = to cook sth slowly in liquid for a long time
10 _____ (verb) = to rub food against a sharp surface in order to cut it into small pieces
11 _____ (verb) = to fill with another type of food
12 _____ (verb) = to make sth become liquid as a result of heating
13 _____ (verb) = to beat very quickly until it becomes stiff, e.g. cream
14 _____ (verb) = to cut food, especially meat, into very small pieces, e.g. to make hamburgers

b Complete the sentence with the correct form of the **bold** word.

1 The real _____ of the film is its witty dialogue. **strong**
2 I need to get someone to _____ my new jeans. **short**
3 The pole-vaulter Sergei Bubka was the first to clear the _____ of six metres. **high**
4 The sauce will _____ as it cools. **thick**
5 I can't express the _____ of my feelings for you. **deep**
6 The team has been _____ by the injury to its top player. **weak**
7 Can you measure the _____ of the window? **wide**
8 The school has decided to _____ the holidays by three days. **long**

c Circle the correct word.

1 We went on a day *journey / trip* to London at the weekend.
2 He'll never be a successful politician, he's too much of *a foreigner / an outsider*.
3 I got completely lost in the old city and ended up *strolling / wandering* round for hours.
4 She *declined / denied* my offer of help.
5 Some people think the government needs to do more to make *emigrants / immigrants* more welcome.
6 He *achieved / succeeded* his ambition of becoming a millionaire by the age of 25.
7 The climber was found lying on the *floor / ground* near the summit.
8 In her old age, she has become *reclusive / shy* and refuses to receive any visitors.

CAN YOU understand this text?

a Read the article once. Do you think it's fair for national football teams to have foreign-born players?

b Read the article again and choose a, b, or c.

1 Players can play for the Moroccan national team _____.
   a if they can speak Arabic b if they were born in France
   c if they have a Moroccan grandparent
2 The teams of _____ reflect their countries' history.
   a Yugoslavia, Senegal, and Switzerland
   b Senegal, Switzerland, and Tunisia
   c France, Switzerland, and Tunisia
3 Players with a choice of countries _____ when they choose which country to play for.
   a go for the most successful team b may be taking a risk
   c cause a lot of problems
4 Vieira was able to play for France because _____.
   a he was born in Senegal
   b he had moved to Europe when he was a child
   c his grandfather had fought for France
5 The writer thinks that Klose's decision to play for Germany was _____.
   a sensible b interesting c unusual

▶ CAN YOU understand these people?

◀) **10.11** Watch or listen and choose a, b, or c.

1 **Alicia** says that _____.
   a her vegan friends are really fussy b soy cheese isn't very nice
   c it's quite tricky to cook for vegans
2 **Vicky** is good at _____.
   a combining unusual ingredients b inventing dishes
   c following recipes
3 **Hywel** thinks that sports commentators are _____.
   a more helpful than annoying
   b more annoying than helpful
   c only useful if you don't watch much sport
4 Living in Germany appeals to **Claire** because _____.
   a it's a place where she's had some wonderful holidays
   b she used to have family there
   c she thinks both the lifestyle and the climate would suit her

Playing for your country?

The players in Morocco's World Cup team receive instructions in three languages: **English, French, and Arabic.** 17 of the current 23-person squad were not born in Morocco: eight in France, five in the Netherlands, two in Spain, and one each in Canada and Belgium. Morocco has a particularly large number of foreign-born players among World Cup squads. Players who were not born in the country are eligible to play for the national team if a parent or grandparent was born in the country, or if they have lived in the country for at least five years. But Morocco is not alone. In 2018, just over 10% of players in teams that qualified for the World Cup were born outside the country they were playing for.

For many national teams, the foreign-born share of players reflects the nation's history. All nine foreign-born players on Tunisia's team, and eight out of the nine on Senegal's, were born in France, the former colonial ruler. Three of the six foreign-born players on Switzerland's team were born in Yugoslavia and migrated to Switzerland in the early 1990s. Immigrants from the former Yugoslavia made up roughly 6% of the population of Switzerland in 2009.

For players with a choice of countries, the decision about which team to play for can be fraught – once they play for a country's senior team in a competitive match, they cannot switch. Sofyan Amrabat, who was born in the Netherlands to parents of Moroccan descent, chose to play for Morocco, even though he had a good chance of being selected by the Dutch national team. It turned out to be a good choice. That year, Morocco made it into the World Cup for the first time in 20 years, while the Netherlands – a much higher-ranked team – did not.

Here are two big-name footballers who have gone on to represent another national team.

Patrick Vieira
We may know the former Arsenal captain as a star of the French midfield, but he was actually born in Senegal. When he was eight, Vieira moved to France with his family and was eligible for French nationality as his grandfather had served in the French army. He played for the French national team 107 times, helped them to win the 1998 World Cup on home soil, and went on to captain the team. He later revealed that Senegal had never asked him to play for them.

Miroslav Klose
As the World Cup's top goal scorer, Miroslav Klose helped shape German footballing history. Born in Poland to a German father, Klose moved to Germany aged eight knowing only two words of the language. In 2001, the Polish coach tried to persuade Klose to join his team. Klose later said it had not been an easy decision to choose Germany, and if the Polish officials had been faster, he would have played for Poland. He did add that he didn't regret his choice though, and with 16 World Cup goals to his name, who can blame him?

 Go online to watch the video, review Files 9 & 10, and check your progress

Communication

1A WHAT'S YOUR PERSONALITY? Students A+B

a Use your four types from p.9 to find out which personality you have, and read the description.

b Now find out what your partner's personality is and read the description.

PLANNER + FACTS + HEAD + INTROVERT = REALIST
How you see yourself mature, stable, conscientious
What you are like loyal, straightforward, good at meeting deadlines, respect facts and rules, can be obsessed with schedules, critical of others, may not have faith in other people's abilities

PLANNER + FACTS + HEAD + EXTROVERT = SUPERVISOR
How you see yourself stable, practical, sociable
What you are like natural organizer and administrator, irritated when people don't follow procedures, other people find you bossy

PLANNER + FACTS + HEART + INTROVERT = NURTURER
How you see yourself gentle, conscientious, mature
What you are like caring, may have trouble making decisions that could hurt others, tend to avoid conflict, others may take advantage of you

PLANNER + FACTS + HEART + EXTROVERT = PROVIDER
How you see yourself sympathetic, easy-going, steady
What you are like warm, caring, traditional, tend to avoid conflict, not afraid to express your beliefs

PLANNER + IDEAS + HEAD + INTROVERT = MASTERMIND
How you see yourself logical, thorough, bright
What you are like efficient, independent, rarely change your mind, critical of those who don't understand you

PLANNER + IDEAS + HEAD + EXTROVERT = LEADER
How you see yourself bright, independent, logical
What you are like organized, good at solving large-scale problems, can be critical and aggressive

PLANNER + IDEAS + HEART + INTROVERT = COUNSELLOR
How you see yourself gentle, peaceful, cautious
What you are like relaxed and creative, deeply private, can be difficult to get to know

PLANNER + IDEAS + HEART + EXTROVERT = MENTOR
How you see yourself intelligent, outgoing, sensitive
What you are like articulate, warm, lively, extremely sensitive to people's needs, may become overbearing

SPONTANEOUS + FACTS + HEAD + INTROVERT = RESOLVER
How you see yourself understanding, stable, easy-going
What you are like independent, rational, good at finding solutions, natural risk-taker, enjoy an adrenaline rush, often focus on short-term results, sometimes lose sight of the bigger picture

SPONTANEOUS + FACTS + HEAD + EXTROVERT = GO-GETTER
How you see yourself inventive, enthusiastic, determined, alert
What you are like resourceful, tough-minded, may become frustrated by routines and constraints

SPONTANEOUS + FACTS + HEART + INTROVERT = PEACEMAKER
How you see yourself steady, gentle, sympathetic
What you are like sensitive to the feelings of others and the world around you, can be self-critical, often difficult to get to know

SPONTANEOUS + FACTS + HEART + EXTROVERT = PERFORMER
How you see yourself enthusiastic, sociable, sensitive
What you are like fun-loving, outgoing, often a good motivator, can be unreliable

SPONTANEOUS + IDEAS + HEAD + INTROVERT = STRATEGIST
How you see yourself bright, logical, individualistic
What you are like quiet, easy-going, intellectually curious, logical, may be critical or sarcastic, can be insensitive to the emotional needs of others

SPONTANEOUS + IDEAS + HEAD + EXTROVERT = BIG THINKER
How you see yourself talkative, curious, logical, self-sufficient
What you are like ingenious, bored by routine, can be rude, rebellious, critical of others

SPONTANEOUS + IDEAS + HEART + INTROVERT = IDEALIST
How you see yourself bright, forgiving, curious
What you are like generally easy-going, flexible, can be stubborn, may refuse to compromise

SPONTANEOUS + IDEAS + HEART + EXTROVERT = INNOVATOR
How you see yourself imaginative, sociable, sympathetic
What you are like energetic, sensitive, creative, sometimes illogical, rebellious, unfocused

2B CHANGING MEANINGS Student A

a Read the notes about how the meaning of the word *deer* evolved, and try to remember the information.

A *deer* /dɪə/ originally meant 'any large animal'

- In Old English, 'deer' meant 'large wild animal', e.g. lion, bear, camel.
- In the 13th century, the French word *beste* entered English and became the word 'beast'.
- 'Beast' also meant 'large wild animal'.
- 'Deer' changed meaning to describe a specific kind of animal.
- By the 15th century, this was the only meaning of 'deer'.

***Naughty* /ˈnɔːti/ originally meant 'having nothing'**

- The word first appeared in English in the 15th century and originally meant 'having nothing'.
- It referred to someone who was very poor and had no possessions, or someone who had no morals or manners.
- Today's meaning emerged in the 17th century, to describe a badly behaved child.
- Subsequently, the other meaning fell out of use.
- We still use the word 'nought', meaning 'nothing', in modern English, e.g. in numbers *0.1*, *0.2*, etc.

---

b Cover the notes and tell **B** as much as you can remember about the 'story' of *deer*.

c Listen to **B** telling you the 'story' of *awful*.

d Repeat for *naughty* and *dismantle*.

3B HISTORICAL INACCURACIES Student A

a Read about the films. Then tell **B** what is fact and what is fiction, and any other information you learn.

The Favourite

In the film
In *The Favourite*, Queen Anne has 17 pet rabbits which represent the 17 children she lost.

The facts
Queen Anne (1665–1714) really did lose 17 children, either during pregnancy or at a very young age. Only one of her children, Prince William, lived beyond the age of two, though he died aged 11. However, the rabbits are an invention of the film's director, Yorgos Lanthimos. In the 18th century, rabbits were viewed either as agricultural pests, or food, and would never have been kept as pets.

Victoria and Abdul

In the film
In *Victoria and Abdul*, the servant Abdul teaches Queen Victoria Hindustani.

The facts
Queen Victoria (1819–1901) was also Empress of India, and was fascinated by the country. She employed Indian servants in the Royal Household, though many people did not approve, and Abdul Karim was the first. They became very close friends and he taught her both Urdu and Hindustani, which Victoria said 'interests me very much.'

---

b Now listen to **B** telling you what is fact and what is fiction in their film and series. Did you guess what really happened and what didn't correctly?

9B COOKING EGGS Student A

a Read López-Alt's recipe for scrambled eggs.

b Explain the recipe to **B**.

> The ingredients are… First, you… Then you…

c Now listen to **B**'s recipe for fried eggs. Make notes as you listen. Then use your notes to tell **B** the recipe again, to check that it's correct.

d How different are the recipes from the way you usually make scrambled or fried eggs? Would you cook them this way in the future? Why (not)?

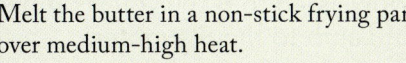

LIGHT AND FLUFFY SCRAMBLED EGGS

4 large eggs
¼ teaspoon salt
1½ tablespoons full-fat milk
1 tablespoon unsalted butter

Combine the eggs, salt, and milk in a medium bowl and whisk for about 1 minute.

Allow to rest at room temperature for at least 15 minutes – the mixture will change colour from yellow to orange, and will cook better.

Melt the butter in a non-stick frying pan over medium-high heat.

Whisk the egg mixture again, then transfer to the frying pan and cook, slowly scraping the bottom and sides of the pan with a silicone spatula as the eggs cook.

Continue to cook until no liquid egg remains, about 2 minutes.

Immediately transfer to a plate and serve.

4A WHAT HAPPENS IN THE END?
Student A

a Read an extract from the end of *The Adventure of the Speckled Band* by Arthur Conan Doyle.

Holmes discovers that if Julia and Helen marry, they can claim money from their stepfather and he will be left virtually penniless. With a motive established, Holmes and his assistant Watson, who narrates the story, go to Dr Roylott's house at night, to lie in wait in Helen's bedroom and find out the reason for the strange whistle. As they wait, they hear a sound in the dark. Holmes leaps up and strikes a match…

At the moment when Holmes struck the match, I heard a low, clear whistle, but it was impossible for me to tell what it was at which my friend lashed so savagely. I could, however, see that his face was deadly pale and filled with horror. He was gazing up at the ventilator when suddenly there broke from the silence of the night the most horrible cry to which I have ever listened. It became louder and louder, a cry of pain and fear and anger all mingled in the one dreadful shriek.

'What can it mean?' I gasped.

'It means that it is all over,' Holmes answered. 'Take your pistol, and we will enter Dr Roylott's room.'

It was an extraordinary sight which met our eyes. On a wooden chair sat Dr Grimesby Roylott. His chin was pointing upward and his eyes were fixed in a dreadful, rigid stare at the corner of the ceiling. Round his forehead, he had a peculiar yellow band, with brownish speckles, which seemed to be wrapped tightly round his head.

'The band! The speckled band!' whispered Holmes.

Then his strange headgear began to move, and there reared itself from among his hair the diamond-shaped head and puffed neck of a vile serpent.

'It is a swamp adder!' cried Holmes, 'the deadliest snake in India. He has died within ten seconds of being bitten.'

Holmes explains that Dr Roylott had trained the poisonous snake to pass from his room, through the ventilator shaft, into the girls' bedroom, hoping that eventually it would bite its victim. He would whistle for the snake to return to him. When Holmes struck at the snake, it was driven back into Roylott's room, where it attacked and killed him.

b Tell **B** what happens at the end of *The Adventure of the Speckled Band*.

c Now listen to **B** tell you what happens at the end of *Lamb to the Slaughter*.

d What did you both think of the endings? Now that you know what happens, would you want to read the stories?

4B WHAT'S GOING ON? Student A

a Look at photo 1 and make speculations and deductions about it.
- When and where could the photo have been taken?
- Who could the people be? What do you think they might be doing and why?
- What might have just happened?
- How might the people be feeling?

b **B** will tell you what's going on. Did you guess correctly?

c Now listen to **B** making speculations and deductions about photo 2. Then tell him / her what's really going on.

This photo was taken in Berlin, at a huge exhibition hall. The people in their pyjamas in camp beds are members of the audience for the performance of a piece of music called *Sleep*, by Max Richter, which lasts for eight hours.

9A THREE ANIMALS Students A+B

a Read what your three animals mean.

> The **first** animal represents how you see yourself.
> The **second** animal represents how others see you.
> The **third** animal represents how you really are.

b Do you agree with any of the results?

6A I NEED SOME HELP Student A

a Read your article carefully and try to work out the meaning of any new words and phrases.

How to survive…
living with your parents

If you are among the quarter of young adults still living at home with Mum and Dad, read on!

Around a quarter of young adults in the UK are living with Mum and Dad, the highest number since records began in 1996. If you are one of them, these tips might help you to survive.

Do your share.

Don't let yourself go into 'child mode' just because it's the house you grew up in. Housework is just as tedious for your parents as for you. Do your share, or you lose the right to call yourself an adult.

Save, save, save.

The major advantage of living at home is the cost. Unless your parents are charging you full market-rate rent (in which case, surely, move out?), you should be able to save some money. If you're working, living at home, and not saving any, you aren't planning for the future at all. It won't end well.

Have an exit plan.

Know how, if not exactly when, you plan to leave. In the darker moments of parent–child cohabitation, when you see in your parents' behaviour a worrying image of the kind of person you might end up being, the knowledge that you have an escape plan will be the only thing that keeps you sane.

Go out. A lot.

Of course, you and your parents love each other very much, but that doesn't mean you like each other all the time. Frankly, if you've lived together all your life and you don't sometimes hate them, there's something wrong with you. So go out.

Get to know them.

This is as good a time as any to find out about your parents' past history. Learning to see them as individuals, and not just as people who are there solely to look after you both physically and emotionally, will make you a better person. It will also make it easier to forgive them when they irritate you beyond belief.

Adapted from The Guardian

b Look at the headings below and remember the tips. Use your own words to explain them to **B**.

Do your share.   Go out. A lot.
Save, save, save.   Get to know them.
Have an exit plan.

c Now listen to **B** telling you about some tips from an article called *The secret to…living with adult children*.

d Are any of the tips from the two articles similar? Which tips do you strongly agree or disagree with?

7A QI QUIZ Student A

a Read the answers to questions 1–6 of the quiz on p.66.

b Explain the answers to 1–6 to **B** in your own words. **B** will then tell you the answers to 7–12.

QI – Everything you think you know is probably wrong…

1 In the last 90 years, 82 Americans have been killed in bear attacks. However, teddy bears, along with other toys, have been responsible for an average of 22 deaths each year. **Teddy bears** are particularly dangerous because of their small parts, like glass eyes, which can cause choking, making them much more deadly than any species of real bear.

2 Not Alsatians (German Shepherds) or Wolfhounds, which physically resemble wolves. Recent DNA analysis has confirmed that **Pekingese**, whose name comes from Peking, the former name for Beijing, are one of the oldest dog breeds, and the most genetically similar to wolves.

3 The reason that the Sun looks yellow to us is because the Earth's atmosphere scatters colours with a longer wavelength, like red, orange, and yellow, less easily. These wavelengths are what we see, which is why the Sun appears yellow. However, the real colour of the sun is **white**.

4 Ice cream was first developed into something resembling its current form by the Italian Giambattista della Porta in the 16th century. It is one of the most complex food products that you will ever consume, a thermodynamic miracle that contains all three states of matter, **solid**, **liquid**, and **gas** at the same time.

5 No, it wasn't Hannibal. Elephants played a critical role in several key battles in antiquity, and continued to be used in combat up till the 19th century in Thailand and Vietnam. The last recorded use of elephants in war occurred in **1987**, when Iraq is alleged to have used them to transport heavy weapons during the **Iran / Iraq war**.

6 We all associate boomerangs with Australia. However, they were used in almost all continents in ancient times, and an Iron Age wooden boomerang was recently found in Holland. In fact, the world's oldest boomerang, made from the tusk of a mammoth, was found in a cave in **Poland**, in 1987.

7B WHICH IS THE FAKE? Student A

a   Describe your picture to **B**, and answer **B**'s questions about the details. Together, find eight differences.

b   Compare your pictures and decide which one you think is an original Vincent van Gogh painting and which is a fake.

8A GUESS THE SENTENCE Student A

a   Look at sentences 1–7 and guess what the missing phrase could be. Remember: ⊞ = positive verb and ⊟ = negative verb.

1   I would love _____ your face when the doctor told you to join a gym. ⊞
2   There's no point _____. He never goes to parties. ⊞
3   It's no good _____ lend you some money. She's completely broke. ⊞
4   We'd rather _____ holiday in August, but we had to because of school holidays. ⊟
5   I don't like _____ to do. I prefer to decide for myself. ⊞
6   The pool wasn't warm enough for us _____. ⊞
7   I really hate _____ the truth. ⊟

b   **B** has the complete sentences 1–7. Read your sentences to **B**. Keep trying different possibilities until you get each sentence exactly right.

c   Now listen to **B**'s sentences 8–14. Tell him / her to keep guessing until he / she gets it exactly the same as yours.

8   Nursing is a very rewarding job that involves **working in** a team.
9   Lucy seems **to be seeing** Dan a lot recently. Do you think they're going out together?
10   We hope **to have found** a new flat by the end of the year.
11   Our plan is **to fly to** Las Vegas and then hire a car.
12   There's absolutely **nothing to do** in this town. There isn't even a cinema.
13   My father was the first person in my family **to go to** university.
14   I really regret **not having known** my grandfather. He died before I was born.

7A   WHAT A RIDICULOUS IDEA!
Student A

a   Read your sentences to **B**. He / She will respond with an exclamation.

- Did you know that you aren't allowed to take soft cheeses in hand luggage?
- I was fined by a police officer yesterday for talking on my phone while I was parked outside my house.
- My sister got married on Saturday and it rained all day.
- I thought we could go to the cinema and then have dinner at the new Thai place down the road.
- My daughter's goldfish died this morning.
- Did you know my parents were both born on exactly the same day?
- You won't believe it, but my brother has just won €200,000 in the lottery!

b   Respond to **B**'s sentences with an exclamation beginning with either *How…!* or *What (a / an)…!* Make sure you use expressive intonation and link the words where appropriate.

9A   MATCH THE SENTENCES   Student A

a   Read your sentences 1–6 to **B**. Make sure you stress auxiliaries where appropriate. **B** will choose a response.

> 1   Have you seen the latest James Bond film?
> 2   I absolutely hate getting up early.
> 3   Is Lina coming swimming this afternoon?
> 4   Your brother lives in Liverpool, doesn't he?
> 5   Your aunt doesn't eat much, does she?
> 6   You do like cabbage, don't you?

b   Now **B** will read you his / her sentences 7–12. Choose a response below. Make sure you stress auxiliaries and *to* where appropriate.

> ☐   He is! He won the under-18 cup this year.
> ☐   I don't, but my partner does. I'm too lazy!
> ☐   No, and neither does her brother. Maybe they were adopted.
> ☐   No, there weren't. I was the only one.
> ☐   She said she wanted to, but she wasn't sure if she'd be able to.
> ☐   We'd like to, but we aren't sure if we can afford to.

c   In pairs, practise all 12 mini-conversations again, making sure you get the stress right.

9B   COOKING EGGS   Student B

a   Read López-Alt's recipe for fried eggs.

FRIED EGGS

2 large eggs
3 tablespoons olive oil
(extra-virgin if you prefer)
salt and freshly ground black pepper

Heat the olive oil in a medium non-stick frying pan over medium heat until it registers 150°C on a thermometer.

Break one egg into a cup and transfer it carefully into the oil. Repeat with the second egg.

Immediately tilt the frying pan so that the oil collects on one side and spoon the hot oil over the egg whites, trying to avoid the yolks as much as possible. Continue doing this until the egg whites are completely set and crispy on the bottom.

b   Listen to **A**'s recipe for scrambled eggs. Make notes as you listen. Then use your notes to tell **A** the recipe again, to check that it's correct.

c   Now explain the recipe for fried eggs to **A**.

The ingredients are… First, you… Then you…

d   How different are the recipes from the way you usually make scrambled or fried eggs? Would you cook them this way in the future? Why (not)?

5A   AM I TOO BUSY?   Students A+B

Between 0 and 4 'yes' answers	Between 5 and 7 'yes' answers	Between 8 and 10 'yes' answers
Amazing! You are on the right track.	You are verging on 'too busy'. Time to rethink.	Seriously? Did you really need to take the quiz?

Of course, this quiz doesn't give any scientific proof about your level of busyness, but it does ask some important questions about how you are using your time, and how you are feeling about it. Question 10 is the critical one – think carefully about how the people closest to you view your busyness.

2B CHANGING MEANINGS Student B

a Read the notes about how the meaning of the word *awful* evolved, and try to remember the information.

b Listen to **A** telling you the 'story' of *deer*.

c Cover the notes and tell **A** as much as you can remember about the 'story' of *awful*.

d Repeat for *naughty* and *dismantle*.

Awful /ˈɔːfl/ **originally meant 'impressive and frightening'**

- In Old English, 'awful' was partly positive and partly negative.
- It described something that was impressive but also frightening, e.g. 'awful mountains'.
- By the 19th century, the positive meaning had disappeared.
- The negative meaning changed to describe something that was very bad.
- Now it is only used to describe something very bad.

To *dismantle* /dɪsˈmæntl/ **originally meant 'to take off your cloak'**

- In the Middle Ages, a 'mantle' was a long cloak.
- 'Dismantle' meant 'to take off your cloak'.
- It was used with this meaning in Shakespeare's play *The Winter's Tale*.
- In the 16th century, its meaning became 'to destroy a castle' (i.e. to 'take off' its walls).
- 'Dismantle' now means 'to take apart' a machine or a structure.

4A WHAT HAPPENS IN THE END?
Student B

a Read an extract from the end of *Lamb to the Slaughter* by Roald Dahl.

Called by Mary, the police arrive and search the house, looking for evidence of an intruder, and the murder weapon…

Sergeant Noonan wandered into the kitchen, came out quickly and said, 'Look, Mrs Maloney. You know that oven of yours is still on, and the meat still inside.'

'Oh dear me!' she cried. 'So it is!'

'I better turn it off for you, hadn't I?'

'Will you do that, Jack. Thank you so much.'

When the sergeant returned the second time, she looked at him with her large, dark tearful eyes. 'Jack Noonan,' she said.

'Yes?'

'Would you do me a small favour – you and these others?'

'We can try, Mrs Maloney.'

'Well,' she said. 'Here you all are, and good friends of dear Patrick's too, and helping to catch the man who killed him. You must be terrible hungry by now because it's long past your suppertime, and I know Patrick would never forgive me, God bless his soul, if I allowed you to remain in his house without offering you decent hospitality. Why don't you eat up that lamb that's in the oven? It'll be cooked just right by now.'

Mary knows that once she has cooked the leg of lamb, and the policemen have eaten it, the murder weapon will never be found and there will be no evidence of her crime.

---

b Listen to **A** tell you what happens at the end of *The Adventure of the Speckled Band*.

c Now tell **A** what happens at the end of *Lamb to the Slaughter*.

d What did you both think of the endings? Now that you know what happens, would you want to read the stories?

7A WHAT A RIDICULOUS IDEA!
Student B

a Respond to **A**'s sentences with an exclamation beginning with either *How…!* or *What (a / an)…!* Make sure you use expressive intonation and link the words where appropriate.

b Read your sentences to **A**. He / She will respond with an exclamation.

- I was at home all morning waiting for the electrician to come, and they didn't turn up.
- We're going to New York on Friday for a long weekend.
- Jack and Sue are going to the theatre for their anniversary, and then they're having dinner at a new French restaurant.
- My parents were burgled last night. They took all my mum's jewellery.
- Even though I got 70% in the exam, the teacher refused to pass me.
- I really put my foot in it at the party last night. I called Tom's wife 'Anna', but that's his ex-wife's name!
- Maria's husband collects photos of famous people's dogs. He has hundreds of them.

3B HISTORICAL INACCURACIES Student B

a Read about the film and the series. Then listen to **A** telling you what is fact and what is fiction in their films. Did you guess what really happened and what didn't correctly?

Mary Queen of Scots

In the film

In *Mary Queen of Scots*, there is a dramatic meeting between Mary and Queen Elizabeth I.

The facts

The relationship between Mary (1542–1587, Queen of Scotland) and Elizabeth (1533–1603, Queen of England) dominated the politics of the two countries for 20 years. Some people believed that Mary should have been queen of both countries, and the two were great rivals. The meeting between them is the dramatic heart of the film. However, although the two Queens wrote many letters to each other, they never actually met.

The Crown

In the series

In *The Crown*, Jackie Kennedy, the US President's wife, criticizes the Queen after a dinner at Buckingham Palace.

The facts

John and Jackie Kennedy were invited to Buckingham Palace for a formal dinner during their first UK visit in 1961. After the dinner, Jackie was reported as saying that the Queen was 'pretty heavy going' and that Buckingham Palace was 'like a provincial hotel'. Later in the episode, Jackie goes to visit the Queen on her own and apologizes. It is true that she had a one-to-one meeting with the Queen nine months after the original meeting, but nobody knows if she actually apologized, and it seems likely that the Netflix series allowed itself some dramatic licence.

b Now tell **A** what is fact and what is fiction in your film and series, and any other information you learn.

9A MATCH THE SENTENCES Student B

a **A** will read you his / her sentences 1–6. Choose a response below. Make sure you stress auxiliaries and *to* where appropriate.

☐	I love it. It's cauliflower I can't stand.
☐	No, she doesn't, but she drinks like a fish.
☐	No, but I'd love to.
☐	She isn't, but her children are. She didn't want to.
☐	So do I. Luckily, I don't often have to.
☐	Yes, and so does my sister.

4B WHAT'S GOING ON? Student B

a Look at photo 1 and listen to **A** making speculations and deductions about it. Then tell him / her what's really going on.

This photo was taken in Germany during the Alpine Skiing World Cup. The people up the tree are sports coaches, watching the competitors training.

b Now look at photo 2 and make speculations and deductions about it.

- When and where could the photo have been taken?
- Who could the people be? What do you think they might be doing and why?
- What might have just happened?
- How might the people be feeling?

c **A** will tell you what's going on. Did you guess correctly?

b Now read your sentences 7–12 to **A**. Make sure you stress auxiliaries where appropriate. **A** will choose a response.

7 Are you going to go skiing at Christmas?
8 Katie doesn't look like her parents, does she?
9 Were there many people waiting at the doctor's?
10 Do you do a lot of gardening?
11 Erica did say she was coming, didn't she?
12 Adam isn't particularly good at tennis, is he?

c In pairs, practise all 12 mini-conversations again, making sure you get the stress right.

6A I NEED SOME HELP Student B

a Read your article carefully and try to work out the meaning of any new words and phrases.

The secret to...
living with adult children

If you are one of the many parents whose adult children have returned to the nest, read on!

Around a quarter of young adults in the UK are living with Mum and Dad, the highest number since records began in 1996. For parents who were expecting a bit of peace and quiet, it can be a difficult situation. Here are some tips to make living with your adult child a little easier.

Get things out in the open.

Whether they are returning after living away, or even if they've never left, you need to set rules about how you're going to live. It's your home. What you were happy to do for them ten years ago, and what you should be doing for them now, are very different. Don't be afraid of bringing up difficult subjects. Talk about money, and don't be afraid of charging them what you think is fair.

Give them space.

If you have the room, allocate them space in the kitchen, or even their own living area. Not to mention their own bedroom, which should not be shared with a sibling.

Don't do it all yourself.

Get them to do their share of the cleaning, washing, cooking – all of these can lead to resentment if the rules aren't established. Don't be a martyr; it's easy to feel like a housekeeper. Be flexible, and expect compromise from them, too.

Treat your child as an adult.

They will have their own life – friends, partners, late nights. But make sure that respect is returned. Don't put up with things that annoy you. You're not obliged to house their friends.

Focus on the positives.

Perhaps you'd forgotten that they love to cook. Or that it's great to come home to someone. Tell them you love them – they may be an adult, but they're still your child.

Adapted from The Guardian

b Listen to **A** telling you about some tips from an article called *How to survive...living with your parents.*

c Now look at the headings below and remember the tips from your article. Use your own words to explain them to **A**.

Get things out in the open.
Give them space.
Don't do it all yourself.
Treat your child as an adult.
Focus on the positives.

d Are any of the tips from the two articles similar? Which tips do you strongly agree or disagree with?

7A QI QUIZ Student B

a Read the answers to questions 7–12 of the quiz on p.66.

b **A** will tell you the answers to 1–6. Then explain the answers to 7–12 to **A** in your own words.

QI – Everything you think you know is probably wrong...

7 In many people's minds, in London, it is permanently raining. However, other European cities primarily associated with sunshine have significantly higher annual rainfall than London, including Barcelona, and also **Rome**, which is the wettest of these three cities.

8 In the UK itself, the highest mountain is Ben Nevis, in Scotland, which is 1,345 metres high. But part of the **Antarctic** is a British territory, and its highest mountain, Mount Hope, measures 3,239 metres, making Ben Nevis seem like a mere hill.

9 Not football or rugby, but **billiards**. Billiards was so popular in the USA that during the American Civil War, billiards results received wider coverage than war news. The first World Championship was held in 1869.

10 The 1896 Summer Olympics, the first of the modern era, were held in Athens, with 14 participating nations. Winners were given a **silver** medal, because gold was considered too expensive, while runners-up received a copper one, and there was no medal for third place. This changed in the 1904 Olympics, in St Louis, USA, to the current gold, silver, and bronze.

11 Although it is named after Gustav Eiffel, he didn't design it himself. He owned an engineering company, and was inspired to build the tower after visiting the Latting Observatory in New York. But the tower was actually designed by two of his senior engineers, **Maurice Koechlin** and **Emile Nouguier**.

12 According to a recent survey, **hairdressers** and **beauticians** have the most injury-prone jobs in Britain. The most common injury involved people cutting themselves. They are closely followed by electricians, plumbers, and police officers.

7B WHICH IS THE FAKE? Student B

a **A** will describe his / her picture to you. Ask questions about the details. Together, find eight differences.

b Compare your pictures and decide which one you think is an original Vincent van Gogh painting and which is a fake.

8A GUESS THE SENTENCE Student B

a Look at sentences 8–14 and guess what the missing phrase could be. Remember: ⊞ = positive verb and ⊟ = negative verb.

> 8 Nursing is a very rewarding job that involves _____ a team. ⊞
>
> 9 Lucy seems _____ Dan a lot recently. Do you think they're going out together? ⊞
>
> 10 We hope _____ a new flat by the end of the year. ⊞
>
> 11 Our plan is _____ Las Vegas and then hire a car. ⊞
>
> 12 There's absolutely _____ in this town. There isn't even a cinema. ⊟
>
> 13 My father was the first person in my family _____ university. ⊞
>
> 14 I really regret _____ my grandfather. He died before I was born. ⊟

b Listen to **A**'s sentences 1–7. Tell him / her to keep guessing until he / she gets it exactly the same as yours.

> 1 I would love **to have seen** your face when the doctor told you to join a gym.
>
> 2 There's no point **inviting him**. He never goes to parties.
>
> 3 It's no good **asking her to** lend you some money. She's completely broke.
>
> 4 We'd rather **not have gone on** holiday in August, but we had to because of school holidays.
>
> 5 I don't like **being told what** to do. I prefer to decide for myself.
>
> 6 The pool wasn't warm enough for us **to go swimming**.
>
> 7 I really hate **not being told** the truth.

c **A** has the complete sentences 8–14. Read your sentences to **A**. Keep trying different possibilities until you get each sentence exactly right.

KEY SUCCESS FACTORS

- using appropriate, professional-sounding language
- conveying a positive image of yourself without appearing overconfident or arrogant
- avoiding basic mistakes which will make you look careless

ANALYSING A MODEL TEXT

a You see the following job advertisement on a travel company website. Would you be interested in applying for the job? Why (not)?

Receptionist

Location: Edinburgh

The receptionist is the first point of contact for staff and visitors. The role involves a variety of tasks including answering and directing calls, welcoming visitors, scheduling meetings, and general admin support.
Core hours are 8 a.m.–6 p.m. and you will need to be available to work earlier shifts some days and later shifts other days.

About you:
The ideal candidate will have a customer-focused personality with a strong can-do attitude. We're looking for someone with proven communication skills for liaising with individuals at all levels in a very fast-moving environment.

Interested? The closing date for applications is Wednesday 18th June – click 'Apply' before this opportunity flies away!

APPLY

b Read the first draft of an email written in response to the advertisement. What information does Agata give in the three main paragraphs?

> **From:** Agata Beck
> **To:** irena.foster@besttravel.net
> **Subject:** Application
>
> Dear ~~Miss~~ *Ms* Foster,
>
> ~~My name is Agata Beck.~~ I am writing to apply for the post of receptionist advertised in your website.
>
> **1** I have recently graduated from Humboldt University in Berlin, where I completed a degree in Business Studies. I have a high level of spoken english (C1 on the CEFR), as I lived in the United States during six months as part of an exchange programm between my school and a high school in Utah. I made many American friends during this period, but we lost touch when I came home.
>
> **2** As you will see from my CV, I have some relevant experience because I am currently an intern at a leading German travel company. I have worked in various roles, including marketing asistant and administrator and my tasks have included organizing and running meetings, and dealing with clients by phone and email. The director of company would be happy to provide a reference. He is, in fact, my uncle.
>
> **3** I am very enthusiastic on travelling and would welcome the chance to be part of such a high-profile and successful company. I believe I would be suitable for the job advertised as, apart of my work experience, I am an outgoing person and get on well with people. Friends describe me as calm and consciensious and I would enjoy the variety and excitement the job would offer. I would definitely not panic when things got busy!
>
> I attach a full CV and if you require a further information, I would be very happy to provide it.
>
> I look forward to hearing from you.
>
> Yours sincerely,
>
> Agata Beck

> 🔍 **Improving your first draft**
> Check your writing for correct paragraphing, mistakes, irrelevant information, and language which is in an inappropriate register.

c Read the draft email again and try to improve it.

1 ~~Cross out~~ three sentences (not including the example) which are irrelevant or inappropriate.
2 Correct ten more mistakes in the highlighted phrases, including spelling, capital letters, grammar, and vocabulary.

d If you were a manager at the travel company, would you have given Agata an interview if she had sent her first draft?

e Look at 1–9 below. How did Agata express these ideas in a more formal way? Use the **bold** words to help you remember. Then look at the model email again to check your answers.

1 This letter is to ask you to give me the job of receptionist. **apply**

_____

2 I've just finished uni, where I did Business Studies. **graduate / degree**

_____

3 I can speak English very well. **high**

_____

4 I've done this kind of job before. **relevant**

_____

5 My tasks have included talking to people on the phone. **deal / clients**

_____

6 I'd love to work for such a famous company. **welcome / high-profile**

_____

7 I'm sending a full CV with this email. **attach**

_____

8 If you need to know anything else, I'll tell you. **require / provide**

_____

9 Hope to hear from you soon! **forward**

_____

PLANNING WHAT TO WRITE

a Read the job advertisement and <u>underline</u> the information you will need to respond to. Then make notes about:
- any qualifications you have.
- any relevant experience you could include.
- what aspects of your personality you think would make you suitable for the job and how you could illustrate them.
- any other information you think you need to include.

GLOBAL STAGE UK

Festival staff required to work at Global Stage UK, a world music event in the west of England, from 12th to 14th July

Responsibilities
- To ensure the safety and comfort of the public and to assist in the running of a successful festival
- To help to manage any crowd-related problems, including maintaining a state of calm to minimize injury
- To prevent unauthorized access to the site by members of the public

Requirements
- You must be aged 18 or over on the date of the festival and be eligible to work in the UK.
- You must be physically fit and healthy and able to work under pressure in a demanding environment.
- You should speak English well and have some experience of dealing with the public.

How to apply Send an email and full CV to Emma Richards: **e.richards@globalstage.org**

b Compare notes with a partner and discuss how relevant you think each other's information is, what you think you should leave out, and what else you might want to include.

TIPS for writing a covering email / letter to apply for a job, grant, etc.:
- Use appropriate sentences to open the email / letter.
- Organize the main body of the email / letter into clear paragraphs.
- Use a suitable style: don't use contractions or very informal expressions. Use formal vocabulary where appropriate, e.g. *require* instead of *need*, *as* instead of *because*.
- The use of a conditional can often sound more polite, e.g. *I would welcome the chance to…*
- When you say why you think you are suitable for the job, be factual and positive, but not overconfident. Be careful not to sound arrogant.
- Use appropriate phrases to close the email / letter.

WRITING

You have decided to apply for the festival job advertised. Write a covering email of between 220 and 260 words.

DRAFT your email.
- Write an introductory sentence to explain why you are writing.
- Paragraph 1: Give personal information including skills and qualifications.
- Paragraph 2: Talk about any relevant experience you have.
- Paragraph 3: Explain why you think you would be suitable for the job.
- Finish the email appropriately.

EDIT the email, checking paragraphing, cutting any irrelevant information, and making sure it's the right length.

CHECK the email for mistakes in grammar, spelling, punctuation, and register.

← p.13

Go online for more Writing practice

Writing An article

ANALYSING A MODEL TEXT

a You're going to read an article about childhood covering the areas below. What information would you include if you were writing about your country?

- What are the main differences between children's lives 50 years ago and children's lives now?
- Why have these changes occurred?
- Do you think the changes are positive or negative?

b Now read the article. Did the writer include any of your ideas? With a partner, choose the best title from the three below and say why you prefer it to the others.

The lost joys of childhood
Children of the past
My forgotten childhood

c Answer the questions with a partner.

1 What is the effect of the direct question in the introduction? Where is it answered?
2 What does paragraph 1 focus on? What examples are given?
3 What are the changes that the writer focuses on in paragraph 2 and what reasons are given for the changes? Do you agree?
4 Underline the discourse markers that are used to link the points in paragraphs 2 and 3, e.g. *First…*

Children's lives have changed enormously over the last 50 years. But do they have happier childhoods today?

1 It's difficult to look back on one's own childhood without some element of nostalgia. I have four brothers and sisters and my memories are all about being with them, playing board games on the living room floor, or spending days outside with the other neighbourhood children, racing around on our bikes or exploring the nearby woods. My parents hardly ever appear in these memories, except as providers either of meals or of severe reprimands after some particularly hazardous adventure.

2 In the UK at least, the nature of childhood has changed dramatically since the 1970s. First, families are smaller and there are far more only children these days. It is common for both parents to work outside the home and far fewer people have the time to bring up a large family. As a result, boys and girls today spend much of their time alone. Another major change is that youngsters tend to spend a huge proportion of their free time at home, inside. This is often due to the fact that parents worry much more than they used to about real or imagined dangers, so they wouldn't dream of letting their children play outside by themselves.

3 Finally, the kinds of toys children have and the way they play is totally different. Computer and video games have replaced the board games and more active pastimes of my childhood. The fact that they can play the games on their own further increases the sense of isolation felt by many young people today. The irony is that so many of these games are called 'interactive'.

4 Do these changes mean that children today have a less idyllic childhood than I had? I personally believe that they do, but perhaps every generation feels exactly the same.

Using synonyms

Try not to repeat the same words and phrases too often in your writing. Instead, where possible, use a synonym or similar expression if you can think of one. This will both make the article more varied for the reader and help to link it together. A good monolingual dictionary or thesaurus can help you.

d Find synonyms in the article for the following words and phrases.

1 at the present time   _____, _____
2 children   _____, _____,
                               _____
3 alone, without adults   _____, _____

Using richer vocabulary

You can make your writing more colourful and interesting to read by trying to use a richer range of vocabulary instead of the most obvious words.

e How are the words in *italics* expressed in the article, to make the style more interesting?

1 …spending days outside with the other *children who lived near us*… _____
2 …*going* around *fast* on our bikes… _____
3 My parents *don't* appear *very often* in these memories… _____
4 …after some particularly *dangerous* adventure. _____
5 …the nature of childhood has changed *in a big way*… _____
6 …*usually* both parents work outside the home… _____
7 …that children today have a less *happy* childhood than I had? _____

PLANNING WHAT TO WRITE

a Look at the exam question.

Many aspects of life have changed over the last 30 years. These include:

dating   communication   education

Write an article for an online magazine about how one of these areas has changed in your country, and say whether you think these changes are positive or negative.

With a partner, brainstorm for each topic…

1 what the situation used to be like.
2 how the situation has changed in your country.
3 whether you think the changes are positive or negative and why.

Now decide which topic you're going to write about and which ideas you want to include.

b Think of a possible title for your article.

TIPS for writing an article:
- There is no fixed structure for an article, but it is important to have clear paragraphs.
- Use discourse markers to link your points or arguments.
- Use a suitable style, neither very formal nor very informal. Think about who your target reader is.
- Choose an interesting or provocative title that makes people want to read the article.
- Make the introduction short. You could ask a question or questions which you then answer in the article.
- Try to engage the reader, e.g. by referring to your personal experience.
- Vary your vocabulary, using synonyms where possible.

WRITING

Write an article of about 260 words.

DRAFT your article, using the topic and title you worked on in the planning stage.

- Write a brief introduction which refers to the changes and asks a question.
- Write two or three main paragraphs saying what the situation used to be like and how it has changed.
- Write a final paragraph which sums up your feelings. If you asked a question in the introduction, then you should answer that question.

EDIT the article, checking paragraphing, cutting any irrelevant information, and making sure it's the right length.

CHECK the article for mistakes in grammar, spelling, punctuation, and register.

← p.17

Writing A review

ANALYSING A MODEL TEXT

a Which of the following would normally influence you to read a book?

- a friend of yours recommended it
- it's a bestseller – everybody is reading it
- you saw and enjoyed a film based on it
- you were told to read it at school
- you read a good review of it

b Read the book review. In which paragraph, 1–4, do you find the following information? Write **DS** if the review doesn't say. Does the review make you want to read the book? Why (not)?

- the strong points of the book
- the basic outline of the plot
- what happens in the end
- where and when the story is set
- the weakness(es) of the book
- whether the reviewer recommends the book or not
- who the author is
- who the main characters are
- who the book is published by
- who the book will appeal to

c Look at these extracts from a first draft of the review. Which words in the **bold** phrases did the reviewer leave out or change to make it more concise? Then read the **Participle clauses** box to check.

> **1** A thriller **which is set in the present day** in a small town in Missouri, USA, it immediately became an international bestseller.

> **2** ...a couple, Nick and Amy Dunne, **who are now living in Nick's hometown** of Carthage...

> **3** Nick owns a bar, **which was opened with his wife's money**, which he runs with his sister Margo.

---

1 *Gone Girl* is the third novel by American writer Gillian Flynn. A thriller set in the present day in a small town in Missouri, USA, it immediately became an international bestseller.

2 The main characters in the novel are a couple, Nick and Amy Dunne, now living in Nick's hometown of Carthage after Nick lost his job as a journalist in New York City. Nick owns a bar, opened with his wife's money, which he runs with his sister Margo. On the day of his fifth wedding anniversary, Nick discovers that Amy is missing. For various reasons, he becomes a prime suspect in her disappearance. The first half of the book is told in the first person, alternately by Nick and then by Amy through extracts from her journal. The two stories are totally different: Nick describes Amy as stubborn and antisocial, whereas she makes him out to be aggressive and difficult. As a result, the reader is left guessing whether Nick is guilty or not. In the second half, however, the reader realizes that neither Nick nor Amy have been telling the truth in their account of the marriage. The resulting situation has unexpected consequences for Nick, Amy, and the reader.

3 The great strength of this book is how the characters of Nick and Amy are revealed. Despite having the typical devices common to thrillers, for example, several possible suspects and plenty of red herrings, the novel is also a psychological analysis of the effect of failure and unfulfilled dreams on someone's personality. My only criticism would be that the first half goes on too long and perhaps could have been slightly cut down.

4 Not only is this a complex and absolutely gripping novel, but it also tackles real problems in society, such as the unhappiness that is caused by economic difficulties, and the effect of the media on a crime investigation. For all lovers of psychological thrillers, *Gone Girl* is a must.

> **Glossary**
> **red herring** an unimportant fact, event, idea, etc. that takes people's attention from the important one

Participle clauses

The writer uses participles (*set, living, opened*) instead of a subject + verb. Past participles replace verbs in the passive, and present participles (*-ing* forms) replace verbs in the active. The subject of the clause is usually the same as the subject of the main clause.

Participle clauses can be used:

- instead of a conjunction (*after, as, when, because, although,* etc.) + subject + verb, e.g. *Having run out of money…* instead of *Because she has run out of money…*
- instead of a relative clause, e.g. *set in the present day / opened with his wife's money* instead of *which is set… / which was opened…*

When you use a participle clause, you do not need to link the next clause with *and*, e.g. *It is set in 1903 and it tells the story of a young girl…* → *Set in 1903, it tells the story…*

d Rewrite the sentences, making the highlighted phrases more concise by using participle clauses.

1 As she believes him to be the murderer, Anya is absolutely terrified.

2 Armelle, who was forced to marry a man she did not love, decided to throw herself into her work.

3 Simon, who realizes that the police are after him, tries to escape.

4 It was first published in 1903 and it has been reprinted many times.

5 When he hears the shot, Mark rushes into the house.

6 It is based on his wartime diaries and it tells the story of a young soldier.

USEFUL LANGUAGE

e Look at the highlighted adverbs. What effect do they have on the words that follow?

> The two stories are totally different…

> …and perhaps could have been slightly cut down.

f Cross out any adverbs that don't fit in these sentences. Tick (✓) if all are possible.

1 My only criticism is that the plot is *somewhat / slightly / a little* implausible.
2 The last chapter is *really / very / absolutely* fascinating.
3 The end of the novel is *rather / pretty / quite* disappointing.
4 The denouement is *absolutely / incredibly / extremely* thrilling.

PLANNING WHAT TO WRITE

a Think of a book or film that you have read or seen recently. Make a list of the main points about the characters and plot that you should cover in a review. Don't include a spoiler.

b Exchange your list with other students to see if they can identify the book or film.

TIPS for writing a book / film review:

- Choose a book or film that you know well.
- Organize the review into clear paragraphs.
- Use a suitable style, neither very formal nor very informal.
- Give your reader a brief idea of the plot, but do not give away the whole story. This is only part of your review, so choose only the main events and be as concise as possible.
- Use the present tense when you describe the plot. Using participle clauses will help to keep it concise.
- Use a range of adjectives that describe as precisely as possible how the book or film made you feel, e.g. *gripping, moving,* etc. (see *p.37*). Use adverbs of degree to modify them, e.g. *absolutely gripping.*
- Remember that an effective review will include both praise and criticism.

WRITING

A student magazine has asked for reviews of recent books and films. Write a review of between 220 and 260 words.

DRAFT your review.

- Paragraph 1: Include the title of the book or film, the genre, the author or director, and where / when it is set.
- Paragraph 2: Describe the plot, including information about the main characters.
- Paragraph 3: Talk about what you liked and any criticisms you may have.
- Paragraph 4: Give a summary of your opinion and a recommendation.

EDIT the review, making sure you've covered all the main points, checking paragraphing, cutting any irrelevant information, and making sure it's the right length.

CHECK the review for mistakes in grammar, spelling, punctuation, and register.

◑ p.39

Writing | A proposal

KEY SUCCESS FACTORS
- organizing your proposal under headings
- describing the current situation
- making logical and persuasive recommendations related to your observations or research
- being clear and concise

ANALYSING A MODEL TEXT

a The managers of a language school would like to expand the business and increase the number of students attending each year. They asked some students to carry out a survey and then write a proposal on how to achieve this. Read the proposal. What recommendations do the students make in the three areas?

b Replace the <mark>highlighted</mark> phrases with the more formal expressions used in the proposal.

1 <mark>What this proposal is for</mark> is…
   The _____ is…

2 …is to <mark>say what things could be better with</mark> the classes and facilities…
   …is to _____
   the classes and facilities…

3 In general, students <mark>think the teachers are very good</mark>.
   In general, students _____.

4 <mark>About the size of the classes</mark>, we suggest that there should never be more than 12 students in a class.
   _____ ,
   we suggest that there should never be more than 12 students in a class.

5 <mark>As for how long the classes last</mark>, lessons officially last an hour…
   _____ ,
   lessons officially last an hour…

6 …<mark>first, we suggest buying</mark> more computers…
   …we suggest, _____
   more computers…

7 …<mark>most students studying at King James at the moment</mark> are positive…
   …_____ are positive…

8 …that <mark>if you make the changes we suggest</mark>, student numbers could be increased by as much as 10%.
   …that _____ , student numbers could be increased by as much as 10%.

A proposal

Introduction
The King James Language School is a successful business which attracts a reasonable number of students every year. However, the school managers think that these numbers could be increased, so we carried out a satisfaction survey with existing students. The aim of this proposal is to suggest a range of improvements to the classes and facilities at the school in order to attract new customers.

1 The classes
In general, students rate the quality of teaching very highly. However, there are some criticisms about class size and the length of classes. As regards class size, we suggest that there should never be more than 12 students in a class. Regarding class duration, lessons officially last an hour, but in practice they are usually only 45 minutes because of latecomers. As a result, we propose that all students who arrive more than five minutes late should have to wait until the next break for admittance.

2 The self-study centre
It is generally thought that the self-study centre, while useful, has two major drawbacks. There are not enough computers, and at peak times they are always occupied. In addition, the centre closes at 7 p.m., so students who come to the later classes cannot use the centre at all. To address these issues, we suggest, firstly, purchasing more computers, and secondly, extending the opening hours to 9 p.m.

3 The cafeteria
The cafeteria was recently replaced by vending machines for drinks and snacks. While there's no doubt that people often had to wait quite a long time to be served, feedback shows that most students greatly prefer to have a cafeteria on the premises. Our final proposal is that the cafeteria should be reopened, serving both healthy snacks and hot meals.

Conclusion
Overall, the majority of students currently attending courses at King James are positive about the school and its facilities. We strongly believe that if the suggested changes are implemented, student numbers could be increased by as much as 10%.

c   Complete the missing words. Some (but not all) are in the model proposal.

Some common expressions for generalizing

1   **In g**_____, people think…
2   **Generally sp**_____, people think…
3   **It is generally co**_____ / thought…
4   **The general v**_____ is that certain improvements need to be made.
5   **Ov**_____, the majority of students think…

d   Rewrite the sentences to make them more formal.

Making recommendations

1   Why don't you make the classes smaller?
    We propose _____
    _____.

2   It would be much better if classes lasted an hour.
    It would be far preferable for classes _____
    _____.

3   Please buy new computers.
    We suggest _____
    _____.

4   The opening hours should be extended until 9 p.m.
    It would be advisable _____
    _____.

5   You really should open the cafeteria again.
    We strongly recommend _____
    _____.

PLANNING WHAT TO WRITE

a   Read the following task and study the relevant information. Then, with a partner, decide:

1   how many headings you will need and what they should be.
2   how to express the main issues in your own words.

> Your school would like to increase the number of students going on four-week study trips to the UK. You have been asked by the school principal to write a proposal with recommendations for getting more students to go on these trips. You have got feedback from the students who went on the most recent trip, including what they were positive about, and what problems they had, and you have made the following notes:
>
> - *People with families much happier than ones who stayed in the halls of residence, because they were able to practise their English with the families.*
>
> - *School OK and classes good, but almost everyone complained about the lunch (just a sandwich). Some thought six hours of classes a day too much.*
>
> - *People not very keen on some weekend cultural programmes. Trips to London and Oxford great, to Bath and Stratford boring. On all trips, too much sightseeing and not enough time for shopping!*

b   Together, suggest improvements to the study trips, beginning with a different expression from **d** each time.

TIPS for writing a proposal:

- Look carefully at who the proposal is for and what they want to know. This will help you choose what information you have to include.
- Decide what the sections of the proposal are going to be and think of headings for them.
- In the introduction, state clearly what the purpose of the proposal is.
- For each paragraph, explain the situation and make a recommendation. Don't forget to say if something is good, as well as bad.
- Use an appropriate style, avoiding very informal expressions.
- Try not to use exactly the same words as in any information you are given.
- Use a variety of expressions for generalizing and making recommendations.

WRITING

Write a proposal of between 220 and 260 words.

DRAFT your proposal, using the headings and recommendations you worked on in the planning stage.

EDIT the proposal, making sure you've covered all the main points, checking paragraphing, cutting any irrelevant information, and making sure it's the right length.

CHECK the proposal for mistakes in grammar, spelling, punctuation, and register.

◀ p.53

KEY SUCCESS FACTORS
- constructing an argument on both sides
- writing an effective introduction and conclusion
- using appropriate discourse markers to contrast and balance points

ANALYSING A MODEL TEXT

a You have been asked to write the following essay:

Do smartphones really improve our lives?

With a partner, discuss three reasons why you think smartphones make our lives better and three reasons why they do not. Order them 1–3 according to their importance, with 1 as the most important.

b Read the essay and check if the writer has mentioned some or all of your arguments. Where does the writer put the main argument in each paragraph?

Do smartphones really improve our lives?

Introduction

Arguments in favour

Perhaps the greatest benefit of smartphones is that they allow us to access an incredible amount of information. They are not just phones – we can also use them as maps, encyclopaedias, novels, entertainment systems, and much more. We live in an age of information, and smartphones help us to make the most of it all. In addition, they allow us to live our lives spontaneously. Whether you need a taxi, have to book a restaurant table, or want to identify stars in the night sky, you can do it straight away. Finally, they keep us in touch with our friends and family, and the social role they play in a fast-moving society is hugely important.

Arguments against

However, there are strong arguments to suggest that what appear to be the advantages of smartphones can also have downsides. One drawback is the cost – monthly contracts are far from cheap and smartphones tend to become obsolete quickly, so people feel they need to buy the latest model. What is more, they are a constant distraction, as they encourage people to spend hours checking social networking sites when they could be doing something more useful. But perhaps the most significant downside is for working people. On the one hand, smartphones offer great convenience, but they also mean that employees can be contacted by their boss or by customers at any time, even while they are on holiday.

Conclusion

> **Introductions and conclusions**
> - In an essay, it is important that the introduction engages the reader. A good introductory paragraph describes the present situation and gives supporting evidence. It should introduce the topic, but should not include the specific points that you are going to mention in the body of the text. It should refer to the statement or question you have been asked to discuss. This can often be done in the form of a question to the reader, which the subsequent paragraphs should answer.
> - The conclusion should briefly sum up the arguments you have made and can include your personal opinion. The opinion you express should follow logically from the arguments you have presented. It is important that this is not just a repetition of your arguments. It is a summary of what you believe your arguments have proved.

c Read the **Introductions and conclusions** box. Then look at the three introductory paragraphs below and choose which one you think is best for the essay. Compare with a partner. Discuss why you think it is the best and why the other two are less suitable. Then do the same with the concluding paragraphs.

Introductions

1 Smartphones dominate the field of personal communications and nowadays virtually everyone owns one. They have many clear benefits, but do they really make our lives better?

2 Smartphones clearly have important advantages and disadvantages. In this essay, I am first going to analyse the advantages of this technology and then I will outline some important disadvantages, before finally drawing my conclusions.

3 Can you imagine life without your smartphone? Probably not, as this fantastic technology has become such a crucial tool for our work and social lives. So how did we manage before smartphones were invented?

argument

Conclusions

1 To sum up, smartphones have both advantages and disadvantages, but all things considered, I believe that their influence is mostly beneficial – after all, we could not live without them.

2 In conclusion, smartphones have improved our lives considerably in my view, especially if you want to use the internet. They are very useful, for example, if you are in a shop and you decide to buy something online instead.

3 On the whole, smartphones are a wonderful tool, but they have both pros and cons and they have to be used wisely. It is very important that we control them, and not the other way round.

USEFUL LANGUAGE

d Complete the missing words. Some (but not all) are in the model essay.

Expressing the main points in an argument
+
1 The greatest **b**_____ is that…
2 **First and most im**_____, smartphones give us an incredible amount of information.
−
3 One **dr**_____ of smartphones is the cost…
4 Another significant **d**_____ to smartphones is that employees can always be contacted.

Adding supporting information to a main argument, or introducing other related arguments
5 **In a**_____,
6 **What is m**_____,
7 **Not o**_____ **that**, but…
8 **Another point in f**_____ is that…

smartphones allow us to live our lives spontaneously.

Weighing up arguments
9 **On the wh**_____,
10 **On b**_____,
11 **A**_____ in a_____,
12 **All things c**_____,

smartphones have both pros and cons.

PLANNING WHAT TO WRITE

a Look at the essay title below and, with a partner, brainstorm the pros and cons of the topic. Then decide on the three main arguments for each side that are relevant to the title.

> The growth of online shopping has greatly improved life for the consumer.

b Write an introduction for the essay. Follow this pattern:
1 Write an introductory sentence about how important online shopping is.
2 Write a second sentence supporting the first one.
3 Ask the main question that you intend to answer in the essay.

c Compare your introduction with a partner. Together, make a final version.

> **TIPS for writing a discursive essay giving both sides of an argument:**
> - Brainstorm points for and against, and decide which two or three you think are the most important.
> - Use a neutral or formal style.
> - Write a clear introduction which engages the reader.
> - An essay is not just a list of ideas and opinions. Link your ideas in a logical sequence. Use phrases to order, contrast, and weigh up the points in your argument.
> - Make sure your conclusion is a summary of what you have previously said and refers back to what you were asked to write about.

WRITING

Write an essay of between 220 and 260 words on the topic above.

DRAFT your essay.
- Paragraph 1: Use your introduction.
- Paragraph 2: Give arguments in favour of online shopping.
- Paragraph 3: Give arguments against online shopping.
- Paragraph 4: Write your conclusion, saying whether you think the advantages outweigh the disadvantages, or vice versa.

EDIT the essay, making sure you've covered the main points, cutting any irrelevant information, and making sure it's the right length.

CHECK the essay for mistakes in grammar, spelling, punctuation, and register.

 p.61

Writing | A discursive essay (2): Taking sides

KEY SUCCESS FACTORS
- constructing an argument
- sustaining your case with examples
- showing that you have considered the opposing viewpoint

ANALYSING A MODEL TEXT

a You have been asked to write the following essay:

> Tourism always does a place more harm than good.

> Discuss the topic with a partner.
> Do you think that the effect of tourism on a country, city, or region is in general more positive or more negative? Why?

> 🔍 **Topic sentences**
> In a well-written essay, the first sentence of a paragraph usually establishes what the paragraph is going to be about. This is sometimes called the *topic sentence*.

b In pairs, read each topic sentence and imagine how the paragraph will continue. Do you think the essay will be for or against tourism?

A The infrastructure of an area is also often improved as a result of tourism.

B It is often claimed that popular tourist destinations are spoiled as a result of overdevelopment.

C Tourism is one of the world's great growth industries.

D Another point in favour of tourism is that governments are becoming aware of the need to protect tourist areas in order to attract visitors.

E The main positive effect of tourism is on local economies and employment.

c Now read the essay and match topic sentences A–E to paragraphs 1–5.

Tourism always does a place more harm than good

1 ☐ People today are travelling further and further, not only in the summer, but throughout the year. Although some people argue that mass tourism has a negative effect on destinations, in my view, its influences are generally positive.

2 ☐ Tourists need places to stay and things to do, and this creates a wide range of jobs for local people. Holidaymakers also spend a great deal of money, which stimulates the economy of the region as well as benefiting the country as a whole.

3 ☐ For example, when tourists start visiting an area, roads and public transport tend to improve, or an airport may be built, all of which benefit local people as well as tourists.

4 ☐ This is leading to better conservation not only of areas of natural beauty and endangered habitats in rural areas, but also of historic buildings and monuments in towns and cities.

5 ☐ For instance, many people argue that tourist development results in ugly hotels and soulless apartment blocks. This may have been true in the past, but nowadays developers recognize that new buildings should blend in with old ones and should not change the character of a place.

6 To sum up, I believe that, on the whole, tourism has a positive influence provided its development is properly planned and controlled. Tourist destinations have a lot to gain from visitors and the business they bring. In my opinion, it is possible for both tourists and local people to benefit and for popular tourist destinations to have a sustainable future.

d Read each paragraph again, with its topic sentence. Answer the questions with a partner.

1 Where does the writer state their overall opinion about tourism?
2 How many arguments are given to support their view?
3 What is the purpose of paragraph 5?

USEFUL LANGUAGE

> 🔍 **Using synonyms and richer vocabulary**
> When you are writing an essay, remember to vary and enrich your vocabulary by using synonyms where appropriate.

e Find synonyms in the essay for the following words and phrases.

1 tourists _____, _____
2 effects _____
3 for example _____
4 in general _____, _____

f Complete the missing words. Some (but not all) are in the model essay.

Giving personal opinions

1 I b_____ that…
2 I f_____ that…
3 In my v_____,…
4 In my o_____,…
5 P_____, I think that…

> the influences of tourism are generally positive.

Introducing opposite arguments

6 Some / Many people ar_____…
7 It is often cl_____…
8 There are th_____ / people who say…

> that popular destinations are spoiled by tourism.

Refuting them

9 This m_____ h_____ been true in the past, but n_____…
10 There are a number of fl_____ in this argument.
11 That is simply not the c_____.

PLANNING WHAT TO WRITE

a Read the essay titles. For each one, decide which side of the argument you're going to take, and think of three or four reasons with examples.

> Our lifestyles are less healthy than our grandparents'.

> The impact of social media on our lives is mostly negative.

b Compare with a partner. Decide which you think are the three most important reasons for each essay. Decide on typical opposing arguments which you could refute.

c Choose which of the essays you're going to write. Decide on the main paragraphs and write topic sentences for each one. Show your topic sentences to a partner and see if you can improve each other's sentences.

> **TIPS for writing a discursive essay where you take one side of an argument:**
> - Organize your essay into paragraphs, with a clear introduction and conclusion (see p.124).
> - Begin each paragraph with a clear topic sentence and then develop the idea.
> - Use synonyms to avoid repeating yourself.
> - Use a variety of phrases for giving your opinion and introducing an opposing argument and refuting it.

WRITING

Write an essay of between 220 and 260 words on one of the topics above.

DRAFT your essay.

- Introduction: Introduce the topic and state your opinion.
- Main argument: Write two or three paragraphs giving your reasons and examples.
- Opposing arguments: Write a paragraph stating one or more common opposing argument(s) and refuting each one.
- Conclusion: Sum up, stating what your arguments have shown.

EDIT the essay, making sure you've covered the main points, cutting any irrelevant information, and making sure it's the right length.

CHECK the essay for mistakes in grammar, spelling, punctuation, and register.

⬅ p.83

Writing A formal email

ANALYSING A MODEL TEXT

a Have you ever had a very bad experience at a restaurant or a hotel? What happened? Did you make a complaint, either in person or in writing? What response did you get?

b Read the formal email. What exactly are the complaints?

c With a partner, discuss which phrase, a or b, is better for each gap and why.

1 a I'm sorry to say
   b I am afraid to say

2 a did not live up to our expectations
   b was a complete disaster

3 a were requested to
   b were told we had to

4 a thought was OK
   b considered reasonable

5 a fed up
   b dissatisfied

6 a that is to say
   b I mean

7 a we had been charged
   b you had charged us

8 a they can eat their food
   b their meal can easily be completed

9 a we are owed an apology
   b you ought to say sorry

10 a some form of compensation
    b a lot of money back

From: a.knight10798@gmail.com
To: manager@fiorellis.co.uk
Subject: Complaint

Dear Sir or Madam,

1 I am writing to complain about the meal which my husband and I had on Thursday 16th March at Fiorelli's in Regent Street. ¹____ that the dinner ²____.

2 First of all, according to our online reservation, the table was booked for 7.00 and we ³____ leave the table by 9.00, which we ⁴____. However, the service was extremely slow, and at 8.45, we had only just been brought our dessert. At this point, the waiter not only brought us the bill, but also asked us to hurry, as he would need the table back very soon. This left us feeling extremely ⁵____.

3 Secondly, when we were ordering our meal, the waiter recommended several dishes from the daily 'specials' board and we both chose *tagliatelli al tartufo*. We assumed that the price of this item would be in line with those on the menu, ⁶____, between £10 and £15. However, when the waiter brought the bill, we discovered that ⁷____ a total of £50, making it more than twice as expensive. When we complained to the waiter, he said that we should have asked the price when we ordered; however, in my opinion, the waiter himself should have pointed out that this dish was considerably more expensive than the other choices.

4 I feel strongly that if customers are given a table which has a time limit, the service should be efficient enough to ensure that ⁸____ within that time. I also think that, while it is understandable that some of the daily 'specials' may be more expensive because of the ingredients used, this should always be made clear from the start.

5 Under the circumstances, I believe that ⁹____ and that I should receive ¹⁰____. I look forward to hearing your views on this matter.

Yours faithfully,

Andrew Knight

d Can you remember how the writer expressed the following in a more formal way? Look at the model email again to check your answers.

1 In this email I want to complain…

_____

2 …it said on our online booking…

_____

3 …the waiter gave us the bill <u>and</u> asked us to hurry…

_____

4 I really think that if customers are given a table…

_____

5 Considering what happened…

_____

6 I'd like to know what you think about this.

_____

PLANNING WHAT TO WRITE

a Read a message Hannah sent to a friend. What problems did she have at the Westfield Hotel?

 **Hannah Jones**

Just got back from Brighton. That's the last time we stay at the Westfield Hotel! We stayed there a couple of years ago and had a good time, so I booked again for a week in July. The website described it just as I remembered and said you could have bar food in the evening – you know what a pain it is to have to go out with the kids – so I just went ahead and booked. Anyway, when we turned up, we were gobsmacked! The kitchen and bar area were being done up and they said that in fact they were now a B&B and didn't do any food except for breakfast. It was too late to find anywhere else, so we decided to stay, but it was a nightmare. The builders started making a noise at 7.30 in the morning, the breakfast was rubbish – just cold food because the kitchen wasn't up and running – and we had to buy drinks and sandwiches and take them back to our room in the evening for dinner. I tried to complain, but somehow the manager was never there, only reception staff who weren't really responsible and obviously felt sorry for us. So I'm going to email the manager, and if I don't hear anything, I'm definitely going to put something on Twitter…

2 hours ago

b You're going to write Hannah's email to the manager of the Westfield Hotel. With a partner:

- <u>underline</u> the relevant information in the message.
- summarize exactly what you are dissatisfied with.
- discuss what it would be reasonable for the hotel to do to compensate you for the inconvenience.
- invent any other details you think might be important to include in the email, for example, the exact dates of your stay, the room number, etc.

TIPS for writing an email / letter of complaint:
- Make a note of all the relevant details you want to include before you start drafting your complaint.
- Decide what action you want the person you are writing to to take.
- Use appropriate expressions for opening and closing the email or letter.
- Use a formal style and be clear and assertive, but not aggressive.
- Use the passive, e.g. _we were told, we are owed an apology,_ etc. to make it more impersonal, or to make it clear that you are not accusing individuals.
- Use a variety of expressions for generalizing and making suggestions.

WRITING

Write a formal email of complaint of between 220 and 260 words based on Hannah's experience.

DRAFT your email.
- Introduction: Explain why you are writing.
- Main paragraphs: Say what the complaint relates to and give the details politely.
- Summary paragraph: Restate your complaints briefly.
- Closing sentences: Ask for some action from the hotel.

EDIT the email, checking paragraphing, cutting any irrelevant information, and making sure it's the right length.

CHECK the email for mistakes in grammar, spelling, punctuation, and register.

◀ p.93

Listening

🔊 1.2

1 These four children would never grow old. The photo, taken around 1906, shows the four daughters of Tsar Nicholas II of Russia. After the Russian revolution in 1917, they and their parents and brother were arrested and imprisoned in a house in Yekaterinburg. There, on 17th July 1918, they were executed on the orders of Lenin. For many years after their assassination, there were rumours that the youngest daughter, Anastasia, on the right of the photo, had managed to escape. Several women claimed to have been Anastasia; the best-known impostor was Anna Anderson, a woman living in Germany, whose claims, though rejected by most surviving members of the Tsar's family, were widely believed. In 1979, the bodies of the Tsar and his wife and three of their daughters were discovered near Yekaterinburg, which fuelled the myth that Anastasia had escaped. However, in July 2007, an amateur historian discovered bones near Yekaterinburg belonging to a boy and a young woman, and in April 2008, DNA tests proved that they belonged to two children of Nicholas II, a son and a daughter – Anastasia. As a result, the story of her survival was conclusively disproved.

2 In this rather touching photo, showing his softer family side, US President John F. Kennedy is greeted by his children, John Jr. and Caroline, on his arrival to spend the weekend with them at their summer home in Massachusetts on 23rd August 1963. His natural joy at seeing them may well have been intensified on this occasion by the fact that, a few weeks previously, his third child, a son named Patrick, had died at just a few days old. Almost exactly three months later, on 22nd November, Kennedy was assassinated in Dallas. His son John Jr., as so many of this ill-fated family, also died young in a plane crash in 1999, and Caroline is the only surviving member of the family.

3 Spanish artist Pablo Picasso is seen here with Francoise Gilot and their son Claude in around 1952. Francoise met Picasso in 1943, when she was 21 and he was over 40 years older. Although they never married, they spent nearly ten years together and had two children, Claude and Paloma. However, Francoise and Picasso's relationship was not a happy one, and in 1964, 11 years after their separation, she wrote a damning description of it in her book called *Life with Picasso*. Picasso tried to stop its publication, but he failed, and it went on to sell over one million copies in dozens of languages. From then on, Picasso refused to see Claude or Paloma ever again.

4 In May 1883, the 13-year-old Mohandas Gandhi was married to 14-year-old Kasturba, following the arranged marriage custom of their region at the time. This photo was taken in 1915, when Gandhi was beginning his 32-year struggle for Indian independence, and it is the earliest known photo of Gandhi and his wife. In the first years of their marriage, Gandhi is said to have been a very controlling husband, but writing many years later, he described the feelings he felt for Kasturba at the time: 'Even at school I used to think of her, and the thought of nightfall and our subsequent meeting was ever haunting me.' Despite frequently being apart, their shared beliefs in national independence and education, not to mention a deep emotional attachment, held them together, and their marriage lasted for over 60 years.

5 The importance of family to the great Russian writer Leo Tolstoy apparently influenced his work, especially his two most famous novels, *War and Peace* and *Anna Karenina*. This photo, taken in 1909, shows him telling a story to two of his grandchildren, Ilya and Sonia. Although his relationship with his children and grandchildren was very close, for most of his marriage he and his wife, Sofia, did not get on. She was strongly opposed to many of his views, especially the idea of giving away his private property, and was also jealous of the attention he gave to his many followers. Shortly after this photo was taken, at the age of 82 and after nearly 50 years of marriage, Tolstoy finally made up his mind to separate from her. He left home in the middle of winter, in the dead of night. He took a train south, but when he arrived at Astapovo station a day later, he became ill and died of pneumonia. According to some sources, he had spent the last hours of his life preaching love and non-violence to his fellow passengers on the train.

6 This photo, taken around 1886, is of scientist Albert Einstein with his sister Maja, as small children. They resembled each other physically, and were extremely close – according to Albert, she was his only friend. After Maja's marriage, she and her husband Paul bought a villa in Italy, near Florence, and Albert frequently visited her. In 1939, at the outbreak of World War II, she was forced to leave Italy because she was Jewish. She sought refuge with her beloved brother in the USA, but she had to leave behind her husband, who could not get a visa. Tragically, in 1946, just after the war had ended, she had a stroke, and was unable to travel. She never saw her husband again, and Albert cared for her until her death in 1951.

🔊 1.13

Part 1

Interviewer So first of all, Emma, how did you actually manage to get the jobs?

Emma Well, I got the jobs through a mixture of networking and cold-calling. So applying to different organizations, finding email addresses online, writing cover letters, explaining my project and attaching my CV. Networking was a big part of it, too. So speaking to someone, aware that they themselves might not work in that area, but they might know someone who does.

Interviewer Was two weeks long enough to get a feel for what doing the jobs more long-term would be like?

Emma For me it was, yes, because it was just meant to be enough to get a sense of whether this is something I want to learn more about or whether it's something that's actually not for me. And I found I was very quickly able to decide whether I wanted to learn more or, or actually maybe not so much. It was just enough to get a flavour of it.

Interviewer Was it an issue that you had none of the qualifications for some of the jobs?

Emma Well, no, because I was doing work shadowing, which is more about following a professional around, shadowing their daily lives, rather than having my own set work and projects to do. I wasn't expected to have qualifications or to lead my own work. And this is the case quite often with young people, who go in and just do some work shadowing, and they just don't have the degree or several years' experience that you would need to do professional-level work. It's just to find out if that's the sort of job they would like to do before they then go and do the qualifications and get the experience.

Interviewer Which job did you enjoy most?

Emma One thing that I enjoyed most was alpaca farming in Cornwall, which is in southern England. And I enjoyed it most because it was one of the most – one of the jobs that challenged all of my assumptions about what being a farmer in the 21st century and earning a sustainable living was like. The first half of each day was traditional farming jobs, so feeding, looking after the animals. But the second half of the day, the farmer was an entrepreneur: she would take her alpacas, shear them, make the wool spun, make the, make the wool into high-end luxury children's clothes that she then sold to department stores across the country. And this was a placement that broke down all of my presumptions and preconceptions about what a job was like.

Interviewer Wow. Were there any jobs that you completely ruled out?

Emma So one that I didn't get on quite so well with was publishing, because I'm very dyslexic and so for me, copy-editing – so spotting typos and grammar mistakes in long pieces of text – I find very challenging. It's not one of my strengths, which in publishing, as an editor, is one of the big things that you have to do.

🔊 1.14

Part 2

Interviewer What did you learn about yourself during this process?

Emma I learned that there's not just one job that is right for me. I went into the experience thinking I will do 25 and I will figure out which is my dream job and that's what I'll go away and do. But what I found out was that that's not necessarily true at all. I discovered the concept of portfolio careers, which is the idea of having multiple, part-time, short-term, freelance contract jobs that make up the equivalent of one permanent role.

Interviewer Do you think young people nowadays have to be prepared to do many different jobs? That the whole idea of going into one career for life doesn't exist any more?

Emma Absolutely! I would completely agree with that: I think the idea of one permanent nine-to-five job is, if not dead yet, it will be in the next 20 years. Young people today will have, on average, five different career changes – not job changes, career changes – over the course of their lives, and to do that, they need to be able to continuously upskill and be able to get on with different people, so I think it's people skills, almost more so than technical skills, that will get us through the longevity of our careers. And bear in mind that people of our age are going to be working well into their 70s – our careers are likely to be ultra-marathons, so we have to like what it is that we're doing.

Interviewer And how do you think we can teach 'people skills'?

Emma So personally, I think our education system, both in terms of secondary school, college, and, and university, needs to be much more focused on skills rather than technical subject-based learning. We need to be teaching young people how to network, for example, which is one of the absolute core skills to progress yourself in your career – it's learning how to walk into a room of people you don't know and to find people that are mutually beneficial that you can develop relationships with.

Interviewer So, what are you doing now?

Emma So what I came away with was several different jobs that I ended up doing. So I now work as a public speaker, as a writer doing bits of journalism, and as a speech writer as well, so altogether they make up the equivalent of one full-time job.

Interviewer Do you think your future career might take off in a completely different direction?

Emma I very much expect it to. So one of the main things that I also learnt from doing the project was that there are different careers that are appropriate for different stages of your life. As you get older, you have different priorities, different financial commitments, different stages of your personal life, and that means that you have different jobs that are relevant at different stages of life. So whilst I adored farming and it was one of my favourite placements, I don't think it is right for me, in my 20s, living in a very urban city like London, but me in my 40s perhaps with a family, I might love to move out to the countryside and start a small, a smallholding farm as part of several other elements of a career!

Interviewer Well, thank you Emma so much for talking to us today.

🔊 2.3
Part 1

Presenter 1 Good afternoon, and welcome to Mind over matter, our regular programme about psychology and mental health. Today we're going to be looking at childhood memories.

Presenter 2 Yes, and we'll be investigating where people's first memories come from and hear a story about the famous Swiss psychologist Jean Piaget. But first, let's hear some early childhood memories sent in by our listeners.

Speaker 1 My, my earliest memory – I must have been about three I guess, possibly two – was when we'd been to, to a fun fair, and I would have gone with my brother, who's a bit older than me, and my parents, and I'd been bought, a, a helium balloon, and for some reason the balloon had a snowman inside it. It was only September; I don't why there was a snowman – but, but there was, and I took it out into the back garden and because it was full of helium obviously it was pulling on the string. It wanted to, to fly away, and I let go. I didn't let go by accident; I remember letting go on purpose, to see what would happen, and of course what happened was the balloon flew up into the sky over the neighbours' trees and disappeared, and I was absolutely devastated – heartbroken – by the loss of the balloon, and stood there crying and crying, and my dad had to go back to the funfair and get me another identical balloon, which did nothing to console me. I kept crying and crying and crying and that's my, my earliest memory – not a very happy one!

Speaker 2 My earliest memory is probably from when I was about three or four years old and it was Christmas and I was at my Nana's house with all my family, and my uncle was reading to me. He was reading The Little Mermaid, except that he was making it up – he wasn't actually reading the words in the book, he was just saying things like, 'Ariel went to buy some fish and chips,' and things like that, and that made me quite annoyed because I was at an age where I couldn't really read myself, but I knew that he was reading it wrong. So I got quite annoyed with him and told him to read it properly, but yeah, that's my earliest memory.

Speaker 3 So, my earliest memory, I think I was around two, or two and a half, anyway, something like that. I know that because we were living in a house that my parents lived in

before we moved to the house that we lived in sort of for the rest of our lives. Anyway, it was Christmastime, because I remember there was a Christmas tree in the corner of the room, of the living room and I remember the carpet, it was a sort of, it was kind of like a dark green check and all the sort of glowing of the baubles on the Christmas tree, anyway I remember my mum putting up these Christmas decorations, new they were, onto the Christmas tree, these new baubles, and they were made out of glass, and then she had to go out of the room for something, and I remember taking one of these new glass baubles in my hand, and I remember putting my finger into the glass and breaking one of them – I don't really know why I did it – anyway, then my mum came back into the room and I remember her shouting at me and, and being really angry because I'd broken one of these new baubles, and I remember feeling actually quite resentful at the time because I didn't really think it was a bad thing to do.

🔊 2.4
Part 2

Presenter 1 So, what age do most people's first memories come from? And are our first memories reliable, or are they sometimes based on something people have told us? John's been looking at some of the research into how our memories work. Let's start at the beginning, then, John. At what age do first memories generally occur?

Presenter 2 Well, according to research, 80% of our first memories are of things which happened to us between the ages of two and four. In fact, a large study by Professor Martin Conway in 2018 concluded that it's impossible to remember events from before the age of two.

Presenter 1 That's interesting, because a lot of people would say they do have earlier memories.

Presenter 2 Yes, in fact the 2018 study asked 6,000 people for their earliest memories, and around 40% of them said they remembered being in their pram or cot, or the first time they walked, or the first word they spoke. But according to research, that just isn't possible.

Presenter 1 Why is that?

Presenter 2 There seem to be three main reasons. The first is that before the age of two, children don't have a clear sense of themselves as individuals – they can't usually identify themselves in a photo. And you know how a very small child enjoys seeing himself in a mirror, but he doesn't actually realize that the person he can see is him. Children of this age also have problems with the pronouns I and you. And a memory without I is impossible – we can't begin to have memories until we have an awareness of self.

Presenter 1 And the second reason?

Presenter 2 The second reason is related to language. According to research, first memories coincide with the development of linguistic skills, with a child learning to talk. And as far as memory is concerned, it's essential for a child to be able to use the past tense, so that he or she can talk about something that happened in the past, and then remember it. And finally, it seems that the part of the brain needed for memories to form doesn't function fully until a few years after birth.

Presenter 1 And what are first memories normally about? I mean, is it possible to generalize at all?

Presenter 2 Early memories seem to be related to strong emotions, such as happiness, unhappiness, pain, and surprise. Research suggests that three quarters of first memories are related to fear, to frightening experiences like being left alone, or a large dog, or having an accident – things like falling off a swing in a park.

And of course this makes sense, and bears out the evolutionary theory that the human memory is linked to self-preservation. You remember these things in order to be prepared if they happen again, so that you can protect yourself.

Presenter 1 So are first memories only related to emotions, or are there any specific events that tend to become first memories?

Presenter 2 The events that are most often remembered, and these are always related to one of the emotions I mentioned before, are the birth of a baby brother or sister, a death, or a family visit. Another interesting aspect is that first memories tend to be very visual. They're almost invariably described as pictures, not smells or sounds. For example, festive celebrations with bright lights are mentioned quite frequently.

Presenter 1 Is it true that first memories are often unreliable, in that sometimes they're not real memories, just things our families have told us about ourselves or that we've seen in photos?

Presenter 2 Absolutely! As I said, some people insist that their first memories are of learning to walk or sitting in a pram, but it's very unlikely that they would form such early memories, for all the reasons I've mentioned. But family stories can definitely be incorporated into our memory. So if your mother tells you the first word you ever said, over the years that becomes your memory – you think you can remember it. A good example of that is the famous case of the Swiss psychologist Jean Piaget…

🔊 2.5
Part 3

Presenter 2 A good example of that is the famous case of the Swiss psychologist Jean Piaget. In the 1890s, when Piaget was a baby, his nanny used to take him for walks around Paris in his pram. Piaget had always thought that his first memory was of sitting in his pram as a two-year-old baby when a man tried to kidnap him. He remembered exactly where it happened, on the Champs-Elysées. He remembered his nanny fighting the kidnapper, and he could remember a policeman appearing, and the man running away. The nanny was then given a watch as a reward by Jean's parents. But many years later, when Piaget was 15, his parents received a letter from the nanny in which she returned the watch to them. The nanny confessed that she'd made up the whole story, and that was why she was returning the watch. Of course, Jean had heard the story told so many times that he was convinced that he'd remembered the whole incident.

Presenter 1 That's fascinating. Thank you very much, John.

🔊 2.9

My earliest memory is from when I must have been nearly three and we were moving house. We moved to a block of flats and I remember arriving and it was, it was dark and we'd had quite a long journey, and we arrived and we went in the door and we turned the lights on and nothing happened, and the whole flat was completely black and dark – no power, no electricity, no light – and I thought this was fantastic, and we had a torch and I was just running around, running around the, the hall and the rooms, finding all these new rooms, all with a torch, and I imagined that it was always going to be like that – that we'd, we'd arrived in a house that wasn't going to have light, so I was always going to have to use a torch. And I thought that was going to be brilliant. My mother was in tears, obviously she, she was very stressed from the journey and arriving somewhere and having no power. But I, I was really, really excited by it, and the next day when the power came on, I was really disappointed.

 Go online to listen to the audio and see all the Listening scripts

2.14

1 **Mairi** I'm from a small village on the south-east coast of Scotland. It's a very small place; not very many people live there. I liked growing up there, but I think it's a better place to visit than it is to actually live because there isn't very much for young people to do there. The people are quite nice and friendly, but most people have spent their whole lives there and their families have been there for several generations, so sometimes it can seem a bit insular.

2 **Diarmuid** I'm from Tipperary, which is in the middle of Ireland. It's quite a rural place. The town I'm from has a population of around 2,000, so it's quite small, but that means that most people know each other. So I'd say the people there are friendly and quite welcoming.

3 **Laura** So, I was born in Kaunas, which is the second-largest city in Lithuania. It is very modern. It has a lot of art galleries, and we even have seven universities in the city, which is quite a lot considering the size of it. It is super green, it has a lot of lakes and within the country it's considered to be a centre for cultural, academic, and economic activities. I would say as well that it's a home to various nationalities, and once you get to know people, they're really friendly, and really welcoming.

4 **Jerry** I'm from Oxford in the south-east of England. I, I was born here and I've, I've lived here my whole life. Difficult to say what the people are like because it's, in a way it's a city of two halves, famous for its university, but also – which obviously has people from all over the world – but also, it's a city in its own right. It has a very large BMW factory, where they make Minis, so, but it's a nice place; I like it. I've lived here my whole life pretty much, so, so there we are.

5 **Andrea** So I'm from Melbourne, which is on the south-east coast of Australia, just in, in the state of Victoria. This is a really cultural city – very European. You've got everything from beaches to art galleries, lots of shopping, and bars and restaurants, so it's a fantastic city to be in. The people are really laid-back and, and quite friendly there. We've got a very big mixture of cultures there, so a very multicultural city. So it's quite diverse and a really interesting place to be.

6 **Anita** I'm from Salamanca in Spain. It's a really beautiful city. It's got an old town with lots of monuments, and people are really nice, because there is a big university as well, there is lots of students, and that means there is always something going on. Students like organizing theatre or music events, lots of different things. And people like going out a lot, so there is always people out in the street, full families, from grandparents to parents to, to children. And there is also lots of tourists throughout the year, so you can always go somewhere and there is something happening.

7 **Lily** I'm from New Jersey and it's a nice mix between rural and city life because it, it has a lot of nature and nice kind of mountain landscapes where you can go hiking or walking, but it also has nice access to the city and lots of nice little shops and restaurants as well.

8 **Paul** OK, I was born in Johannesburg in the late, in the late 50s. I moved to Cape Town when I went to university and of course it's a very beautiful old colonial centre, with lovely buildings, and the aspect of Table Bay with the beautiful backdrop of Table Mountain, wonderful vegetation, and a wonderful friendly community of people. It's very vibrant and exciting, people like bright colours in the strong sunlight, it's a very creative environment.

3.4

Challenge one: Approach a stranger
James suggested that I talk to guys in bookshops, mainly because I love books, but also because, as he pointed out, bookshops are a nice calm space to start a conversation, much better than a packed Tube train. So I had a go, but it was absolutely terrifying. I tried smiling and saying, 'Ooh, that one's very good', but it just didn't feel natural at all, and even though a couple of guys responded positively, I just couldn't move from 'that one's very good' to natural conversation. So, in the end, I left the shop with zero phone numbers and more books to gather dust on my shelves.

I can sort of see how this method might work for some people, but I'd still rather use my thumb and my phone. I'd give this challenge 2 out of 5.

Challenge two: Try a new activity
OK, so my next challenge was to try something new, and I thought I'd take my housemate, Charlie, to a club that had minigolf. This challenge was Hayley's idea, and she suggested I shouldn't use conventional chat-up lines, like, I don't know, 'Do you come here often?' and that I should try and be as natural as possible.

Anyway, so after our game of minigolf, I managed to catch the eye of a guy who was sipping a pint of beer across the bar. He was tall and had dark hair, my typical type in fact. I remembered Hayley's advice, and I walked over to him, with Charlie to help me feel more confident, and I told him that Charlie and I had a bet to guess his name. Of course our guesses were all wrong and we ended up laughing hysterically. He turned out to be called Rob – our idea was Harold – and though I was nervous talking to him at first, it quite quickly felt as easy as talking to a friend at a party. And guess what? We exchanged numbers and have been chatting online ever since. So, I'd definitely recommend trying something new, outside of your comfort zone, 5 out of 5.

Challenge three: Go to an event for singles
I decided to go to a singles' event, because I thought that before dating apps existed, these must have worked. I sort of imagined there'd be professional people who live in London, a bit like me, people who'd signed up because they were too busy to go looking for dates, or perhaps who were also fed up of apps.

So, as soon as I got there, I had two glasses of wine and that meant I was happy to chat with pretty much anyone, but the awkward atmosphere was painful and sort of embarrassing. No one was talking – they were just standing in small groups of either men or women and sort of looking round at the others in the room. Anyway, I plucked up the courage and went up to a couple of guys, but they both made it clear that they weren't interested in me. And then I tried chatting to another guy eating a burrito, but he seemed more interested in the burrito than me. So I felt like a bit of a failure, and to be honest I'd only give singles events 1 out of 5.

Challenge four: Ask a friend to set up a blind date
A blind date is one of the most classic dating techniques I could think of, so I texted a few friends and asked them to set me up. They took ages, but after a while I finally managed to get a friend to organize a date for me. She gave me his first name, which was Tom, and a photo, and told me to head to a restaurant that night at 7.30. Of course, I really wanted to look him up on every social media site in order to prepare, but then I reminded myself that this was supposed to be real life. But because I knew nothing about him, I got way more nervous than before any other first date I'd been on.

Tom was a bit late, but we immediately got chatting about American politics, and I think I was probably more 'myself' than I'd ever been on a date from a dating app. The fact that we didn't know anything about each other meant we discovered things on equal terms, and that was a nice change. And he was funny, and asked interesting questions, and all that showed me that dating in real life can be fun. And I'd only just left the restaurant when he texted me to say that he'd had a great time. So that was a good experience, 4 out of 5.

3.6

The verdict
Well, after the four challenges I think the main thing I learnt was that pushing myself out of my comfort zone, and actually looking at men outside of a screen showed me just how many opportunities there are to meet people in real life. Catching a stranger's eye started off as terrifying, but it also gave me a real buzz, and I really surprised myself, that I was able to chat someone up for the first time in my life.

Obviously, I didn't find love, and sadly the texting with Rob and Tom has dried up – but those positive experiences taught me a lot, and I won't rule out real-life flirting in the future. But although I found the experience confidence-boosting, I'm not sure I'm completely converted. I found that approaching guys with no idea even whether they're single or not was more stressful than fun. If I get a match on an app, we already have things in common, and I know they're looking for a match too. So I'm not giving up my apps just yet.

3.14

Part 1
Interviewer How important is historical accuracy in a historical film?

Adrian The notion of accuracy in history is a really difficult one in drama because, you know, it's like saying, 'Well, was Macbeth accurate? Was – is – Shakespearean drama accurate?' The iro– the thing is, it's not about historical accuracy, it's about whether you can make a drama work from history that means something to an audience now. So I tend to take the view that, in a way, accuracy isn't the issue when it comes to the drama: if you're writing a drama, you, you have the right as a writer to create the drama that works for you, so you can certainly change details. The truth is nobody really knows how people spoke in Rome or how people spoke in the courts of Charles II or William the Conqueror or Victoria, or whoever; you have an idea from writing, from books, and plays, and so on. We know when certain things happened, what sort of dates happened. I think it's really a question of judgement: if you make history ridiculous, if you change detail to the point where history is an absurdity, then obviously things become more difficult. The truth is, the, the more recent history is, the more difficult it is not to be authentic to it. In a way, it's much easier to play fast and loose with the details of what happened in Rome than it is to play fast and loose with the details of what happened in the Iraq War, say, you know. So it, it, it's all a matter of perspective in some ways. It, it, it's something that you have to be aware of and which you try to be faithful to, but you can't ultimately say a drama has to be bound by the rules of history, because that's not what drama is.

Interviewer Do you think that the writer has a responsibility to represent any kind of historical truth?

Adrian Not unless that's his intention. If it's your intention to be truthful to history, and you, and you put a piece out saying this is the true story of, say, the murder of Julius Caesar exactly as the historical record has it, then of course, you do have an obligation, because if you then deliberately tell lies about it, you are, you know, you're deceiving your audience. If, however, you say you're writing a drama about the assassination of Julius Caesar purely from your own perspective and entirely in a fictional context, then you have the right to tell the story however you like. I don't think you have any obligation except to the, to the story that you're telling. What you can't be is deliberately dishonest; you can't say this is true when you know full well it isn't.

3.15
Part 2

Interviewer Can you think of any examples where you feel the facts have been twisted too far?

Adrian Well, I think the notion of whether a film, a historical film, has gone too far in presenting a dramatized fictional version of the truth is really a matter of personal taste. The danger is, with any historical film, that if that becomes the only thing that the audience sees on that subject – if it becomes the received version of the truth, as it were, because people don't always make the distinction between movies and reality and history – then obviously if that film is grossly irresponsible or grossly fantastic in its, in its presentation of the truth, that could, I suppose, become controversial. I mean, if you – you know, I think that the only thing anybody is ever likely to know about Spartacus, for example, the movie, is Kirk Douglas and all his friends standing up and saying, 'I am Spartacus, I am Spartacus', which is a wonderful moment and it stands for the notion of freedom of individual choice and so on. So Spartacus, the film made in 1962, I think, if memory serves, bec– has become, I think, for nearly everybody who knows anything about Spartacus, the only version of the truth. Now in fact, we don't know if any of that is true, really. There are some accounts of the historical Spartacus, but very, very few, and what – virtually the only thing that's known about it is that there was a man called Spartacus and there was a rebellion and many people were, you know, were crucified at the end of it, as in, as in the film. Whether that's irresponsible, I don't know. I, I can't say that I think it is. I think, in a way, it's, it's, it's… Spartacus is a film that had a resonance in the modern era.

There are other examples, you know: a lot of people felt that the version of William Wallace that was presented in Braveheart was really pushing the limits of what history could stand. The whole, in effect, his whole career was invented in the film, or at least, yeah, built on to such a degree that some people felt that perhaps it was more about the notion of Scotland as an independent country than it was about history as an authentic spectacle. But you know, again, these things are a matter of purely personal taste – I mean, I enjoyed Braveheart immensely.

4.1

A Well, I, I remember reading *Catch 22* by I think it's Joseph Heller. And I actually started it one night – it was, we'd gone to, to France, to this campsite and they'd all gone to bed, so I went ahead and started it that night. And when I woke up the next morning, I just sat under a tree in the shade and read the whole thing from start to finish. Yeah, I think it's the only book I've ever done that with, didn't do it before or since, yeah.

B Yeah, yes, so there is a book that, well, it's a, a book from my childhood and it's called *Carbonel*, by Barbara Sleigh. And I always really feel that, well, you know, it's got everything, it's got…what's in it? It's got a, a talking cat, a curse, there's a witch, there's loads of children. And I really just don't understand why this hasn't been made into a children's film or even an animated film really, to be honest. It's, it's just such a good story, and it's got really great characters, and it's, it's a very visual book. So a lot of the things that it describes, you can, you can just sort of see it, and I think it's a missed opportunity. I really think someone in Hollywood should definitely pick this one up.

C Well, there's been a couple of things recently that I've seen on television and then read the book afterwards, and one of those was *Big Little Lies*. So, that was turned into a TV series on HBO, I think. And another was on, it was

a film on Netflix and it was called *To all the boys I've loved before*, which is a young adult book that I then went on to read afterwards, it wouldn't usually be my thing, but I read the whole series of three books, it was fantastic.

D So, there's a book I've started a couple of times, it's called *The Silmarillion* by Tolkien, and like, it's sort of more information about the world that *The Lord of the Rings* saga happens in. But I just find the beginning so boring and I cannot finish it, and I know that a friend of mine has told me about some really interesting bits that come up later on, but I cannot get to them. I just keep reading about someone, son of someone and it gets really, really boring, really, really soon. So I think I'll have to try again, but I still have not managed to get to the end of it.

E I remember we had to read *The War of the Worlds*, by H. G. Wells, when I was at school. I was about ten at the time, and I remember thinking oh, this looks, you know, really exciting, 'cause I really, I really was into science fiction as a kid, and, and, the cover looked, you know, like really exciting. So I thought this is going to be fantastic; we're going to be, you know, doing something really this exciting, it's, you know, we're really lucky, but…I started it and oh, it was, it was just too hard for somebody, well I think if ten years old. The, the vocabulary was difficult; the sentences went on forever, it was really hard to follow them. And it was just frustrating, because I was just sort of looking at the words and I sort of knew when to turn the page, but I hadn't really remembered what I'd just read. So yeah, I didn't get to understand the story at all, and I – the thing is, it sort of put me off H.G. Wells, because I've not really read any since.

F Well I've got to say, I've hardly read any classics at all, or any of those ones that win prizes, and, and stuff, that get reviewed in, in papers. So, like, I've never read *To Kill a Mockingbird*, for example, yeah, you know, all those, those classics. Think I've read one Jane Austen book. And I, I feel as if I should address this, maybe read some Charles Dickens or…and I just can't concentrate on it, to be honest. It's just…, and for me, reading is a way of switching off, so I don't really want to read anything that's quite a struggle.

4.4
Part 1

Interviewer What made you want to be a translator?

Beverly It was something that I'd done when I was at university, and when I moved to Spain, it was difficult to get a job that wasn't teaching English, so I went back to England and I did a postgraduate course in translation. After doing the course, I swore that I would never be a translator – I thought it would be too boring – but I kept doing the odd translation, and eventually I, I came round to the idea because I liked the idea of working for myself, and it didn't require too much investment to get started. And, and actually, I enjoy working with words, and it's, it's very satisfying when you feel that you've produced a reasonable translation of the original text.

Interviewer What are the pros and cons of being a translator?

Beverly Well, um, it's a lonely job I suppose – you know, you're on your own most of the time. It's hard work – you're sitting there and, you know, you're working long hours, and you can't programme things because you don't know when more work is going to come in, and people have always got tight deadlines. You know, it's really rare that somebody'll, 'll ring you up and say, 'I want this translation in three months' time'. You know, that, that just doesn't really happen.

Interviewer And the pros?

Beverly Well, the pros are that it, it gives you

freedom, because you can do it anywhere if you've got an internet connection and electricity, and I suppose you can organize your time, 'cause you're freelance – you know, you're your own boss, which is good. I, I like that.

Interviewer What advice would you give someone who's thinking of going into translation?

Beverly I'd say that – I'd say, in addition to the language, get a speciality. Do another course in anything that interests you, like economics, law, history, art, because you really need to know about the subjects that you're translating into.

4.5
Part 2

Interviewer What do you think is the most difficult kind of text to translate?

Beverly Literary texts, like novels, poetry, or drama because you've got to give a lot of consideration to the author, and to the way it's been written in the original language.

Interviewer In order to translate a novel well, do you think you need to be a novelist yourself?

Beverly I think that's true ideally, yes.

Interviewer And is that the case? I mean, are most of the well-known translators of novels, generally speaking, novelists in their own right?

Beverly Yes, I think in English, anyway. People who translate into English tend to be published authors, and they tend to specialize in a particular author in the other language. And of course, if it's a living author, then it's so much easier because you can actually communicate with the author and say, you know, like, 'What did you really mean here?'

Interviewer Another thing I've heard that is very hard to translate is advertising – for example, slogans.

Beverly Yeah, well, with advertising, the problem is that it's got to be something punchy, and, and it's very difficult to translate that. For example, one of the Coca Cola adverts, the slogan in English was 'the real thing', but you just couldn't translate that literally into Spanish – it, it just wouldn't have had the same power. In fact, it became Sensación de vivir, which is 'sensation of living', which sounds, sounds really good in Spanish, but it, it would sound weird in English.

Interviewer What about film titles?

Beverly Ah, they're horrific, too. People always complain that they've not been translated accurately, but of course it's impossible because sometimes a literal translation just doesn't work.

Interviewer For example?

Beverly OK, well, think of, you know, the Julie Andrews film *The Sound of Music*. Well, that works in English because it's a phrase that you know – you know, like, 'I can hear the sound of music'. But it doesn't work at all in other languages, and in Spanish it was called *Sonrisas y Lágrimas*, which means 'Smiles and Tears'. Now let me –, in German it was called *Meine Lieder, meine Träume*, which means 'My Songs, My Dreams', and in Italian it was *Tutti insieme appassionatamente*, which means, I think, 'All Together Passionately', or, I don't know, something like that. In fact, I think it was translated differently all over the world.

Interviewer Do you think there are special problems translating film scripts, for the subtitles?

Beverly Yes, a lot. There are special constraints, for example the translation has to fit on the screen as the actor is speaking, and so sometimes the translation is a paraphrase rather than a direct translation, and of course, well, going back to untranslatable things, really the big problems are cultural, and humour, because they're, they're just not the same. You can get across the idea, but you might need pages to explain it, and, you know, by that time

 Go online to listen to the audio and see all the Listening scripts

the film's moved on. I also sometimes think that the translators are given the film on DVD – I mean, you know, rather than a written script – and that sometimes they've simply misheard or they didn't understand what the people said. And that's the only explanation I can come up with for some of the mistranslations that I've seen. Although sometimes it might be that some things like, like humour and jokes, especially ones which depend on wordplay, are just, you know, they're, they're simply untranslatable. And often it's very difficult to get the right register, for example with, with slang and swear words, because if you literally translate taboo words or swear words, even if they exist in the other language, they may well be far more offensive.

🔊 **4.14**

1 My next-door neighbours have just got a dog. I've always really liked dogs, but this one just absolutely drives me mad. It barks at everything. It barks at the rain, it barks at traffic, barks at the wind. And it's got a really high-pitched yappy bark. And, yeah, it barks all day, all night, it drives me mad.

2 A sound that I really can't stand, I actually detest this sound, is the sound of my daughter eating popcorn whenever we go to the cinema together. I always make her buy a small box, because otherwise it takes her forever to finish and get to the bottom. But it's the, the crunch, the sound of the little kernels in her mouth, the, the, the chew, the, the, all the sounds inside her mouth. It's just so irritating.

3 I do this quite funny thing, so when my kids are in bed, I often go in and I just listen to them breathing when they're asleep. And it's – really calms me down, this sort of, steady breathing. And it makes me feel really happy and calm, and reassured that they're healthy, and they're at home, and well actually, also the fact that they're fast asleep! So I can get some time to myself, you know, some peace and quiet.

4 I find the sound of the sea just, just makes me feel relaxed, it makes me at peace. Doesn't matter if it's a gentle sea against a beach, or ocean crashing against rocks, I just, it just calms me down. I love it. I've even got an app on my phone of sea sounds which helps me if I'm travelling and I can't get to sleep somewhere. I always put that on, helps me relax.

5 I think it's when I hear the constant beeping of all my different kitchen appliances, you know, the washing machine, or the dishwasher. And…when you think they've, they've finished, and, but you don't know and then it goes beep, and then a minute later, beep, beep, beep and it gets louder, just so you know it's really finished what it's doing, you know, it's talking to you. I just find it so annoying. It really annoys my husband too, you know, you're sitting there, trying to have a nice relaxing evening watching the TV and then, you know, one of you has to get up and go and attend to it, go and turn it off.

6 Well, the sound of a baby laughing – or like, giggling, I love that. I was watching something on YouTube the other day, and, with like, young babies and pets, and the babies were just giggling all over the place, they were roaring with laughter, and I t thought it was one of the happiest, like, sweetest sounds I'd ever heard.

7 Listening to music played very quietly so that you can't actually hear it. Music should be something that you want to hear properly and more loudly, not just there, playing quietly, irritating you. And the other thing is background music, like lift music, that you don't want to hear at all. I don't like hearing any music 'unwillingly'!

8 Well, the sound of the train – I, I find it really relaxing, because the sound fits perfectly along with the movement of the train, moving along and the jolting backwards and forwards, and…

Oh, but I do need to be sitting facing forwards rather than backwards, because otherwise I feel really train-sick.

🔊 **5.1**

The Chocolate Meditation
Again and again people tell us that mindfulness greatly enhances the joys of daily life. In practice, even the smallest of things can suddenly become captivating again. For this reason, one of our favourite practices is the chocolate meditation. In this, you ask yourself to bring all your attention to some chocolate as you're eating it. So if you want to do this right now, choosing some chocolate, not unwrapping it yet, choosing a type that you've never tried before, or one that you've not eaten recently. It might be dark and flavoursome, organic, or Fairtrade, or whatever you choose. Perhaps choosing a type you wouldn't normally eat, or that you consume only rarely.

Before you unwrap the chocolate, look at the whole bar or packet – its colour, its shape, what it feels like in your hand – as if you were seeing it for the very first time. Now very slowly unwrapping the chocolate, noticing how the wrapping feels as you unfold it, seeing the chocolate itself. What colours do you notice? What shapes? Inhaling the aroma of the chocolate, letting it sweep over you. And now taking or breaking off a piece and looking at it as it rests on your hand, really letting your eyes drink in what it looks like, examining every nook and cranny. At a certain point, bringing it up to your mouth, noticing how the hand knows where to position it, and popping it in the mouth, noticing what the tongue does to receive it. See if it's possible to hold it on your tongue and let it melt, noticing any tendency to chew it, seeing if you can sense some of the different flavours, really noticing these.

If you notice your mind wandering while you do this, simply noticing where it went, then gently escorting it back to the present moment.

And then, when the chocolate has completely melted, swallowing it very slowly and deliberately, letting it trickle down your throat.

What did you notice? If the chocolate tasted better than if you'd just eaten it at a normal pace, what do you make of that? Often we taste the first piece and perhaps the last, but the rest goes down unnoticed. We're so often on autopilot, we can miss much of our day-to-day lives. Mindfulness is about bringing awareness to the usual routine things in life, things that we normally take for granted. Perhaps you could try this with any routine activity, seeing what you notice? It could change your whole day.

🔊 **5.2**

How long is it before we get frustrated at people talking during a movie, or waiting for a date who hasn't shown up? I veer wildly between patience and impatience. It's probably good to know whether you're more or less patient than the average person, so I was interested to read the results of a survey by the watch company Timex asking people how long they were willing to wait in various situations before losing patience. Some of the results seem about right. However, some seem wildly unlikely, based on my experience of how people tend to behave.

First, a car in front of you at a green light – average time before getting annoyed, 50 seconds. This is the one result that seems least believable to me. FIFTY SECONDS waiting behind someone at a green light? From what I've observed, it's more like five seconds, maybe even less.

Then, waiting for people to stop talking in a movie theater – average wait, 1 minute, 52 seconds. This also seems a long time. For me, it depends – if it's a really sad or emotional story, and they're ruining the atmosphere, I shush them after five seconds, but if it's a full-blown action movie, then it doesn't really bug me.

Next, crying babies. Apparently, it takes almost

three minutes (2 minutes, 41 seconds, to be precise) before someone gives parents a dirty look because their baby is screaming. That sounds quite a long time to me, and what they didn't ask was how long people would wait to ask a flight attendant if they can switch seats when they realize they're sitting right next to a screaming baby. That would have to be in the 30-second range, right?

Waiting to see the doctor is something everyone expects to take a while. 32 minutes on average before people get mad doesn't seem unreasonable. I suppose there are always magazines to read, even though they're usually several years out of date.

Now, what about waiting for your partner to get ready? Average wait, 21 minutes. I assume that means 21 minutes after you're ready yourself? I think that's too long to wait. I can get ready to go out in approximately 10 minutes – shower, change, coat on, ready! My wife, on the other hand…

The next one also seems pretty long. Maybe from entering the coffee shop to actually drinking your coffee could take 7 minutes. But just waiting in line? Presumably not during rush hour, when customers just want a takeout and the baristas generally know what they're doing?

What about if your blind date is late? The survey says that the average time before people get angry and leave is 26 minutes. That seems like the right amount of time for you to experience that scene from romantic comedies where the main character is sitting at a table, checking his or her phone, and finally decides to leave when the server offers them 'More bread?' for the fourth time.

Finally, the average wait before angrily asking some over-confident business-type next to you talking loudly on a cellphone to quiet down – 2 minutes, 25 seconds. Well, everyone in the world must be more patient than me. But my tip here is: just make facial expressions to let them know you're annoyed. Really exaggerated facial expressions. Works every time.

🔊 **5.3**

1 One thing I really, really hate is waiting at home for a delivery, 'cause sometimes they'll, they'll give you a, a delivery slot of, of, of two hours and that's fine you know when it's coming, but more often they'll say it could be any time from 7 a.m. to 7 p.m., and then you're just stuck in the house – you don't even dare go out in case you miss them – and of course it always ends up coming at two minutes to seven, and you've just spent the whole day waiting, wasting your time at home.

2 So, what annoys me is, oh, you know when you have to wait for ages for like, films and TV programmes to download? It doesn't really happen so much nowadays, but from time to time, I'll be somewhere where there's like, really bad internet connection and it really irritates me. I'll be sort of sitting there, watching that little download icon moving at, at an absolute snail's pace.

3 I really hate waiting for anything where I've been given an appointment time for a specific hour – you know, a specific time – and then having to wait for ages before I actually have it, so, well, you know, for example a hairdresser or a dentist or a doctor. I mean, I'm very punctual, so I always turn up on time – in fact, usually at least five minutes early – and it really, really annoys me if I have to wait for a long time. Anything more than 15 minutes over the appointment time drives me completely insane.

🔊 **5.14**

Interviewer So, Alessandro, how did the idea of Pasta Evangelists come about?

Alessandro Well, I'm half Italian, half English; and I've always been interested in, in the sector of food and beverages; and I'd been thinking about creating a new brand in the food and beverage sector for quite a while. And I saw an opportunity of creating potentially the first premium, artisanal fresh pasta brand in the UK, even internationally, and so two and a half years ago we started by selling gnocchi to my friends.

Interviewer Where are you based?

Alessandro Our business is based in London, however our product is distributed and sold everywhere in the UK. We have an office in Farringdon, our kitchen is in East London, and we also have a concession, a Pasta Evangelist concession, in Harrods.

Interviewer Who actually makes the pasta?

Alessandro So, so, yeah, we have a whole team of sfoglini, Maria Rosaria, Olivia, Michelangelo, Federica, Francisca, who make fresh pasta every day. So, sfoglini is an Italian word which means 'pasta artisans', and it derives from the word sfoglia, which is the pasta sheet. All our sfoglini are Italians. Having said that, we are also training non-Italians to, to make pasta, such as Dorina, Semeya, Veronica – so people from Poland, Russia, Bangladesh – why not?

Interviewer Where do you get your ingredients from?

Alessandro We have a quite extensive number of different suppliers for our ingredients because we make hundreds of different recipes. So we're always, always working with new suppliers, veg, meat, fish, eggs, flours, and I would say that we, we, we work with a mix of both Italian suppliers for some ingredients, but also British suppliers, and I think I would say that the quality and the freshness of the produce is what we're most after, as well as the authenticity, whether it's the pistachios from Sicily or hazelnuts from Piemonte. It really depends.

Interviewer Approximately how much money did you need to raise to get the project off the ground?

Alessandro So, whilst it was relatively inexpensive to get the business started, i.e. I invested £2,000, and even the second step was relatively – well, was not colossal, i.e. £60,000 – once we were keen to increase growth, we had to raise larger amounts of money, i.e. we raised half a million and then £1.7 million.

Interviewer One of the ways in which you tried to get more investment was appearing on *Dragons' Den*. What happened when you went on the programme?

Alessandro The *Dragons' Den* was really an amazing, an amazing experience. We, we really enjoyed it. It gave immediate visibility to the brand to approximately two million individuals across the UK. It was free. And the brand was shown in a very positive light and we were able to showcase our products, our craftsmanship, and our story. Having said that, we didn't raise the capital from the Dragons.

Interviewer What would you say is the unique selling point, the USP, of Pasta Evangelists?

Alessandro The USP is probably the quality, the quality of the product, which is reflected, which is a reflection of the artisanality, the freshness, the originality, the ingredients themselves, the craftsmanship of the product, the fact that it's made by hand. So, yeah, a hand-made fresh product probably is our USP.

Interviewer Who are your main competitors?

Alessandro I don't think there is direct competition, i.e at the moment, to our knowledge, there aren't companies doing what we're doing – exactly what we're doing. Having said that, the food industry itself is massively competitive and therefore we're fighting for the same shares of wallets as thousands of other companies. Especially in the UK, in London, people are bombarded with different offers, different companies, new brands, existing brands, restaurants, takeaway, Deliveroo, recipe boxes, so it is very competitive overall.

Interviewer How do your prices compare with having an Italian pasta dish in a restaurant?

Alessandro I'm glad you, you suggested that our competition is Italian restaurants, rather than supermarket pasta or takeaway pasta, or other recipe boxes, because indeed we see ourselves as 'restaurant quality' delivered to your home. Having said that, our dishes are on average 20, 30, in some cases 40% less expensive than an equivalent dish sold in a restaurant in London, an Italian restaurant. And our pricing varies depending on what dish it is. We've done more than 200 different pasta recipes to date, and the pricing varies from six pounds to perhaps a more, let's say, simple dish, to twelve pounds for a more luxurious pasta dish.

Interviewer How would you describe a typical customer?

Alessandro It's hard to say, because we do have, our product is…we, we define it as quite democratic, in that it's a product which appeals to several different types of customers – we have families, we have younger couples, we have people who buy it as a special occasion for dinner parties.

Interviewer Where do you sell your products?

Alessandro So, roughly a third of our sales are in London; two thirds are outside of London. So every day we ship hundreds of boxes from Cornwall, to Scotland, to Wales, to the Isle of Man, everywhere, everywhere, we find and we actually find that most locations where we ship to, apart from London, are small villages we've never heard of, where there is less availability of high, you know, high-quality convenience food, where, where it's more difficult to find a product like ours.

Interviewer Are you hoping to expand your business?

Alessandro So, yeah, we, we think that the market for our products in the UK is, is fairly vast. We think we've just scratched the surface. There's much more we can do. And we just started only two years ago, and so our plan is certainly to grow. Hopefully we can grow four-fold this year.

Interviewer Yes, well thank you very much Alessandro, it's been lovely talking to you.

🔊 6.1

Nowadays, we're surrounded by some powerful ideas about the sort of things that will make us happy. The first of these is that we tend to think that really to deliver satisfaction, the pleasures we should aim for need to be rare. We've become suspicious of the ordinary, which we assume is mediocre, dull, and uninspiring, and likewise we assume that things that are unique, hard to find, exotic, or unfamiliar are naturally going to give us more pleasure.

Then, we want things to be expensive. If something is expensive, we value it more, whereas if something is cheap or free, it's a little harder to appreciate. The pineapple, for instance, dropped off a lot of people's wish list of fruit when its price fell from exorbitant (they used to cost the equivalent of hundreds of pounds) to unremarkable. Caviar continues to sound somehow more interesting than eggs.

Then, we want things to be famous. In a fascinating experiment, a well-known violinist once donned scruffy clothes and busked at a street corner and was largely ignored, though people would flock to the world's greatest concert halls to hear just the same man play just the same pieces.

Lastly, we want things to be large-scale. We're mostly focused on big schemes that we hope will deliver big kinds of enjoyment: marriage, career, travel, getting a new house.

These approaches aren't entirely wrong, but they unintentionally create an unhelpful bias against the cheap, the easily available, the ordinary, the familiar, and the small-scale. As a result, if someone says they've been on a trip to a Caribbean island by private jet, we automatically assume they had a better time than someone who went to the local park by bike. We imagine that visiting the Uffizi Gallery in Florence is always going to be nicer than reading a paperback novel in the back garden. A restaurant dinner at which lobster thermidor is served sounds a good deal more impressive than a supper of a cheese sandwich at home. The highlight of a weekend seems more likely to be a hang-gliding lesson, rather than a few minutes spent looking at the cloudy sky. It feels odd to suggest that a modest vase of lily of the valley (the cheapest flower at many florists) might give us more satisfaction than a van Gogh original.

And yet the paradoxical and cheering aspect of pleasure is how unpredictable it can prove to be. Fancy holidays are not always 100% pleasurable. Our enjoyment of them is remarkably vulnerable to emotional trouble and casual bad moods. A fight that began with a small disagreement can end up destroying every benefit of a five-star holiday resort. Real pleasures often seem insignificant – eating a fig, having a bath, whispering in bed in the dark, talking to a grandparent, or scanning through old photos of when you were a child – and yet these small-scale pleasures can be anything but small. If we actually take the opportunity to enjoy them fully, these sort of activities may be among the most moving and satisfying we can have. Fundamentally, this isn't really about how much small pleasures have to offer us. It's about how many good things there are in life that we unfairly neglect. We can't wait for everything that's lovely and charming to be approved by others before we allow ourselves to be delighted. We need to follow our own instincts about what is really important to us.

🔊 6.6

Interviewer How much do you depend on your phone in daily life?

Clive I'm a journalist, and when you're a journalist, it's very difficult to turn your phone off. My job can be unpredictable – for example, being sent to Las Vegas to cover the worst shooting in American history. You know, I get a phone call and I'm on the next flight out.

Interviewer Would you describe yourself as a techie?

Clive Not really. I only really use WhatsApp and Twitter. I know there's a whole world of apps out there, but I don't feel as if I'm missing out – I mean, I don't sit on the Tube frantically playing games on my phone.

Interviewer So deleting apps wasn't a problem for you?

Clive Well, I missed the two I normally use. But my phone's mainly for reading newspapers and getting information for stories.

Interviewer How did you find the challenges?

Clive Days one to four weren't a problem at all. In the evening, it feels absolutely fine to put my phone away. When I go out for dinner with my wife and leave my phone behind, it makes no difference because it would never ever be on the table. In fact, I get a little irritated if I'm in a group and someone is scrolling through a phone. I don't say anything; I just quietly get wound up.

Interviewer So there was nothing you missed?

Clive Not really. My only real guilty pleasure is checking the football, but the bottom line is, if I wasn't at work, I could live without my phone.

Interviewer What about the last three days?

Clive Days six and seven were more difficult. At the weekend, I normally work from 1 p.m. until after my programme ends, News At Ten, about 11 p.m., and without a phone it's tricky to get a heads-up on the stories before work. I considered going out and buying the papers, but part of the attraction of the phone is you don't have to go out in the cold, so I broke the rule and turned my phone on to go through the papers. I was also panicking that if the Queen dropped down dead, or some other big news story, they wouldn't be able to get hold of me, and I'd quite like to keep my job, so I decided to keep my phone on, but just not to look at it.

Interviewer What did you learn from the challenges?

Clive What I learned is that I use my phone more than I thought. By the end of the week, I was actually using it more than when I started. I still like to think I prefer talking face-to-face, but I missed not being able to pick up the phone when I wanted to use it. And I use Twitter more than I thought.

Interviewer What did you decide you couldn't cope with?

Clive I couldn't cope with not being kept in the loop with friends on WhatsApp. There were group messages I couldn't read or respond to.

Interviewer And what can you do without?

Clive I still think I can do without social media, but as a journalist, I have to play along with it up to a point, because this is how the world works.

Interviewer Clive's results were surprising. His daily phone screen time had actually gone up from 45 to 50 minutes, and his number of pick-ups a day from 11 to 16. So maybe he just didn't need to divorce his phone in the first place!

🔊 6.8

A My nephew Sacha is absolutely obsessed with Lego. He's nine years old now, but he's been crazy about Lego since he was, well, since he was about three or four years old, and he is so good at assembling the things that he makes – he never asks for help, he never has done, what he does is he just reads the instructions and then he does it himself. When he wrote his letter to Santa this year, he just put Lego, Lego, and more Lego. Then a couple of days after Christmas, his parents, that's my brother and my sister-in-law, had a lunch party and a load of people came with kids, kids who were friends of his, and he just refused to come out of his room and he wouldn't play with them because all he wanted to do was carry on making one of the Lego sets he got for Christmas. I've never seen a kid quite so obsessed, and for such a long time, with one particular toy.

B My sister-in-law, Miriam, she's really into baking. She has a very demanding job: she's a surgeon, but she spends loads of her time baking. I think she's got every single cookery book, baking book, that's in print, and in her kitchen she has a million and one different cake tins and equipment. I have to say she's incredibly good – makes the most amazing cakes, biscuits, whatever – but the weird thing is, as far as I'm concerned, is that she doesn't really like eating what she makes. In fact, I don't think she has a sweet tooth. Very weird.

C So, my partner, Miguel, is totally obsessed with his health, you know, absolutely obsessed, and it drives me up the wall. He's always talking about how he feels, and taking his blood pressure on this wee machine he's got for it and how everything he's eaten has affected his body and, like, he talks about how many times he's been to the loo, I mean, seriously. And he also takes all these, you know, like vitamins, you know, supplements and stuff, like the fridge is full of them. I wouldn't exactly say he was a hypochondriac, because he doesn't often go to the doctor, but I do think it's an obsession, and nothing makes him happier than sitting down with a lovely herbal tea and a mate and going on and on about his health problems. And of course, you know, at the end of the day there's actually nothing wrong with him, he's like the healthiest person you've ever met, so it's quite a joke really.

D I've got a Polish friend called Dagmara who

has a bit of an obsession with cats. She's got this small plot of land with like, a shed near where she lives, and she's got about 40 cats there which she goes and feeds every day and they've all got names. And she's always rescuing new cats she finds all over the place and taking them there. She also has two or three that live in her flat, and she even used to have one that lived in her office, but I think it died. And everything in her house, like mugs towels, crockery, all of it has got something to do with cats. And like, she's so normal in about every other way, but she does have a thing about cats. It's kind of weird.

E A mate of mine, well, his girlfriend Silvia, really likes, actually, I think it's fair to say she's obsessed with Disney. Anything Disney, the films, she collects the films themselves and as much merchandising as she can. She has dolls from the films, small toys, and anything she can find. She even wears clothes, and the clothes have pictures of Disney characters all over them. Right now it's getting a bit out of hand, because she doesn't have a very big flat and there's Disney stuff everywhere and it takes up all the room, there's toys all over her bed. Her boyfriend's getting a bit fed up with the whole thing and I can't say I blame him.

🔊 7.1

Part 1

When TV producer John Lloyd thought of a formula for a new quiz show, he decided to call it *QI*, which stands for Quite Interesting, and which is also IQ backwards. It's a comedy quiz where panellists have to answer unusual general knowledge questions, and it is perhaps surprising that it's particularly popular among 15- to 25-year-olds. Along with co-author John Mitchinson, Lloyd has since written a number of QI books, and these have also been incredibly successful. Lloyd's basic principle is very simple: everything you think you know is probably wrong, and everything is interesting. *The QI Book of General Ignorance*, for example, poses 240 questions, all of which reveal surprising answers. So we learn, for example, that you are more likely to be killed by an asteroid than by lightning, or that Julius Caesar was not, in fact, born by Caesarian section.

The popularity of these books proves Lloyd's other thesis: that human beings, and children in particular, are naturally curious and have a desire to learn. And this, he believes, has several implications for education. According to Lloyd and Mitchinson, there are two reasons why children, in spite of being curious, tend to do badly at school. Firstly, even the best schools can take a fascinating subject, such as electricity or classical civilization, and make it boring, by turning it into facts which have to be learnt by heart and then regurgitated for exams. Secondly, QI's popularity seems to prove that learning takes place most effectively when it's done voluntarily. The same teenagers who will happily choose to read a QI book will often sit at the back of a geography class and go to sleep, or worse still, disrupt the rest of the class.

🔊 7.2

Part 2

So how could we change our schools so that children would enjoy learning? What would a 'QI school' be like? These are Lloyd and Mitchinson's basic suggestions.

The first principle is that education should be more play than work. The more learning involves things like storytelling and making things, the more interested children will become.

Secondly, they believe that the best people to control what children learn are the children themselves. Children should be encouraged to follow their curiosity. They will end up learning to read, for example, because they want to, in order to read about something they are interested in.

Thirdly, they argue that children should also be in control of when and how they learn. The QI school would not be compulsory, so pupils wouldn't have to go if they didn't want to, and there would be no exams. There would only be projects, or goals that children set themselves with the teacher helping them. So a project could be something like making a film or building a chair.

Fourthly, there should never be theory without practice. You can't learn about vegetables and what kind of plants they are from books and pictures; you need to go and plant them and watch them grow.

The fifth and last point Lloyd and Mitchinson make is that there's no reason why school has to stop dead at 17 or 18. The QI school would be a place where you would be able to carry on learning all your life, a mini university where the young and old could continue to find out about all the things they are naturally curious about.

🔊 7.6

Part 1

Trafalgar Square in London has a plinth, that is, a stone base for a statue, in each of its four corners. On three of them, there are statues of famous historical figures. The fourth plinth was originally intended to hold a statue of King William IV on a horse, but, due to insufficient funds, the statue was never built. The use of the fourth plinth was debated for over 150 years, and finally, in 1998, the Royal Society for the encouragement of Arts commissioned three contemporary sculptures to be displayed there temporarily. Shortly afterwards, the authorities decided to seek opinions from public art commissioners, critics, and members of the public as to the future of the plinth. Although various proposals were put forward for permanent statues, such as of Nelson Mandela or Margaret Thatcher, it was finally agreed that, rather than having anything permanent, works of art would be commissioned from leading national and international artists and be displayed there on a temporary basis. In 2005, the first work was unveiled, a sculpture of a pregnant woman by Marc Quinn, and since then, there has been a succession of new works. It is considered the world's most famous public art commission. However, it is thought that the reason for not accepting any permanent statue there may be because the fourth plinth is being reserved for a statue of Queen Elizabeth II.

🔊 7.7

Part 2

This sculpture, called *Nelson's Ship in a Bottle*, was unveiled in May 2010, and was the first artwork on the fourth plinth to relate directly to Admiral Horatio Nelson, who stands at the top of the column in Trafalgar Square. It was created by the British artist Yinka Shonibare. The ship inside is a model of Nelson's ship *HMS Victory*. The bottle was made out of glass and was constructed by aquarium specialists in Rome, along with the giant cork. Unlike Nelson's ship, however, this ship's sails were made of different African cloths; Shonibare said of his sculpture that it was designed to specifically reflect on the relationship between the birth of the British Empire and Britain's present-day multicultural context. The sculpture, the fourth work of art to be displayed there, was on show until January 2012, and in 2015 it was voted by the public to be the best of all the sculptures that had been displayed up to that point. When the sculpture was removed, money was raised to buy it from the artist, and it was the first of the fourth plinth commissions to be relocated in London. It is now on permanent display in the National Maritime Museum.

This statue of a boy on a rocking horse is called *Powerless Sculptures, Figure 101*. It was created by two Scandinavian artists, Michael Elmgreen from Denmark and Ingar Dragset from Norway. It was the fifth work to occupy the fourth plinth, and was on display from February 2012 to April 2013. The statue, which is 4.1 metres high, was made entirely of bronze. The two artists based their concept around the idea of the many memorial statues of men on horseback which celebrate victory in war. This boy on horseback is vulnerable; unlike traditional heroes, he is not competitive or aggressive; rather, he represents the heroism of a child growing up. Talking about their work, the artists said, 'We thought maybe we should celebrate some generations to come, and hope that there will be a future where there are not so many war monuments.'

Installed in March 2018, and displayed until March 2020, the ninth work of public art was by Iraqi-American artist Michael Rakowitz. In 2006, Rakowitz started a project to recreate more than 7,000 objects of Iraqi art which had been lost forever, either looted from the Iraq Museum in 2003, or destroyed at archaeological sites during the Iraq War. For the fourth plinth commission, Rakowitz created a sculpture that was part of this ongoing project, called *The invisible enemy should not exist*. It was a life-size recreation of the lamassu, the winged god that stood at the entrance to Nergal Gate in Nineveh in present day Iraq from 700 BC until it was destroyed in 2015. This lamassu was made out of 10,500 empty Iraqi date-syrup cans, which symbolize not only how so much art was destroyed during the war, but also how Iraq's date industry, the country's second-biggest export after oil, was decimated by the destruction of millions of its date palm trees. While his sculpture was on display, Rakowitz also set up a pop-up kiosk across the square, which sold small books of recipes using date syrup, as well as small cakes and biscuits.

🔊 7.10

Presenter First of all, the programme needed to know where Jon got the painting from in the first place.

Interviewer So Jon, how did you get the painting?

JT I was given the painting by Denis Wirth-Miller, who was at the East Anglian School of Painting and Drawing with Lucian Freud, and I was given it when I was staying the weekend at Denis Wirth-Miller's house in Wivenhoe, in Essex.

Interviewer So it was a present?

JT It was a present. Yep.

Presenter The programme then decided to look into how Denis Wirth-Miller had got hold of the painting, especially since he and Lucian Freud were not friends.

Interviewer So, Jon, do you think that Freud gave the painting to Denis?

JT There was never, there was never a case that Freud had given it to Denis. The case was that Denis had taken it from the barn.

Presenter The story was that during the Second World War, when Denis and Freud were students, it was very difficult to get hold of canvases to paint on, so students often just left their used canvases in a barn at the school, and then the canvases were reused. Denis told Jon that he had just picked up the canvas, Freud's painting, to reuse, but then he didn't; he just kept it.

The next question the programme focused on was who the portrait was of, in case this might give some more clues about the identity of the painter. After some research into the archives, a note in Denis's handwriting was found, which identified the man in the portrait, *The Man in the Black Cravat* as a certain John Jameson. The programme found letters written by John Jameson, which made it clear that he knew Lucian Freud quite well, and had met him on a number of occasions, including at the painting school in 1939. So it was perfectly credible that Freud had painted Jameson exactly at the time that Denis had said.

The programme then decided to focus on the canvas itself, and took it to an expert in the scientific analysis of paintings, called Libby Sheldon. Sheldon put the painting under the microscope and made a fascinating discovery. There was a long hair embedded in the picture, which looked like a human hair, and which might give them some DNA evidence. The hair was removed from the picture and taken to be analysed, and at the same time, they were able to get a DNA sample from one of Freud's cousins to compare it with.

Interviewer Jon, what did you think when Libby Sheldon found a hair in the painting?

JT I was absolutely gobsmacked. I hadn't even thought that there'd be a possibility that anything like that could exist.

Interviewer Did you assume it was Freud's hair?

JT I didn't. I didn't assume it was Freud's.

Interviewer And when the results came back, unfortunately it was not a match. The hair was definitely not Lucian Freud's. How did you feel, Jon, at that moment?

JT I was very disappointed when I found that it wasn't a hair from Lucian Freud's head, because I got swept along with adrenalin and excitement that goes with one of these TV shows, because of course you're not only dealing with the presenters, you have the producers and the researchers, and the film crew, we got to know each other so well at this stage, and none of us knew. So we were all biting our nails at this moment, and, as that, when that was delivered, none of us knew the result, and so we'd been sitting in the laboratory for three hours before that was delivered and I was really biting my fingernails right down.

Presenter The real mystery of course remained – if it really was a Freud painting, why had he denied it? Was it because it was an early work and he was ashamed of it, and didn't want to be associated with it? Fake or Fortune's experts contacted Freud's solicitor, Diana Rawstron, who had known him very well. They had often talked about his paintings, and when she checked back through her records, she found that in 2006 they had discussed The Man in the Black Cravat, and Freud admitted that in fact he had started the painting – he had painted the body, the shirt, the neck and part of the face – but that someone else had completed it. This was very exciting. The programme now had first-hand evidence that the painting was partly by Freud. So they went back to Libby Sheldon, the expert in the scientific analysis of paintings, and asked her to see whether she thought it was possible that the painting had been made by two different people. After examining all the paint pigments and the brushstrokes, she had no hesitation in saying that she was absolutely certain that the painting was done by a single artist, so she thought that as Freud admitted to having started it, then he must have finished it, too.

Interviewer Jon, what did you think when you heard the news that Freud had admitted to starting the painting?

JT I could have fallen over backwards. It was one of those moments when I did the action you're told not to do. I looked off camera straight at the producer, who had been, who had become actually a friend and I was very close to at that stage, just looked at her in just utter disbelief that, that this had happened.

Finally, after collecting together all the evidence they had uncovered, the programme asked three experts on Freud to give their verdict. The letter with their decision was opened live on camera at the end of the programme. And this is what they said…

🔊 7.11

Presenter Finally, after collecting together all the evidence they had uncovered, the programme asked three experts on Freud to give their verdict. The letter with their decision was opened live on camera at the end of the programme. And this is what they said…

Expert 'We believe this to be a work that Lucian Freud did at art school, most probably in 1939.'

Interviewer Jon, you must have been over the moon! Why do you think Freud denied that he had done the painting?

JT I'm absolutely certain that the reason he denied having done the painting to other people was because the war that was going on between him and Denis Wirth-Miller. They fell out when they were aged, he was 17 and Miller, when Denis Wirth-Miller was 21 or so, and there were times when they were together and it was OK. Denis was certainly a very, very difficult character.

Interviewer And regardless of the fact that it's by Freud, do you love the painting?

JT That's – whether I love the painting or not – is a very interesting question, because a lot of people, particularly on social media when it was seen on the television were saying, 'But it's hideous; it's absolutely terrible.' I love it. I've always loved it and particularly because it just clicked straight away with me that it was so like Freud's early drawings. I love the shadows; I love the way, the exaggerated face. Everything about it just appeals to me greatly.

Interviewer Would your feelings have changed if it had turned out not to be by Freud, or to be a fake?

JT My feelings for the painting certainly wouldn't have changed if I'd found it wasn't a Freud, because it mustn't be forgotten that I have been at that stage for many occasions. I've been to meet people, very important people who've told me it is the most wonderful early Freud they've ever seen, and then snapped at me, saying it's a fake, three weeks later, with no explanation as to why we've gone from hot to cold. And, so my emotions have gone really high, thinking, 'Wow, I now know this is a Freud', to absolutely crashing down, to saying it isn't. And I know from that that my emotion towards the painting has never changed.

Interviewer Would you ever sell it?

JT What I'd always said that I was going to do with the canvas was put it into my estate and set up a trust to pay for people to go to the Royal College of Art. I was in a situation where there was no money for me to do further education. And I got a bursary, a state bursary, like a scholarship to go to the Royal College of Art, and that saw me through my time there, so it would seem appropriate that it should go towards helping someone who otherwise wouldn't be able to get there to do further education.

Interviewer Jon, thank you very much.

🔊 8.1

1 Tony Well, I've had back pain for a while now and I went to see a chiropractor, who did sort me out partially, but she also does acupuncture, and she said one day would I like to try it, and, well actually, to my surprise it seemed to do some good and for a few days it felt better. Now, I don't know whether it was a real effect or a placebo, but yeah, it did some good. I've had it three times now – I don't know if I'd call it a 'proper' therapy, but yeah, I, I think it worked, and the funny thing is, it's amazing she got me to go back, because I have a complete phobia of needles.

2 Katie So, I went to a Chinese medicine practitioner that was recommended to me because I had some skin problems, and I went along and it was very nice, sort of a, very calm office – he seemed really professional, anyway. He prescribed me some herbal medicine, it was some tea – a Chinese tea made of bark and leaves and so on – and I had to boil it up three times a day and then drink the liquid, and the liquid just smelled revolting; it was really bad, made the whole house smell and it tasted even worse. It was really expensive as well, the consultations and the dead leaves, but I stuck to it for a few weeks. And I have to say, although I was very sceptical about it, I really do think it made a difference – didn't solve the problem completely, but it did actually improve the quality of my skin. So yeah, maybe I would try it again if I needed to.

3 **Jen** I don't use alternative medicine, because I think it's a waste of time and it doesn't work. If alternative medicine worked, it wouldn't be alternative, it would be actual conventional medicine. The reason that it is alternative is because we don't have any solid proof that it works. You only ever hear anecdotal evidence that it's worked for individual people – that's not real evidence, and I would say to anyone who's heard stories like that, look up 'the placebo effect'. There's no evidence that alternative medicine works beyond the placebo effect, and so as far as I'm concerned, it's a waste of time and money, and at its worst it could even be dangerous or harmful if people are using it in place of real medicine that might cure their very real illness.

4 **Chris** My neighbour who lives in the flat above me is a homeopathic doctor and also a hypnotherapist, and at one point because I'd been trying to give up smoking for a long time, I decided to try hypnotherapy to see whether it would have any effect. I was pretty sceptical about the whole idea of hypnotherapy, but I very much like and respect my neighbour, so I thought, 'Why not give it a go?' Anyway, I went to her clinic and sat in a chair – and there weren't any golden pendulums or anything like that, but she did tell me to close my eyes and I suppose she asked me several questions or talked to me. But I didn't go into a trance; I was conscious all the time, and the one thing I remember is that she told me to imagine that I was in a forest, walking in a beautiful forest with lots of trees, and green trees, and then to imagine that the forest was slowly dying and that all the trees were dead wood and that this was the effect that smoking was having on me, and that if I stopped, it would go back into the green beautiful forest that I'd imagined in the first place. Sadly, it had no effect on me whatsoever. Maybe if I'd believed in it – she said that anyway, I wasn't yet ready to stop smoking, so maybe that is the answer, and hopefully one day I will stop smoking.

5 **Mary** So, I've used aromatherapy, which I have with a massage whenever I can, because I've got loads of back problems and shoulder problems. Anyway, with an aromatherapy massage, like, they use specific oils from plants which either relax you or they invigorate you, and I always go for the relaxing one because I think that's the whole point of a massage. And so they massage these plant oils and you breathe them in, and then they soak into your skin, and I am pretty sure, I'm, yeah, I'm certain that the oils makes a difference to the effectiveness of this treatment, or you know, it does for me. I don't know if that's a placebo or it's real, but, it's a question worth thinking about. Have I – I don't think anybody really knows; maybe there are some trials. I do know that recently there was a study by some university or, or other on the use of lavender oil for children, and they found that lavender oil really does have a big effect on them, helping them sleep better and on their behaviour – it improves behaviour in over-active children, apparently. So, you know, based on that evidence, I'd, I'd say it's a real therapy; it's just one that doctors don't prescribe, yet – normally, anyway.

🔊 **8.4**

Interviewer So, tell us what you think about it, we'd love to hear from you. Now, you may have heard in the news that the government has been consulting on ways to reduce dependence on prescription drugs, especially those which people take long-term, such as painkillers and antidepressants. Today we have Mark in the studio, and Mark's a research scientist – welcome – and you're going to tell us about something called 'social prescribing'…

Mark Hi, Liz. Thanks for inviting me on the show. Yes, so my area is public health research, and I've been working with the Department of Health on this issue. Of course, often patients do need to be prescribed drugs, but the concern is that too many people are getting them almost automatically, when in fact there may be other ways to deal with their health problems.

Interviewer Right.

Mark My research has shown that patients who take up social activities or hobbies are far less likely to need some types of prescription medicine, and obviously that's something we want to encourage. So this is what we're calling 'social prescribing', the idea that doctors will suggest to patients that instead of taking medicine, they take up a specific hobby or leisure activity that will improve their particular health issue.

Interviewer I see. So, what kind of things are we talking about?

Mark Well, different hobbies offer different health benefits. Let's take dancing. Dancing of any kind is good for both your fitness and your mood, but a German study published last year showed that dancing can also slow down brain ageing. In this study, volunteers took part in a dance class once a week for 18 months. At the end of the 18 months, the participants showed an increase in the area of the brain that plays an important role in memory and learning.

Interviewer Wow.

Mark So that's clearly something for people to consider as they get older. Another example: cycling. As we get older, the thymus – this is the organ which makes the so-called T-cells that we need to help us resist disease – starts to get smaller, to shrink. But it's now been shown that cycling can actually boost your immune system – recent research has found that the thymus in older cyclists produces as many T-cells as in young people.

Interviewer Fascinating. So dancing and cycling are both things that a doctor might consider prescribing for patients to increase their long-term health. Although both of those activities are fairly energetic, and not all patients would be able to do them…?

Mark Sure, so there's also yoga. It's well known that yoga can improve body flexibility and make you feel calm, but doing yoga regularly can also significantly reduce your blood pressure. It's the stretching and deep breathing that makes a significant difference. Doing yoga for 15 minutes a day can reduce blood pressure by as much as 10%. Then there's golf – already a really popular sport – and there's now evidence that playing golf can actually help to offset the risk of getting diabetes and some types of cancer. In fact, golf can reduce your chances of developing up to 40 chronic diseases. Research shows that golfers live longer and feel better than the general population.

Interviewer Well, that sounds very positive, but what about people like me, who aren't so keen on sporting activities? What could doctors prescribe for them?

Mark Absolutely. Well, in terms of getting outdoors, how do you feel about gardening?

Interviewer Mmm, well, maybe…

Mark Researchers have repeatedly shown that doing things in the garden will lower levels of stress and anxiety. Looking after your plants for just half an hour a week can almost instantly reduce feelings of tension and fatigue, and make you less likely to suffer from depression. And another really effective thing is owning a pet. You get great exercise from walking a dog, but also, and rather surprisingly, living with a pet really helps reduce the likelihood of allergies. One study showed that stroking a dog for 18 minutes a day makes a difference to how the body reacts to animals. Children who live with a pet are less prone to developing allergies such as asthma, because they are exposed to fur and animal saliva from a young age.

Interviewer And is there anything for the more creative types?

Mark Yes, one of the most intriguing findings is about knitting, which you might think is a rather old-fashioned hobby, but actually it's now enjoying a bit of a comeback. A study at Harvard Medical School found that knitting lowers the heart rate by an average of 11 beats a minute, and another trial involving women with eating disorders who were taught to knit showed that 74% of them said knitting helped them feel better about themselves. And I should just point out that it's not only about being a bit more active – most of the hobbies I've mentioned are things you can do with other people, which in itself has a beneficial effect on your health.

Interviewer Well, Mark, I'm totally convinced, so next time I go to the doctor, I'm hoping I'll get a prescription for a course of dance classes and some knitting needles!

Mark Exactly. Let's hope so…

🔊 **8.10**

Clive *So I was living in Spain at the time, and I was travelling back from Spain to the UK with my wife and two young children. It was two days before Christmas, and we were travelling back to London to visit my family there, it was an evening flight, from Valencia to London Gatwick.*

Clive Come on, kids, are you nearly ready? We're leaving for the airport in 15 minutes.

Kids Coming daddy!

MA What time do we need to check in?

Clive Well, the flight leaves at 10.15. Don't worry, we've got plenty of time.

Annnouncer Departure for flight Iberia 6845. Please passengers proceed to gate number A6.

Clive *The weather in Spain was really good, but just before we were going to take off, I was just reading my messages at the last minute and I saw there was a message from my brother, Russ.*

Clive Oh look, there's a message from Russ – oh, he's asking whether the flight's been cancelled. Apparently, there's a really bad storm in London, with gale-force winds.

MA Oh, really? That doesn't sound good.

Clive I know. Anyway, we're about to take off. I'll let him know we're already on the plane.

Clive *So we took off, but obviously, we were a bit worried about what the weather was going to be like when we got there.
It was a two-hour flight, and everything was fine, until we were approaching Gatwick, when the pilot made an announcement.*

🔊 **8.11**

Pilot Ladies and gentlemen, this is your pilot speaking. We're about 20 minutes from Gatwick, but unfortunately, we can't land yet because we've been told that there's really windy weather there, so we're going to circle for a while and assess the situation. Please make sure that your seatbelts are fastened, as it may be a bit bumpy.

Clive *So the plane started circling, and then we started getting the worst turbulence I've ever, ever experienced. The plane just seemed to be going up in the air, then dropping down, then rising up again, then dropping.*

Pilot Ladies and gentlemen, thank you for your patience. We're going to attempt a landing now.

Clive *We could see now that the wind was incredibly strong – we could see the wings of the plane moving up and down out of the window. I'm sure everyone on the plane was thinking the same thing: 'He's never going to be able to land the plane. We're going to crash.' Then just at the very last moment, the pilot obviously realized that it was impossible to land, and he changed his mind and the plane suddenly rose back up into the air. It was an absolutely terrifying moment. The plane just kept climbing and climbing, going further and further away from the airport. Then the pilot made another announcement.*

Pilot Ladies and gentlemen, well, I'm very sorry, but it was too dangerous to land; it was too windy, and I'm afraid we can't land at Gatwick now because the airport's been closed. In fact, I have to tell you that we can't land anywhere in the UK because all the airports are closed.

🔊 8.12

MA So, where are we going to land if the airports are closed?

Clive *I've no idea. Maybe Paris?*

MA Paris?! What if we don't have enough fuel to get there?

Clive *Then the pilot made another announcement.*

Pilot Ladies and gentlemen, we're going to try to land at Amsterdam because the weather conditions there are a little better, so we're heading towards the Netherlands now. We're due to land at Schiphol in approximately one hour.

Clive *After that, we had about an hour's journey to Holland. That was OK – fairly normal – and then as we got closer to Amsterdam, the pilot came back on again.*

Pilot Good evening, everyone. We'll be landing shortly at Schiphol Airport. It's going to be a bit windy here, too, but not as bad as at Gatwick, you'll be happy to hear.

Clive *And it was quite a good landing – a little bit bumpy – but everyone was very, very relieved to get down on the ground. And we all started getting up – to be honest, we couldn't wait to get off, to get our feet back on firm ground again – and we got up and we started to get all our things from the overhead locker. But then there was another announcement…*

Cabin crew Your attention, everyone. We aren't going to disembark here in Amsterdam. We're going to refuel and then we'll be flying back to the UK, because we've been told that in a couple of hours, the weather may be a bit better at Gatwick.
However – ladies and gentlemen, if you want to get off, you can get off, but unfortunately, there won't be a hotel for you to stay at tonight, because this plane's travelling back to Gatwick.

🔊 8.13

Clive *So basically, then everyone had a dilemma – to stay on the plane or to get off and spend the rest of the night in Amsterdam.*

Clive What do you want to do? Get off here? Or try getting back to London tonight? To be honest, I think we should get off.

MA Yes, absolutely, let's get off now – I don't want to be on this plane a minute longer. Come on, kids, get your things.

Clive *More or less everyone with children got off the plane, but a lot of the passengers stayed on board. I suppose for some people the idea of being stuck in Amsterdam on Christmas Eve was even worse than flying back to Gatwick and trying to land again. But personally, we were really happy to get off that plane, and we spent the night in Amsterdam Airport, then in the morning we got a train from Amsterdam to*

Belgium. In Brussels, we picked up the Eurostar, and that took us through France, under the Channel, and safely back to London. So, after travelling all day, we finally got to my parents' house at around seven o'clock in the evening on Christmas Eve, just in time for the children to hang up their stockings. That flight was definitely the most frightening experience I've ever had.

🔊 9.8

John Good afternoon and welcome to A Question of Food , where each week we look at a different aspect of food and the food industry. This week we're talking about veganism. Well over half a million people in the UK now describe themselves as vegan, an increase of over 500% in ten years, and 20% of people under the age of 35 have tried a vegan diet. So what are the arguments for and against veganism, and is it here to stay? We have two experts here to explore the arguments: Jimmy, a vegan activist who also runs a vegan restaurant in East London – hello, Jimmy…

Jimmy Hello.

John …and Simone, a dietician and omnivore.

Simone Hello.

John Jimmy, let me start with you. What, in your view, are the main reasons for the explosion of interest in veganism?

Jimmy For me, there are two main reasons. The most obvious reason for veganism is to do with animal rights, and this argument has been around for a long time. In fact, writer Leo Tolstoy had this to say in 1886, and it sums up my feelings very well: 'A man can live and be healthy without killing animals for food; therefore, if he eats meat, he participates in taking animal life merely for the sake of his appetite. And to act so is immoral.' I think this is at the heart of why so many people are now becoming vegans, the idea that killing and eating animals, and modern farming practices, are simply immoral. And the second big reason is that being a vegan helps the environment: it reduces your carbon footprint. There was a recent study at Oxford University which concluded that adopting a vegan diet can reduce your carbon footprint by 73%, which is far more significant than cutting down on flights or buying an electric car.

John Simone, can I bring you in here? These both seem pretty strong arguments; what do you think of those two points?

Simone Well, the first point, the point about your moral position, I do think that's a very personal decision, whether to eat meat or not, and I personally, I don't think it's immoral. But I think everybody needs to decide for themselves. An unfortunate aspect of veganism is that it's easy for vegans to believe that their position is morally superior, and so they make meat-eaters feel morally inferior, which of course meat-eaters resent, so immediately you have this conflict, which I really think is unfortunate.

John Jimmy, can I ask you, do you feel morally superior to Simone?

Jimmy Yes, yes, I do feel superior. I do think that veganism is a morally strong position, but it's not about being better than other people, it's just about doing what's right.

John And Simone, what about Jimmy's second point, about the environment?

Simone Well, broadly speaking, Jimmy is right: being a vegan can reduce your carbon footprint. But it isn't quite as simple as that. Some foods that are a real favourite with vegans, like avocados and quinoa and soya beans, are grown a long way from the UK. I mean, the biggest producers of quinoa are Peru and Bolivia, and avocados come to the UK from Mexico, the Caribbean, Africa, and soya beans from Brazil. And there's a significant environmental impact associated with bringing those foods to Britain, and they are often not grown in a sustainable way – growing

food crops can be just as damaging to the environment as farming animals. And there's also the problem that demand for those foods is now so high in, for example, Britain and the States, that there isn't enough left for the country that actually grows the food – so for example, Kenya has recently banned the export of avocados, because they were all going abroad, with none left for the Kenyans.

John OK, Simone, that's a valid point. As a dietician, what do you think are the health implications of being vegan? We hear a lot about vitamin deficiency and so on; is that something we should be concerned about?

Simone Yes, it is true that it's harder to maintain a balanced diet if you're vegan, and that may present a serious health risk, especially for children and teenagers, who I absolutely believe should not be vegan. Humans are designed to be omnivores, so obviously if you eat a bit of everything, like me, then you get plenty of vitamins and minerals and so on, but vegans have to really make sure that they get enough of these things. The classic example is vitamin B12. If you're vegan, you need to take B12 supplements, or eat food fortified with B12. If you don't, you can become quite ill quite quickly.

Jimmy Of course you do need to take a bit of care, but that goes without saying. There's nothing wrong with taking vitamin supplements, and lots of people who aren't vegans do the same thing. But I think you're missing the important point, which is that overall, being vegan is hugely positive for your health. Less risk of heart disease, less risk of diabetes, and how many vegans do you know who are overweight?

Simone That may be true to some extent, but fundamentally, I still don't see why anyone would choose to eat a diet that doesn't deliver the right nutritional balance for the human body.

John One thing I want to ask you both about is what you could call the social side of being vegan. I mean eating out – that can be very difficult.

Jimmy Well, actually, I think that problem has disappeared now. Being vegan is becoming more and more mainstream, and most restaurants offer vegetarian and vegan options.

John Well, one if you're lucky!

Simone Yes, and that's only true in big cities and in certain countries. I mean, there are some countries where avoiding all animal-based food is more or less impossible.

John And Jimmy, what about when you go round to somebody's house for dinner? Does that create problems?

Jimmy Not at all. Most of my friends are vegan, anyway, and all my other friends are really getting into trying vegan recipes.

Simone I'm afraid you'd have a problem if you came to my house – I think it's really inconsiderate to expect the host to cook something specially for you, or for everybody to have to eat the food that only you actually want. You'd expect me to cook something special for you, but would you be prepared to cook a steak for me?

Jimmy I'm sorry, but I wouldn't.

John So can I ask you both just to round off, is veganism the future?

Jimmy Absolutely it is.

Simone I think it'll always be an option, but it'll never be for everyone.

🔊 9.15

How to Eat Out

Tip 1 Always order the fish.

Really good fresh fish is very hard to find, very hard to store and keep fresh – you've got to really cook it as soon as you buy it or there's no point. It's often fiddly to prepare and very smelly to cook. It's what

---

🔊 **Go online** to listen to the audio and see all the Listening scripts

restaurants are FOR! It just amazes me that people will go into a restaurant and order the steak. A thing you can buy almost anywhere, keep for weeks, and cook however you like without doing anything to it and it'll always basically be OK.

Tip 2 Never eat the bread.
An ex-girlfriend of mine eats nothing all day. She claims she doesn't get hungry. So, whenever we meet for dinner, she is utterly starving and gobbles up the entire bread basket and three pats of butter without pausing for breath. Then halfway through her main course she starts poking about and saying, 'I don't know why they give you such large portions. I'll never eat all this!' I just don't know why people eat the bread. You shouldn't be that hungry. Ever. Bread is not a first course. It's a breakfast food, an accompaniment to certain terrines. At an expensive place with a TV chef and a whole range of exciting things to chew on for the next couple of hours, why would anyone want to fill up with bread? I always tell them, as soon as I arrive, to bring no bread. But sometimes they do and you must tell them to take it away.

Tip 3 Have the vegetarian option – but not in a vegetarian restaurant.
As a rule, the best vegetarian food is cooked by meat-eating chefs who know how to cook, rather than by bearded hippies. For this reason, if you want good vegetarian food, go to a normal, that is omnivorous, restaurant. There may not be much choice, but personally, I would much rather restaurants focused on doing one or two things brilliantly than offered a whole load of stuff that was just about OK.

Tip 4 Never sit at a table outside.
Why on earth would you want to eat outside? I suppose in a hot country where there's no air-conditioning, it might be nice to sit outside in the shade, overlooking the sea. But on a busy London street? Crazy. Go indoors. Also, in most restaurants the outside tables are ruined by smokers. If you want to eat outside in London, take sandwiches and eat them in one of the wonderful parks.

Tip 5 Insist on tap water.
We have invested years and years and vast amounts of money into an ingenious system which cleans water and delivers it very cheaply to our homes and workplaces through a tap. And yet last year, we bought three billion litres of bottled water. That's just free money for the restaurant, so don't order mineral water! Ask for a jug of tap.

Tip 6 How to complain – and get a result.
Complain nicely, politely, apologetically. But firmly, and at the very moment of disappointment. 'I'm awfully sorry to make a fuss,' you might say, 'but this fish really isn't as fresh as I'd hoped. I really can't eat this. What else might I have as a replacement that can come quickly?' There's simply no way you can lose with that. The end result is likely to be free main courses, a jolly time, and an amicable departure.

Tip 7 Be nice to the staff.
Just be nice to them, that's all. You should always be nice to everybody, obviously, but if you're not, make being nice to staff in restaurants your only exception. Don't flirt with them, and don't ask foreign staff where they're from. Just smile, and say please and thank you, and look at them when you're ordering. And then shut up and eat.

🔊 **10.1**

1 Off and running! Brilliant start from Lorraine Stewart; she's flying out. Browning's getting into her stride, she's trying to chase her down; now Harris is coming up in lane six, she's coming up on Stewart, she's coming hard, but Stewart is going to get there, she dips for the line. 10.72! Stewart takes the gold in a new championship record.

2 Brian Marks to putt now, and he…he's had a tough time in this competition: nothing has gone right for him. And we haven't seen him make a long putt in a while. He would love this to go in for a birdie and try to get his round back on track. It must be 30, 32 feet, with a slight break to the left, and he needs enough speed on it. He's hit it well, it's looking good, come on, come on…and he makes it! That was beautiful!

3 Surely the attack is going to come soon – Fernández can't afford to wait any longer: she doesn't have a sprint finish; she needs to go now. Coming to the foot of the final climb of the day, eight kilometres at an average gradient of 12%, this could be very interesting. And she's gone! Fernández has gone! Brankart is trying to follow, but the gap is opening! And Fernández has 20 metres, 30 metres, and she looks round once, and she knows this is her chance.

4 The Cuban has got the arm lock, Asaka desperately trying to keep his elbow turned. That was a moment of real danger; he needs to settle himself here. He might have hurt his arm. Thirty seconds to go now. This is fraught with danger: every time you take a step towards your opponent, you put yourself in danger, but you've got to take that step to win the gold.

5 What has happened to Australia? They cannot contain Brazil; they're trying to come back at them, but Australia have lost their rhythm. Very consistent throwing from Brazil – there's another three-pointer; that's a nice move; they're running away with this now. Only a few seconds left – and that's it, it's two more points to Brazil and it's all over. Brazil are safely through to the semi-final, 71 to 40.

6 Fantastic start from Ivanova: triple Salchow, triple toe, great elevation on both jumps. And again, amazing elevation; that was a flip. She looks so relaxed; she's completely in control here. Triple flip, double toe, ooh, a little bit of a stumble, but she comes out of it well. Last jump coming up now; it's a double Axel, and oh no! She's down on the ice, and she's back up, but that's going to be the end of her hopes for a medal. That is a disaster for Ivanova.

🔊 **10.2**

Interviewer So, Olly, have you always been interested in sport?

Olly Yes, I have. I was always a huge sports fan as a child, particularly tennis and football. They were the ones that I played. My mother was a tennis player; my dad was a footballer. So they…those were the sports that I got into. But I always loved watching most sports. My grandfather – both of my grandfathers – were huge fans of sport. So watched a lot and, and then just became very curious about the language of television, sometimes even more than the action of the sport.

Interviewer Do you do a lot of sport or exercise yourself?

Olly I could tell you yes, but that would be a lie. Especially about the exercise bit. I do probably not enough exercise. I play football, I play tennis a little bit, but that's about it. And I would never – because I'm a sports commentator – I would never call myself an athlete, because I know what an athlete really is, and it isn't me.

Interviewer What made you want to be a commentator?

Olly When I was a child, I commentated on everything that was happening. That, that's the thing that unites all sports commentators. When you go back to their childhood, they're the ones that commentated when people were playing football in the playground. I, when I was playing sport in the back garden, I would add in a running commentary to it. I made cassette tapes that I've still got, when I was 11 years old, of radio broadcasts of pretend football matches. So I always had this love of language. My grandfather was somebody who absolutely loved words, and I think in my family we grew up with a passion, a curiosity, for language, so that was always there. And then when my love of sport developed, I think the two married together very nicely.

Interviewer What's your favourite sport to commentate on?

Olly My number one is definitely gymnastics, which I love because of the variety: there's just so many different forms of gymnastics. It could be trampolining or aerobics, or rhythmic gymnastics – that's beautiful and exciting to do so many different things.

Interviewer Do you have to be an expert in all the sports you commentate on?

Olly There are some sports that you have to have extremely strong knowledge of. Gymnastics is full of technical moves, complex rules, complex scoring – you have to know the vocabulary; you have to understand it.

Interviewer I'm sure.

Olly There are other sports that are definitely something you can commentate without being an expert. For example, a race. Now if you're doing a race, in swimming, in horseracing, in athletics, it's still just a race. The most important thing is: tell the story of the race.

Interviewer What would you say is the most difficult thing about commentating?

Olly Shutting up is definitely the hardest thing about commentating, because pictures are beautiful. Sound is beautiful. The sound of a crowd is a beautiful thing; the sound of a player screaming with excitement when they hit the winning point is wonderful. It's very easy as a commentator to forget that there are pictures – and we use a phrase in the broadcasting world: we say, 'Let the picture breathe', and I think that's really important to do.

Interviewer That's so interesting. Do you ever disagree with the referee or the judges when you're commentating?

Olly Absolutely, but the important thing is: do not destroy them. As a broadcaster, do not attack referees or judges. They are human beings; they are doing a job. They get it right sometimes; they get it wrong sometimes. Unless a referee is obviously cheating, which is very, very, very unusual, then you have to be understanding and kind because athletes make mistakes, referees make mistakes, commentators make mistakes.

Interviewer So, have you ever seen anyone, a player or an athlete, cheating during an event?

Olly Very occasionally. I would say that most athletes actually have great integrity. They are very honest people. It's rare that it happens. When it does happen, it can be quite difficult, actually. You have to choose your words very carefully because to…maybe to me or to you it's very obviously cheating, but it's not to them. Sometimes a footballer dives. But did they dive or did they fall? And actually, I…it's not my job to try to inhabit the mind of the athlete and tell you what they were thinking at the time. Where it is also difficult is maybe if an athlete has returned after a ban because they had taken drugs or they had cheated – then you have to refer to that ban, but it's important not to be stuck in the past too much.

Interviewer What do you think commentary adds to the experience of a television viewer?

Olly Commentary should be furniture, not wallpaper; I think that's a term that we use quite often in broadcasting. It should make it easier for the viewer to place themselves in the action. It shouldn't just be decoration; it shouldn't be something that distracts you from the really important things. If you use too many words, if you start to tell meaningless stories, then the viewer will switch off from the things that you're saying. I think the point of commentary is to provide drama, it is to help explain why things have happened, and it's also to introduce new viewers to a sport.

Interviewer I see. What are the most memorable moments of your career so far?

Olly You never forget your first Olympic Games. The feeling of arriving at the stadium, staring up at the Olympic rings, probably the most famous logo in all of sport – you look at it and you realize this is what you are doing. You are part of the Olympic movement, and that's incredible. And the Olympic Park is full of energy; the atmosphere is unbelievable there. And you get to broadcast the greatest moments of people's careers at the Olympic Games, which is an incredible feeling.

🔊 **10.3**

Interviewer Can you tell us about one really special moment that you remember?

Olly There was one very special moment for me that happened in the Rio 2016 Olympics. Sometimes it's not the biggest moments – they're not always the most memorable. Sometimes it's small things that have a particular story. And there was a Norwegian wrestler, a gentleman called Stig-André Berge. He was 33, it was his third Olympic Games, and he had never even come close to winning a medal in his previous attempts. He was a very good wrestler, but he had never come close. Just before the Olympic Games, he discovered that his mother had terminal cancer, and he made it home from the qualification tournament for the Olympic Games in time to see her for the last time.

Interviewer Wow.

Olly And he promised her in that last meeting that he would win her an Olympic medal. And we got to the Olympic Games in Rio a few months later, and every match he won by the most narrow of margins; it was so tight and so close. And then he won the crucial match that gave him a chance to go for the bronze medal. And when he won that match, he looked up into the sky and he just pointed upwards. And I realized that this was now the time to start telling that story. Because I didn't want to start telling it too early or make it too sentimental, so I mentioned the story about his mother. And then he won the bronze medal. And it was so close. And at the end, his coaches ran…he burst into tears, his coaches ran on; they were three of them lying on the ground, holding each other, crying. And I was able to put into words that story of the promise he'd made to his mother. I felt very honoured to be the person trusted to tell his story.

Interviewer Wow, what a moment that must have been. Thank you so much, Olly, and thank you for sharing that story with us.

🔊 **10.5**

Part 1

Interviewer Why did you decide to leave the UK and live abroad?

Emma Well, actually it was David who convinced me it was a good idea. A long time ago, going back, I was studying at the…my final year at University of Warwick and David was working at that time in Majorca, and we met in England and then he returned to work in Majorca. And then it was, it was very…we kept in touch by letters and it was very easy to be seduced by the, the lifestyle he had there, the lovely swimming, the barbecues in the mountains, the, the fishing for octopus. So I was sitting finishing my le–, my essays in the, the library windows covered with rain and, yes, so when I graduated, I, I went very happily out to, to Spain to be with him and we both got jobs in Vigo in, in Spain, working as language teachers in a private school, and we had a lovely time. We just…we worked, and when we weren't working, we spent the time discovering the area, going out on our bikes and learnt to

windsurf – yes, that was a great year.

Interviewer So a very happy introduction to Spain for you. And how did you both end up in Mairena?

David Well, it was by chance, really. We'd, we'd been working as English teachers for, for several years – ten years perhaps in my case – and we realized that we had the opportunity to, to take a year off, a sabbatical year as it were, with a view to then going back to, to teaching again. And we had a friend who had a, a small house in the, in, in a village in the mountains south of Granada, and he'd agreed to, to let us rent this house for, for next to nothing for a year, so that's what we did – but whilst we were there, we wandered around and cycled around and finally stumbled on this little village of Mairena, where we live now, and fell in love with the village, fell in love with the house that we, we lived in for a while at first, and realized at the end of the year that we were, we were having a ball and enjoying it too much, really, to, to want to go back. So at that point, we realized that we had to, to find a way of, of earning a living, because we didn't have any money, and so we…I, I got a job in Granada in fact, just teaching for a year or so, and then we opened what's now Las Chimeneas, our little hotel and restaurant.

Interviewer How integrated do you feel in the local community?

David Well, one of the things that made me feel very integrated and indeed very, very proud, in fact, was, was being invited to, to join the local council, and I worked for six years as the, the Deputy Mayor – and not necessarily a very good Deputy Mayor, but I kind of enjoyed it, and it was, you know, I consider it as an honour to be, to be involved and asked to get involved in, in local politics. And it's, it's a useful thing as well, rather than just being on the outside protesting at decisions taken after the event, it's quite useful to be part of the decision-making process as well. And…

Emma I think for me, the, the thing that really made a difference was when we had children, because especially, as being, being, you know, a mother in the village, it meant that you met other mothers and people felt that it was a reason to talk, and our children are friends with the other kids – they come round to play now – so yeah, that was a big difference for me.

David And having the business as well, because we, you know, people can see that we're, we're actually working, and we're working alongside our neighbours, because, you know, we're lucky – we're…enough to be in a position where we've been able to employ quite a lot of the local villagers as, you know, as cooks, and chefs, and taxi drivers, and so on.

🔊 **10.6**

Part 2

Interviewer What do you like most about living in Mairena?

Emma The obvious thing, and almost a cliché, is the weather, but you can't underestimate that – I mean, the weather does affect your everyday life – and also simple things like the incredible clear skies and the light. But I think it's something more than that: as long as I can remember, I always had a hankering – I really wanted to live in a very small community; I remember even as a child it was something that I always had an ambition to do. And I think something about living in a very small village: everything seems very kind of human, very manageable; you, you know everybody, you literally know everybody in the village. And what's also been great the last few years is that we bought some land which is filled with almonds and olive and fruit trees, so we spend a lot of tr–, time down there and learning how to farm like the locals do, because they have

very complicated watering techniques, so we've had to speak to locals and learn how to farm the land.

Interviewer Are there any downsides to living there?

Emma It's the travelling, isn't it? We have to spend probably more time than we would like in a car to, to buy something simple. On, on the one hand, it's great being away from shops – it's like a kind of a, real kind of consumer detox – but on the other hand, when you actually have to buy something, it means you have a long journey, which I could do without.

David And there's lots of paperwork as well. Spain is a very heavily bureaucratic country as well, and so there's lots of certification and permits and so on that we've got to, we've got to get together, and that always means a drive of a couple of hours to, to get to, to Granada, the local centre, to, to get paperwork sorted out.

Interviewer Is there anything you miss about the UK?

David Well, obviously we miss friends and family – I mean, that's the, the big thing, but we're lucky we live in a, a nice part of the world and so we, we get lots of visitors who come out and, and stay with us, which is nice. And then, you know, often it's very trite, silly little things that you miss: I mean, I miss pubs with carpets and soft lighting and you, you know, polite dog walkers – that kind of thing.

Emma The fact that, actually, when we come back, we often come back to London, so… what I really like about the UK is, is that sense of cultural diversity. Just travelling on public transport in London, you're very aware of the, the, the very wide range of people living here, which obviously you wouldn't get in a, a small rural community. And, of course, the, the great thing about that is being in London is, yeah, you can choose, the, the, you know, rest–, any kind of restaurant. That's a big treat to come back and be able to choose what kind of food you want to eat.

Interviewer Do you think you'll come back to the UK one day?

David Well, you never know. I mean, we, we, we never took a, a decision that we would stay in Spain forever, so it was kind of by chance – by accident – that we've been in Spain so long, so we, we've never really ruled it out. It would be tricky, I think, to come back, largely for economic or financial reasons. Britain is a very expensive place to buy a house at the moment, and then of course there's the boys, the boys – our two sons are now aged 7 and 13, so they were born and brought up in Spain, so it would be…they would be really uprooted for them. To take them back to the UK, I think now, that would be perhaps a, a bigger hurdle.

Emma Yeah, for sure, that's the main reason why, why I can't see us going back is definitely Dan and Tom, but of course, I think once you've spent 15 years building up a business, then also that's something you don't want to, to easily turn your back on. Of course, the other thing we need to think about is the impact of Brexit. It might be that we end up applying for Spanish nationality. I think for now we're just going to see how things go.

 Go online to listen to the audio and see all the Listening scripts

have: lexical and grammatical uses

different uses of *have* as a main verb

1. I **have** a large extended family.
2. I**'m having** problems with my wi-fi.
3. **Do** we really **have to** spend Christmas with your parents again?
4. We're going to **have** our house **repainted** next week.
   I **had** my phone **stolen** when I was paying at the checkout.

- We don't usually contract *have* when it is a main verb.
1. We use *have* as a main verb for possession.
- *have* with this meaning is a stative (non-action) verb and is not used in continuous tenses. *have* is also a stative verb when used to talk about relationships or illnesses.
2. We use *have* + object as a main verb for actions and experiences, e.g. *have a bath, a drink, a problem*, etc.
- *have* with this meaning is a dynamic (action) verb and can be used in continuous tenses.
3. We use *have to* as a main verb to express obligation, especially obligation imposed by others, and rules and regulations.
4. We use *have* as a main verb + object + past participle to say that you ask or pay another person to do something for you, or that something bad has been done to you.

different uses of *have* as an auxiliary verb

1. We**'ve got** two sons, but we **haven't got** a daughter.
2. I **haven't** the time to go to the bank.
3. I**'ve got to** go now – I'm meeting my girlfriend for lunch.
4. They**'ve been** married for 15 years.
   How long **has** Anna **been going** out with James?
5. She'll **have** finished lunch in a few minutes, so call her then.
   If I **hadn't** taken a taxi, I wouldn't **have** arrived in time.

- *have* as an auxiliary verb is often contracted.
1. We often use *have got* for possession.
- We normally use *had* for the past, not *had got*, e.g. *My grandparents had six children.* **NOT** ~~*My grandparents had got…*~~
2. In negative sentences, we occasionally leave out *got*, especially in fixed expressions like *I haven't time, I haven't a clue.*
3. We use *have got to* to express obligation, especially in informal English.
- *have got to* is normally used for a specific obligation rather than a general or repeated obligation. Compare:
  I've got to make a quick phone call. (= specific)
  I have to wear a suit to work. (= general)
4. We use *have* as an auxiliary verb to form the present perfect simple and continuous.
5. We also use *have* for other perfect forms, e.g. the future perfect, the perfect infinitive, the past perfect, etc.

have or *have got* in idioms and expressions

1. I think my sister has been borrowing money from my mother. I'm going to **have it out with** her. (= talk openly about it)
   You're getting married? You're **having me on**! (= play a joke on sb)
   I'm going to **have a go** at making home-made pasta. (= try)
   We **had** such a **laugh** at the party last night. (= enjoy yourself)
   That's it. I**'ve had it** with Mark. I'm never going to speak to him again. (= have had enough of sb/sth)
2. My boss is constantly asking me to work late. She really **has it in for me**. (= not like sb and be unpleasant to them)
   I don't think I**'ve got it in me** to find somebody new. (= feel capable of sth)

- There are many idioms and expressions with *have*, some of which can also be used with *have got*.
1. These expressions only exist with *have*.
2. These expressions exist with both *have* and *have got*.

a Right (✓) or wrong (✗)? Correct the mistakes in the highlighted phrases.

I'm exhausted! I've been looking after my sister's kids all day. ✓

1. I don't think you should drive until you've had your brakes fixed.
2. I can't come on holiday because I haven't got any money.
3. Has your husband to work tomorrow?
4. The staff don't have to dress formally in this company – they can wear what they like.
5. How long have you been having your flat in London?
6. What time are we having dinner tonight?
7. My parents had got a lot of problems with my sister when she was a teenager.
8. I don't have a holiday for 18 months. I really need a break.
9. Have we got to do this exercise now?

b Complete the second sentence so that it means the same as the first. Use a form of *have* or *have got*.

Her brother moved to Canada in 2011 and he still lives there.
Her brother*'s been living in Canada* since 2011.

1. She's an only child.
   She _____ brothers or sisters.
2. We used to pay someone to take a family photograph every year.
   We used _____ every year.
3. Having car insurance is compulsory for all drivers.
   All _____ car insurance.
4. He's seeing his father tomorrow. He last saw him two years ago.
   He's seeing his father tomorrow. He _____ two years.
5. He lacks the right qualifications for this job.
   He _____ for this job.
6. It isn't necessary for us to do it now; we can do it later.
   We _____; we can do it later.
7. The sea was amazingly clear and warm – we swam every morning.
   The sea was amazingly clear and warm – we _____ every morning.
8. When did you start to get on badly?
   How long _____ badly?
9. I need someone to fix the central heating.
   I need _____.

c Complete the sentences with one word.

1. He was a good interviewee, but I don't think he has it in _____ to do the job.
2. We went on a girls' night out last weekend, and we had a real _____.
3. Are you really going to do a bungee jump or are you having me _____?
4. My maths teacher has really _____ it in for me. She's much stricter with me than with the rest of the class.
5. I've _____ it with always tidying up after you.

p.7

discourse markers (1): linkers

result

> 1 I have a job interview next week, **so** I've bought myself a suit!
> 2 It had snowed hard all night. **As a result**, the airport was closed until 11.00 a.m.
> We regret that you do not have the necessary qualifications and **therefore** / **consequently** we are unable to offer you the job.

1 *so* is the most common way of introducing a result or a logical connection.
2 *as a result*, *therefore*, and *consequently* (more formal than *so*) are often used at the beginning of a sentence or clause.
• *therefore* and *consequently* can also be used before a main verb, e.g. *We have therefore / consequently decided not to offer you the job.*

reason

> 1 I've stopped emailing her, **because** / **as** / **since** she never answers me.
> Can I go home, **seeing as** / **seeing that** there's no work to do?
> 2 The plane was late **because of** the fog.
> Flight 341 has been delayed **due to** / **owing to** adverse weather conditions.

1 *because*, *as*, and *since* (more formal) are synonyms and are used to introduce clauses giving a reason. *as* and *since* are often used at the beginning of a sentence, e.g. *As / Since the rain hasn't stopped, we've decided not to go out.*
• We can use *seeing as* / *that* to give a reason for what we're saying.
2 *because of*, *due to*, and *owing to* also express the reason for something. They are usually followed by a noun, a gerund, or *the fact that* + clause.
• *due to* and *owing to* are more formal than *because of*.

purpose

> 1 I did a language course **to** / **in order to** / **so as to** improve my English.
> 2 He closed the door quietly **so as not to** / **in order not to** wake the baby.
> 3 They moved to London **so (that)** they could see their grandchildren more often.
> 4 I'm not going to tell Amy, **in case** she tells everyone else.

1 *to*, *in order to*, and *so as to* introduce a clause of purpose and are all followed by an infinitive. *to* is the most informal.
2 For negative purpose we use *so as not to* or *in order not to*.
3 We can also use *so (that)* + *can* / *could* + verb or *will* / *would* + verb to express purpose. *that* can be left out in informal English.
• Use *so (that)* when there is a change of subject in the clause of purpose, e.g. *She put a blanket over the baby so (that) he wouldn't be cold.*
4 We use *in case* + a clause when we do something in order to be ready for future situations / problems, or to avoid them.

contrast

> 1 The meeting was OK, **but** the journey home was a nightmare.
> Agnes was attracted to the stranger, **yet** something in her head was telling her not to get close to him.
> It's a really good idea. **However**, it may be too expensive.
> The moon shone brightly. **Nevertheless**, it was hard to find our way.
> 2 We enjoyed the film **although** / **even though** / **though** it was long.
> 3 **In spite of** / **Despite** being 85, she still travels all over the world.
> **In spite of** / **Despite** her age…   **In spite of** / **Despite** the fact that she's 85…

1 *but* is the most common and informal way of introducing contrast and is normally used to link two contrasting points within a sentence. *yet* is used in the same way, but is more formal / literary.
• *however* and *nevertheless* are normally used at the beginning of a sentence to connect it to the previous one and are usually followed by a comma.
• *nevertheless* (or *nonetheless*) is more formal / literary than *however*.
2 *even though* is more emphatic than *although*. *though* is more common in informal speech.
3 After *in spite of* and *despite*, use a gerund, a noun, or *the fact that* + clause.

---

a Circle the correct linker.

Even though / *Despite* she's working really hard, I don't think she'll be able to catch up.

1 We can't afford to have a holiday this year *as* / *yet* we've got an overdraft at the bank.
2 Could we rearrange my timetable *so that* / *in case* I don't have so many classes on Fridays?
3 I got to the interview on time *due to* / *in spite of* the fact that my train was late.
4 It isn't worth phoning John, *seeing that* / *so that* he's arriving in five minutes.
5 He gets a good salary *though* / *since* the job itself is quite monotonous.

b Circle the better option according to register.

Sales have increased over the last six months. *So* / *Therefore* we will be taking on five new employees.

1 I've been off work for the last three days *because of* / *owing to* this nasty cough I've got.
2 The organization has severe financial problems, and *so* / *consequently* half the staff have been laid off.
3 The company has reported declining sales this year. *Nevertheless* / *But*, they have so far managed to avoid any staff cuts.
4 I stopped at a service station *to* / *in order to* fill up with petrol.
5 I thought it was an amazing book. It was a bit depressing, *though* / *however*.
6 We regret to announce that the performance has been cancelled *due to* / *because of* technical problems.

c Join the sentences using the **bold** word(s), making any necessary changes.

We only use energy-efficient light bulbs. We don't want to waste electricity. **so as**
We only use energy-efficient light bulbs so as not to waste electricity.

1 Our seats were a long way from the stage. We enjoyed the play. **In spite**
We _____.
2 It took us ages to get there. The traffic was heavy. **because of**
It _____.
3 I took the price off the bag. I didn't want Becky to know how much it had cost. **so**
I _____.
4 Keep the receipt for the sweater. Your dad might not like it. **in case**
Keep _____.
5 Susanna is an only child. She isn't at all spoilt. **Even though**
Susanna _____.
6 Prices have risen. Production costs have increased. **due to**
Prices _____.

p.13

the past: habitual events and specific incidents

narrative tenses: describing specific incidents in the past

This **happened** when I **was** about five years old. My father **had gone away** on business for a few days and my brother and I **were sleeping** in my parents' bedroom. Before we **went** to bed that night, I **had been reading** a very scary story about a wicked witch. In the middle of the night, I **woke up** with a start and **saw** that a figure in a dark coat **was standing** in the doorway. I **screamed** at the top of my voice.

When we describe specific incidents in the past, we use **narrative tenses**, i.e. the past simple, past continuous, and past perfect simple or continuous.

- We use the past simple to talk about the main actions in a story (*We went to bed…, I woke up…, I screamed*).
- We use the past continuous to set the scene (*We were sleeping in my parents' bedroom*) and to describe actions in progress in the past (*Somebody was standing in the doorway*).
- We use the past perfect and the past perfect continuous to talk about the earlier past, i.e. things which happened before the main event (*My father had gone away…, I had been reading a story*).

used to and would: describing habitual events and repeated actions in the past

1. Every summer, my family **used to rent** an old house in the south of France. My sister and I **often walked** to the harbour in the morning, where we **used to watch** the fishermen cleaning their nets.
2. Every night before we went to bed, my mother **would tell** us stories, but she **would never read** them from a book – she **would always make them up** herself.
3. When I was a teenager, my friends **were always teasing** me because of my red hair.

1. We often use *used to* + infinitive as an alternative to the past simple to talk about things that we did repeatedly in the past.
- We can also use *used to* + infinitive to talk about situations or states which have changed, e.g. *I used to have much longer hair when I was younger.*
2. We use *would* + infinitive as an alternative to *used to* to talk about things that we did repeatedly in the past over a period of time.
- We <u>don't</u> use *would* with stative verbs, i.e. to talk about situations or states which have changed. **NOT** I would have much longer hair when I was younger.
- We don't use *would* without a time reference, e.g. *I used to play the violin.* **NOT** I would play the violin.
3. We can also use *always* + past continuous for things that happened repeatedly, especially when they were irritating habits.

🔍 ***used to and be / get used to***
Be careful not to confuse *used to* and *be / get used to. used to* only describes states or repeated actions in the past, *be / get used to* means *be / get familiar with*, e.g. **We used to live** in London. We moved to the country last year, but **we're still not used to it**. It's too quiet for me, and **my husband can't get used to** having to drive everywhere.

a Circle the correct form. Tick (✓) if both are possible.

Corinne and I *used to be* / *would be* very close, but recently we've grown apart.

1. When I came into the room, my aunt *sat* / *was sitting* with her back to me. When she turned round, I could see that she *had been crying* / *had cried*.
2. Our grandmother *always used to have* / *would always have* a surprise waiting for us when we visited.
3. My sister *used to live* / *would live* on her own, but then she *was buying* / *bought* a flat with her boyfriend.
4. My brother *didn't use to look* / *wouldn't look* at all like my father, but now he does.
5. When I was small, I *was always getting* / *always used to get* into trouble at school and my parents *used to punish* / *would punish* me by not letting me play with my friends at the weekend.
6. Suddenly, we heard a tremendous bang and we saw that a car *crashed* / *had crashed* into a tree and petrol *poured* / *was pouring* onto the road.

b Complete the text with the verb in brackets using a narrative tense or *would* / *used to*.

My earliest memory

When I was about four or five, my grandmother, who was Polish, <u>was living</u> (live) in London and we children often ¹_____ (spend) weekends at her flat. My grandfather ²_____ (die) a couple of years earlier, so I suppose she was in need of company. We loved going there, as my grandmother ³_____ (cook) special meals for us and ⁴_____ (take) us for lovely walks in Regent's Park, which was quite nearby. One occasion that I remember really well was when she ⁵_____ (invite) me to stay with her on my own, without my brothers and sisters. On the first day, after lunch, my grandmother ⁶_____ (go) for her rest. I ⁷_____ (try) to sleep too, but I couldn't, so after a while I ⁸_____ (get up) and ⁹_____ (decide) to explore the flat. Everything was very quiet, so I was convinced that my grandmother ¹⁰_____ (sleep). The room I most ¹¹_____ (want) to explore was my grandfather's study, I imagine, precisely because she ¹²_____ (tell) me not to go in there. I opened the door and went in, and was immediately drawn to his large old desk. I ¹³_____ (climb) onto the chair and ¹⁴_____ (see) on the desk a green pen in a kind of stand, with a bottle of ink. I ¹⁵_____ (ask) my parents for a real pen for a long time, but they ¹⁶_____ (refuse), foreseeing the mess that I was almost bound to make with the ink. I picked up the pen and then tried to open the bottle of ink. At that moment, I ¹⁷_____ (hear) my grandmother's voice saying, 'Christina? Where are you? What are you doing?' To my horror, I ¹⁸_____ (realize) that my grandmother ¹⁹_____ (get up) and ²⁰_____ (come) towards the study. Two seconds later, she ²¹_____ (open) the door. I will never forget the awful feeling of shame that she ²²_____ (catch) me doing something that she ²³_____ (forbid) me to do.

← p.17

2B

pronouns

generic pronouns

> 1 If **you** mispronounce a word, people might not understand **you**.
> 2 **One** tends to have problems understanding very strong accents.
> 3 When **we** talk about an accent, **we** must not confuse this with pronunciation.
> 4 **They** always say that it's never too late to learn a new language.
>   **They** should make it compulsory for people to learn two languages at school.
> 5 If someone phones me, tell **them** to call back later.
>   Could the person who left **their** bag in the library please come and see me?

1 We often use *you* to mean people in general.
2 We can also use *one* + third person singular of the verb to mean people in general. *one* is much more formal than *you* and is very rarely used in spoken English.
• We can also use *one's* as a possessive adjective, e.g. *When confronted with danger, one's first reaction is often to freeze.*
3 *we* can also be used to make a general statement of opinion which includes the reader / listener.
4 In informal English, we often use *they* to talk about other people in general, or people in authority, e.g. ***They** always say…* (*They* = people in general); ***They** should make it compulsory…* (*They* = the government).
5 We use *they, them,* and *their* to refer to one person who may be male or female, instead of using *he* or *she, his* or *her*, etc.

reflexive and reciprocal pronouns

> 1 You need to look after **yourself** with that cold.
>   He's very egocentric. He always talks about **himself**.
> 2 I managed to complete the crossword! I was really pleased with **myself**.
> 3 We decorated the house **ourselves**.
>   There's no way I'm going to do it for you. Do it **yourself**!
> 4 I don't feel very comfortable going to the cinema **by myself**.
> 5 My ex-husband and I don't talk to **each other** any more.
>   My mother and sister don't understand **one another** at all.

1 We often use reflexive pronouns when the subject and object of a verb are the same person.
• We don't usually use reflexive pronouns with some verbs which may be reflexive in other languages, e.g. *wash, shave,* etc. **NOT** ~~He got up, shaved himself, and …~~
• *enjoy* is always used with a reflexive pronoun when not followed by another object, e.g. *Enjoy your meal!* **BUT** *Did you enjoy **yourself** last night?*
2 We can also use reflexive pronouns after most prepositions when the complement is the same as the subject.
• After prepositions of place we use object pronouns, not reflexive pronouns, e.g. *She put the bag next to her on the seat.* **NOT** ~~next to herself~~
3 We can use reflexive pronouns to emphasize the subject, e.g. *We decorated the house ourselves.* (= we did it, not professional decorators)
4 *by* + reflexive pronoun = alone, on your / her, etc. own.
5 We use *each other* or *one another* for reciprocal actions, i.e. A does the action to B, and B does the action to A.

it and *there*

> 1 **It's** 10 o'clock. **It's** 30 degrees today. **It's** five miles to the coast.
> 2 **It was** great to hear that you and Martina are getting married!
>   **It used to be** difficult to buy fresh pasta in the UK, but now it's everywhere.
> 3 **There have been** a lot of storms recently. **There used to be** a cinema in that street.

1 We use *it* + *be* to talk about time, temperature, and distance.
2 We also use *it* + *be* as a 'preparatory' subject before adjectives. *It was great to hear from you.* **NOT** ~~To hear from you was great.~~
3 We use *there* + *be* + noun to say if people and things are present or exist (or not). You cannot use *It…* here. **NOT** ~~It used to be a cinema in that street.~~

---

a Circle the correct pronoun. Tick (✓) if both are possible.

> They helped **one another** / *themselves* to prepare for the exam.

1 *One / You* can often tell where people are from by the way they speak.
2 Can you put my case on the rack above *yourself / you*?
3 Sally and her sister look incredibly like *each other / one another*. Are they twins?
4 Steve is a really private person – he rarely talks about *him / himself*.
5 Either Suzie or Mark has left *her / their* book behind.
6 When a person goes to live abroad, it may take *them / him* a while to pick up the language.
7 *They / One* say that eating tomatoes can help protect the body against certain diseases.

b Complete the sentences with a pronoun.

> Don't tell him how to spell it. Let him work it out by *himself*.

1 If anyone has not yet paid _____ course fees, _____ should go to registration immediately.
2 Isabel is very quick-tempered. She finds it very hard to control _____.
3 I wouldn't stay in that hotel – _____ say the rooms are tiny and the service is awful.
4 They've never got on. They just don't like _____ at all.
5 Did they enjoy _____ at the festival?
6 Are you going to have the flat repainted, or will you and Jo do it _____?
7 It's always the same with taxis. _____ can never find one when _____ need one!

c Complete the sentences with *it* or *there*.

> *There* was a very interesting article about language learning in *The Times* yesterday.

1 Look. _____'s a spelling mistake in this word. _____ should be *j*, not *g*.
2 _____'s illegal to use a handheld mobile while you're driving. _____ used to be a lot of accidents caused by this.
3 How many miles is _____ to Manchester from here?
4 _____'s scorching today. _____ must be at least 35 degrees.
5 _____'s no need to hurry. The train doesn't leave for ages.
6 _____'s not worth reading the paper today. _____'s absolutely nothing interesting in it.

◀ p.21

get

1 I **got** a message today asking me on a date!
If you're going to the post office, could you **get** me some stamps?
Let's not bother with a taxi – we can **get** the bus.
When do you think we'll **get to** Paris?

2 We'd better go home. It's **getting dark**.
I seem to have **got** very **forgetful** recently.
The traffic **gets worse** in the city centre every day.
I don't think my mother will ever **get used to** living on her own.

3 Did you know Dan **got sacked** last week?
My husband **got caught** on the motorway driving at 150 km/h.

4 I'm going to **get my hair cut** next week.
I need to **get my passport renewed** – it runs out in a couple of months.

5 Could you **get Jane to finish** the report? I'm too busy to do it this afternoon.
We need to **get someone to fix** the central heating – it's not working properly.

- **get** is one of the most common verbs in English and can be used in many different ways.

1 **get** + noun / pronoun usually means 'receive', 'bring', 'fetch', 'obtain', 'buy', or 'catch'; with **to** + a place it means 'arrive at / in'.

2 We use **get** + adjective or comparative adjective to mean 'become'.

- Compare **be** + adjective and **get** + adjective:
It's dark. It's getting dark.
I'm used to the climate in England now. I'm getting used to the climate in England.

3 We can use **get** + past participle instead of **be** to make a passive structure. This is more informal than using **be** and is often used to talk about bad or unexpected things that have happened.

4 In informal spoken English, we sometimes use **get** + object + past participle instead of **have** + object + past participle to say that you ask or pay another person to do something for you.
See **1A** p.142.

5 We can use **get** + object + infinitive with **to** to mean 'make', 'tell', 'persuade' somebody (to) do something.

- **have** can also be used in this way (without **to**), especially in American English, e.g. *I'll have someone send you the details.*

a Replace **get** with another verb in the correct form so that the sentences mean the same.

He **got** blamed for the break-up of their   *was*
marriage.

1 My father **is getting** increasingly   _____
bad-tempered in his old age.

2 Do you know anywhere near here where   _____
I can **get** something to eat?

3 Could you **get** your brother to lend you   _____
the money?

4 We had to **get** the roof repaired, as it was   _____
damaged in the storm.

5 I **got** an email out of the blue today from an   _____
old school friend.

6 If I **get** the 7.30 train, would you be able to   _____
pick me up at the station?

7 What time do you think we'll **get to** the   _____
hotel?

8 If you're going upstairs, could you **get** me   _____
my jacket? It's on the bed.

9 You're going to **get** fined if you park there.   _____

10 How can I **get** you to change your mind?   _____

b Complete the sentences with the correct form of **get** and the words in brackets.

I think we ought to stop playing now. It's *getting cold.*
(cold)

1 I only just _____ in time. It was about to run out. (my work permit / renew)

2 My husband has only been in the UK for two months and he just can't _____ on the left. (used / drive)

3 Monica's fiancé _____ in a car crash. He only just survived. (nearly / kill)

4 I can _____ tomorrow night so we can go out. (my sister / babysit)

5 If you can't find your keys, we'll have to _____. (all the locks / change)

6 We _____ by the police today. They were looking for a stolen car. (stop)

7 I went to the optician's yesterday to _____. (eyes / test)

8 We could drive there if you could _____ their car. (your parents / lend)

9 My job has _____ over the last few years. (more stressful)

10 We really want to _____ soon. (the kitchen / replace)

p.29

discourse markers (2): adverbs and adverbial expressions

Expression	Use
A I really like your shirt. Hasn't Harry got one just like it? **B** Yes he has. **Talking of / Speaking of** Harry, did he get the job?	To change the direction of a conversation, but making a link with what has just been said.
So let's meet at five o'clock then. **By the way / Incidentally**, could you possibly lend me some money?	To introduce something you have just thought of, or to change the subject.
A Did you see the match last night? **B** No. **Actually / In fact / As a matter of fact**, I don't really like football.	To introduce additional surprising or unexpected information.
We didn't go away at the weekend because I had too much work. **In any case / Anyway** the weather was awful, so we didn't miss much.	To introduce the idea that what you said before is less important than what you are saying now, or to return to the main topic after a digression.
Yes, it was a bad accident. **At least** nobody was killed, though. Tom's coming to the meeting, or **at least**, he said he was.	To introduce a positive point after some negative information, or to qualify what you have just said or to make it less definite.
As I was saying, if Mark gets the job, we'll have to reorganize the department.	To return to a previous subject, often after you have been interrupted.
He's still a great director but, **on the whole**, I prefer his earlier films.	To generalize.
I like both flats, but **all in all**, I think I prefer the one next to the cathedral.	To say that you are taking everything into consideration.
I think we should buy them. **After all**, we'll never find them anywhere cheaper than this.	To introduce an argument that the other person may not have considered.
I don't think I'll come to Nick's party. It will finish very late. **Besides**, I won't know many people there.	To introduce an additional point.
Basically, my job involves computer skills and people skills.	To introduce the most important or fundamental point.
Obviously, you can't get a real idea of life in Japan unless you can speak the language.	To introduce a fact that is very clear to see or understand.
She's very selfish. **I mean**, she never thinks about other people at all.	To make things clearer, or give more details.
A lot of people booed and some people even left early. **In other words**, it was a complete disaster.	To say something again in another way.
Try not to make a mess when you make the cake. **Otherwise** I'm going to have to clean the kitchen again.	To say what the result would be if something did not happen or were different.
…and that's all you need to know about the travel arrangements. **As far as** accommodation is **concerned**, … **As regards / Regarding** the accommodation, …	To introduce a new topic or to announce a change of subject.
There are plans to help first-time buyers. **That is to say**, mortgages will be more easily available.	To introduce an explanation or clarification of a point you have just made.
On the one hand, more young people today carry knives. **On the other hand**, the total number of violent crimes has dropped.	To balance contrasting facts or points. • *On the other hand* is also used alone to introduce a contrasting fact or point.

a Circle the correct discourse marker.

  A What a good film! I really enjoyed it. And you?

  B *Actually / Incidentally* I didn't like it very much.

  A Why not?

  B [1] *Basically / After all*, I thought the plot was completely unbelievable.

  A I wouldn't call it unbelievable. [2] *In other words / In any case*, it wasn't supposed to be a true story.

  B I know, but it was set in a specific historical period. [3] *Otherwise / Obviously*, you can't expect the dialogue to be totally authentic, [4] *I mean / on the other hand*, nobody knows exactly how people spoke in Roman times, but [5] *besides / at least* the details should be right. There were cannons in the battle scene and they weren't invented till a thousand years later! [6] *All in all / That is to say*, I thought it was a pretty awful film.

  A We'll have to agree to disagree then. [7] *By the way / As a matter of fact*, do you know what time the last bus leaves? I don't want to miss it. [8] *Otherwise / In any case*, I'll have to get a taxi home.

  B 11.40. Don't worry, we've got plenty of time. [9] *In fact / Besides*, I think we've even got time to have something to eat. There's a good Italian restaurant just round the corner.

  A Good idea. [10] *As I was saying / Talking of* Italian food, I made a wonderful mushroom risotto last night…

b Complete the sentences with a discourse marker. Sometimes more than one answer is possible.

  The film was a box office disaster. *That is to say*, it cost more to produce than it made in receipts.

1 **A** Did you buy the shoes in the end?

   B No, they were too expensive. And _____, I decided that I didn't really like them that much.

2 I really think you ought to apply for the post of Head of Department. _____ you've got nothing to lose.

3 **A** I've just read a brilliant book that Simon lent me.

   B _____ Simon, did you know he's moving?

4 **A** How was your day?

   B Fine. I finished work earlier than usual. _____, did you remember to get a birthday present for Mum?

5 _____ salary, you will be paid on the last day of each month, with a bonus in December.

6 It was a very overcast day, but _____ it didn't rain.

7 I'm not sure what the best solution is. _____, buying our own place would mean not paying rent, but _____, I'm not sure we can afford a mortgage.

8 They've employed me as a troubleshooter – _____, somebody who sorts out any problems.

9 The food was delicious and the service was excellent. _____, the meal was a great success.

10 **A** Do your wife's parents live near you, then?

   B _____, they live in the flat below us. It's not ideal, but it does have some advantages.

11 You'd better hurry up with your homework, _____ you won't be able to watch TV tonight.

↩ p.32

adding emphasis (1): inversion

1 **Not only is the plot** great, (but) it's also very well written.
   Not until you can behave like an adult **will we treat** you like an adult.
   Never have I heard such a ridiculous argument.
   Never again will I believe a word he says.
   No sooner had the football match started than it began to snow heavily.
2 **Not only did you forget** to shut the window, (but) you also forgot to lock the door!
   Not until you become a parent yourself **do you understand** what it really means.

3 The train began to move. **Only then was I able to** relax.
   Only when you leave home **do you realize** how expensive everything is.
   Hardly had I sat down when / **before** the meeting began.
   Rarely have I met a more irritating person.

- In formal English, especially in writing, we sometimes change the normal word order to make the sentence more emphatic or dramatic.
1 This structure is common with negative adverbial expressions such as *Not only…*, *Not until…*, *Never (again)…*, and *No sooner…* (= a formal way of saying *as soon as*).
- When we use inversion after the above expressions, we change the order of the subject and (auxiliary) verb. **NOT** ~~Not only the plot is great,…~~
   Compare:
   I have never heard such a ridiculous argument. (= normal word order)
   Never have I heard such a ridiculous argument. (= inversion to make the sentence more emphatic)
2 In the present simple and past simple tense, rather than simply inverting the subject and verb, we use *do / does / did* + subject + main verb. **NOT** ~~Not only forgot you to shut the window…~~
3 Inversion is also used after the expressions *Only then…*, *Only when…*, *Hardly / Scarcely…*, *Rarely…*

🔍 **Overuse of inversion**
   Inversion should only be used occasionally for dramatic effect. Overusing it will make your English sound unnatural.

Rewrite the sentences to make them more emphatic.

I had just started reading when all the lights went out.
No sooner *had I started reading than all the lights went out*.

1 I didn't realize my mistake until years later.
   Not until _____.
2 We had never seen such magnificent scenery.
   Never _____.
3 They not only disliked her, but they also hated her family.
   Not only _____.
4 We only understood what he had really suffered when we read his autobiography.
   Only when _____
   _____.
5 We had just started to eat when we heard someone knocking at the door.
   Hardly _____
   _____.
6 I have rarely read such a badly written novel.
   Rarely _____.
7 Until you've tried to write a novel yourself, you don't realize how hard it is.
   Not until _____
   _____.
8 The hotel room was depressing – it was cold as well.
   Not only _____.
9 We only light the fire when it is unusually cold.
   Only when _____.
10 Shortly after he had gone to sleep the phone rang.
   No sooner _____.
11 I only realized the full scale of the disaster when I watched the six o'clock news.
   I watched the six o'clock news. Only then
   _____.
12 He has never regretted the decision he took on that day.
   Never _____.
13 I spoke to the manager and the problem was taken seriously.
   Only when _____.
14 He had scarcely had time to destroy the evidence before the police arrived.
   Scarcely _____
   _____.
15 He would never see his homeland again.
   Never again _____.

◀ p.37

speculation and deduction

modal verbs: *must, may, might, can't, could, should, ought*

1 That **must be** an electric car – it isn't making any noise at all.
You **must have seen** him – he was standing right in front of you!

2 They **can't be playing** very well – they're losing 3–0.
You **can't** / **couldn't have spent** very long on this essay – you've only written 100 words.

3 I haven't seen the Sales Manager today. He **may** / **might** / **could be** off sick.
The keys of the store cupboard have disappeared. Do you think someone **may** / **might** / **could have taken** them?
He **may** / **might not have heard** the message I left.

4 If I post the letter today, it **should** / **ought to arrive** on Friday.
I posted the letter a week ago, it **should** / **ought to have arrived** by now.

---

1 As well as using *must* for obligation, we also use *must* + infinitive to say that we are almost sure something is true about the present and *must have* + past participle to say that we are almost sure something was true or happened in the past.

2 We use *can't* + infinitive to say that we are almost sure that something isn't true in the present and *can't have* / *couldn't have* + past participle to say that we are almost sure that something wasn't true / didn't happen in the past.
• We don't use *mustn't* / *mustn't have* with this meaning.

3 We use *may* / *might* / *could* + infinitive and *may have* / *might have* / *could have* + past participle to say that we think it's possible that something is true in the present, or was true / happened in the past.
• We only use *may not* or *might not* to talk about a negative possibility. **NOT** *couldn't*

4 We use *should* / *ought to* + infinitive to describe a situation we expect to happen. We use *should have* / *ought to have* + past participle to describe a situation we would expect to have happened in the past.

> 🔍 **Infinitive or continuous infinitive after modals?**
>
> He **must work** really hard. He never gets home before 9.00 p.m.
> (= deduction about a habitual action)
>
> There's a light on in his office. He **must** still **be working**.
> (= deduction about an action in progress at the moment of speaking)

adjectives and adverbs for speculation

1 He's **bound** / **sure to** be here in a minute. He left an hour ago.
She's **bound** / **sure to** know. She's an expert on the subject.

2 I think she's **likely** / **unlikely to** agree to our proposal.
It is **likely** / **unlikely** that the government will raise interest rates this year.

3 She'**ll definitely pass** the exam. She's worked really hard.
She **definitely won't** pass the exam. She hasn't done any work at all.
He'**ll probably be** here around 8.00. He usually leaves work at 7.30.
He **probably won't be** here until about 8.15. He's stuck in a traffic jam.

---

1 *bound* and *sure* are adjectives. We use *be bound* or *be sure* + *to* + infinitive to say that we think something is certain to be true or to happen.

2 *likely* and *unlikely* are also adjectives (not adverbs). We can use subject + *be likely* / *unlikely* + *to* + infinitive, or *it is likely* / *unlikely* + *that* clause.

3 *definitely* and *probably* are adverbs. They go before a main verb and after the auxiliary if there is one in ⊞ sentences and before the auxiliary in ⊟ sentences.
• With *be* they go after the verb in ⊞ sentences and before the verb in ⊟ sentences, e.g. *He's probably British. The painting definitely isn't genuine.*

---

a Right (✓) or wrong (✗)? Correct the mistakes in the highlighted phrases.

Jim didn't leave work until 6.00, so <mark>he won't likely be here</mark> before 7.00. ✗
Jim didn't leave work until 6.00, so he's unlikely to be here before 7.00.

1 My glasses aren't in their usual place. <mark>Someone must move them.</mark>

2 **A** Do you know where Emma is?
B <mark>She should be in the library.</mark> That's where she said she was going.

3 **A** What's that noise in the garage?
B <mark>I think it can be</mark> the neighbour's cat.

4 I'm sure Chelsea will win tonight. <mark>They're unlikely to lose</mark> three times in a row.

5 I think you should delete that photo of Tina. <mark>She won't definitely like</mark> it.

6 <mark>Julian is bound be late</mark> – he always is.

7 No one's answering the phone at the shop. <mark>I'd say they've probably gone home.</mark>

8 I don't think Marta has gone to bed yet. <mark>I think she must still study.</mark>

9 <mark>It's quite likely that the boss will retire</mark> in a year or two.

b Complete the sentences using the **bold** word.

Perhaps Luke has got lost. He has no sense of direction. **might**
Luke *might have got lost*. He has no sense of direction.

1 I don't think he'll have time to call in and see us. He has a very tight schedule. **probably**
He _____. He has a very tight schedule.

2 I'm not sure she'll ever get over the break-up. **may**
She _____ the break-up.

3 They will probably have heard the news by now. **ought**
They _____ now.

4 I didn't leave my credit card in the restaurant.
I remember putting it in my wallet. **can't**
I _____.
I remember putting it in my wallet.

5 I'm sure your sister will like the scarf – it's just her style. **bound**
Your sister _____. It's just her style.

6 The company director probably won't resign, despite the disastrous sales figures. **unlikely**
The company director _____, despite the disastrous sales figures.

7 I'm sure he was in love with her, otherwise he wouldn't have married her. **must**
He _____, otherwise he wouldn't have married her.

8 Are you sure you locked the back door? **definitely**
Did _____ lock the back door?

9 According to press reports, the couple will probably get divorced soon. **likely**
According to press reports, it's _____ soon.

 p.41

 Go online to review the grammar for each lesson

distancing

seem / appear

> 1 **It seems / appears that** when older people stay busy, they are in fact much healthier.
> The new Head of Department **seems / appears to be** quite friendly.
> Excuse me. **There seems / appears to be** a mistake with the bill.
> 2 **It would seem / appear that** Mr Young had been using the company's assets to pay off his private debts.

1 We often use *seem* and *appear* to give information without stating that we definitely know it is true, in this way distancing ourselves from the information.
   We can use *It seems / appears + that + clause*, or *subject + seem / appear + infinitive*.

2 We use *It would seem / appear + that + clause* to distance ourselves even further from the information, making it sound even less sure. This is more formal than *It seems / appears…*

the passive with verbs of saying and reporting

> 1 **It is said that** using a washing machine saves people on average 47 minutes a day.
> **It has been announced by** a spokesperson **that** the President has been taken to hospital.
> 2 The company director **is expected to resign** in the next few days.
> The missing couple **are understood to have been living** in Panama for the last five years.
> 3 There **are thought to be** over a thousand species in danger of extinction.

• Another way of distancing ourselves from the facts, especially in formal written English, is to use the passive form of verbs like *say*, *think*, etc. to introduce them. We can use:

1 *It + passive verb + that + clause*.
• Verbs commonly used in this pattern are: *agree, announce, believe, claim, expect, hope, say, suggest,* and *think*.

2 *subject + passive verb + to + infinitive*.
• Verbs commonly used in this pattern are: *believe, consider, expect, report, say, think,* and *understand*.

3 *There* can also be used + *passive verb + to + infinitive*. Compare:
• *It is said that there are more than five million people living in poverty in this country.*
• *There are said to be more than five million people living in poverty in this country.*

other distancing expressions: *apparently, according to, may / might, claim*

> 1 **Apparently**, Jeff and Katie have separated.
> 2 **According to** new research, the idea that we have to drink two litres of water a day is a myth.
> 3 Dinosaurs **may have died out** due to extremely rapid climate change.
> There are rumours that the band, who broke up ten years ago, **might be planning** to reform and record a new album.
> 4 The health minister **claims** to have reduced waiting times.

1 We use *apparently* (usually either at the beginning or the end of a phrase) to mean that we have heard / read something, but that it may not be true. This is very common in informal conversation.

2 We use *according to* to specify where information has come from. We use it to attribute opinions to somebody else. **NOT** ~~According to me…~~

3 Using *may / might* also suggests that something is a possibility, but not necessarily true.

4 We can say that somebody *claims* something when there is some doubt about whether it is true.

---

a Complete the sentences with one word to distance the speaker from the information. Sometimes more than one answer is possible.

> *Apparently*, people who multitask often have concentration problems.

1 It _____ that the less children sleep, the more likely they are to behave badly.
2 It _____ appear that someone has been stealing personal items from the changing rooms.
3 Matt _____ to have aged a lot over the last year.
4 He may not look it, but he is _____ to be one of the wealthiest people in the country.
5 _____ to some sources, the latest research is seriously flawed.
6 Despite the fact that there will be an autopsy, his death is _____ to have been from natural causes.
7 _____ are thought to be several reasons why the experiment failed.
8 The troubled celebrity is believed _____ have had financial difficulties.
9 It is understood _____ the minister will be resigning in the near future.

b Complete the second sentence so that it means the same as the first.

> People say that mindfulness helps people to deal with stressful work environments.
> It is *said that mindfulness helps people to deal with stressful work environments.*

1 Apparently, people who work night shifts die younger.
   It would _____ die younger.
2 It is possible that the prisoners escaped to France.
   The prisoners may _____ to France.
3 We expect that the Prime Minister will make a statement this afternoon.
   The Prime Minister is _____ this afternoon.
4 The company has announced that the new drug will go on sale shortly.
   It _____ will go on sale shortly.
5 People believe that stress is responsible for many common skin complaints.
   Stress _____ for many common skin complaints.
6 The instructions say that the battery lasts for at least 12 hours.
   According _____ for at least 12 hours.
7 It appears that the government is intending to lower the top rate of income tax.
   The government _____ the top rate of income tax.
8 People have suggested that birth order has a strong influence on children's personalities.
   It _____ a strong influence on children's personalities.
9 It seems that there are more cyclists on the road than there used to be.
   There _____ than there used to be.

← p.47

5B

unreal uses of past tenses

1 It's so expensive! I **wish** I **could** afford it!
  I **wish** (that) you **hadn't spoken** to Julie like that – you know how sensitive she is.
2 **If only** he **were** a bit less stubborn! Then we wouldn't have so many arguments!
  If only you **hadn't forgotten** the map, we'd be there by now.
3 I **wish** she **were** a bit more generous.
  If only the weather **were** a bit warmer, we could walk there.

4 **I'd rather** you **left** your dog outside – I'm allergic to animals.
  Are you sure this is a good time to talk? **Would you rather** I **called** back later?
5 Don't you think **it's time** you **found** a job? It's six months since you finished university!

1 We use *wish* + past simple to talk about things we would like to be different in the present / future (but which are impossible or unlikely).
  We use *wish* + past perfect to talk about things which happened / didn't happen in the past and which we now regret.
• We sometimes use *that* after *wish*.
2 We sometimes use *If only...* instead of *I wish...* It is less common and more emphatic. It can be used by itself, e.g. *If only I hadn't said it!* but it can also be used with another clause, e.g. *If only I hadn't said it, none of this would have happened!*
• When we want to talk about things we want to happen or stop happening because they annoy us, we use *wish* or *If only* + person / thing + *would* + infinitive, e.g. *I wish the bus would come! If only he wouldn't keep whistling when I'm working!*
3 We can use *were* instead of *was* for *I / he / she / it* after *wish* and *if only*.
4 We use *would rather* + subject + past tense to express a preference.
• We can also use *would rather* + infinitive without *to* when there is no change of subject, e.g. *I'd rather **not talk** about it.* However, we cannot use this structure when the subject changes after *would rather*, e.g. *I'd rather **you didn't talk** about it.* **NOT** ~~I'd rather you not talk about it.~~
5 We use the past simple after *It's (high) time* + subject to say that something has to be done now or in the near future.
• We can also use *It's time* + *to* + infinitive when we don't want to specify the subject, e.g. *It's time to go now.*

a Complete the sentences with the correct form of the verb in brackets.

I wish I *hadn't lent* Gary that money now. Who knows when he'll pay it back? (not lend)

1 It's high time the government _____ that most people disagree with their education policy. (realize)
2 My wife would rather we _____ a flat nearer the city centre, but we can't afford it. (buy)
3 I wish you _____ to stay a bit longer last night – we were having such a good time! (be able)
4 Would you rather we _____ the subject now? (not discuss)
5 I think it's time the company _____ expecting us to do overtime for no extra pay. (stop)
6 If only I _____ a bit more when I was earning a salary, I wouldn't be so hard up now. (save)
7 I'd rather you _____ me in cash, please. (pay)
8 If only we _____ the name of the shop, we could google it and see where it is. (know)
9 Do you wish you _____ to university or are you glad you left school and started work? (go)

b Complete the sentences using the **bold** word or phrase.

The children ought to go to bed. It's nine o'clock. **time**
It's time the children went to bed. It's nine o'clock.

1 I'd prefer you not to wear shoes in the living room, if you don't mind. **rather**
  _____, if you don't mind.
2 I would like to be able to afford to travel more. **wish**
  _____ travel more.
3 We shouldn't have painted the room blue – it looks awful **if only**
  _____ – it looks awful!
4 Don't you think you should start looking for your own flat? **time**
  Don't you think _____ for your own flat?
5 He's so rude, he's really difficult to work with. **if only**
  _____, he'd be easier to work with.
6 Would you prefer us to come another day? **rather**
  _____ another day?
7 I should have bought the tickets last week. They would have been cheaper then. **wish**
  _____ last week.
  They would have been cheaper then.
8 It's really inconvenient when he turns up without letting us know. **if only**
  _____ before he turns up.

← p.52

verb + object + infinitive or gerund

verb + object + *to* + infinitive

> 1 She **advised him not to travel** by train.
> We **expect the flight to arrive** at 19.50.
> It **took us ages to get** there.
> 2 I'm **waiting for my friend to arrive**.
> We've **arranged for a taxi to come** at 6.30.
> 3 I **want Arsenal to win**.
> I **would hate you to think** that I don't appreciate your offer of help.
> I'd **like you to send** me the bill.

1 We often use the following verbs + object + (not) to + infinitive: *advise, allow, ask, beg, cause, enable, encourage, expect, force, help, intend, invite, mean, order, persuade, remind, take (time), teach, tell, warn*.
  • After *advise, persuade, remind, teach, tell*, and *warn* you can also use an object + *that* clause, e.g. *She advised him that he shouldn't travel by train.*

> 🔍 **Other patterns**
> After *advise, allow, encourage*, or *recommend*, if we want to use another verb, but without an object, a gerund is needed, e.g. *We don't allow eating and drinking on the premises. I recommend visiting the castle.*
> After *recommend* we can also use a *that* clause, e.g. *He recommended that I took some cash.*

2 After some verbs including *arrange, ask, plan*, and *wait* we put *for* immediately after the verb before the object + *to* + infinitive.
3 We also often use verb + object + *to* + infinitive with *want, would like, would love, would prefer*, and *would hate*.
  • After all these verbs a *that* clause is impossible. **NOT** ~~I want that Arsenal wins. I would hate that you think…~~

verb + object + infinitive without *to*

> Please **let me explain**!
> He **made me feel** really guilty.
> My parents **helped me buy** a car.

  • We can use object + infinitive <u>without</u> *to* after *let, make*, and *help*.
  • *help* can be followed by object + infinitive with or without *to*, e.g. *She helped me (to) make the dinner.*

> 🔍 **Passive form of *make sb do sth***
> When *make sb do sth* is used in the passive, it is followed by the infinitive with *to*, e.g. *We were made to clean our rooms every morning.*

verb + object + gerund

> Please don't **keep me waiting**!
> I **dislike people telling** me what to do.
> I **don't mind you watching the TV**, but please could you turn the sound down a bit?

  • We often use the following verbs + object + gerund: *dislike, hate, imagine, involve, keep, mind, prevent, remember, risk, stop*.

Complete the second sentence so that it means the same as the first.

> 'Take special care because of the snow and ice,' the police told motorists.
> The police warned <u>motorists</u> <u>to</u> <u>take</u> <u>special</u> care because of the snow and ice.

1 You sit down – I'll make the coffee.
   You sit down. Let _____ _____ the coffee.
2 I felt uncomfortable because of the situation at work.
   The situation at work made _____ _____ _____.
3 You are going to stay with a British family. We have made the arrangements.
   We have arranged _____ _____ _____ _____ with a British family.
4 I don't have a problem if Sarah comes, but I'd rather her boyfriend didn't.
   I don't mind _____ _____, but I'd rather her boyfriend didn't.
5 Please don't think that I didn't enjoy myself, because I did!
   I would hate _____ _____ _____ that I didn't enjoy myself, because I did!
6 You paid for everything, which wasn't what I expected.
   I didn't expect _____ _____ _____ for everything.
7 It would be wonderful if you visited for a few days.
   I would love _____ _____ _____ for a few days.
8 If you want to live at home again, your younger sisters will have to share a bedroom.
   Living at home again will involve _____ _____ _____ _____ to share a bedroom.
9 I told Hannah not to forget to do her homework.
   I reminded _____ _____ _____ her homework.
10 Did you really use to be shy? I can't imagine it!
   I can't imagine _____ _____ shy!
11 We were able to buy a bigger flat thanks to the money my uncle left me.
   The money my uncle left me enabled _____ _____ _____ a bigger flat.
12 The guards wouldn't let us cross the border.
   The guards prevented _____ _____ _____ the border.
13 I could call back later if you're busy now.
   Would you prefer _____ _____ _____ _____ later?
14 The car might break down on holiday. We don't want to take the risk.
   We don't want to risk _____ _____ _____ while we're on holiday.
15 I don't like it when people answer their phones in restaurants.
   I dislike people _____ _____ _____ in restaurants.
16 When I was an intern, the secretaries made me do all the photocopying.
   When I was an intern, I _____ _____ _____ _____ all the photocopying.

p.57

conditional sentences

real and unreal conditionals

1 You **won't get** a phone upgrade unless you**'ve got** a contract.
Can I borrow your laptop a moment if you**'re not using** it?
If it **stops** raining, I**'m going to** walk into town.
2 How **would** you **know** if he **wasn't telling** the truth?
If we **had** a bit more time here, we **could go** to the museum.
3 I **would have bought** that jacket if they**'d had** it in my size.
If you**'d been looking** where you were going, you **might not have tripped**.

1 First conditional sentences are used to talk about a possible present or future situation and its result.
We use any present tense in the *if*-clause and any form of the future or a modal verb in the other clause.
2 Second conditional sentences are used to talk about hypothetical or improbable situations in the present or future.
We use the past tense (simple or continuous) in the *if*-clause and *would* (or *could* / *might*) + infinitive in the other clause.

> 🔍 *was* or *were* in the *if*-clause?
> We can use *were* instead of *was* after *I / he / she / it* in the *if*-clause and we <u>always</u> use *were* in the expression *If I were you…*

3 Third conditional sentences are used to talk about a hypothetical situation in the past.
We use the past perfect (simple or continuous) in the *if*-clause and *would have* (or *could* / *might have*) + past participle in the other clause.

mixed conditionals

I **wouldn't be** in this mess if I **had listened** to your advice.
If Jenny **didn't** still **love** Mike, she **would have left** him by now.

- If we want to refer to the present and the past in the same sentence, we can mix tenses from two different types of conditional, e.g. *I wouldn't be in this mess* (second conditional) *if I had listened to your advice* (third conditional). *If Jenny didn't still love Mike* (second conditional), *she would have left him by now* (third conditional).

alternatives to *if* in conditional sentences

1 I'll tell you what happened **as long as** / **so long as** you promise not to tell anyone else.
Provided / **Providing** (**that**) the bank gives us a mortgage, we're going to buy that flat.
My boss agreed to give me Friday off **on condition** (**that**) I worked over the weekend.
2 I'm going to sell the car **whether** you agree with me or not.
3 **Even if** I get the job, I'm going to carry on living with my parents for a while.
4 **Supposing** / **Suppose** you lost your phone, what would you do?
5 **Had I seen** the sign, I would have stopped.

1 We often use *as long as / so long as*, *provided / providing* (*that*), and *on condition* (*that*) instead of *if* to emphasize what must happen or be done for something else to happen.
- *that* is often omitted in spoken English. *on condition* (*that*) is slightly more formal than the other expressions.
2 We can use *whether* + subject + verb + *or not* instead of *if* to emphasize something is true in either of two cases.
- The word order can also be: *I'm going to sell the car* **whether or not** *you agree with me*.
3 We can use *even if* instead of *if* for extra emphasis.
4 We can use *supposing / suppose* when we ask someone to imagine that something is true or might happen. It is usually used at the beginning of a sentence.
5 In third conditionals, we can invert *had* and the subject and leave out *if*. *Had I seen…* = If I had seen…

---

a Right (✓) or wrong (✗)? Correct the mistakes in the highlighted phrases.

If you hadn't been here last night, I don't know what I would do. ✗
If you hadn't been here last night, I don't know what I would have done.

1 They wouldn't have made you Marketing Manager if they didn't think you were right for the job.
2 The government would accept more refugees if the camp isn't so crowded.
3 If you've done all your homework, you can go out this evening.
4 We wouldn't be living in Singapore now if my company hadn't been taken over by a multinational.
5 Louisa would be in the team if she didn't get injured last month.
6 If you've ever been to New York, you will know exactly what I'm talking about.
7 They would get divorced ages ago if they didn't have young children.
8 If the storm wasn't at night, more people would have died.
9 If their flight hasn't been delayed, they will have arrived by now.
10 I wouldn't have bought the flat if I knew I was going to have so many problems with it.

b Complete the sentences with one word. Don't use *if*.

Supposing we can't find a taxi, how will we get home?

1 My father has agreed to lend me the money _____ I pay it back by the end of the year.
2 _____ if I had played my best, I still wouldn't have beaten him.
3 I'll tell you what happened to the car, as _____ as you promise not to be cross with me.
4 _____ the rebels not surrendered, there would have been a lot more casualties.
5 The company will only employ me _____ condition that I sign a two-year contract.
6 We've decided we're going to go ahead with the event _____ we sell all the tickets or not.
7 Amy will only get back together with her boyfriend on _____ that he apologizes.
8 _____ we do buy a dog, who's going to take it for walks?
9 I can meet you for lunch on Friday provided _____ I don't have any meetings.
10 _____ the plane not caught fire, there would have been more survivors.

 p.62

🖱 **Go online** to review the grammar for each lesson

permission, obligation, and necessity

can / could, must, should, ought to, had better

> 1 **Can** I use your phone, as my battery seems to have died?
> I **couldn't** take any photos in the gallery, so I bought some postcards.
> If you want to apply for this job, you **must** be able to speak Spanish.
> We **should / ought to** drive – it'll be much quicker.
> 2 We **should have / ought to have** driven – it would have been quicker.
> 3 You**'d better** post the parcels today or they won't get there in time.

1 The most common modal verbs for talking about permission and obligation are *can / could*, *must*, and *should / ought to*.
- We can also use *May I...?* to ask for permission, e.g. *May I use your phone?*
2 We can use *should have* or *ought to have* + past participle to talk about past events which did not happen and which we regret.
3 *had better* is stronger and more urgent than *should / ought to* and is often used to give strong advice or a warning. It normally refers to the immediate future.
- The negative is *had better not* **NOT** ~~hadn't better~~

mustn't / don't have to

> You **mustn't** take photos during the performance.
> You **don't have to** tip here unless you think the service was especially good.

- *mustn't* and *don't have to* are completely different.
  - *mustn't* is used to express an obligation <u>not</u> to do something.
  - *don't / doesn't have to* is used to express an absence of obligation.
See **1A** *p.142* for information about *have to* and *have got to* to express obligation.

need

> 1 You usually **need to** check in at least two hours before a flight leaves.
> You **don't need to** take a jacket. It's going to be hot today.
> 2 We **needn't** lock the car. Nobody will steal it in this village.
> 3 We **needn't have booked / didn't need to book**. The restaurant is empty!
> 4 We knew the way, so we **didn't need to use** the satnav.

1 We use *need / don't need* + *to* + infinitive to say that something is necessary / unnecessary. You can use these forms for habitual, general, and specific necessity.
2 When we want to say that something is unnecessary on a specific occasion, we can also use *needn't* + infinitive without *to*.
3 When something was not necessary, but you did it, you can use either *needn't have* + past participle or *didn't need to* + infinitive.
4 When something was not necessary, so you did <u>not</u> do it, you must use *didn't need to*. Compare:
We didn't need to book. (= It wasn't necessary. We may have booked or we may not.)
We needn't have booked. (= We booked, but it wasn't necessary.)

be able to, be allowed to, be permitted to, be supposed / meant to

> 1 From tomorrow we **won't be able to** park in this street.
> You**'re not allowed / permitted to** smoke in any public buildings in our country.
> 2 It **is not permitted to** take phones into the exam room.
> 3 We **are supposed / meant to** check out by 12.00. What's the time now?
> You **aren't supposed / meant to** park here – it's reserved for teachers.

1 We often use person + *be able to* or *be allowed to* + infinitive instead of *can* to talk about what is possible or permitted.
2 *it* + *be permitted to* + infinitive is used in formal situations, e.g. notices and announcements, to say what can / can't be done according to the law or to rules and regulations.
- We <u>don't</u> use *it isn't allowed to...* **NOT** ~~It isn't allowed to take phones into the exam room.~~
3 We can also use *be supposed to / be meant to* + infinitive to say what people should or shouldn't do, often because of rules. There is often a suggestion that the rules are not necessarily obeyed, e.g. *Students are not supposed / meant to have guests after 12.00, but everyone does.*

a Circle the correct form. Tick (✓) if both are possible.

> We *couldn't / weren't allowed to* go out at night when we were at boarding school. ✓

1 You *aren't supposed / aren't meant* to use your phone here, but everyone does.
2 You*'d better not / don't have to* use his computer. He hates other people touching it.
3 I *shouldn't have / mustn't have* lost my temper last night. I feel really guilty about it.
4 It is *not permitted / not allowed* to take flash photographs in this museum.
5 You *can / need to* pay cash here as they don't accept credit cards.
6 You are *allowed / able* to drive in the UK when you are 17.
7 We *didn't need to get / needn't have got* a visa, which was lucky, as we only booked our holiday at the last minute.
8 You really *ought to have / should have* got specialist advice about your back problem.
9 Japanese people *don't need to / needn't* get a visa to travel to China.
10 You *don't have to / needn't* bring your car – we can go in mine.

b Complete the sentences with three words. Contractions count as one word.

> If you don't finish your homework, you won't be *able to watch* TV.

1 You don't _____ _____ _____ to go into the art gallery. Entrance is free.
2 We remind you that this is a non-smoking flight. Smoking _____ _____ _____ anywhere on the aircraft.
3 You'd _____ _____ _____ late – you know what Helen is like about punctuality!
4 You _____ _____ _____ back until next month. I'm in no hurry for the money.
5 You _____ _____ _____ you didn't like the pasta. You know how sensitive Daniel is about his cooking.
6 It was a difficult journey because we _____ _____ _____ trains three times.
7 A lot of people think that governments _____ _____ _____ more to protect young people's health.
8 You aren't _____ _____ _____ e-cigarettes in pubs in the UK.
9 We just looked into each other's eyes – we _____ _____ _____ say anything.
10 Am I _____ _____ _____ a suit to the wedding, or is it quite informal?

→ p.69

perception and sensation

see, hear, smell, feel, taste

> **Can** you **see** that tiny figure at the top of the painting?
> I **can hear** a weird beeping noise coming from the kitchen.
> I **can smell** burning. Are you sure you turned the gas off?
> I **can feel** a draught – is there a window open?
> I **can't taste** the garlic in the soup.

- The five basic verbs of the senses, *see*, *hear*, *smell*, *feel*, and *taste* are stative (non-action) verbs and are not normally used in the continuous form.
- We normally use *can* with these verbs to refer to something happening at the moment, instead of the present continuous, e.g. *I can smell burning.* **NOT** ~~I'm smelling burning.~~

see / hear / watch / feel + infinitive or gerund

> 1 I **saw** a man **hit** his dog really aggressively.
>   I think I **heard** the alarm **go off**.
> 2 I **saw** the man **hitting** his dog really aggressively.
>   I think I **heard** the alarm **going off**.
> 3 I **watched** a street artist **draw / drawing** a caricature.
>   I **felt** someone **touch / touching** my shoulder.

1 We often use *see / hear* + object + verb in the infinitive. This means you saw or heard the whole action.
2 We can also use *see / hear* + object + gerund. In this case the meaning is slightly different, meaning you saw / heard an action in progress or a repeated action.
3 The distinction above also applies to verbs after *watch*, *feel*, *notice*, and *listen*.

look, feel, smell, sound, taste

> 1 That sofa **looks** really uncomfortable.
>   Does that noise **sound like** thunder to you?
>   It smells **as if / as though** someone has been making a curry.
> 2 **A** I love your new perfume. It **smells of** orange blossom.
>   **B** Yes, I love it too. In fact it **smells** a bit **like** yours.
>   This sauce **tastes of** flour. I don't think you've cooked it for long enough.
>   This sauce **tastes like** one my mother used to make.

- When we talk about the impression something or someone gives us through the senses, we use *look, feel, smell, sound,* and *taste* followed by an adjective, *like* + noun or *as if / as though* + clause.
- Nowadays *like* is often used as an alternative to *as if / as though* e.g. *It looks like it's going to rain.*
2 Compare *smell / taste of* and *smell / taste like*:
  It smells / tastes of... (= it has that smell / taste)
  It tastes / smells like... (= it has a similar smell / taste)

seem

> 1 You **seem** worried. Is something wrong?
>   It **seemed like** a good idea at the time, but in fact it wasn't.
>   It **seems as if / as though** every time I clean the car it rains.
> 2 You **seem to be** a bit down today. Are you OK?
>   The waiter **seems to have made** a mistake with the bill.
>   The couple next door **seem to be arguing** a lot more than they used to.

1 We can use *seem* followed by an adjective, *like* + noun or *as if / as though* + clause. Compare:
  You seem worried. (= I get this impression from the way you are behaving in general – voice, actions, etc.)
  You look worried. (= I get this impression from your face.)
2 We can also use *seem* + an infinitive (simple, perfect, or continuous).

---

a Right (✓) or wrong (✗)? Correct the mistakes in the <mark>highlighted</mark> phrases.

> <mark>I'm smelling something funny</mark> in here. What on earth is it? ✗
> *I can smell something funny in here. What on earth is it?*

1 I don't know what happened, but <mark>he seems like very angry</mark>.
2 We could hardly sleep at all, <mark>as we could hear the wind howling</mark> in the trees all night.
3 I was very near when it happened. <mark>I actually heard the bomb exploding</mark>.
4 Do you know what this piece is? <mark>It sounds of Beethoven's 7th</mark>, but I'm not quite sure.
5 I think we should send the wine back. <mark>It tastes like vinegar</mark>.
6 They said this bag was leather, but <mark>it's feeling more like plastic</mark>.
7 You and Raquel <mark>seemed to be getting on very well</mark> last night. What did you think of her?

b Circle the correct verb form. Tick (✓) if both are possible.

> The waiter *looks /* (*seems*) to have forgotten about us.

1 He *looked / seemed* very angry about something.
2 It *looks / seems* as if it's going to rain very soon.
3 It doesn't *look / seem* possible that ten years have passed since we last met.
4 Cathy *is looking / is seeming* very tired, don't you think?
5 You *look / seem* much more like your father than your mother. You've got his eyes.

c Complete the sentences with one word. Sometimes more than one answer is possible.

> The clouds are very low. It looks *as* if it's going to snow.

1 This tastes a bit _____ a soup my grandmother used to make. What's in it?
2 I haven't met the boss yet, I've only spoken to him on the phone. He _____ quite nice though.
3 I assume she's gone out because I heard the door _____ about five minutes ago.
4 The engine sounds as _____ there's something wrong with it. I think we should stop.
5 My favourite perfume is one that smells _____ roses. Apparently it's made from thousands of petals.
6 We saw hundreds of people _____ selfies instead of enjoying the view.
7 Could you possibly speak up a bit? I _____ hear you very well.

◀ p.71

advanced gerunds and infinitives

different forms of gerunds and infinitives

1. She hates **being told** she should do more exercise.
   I'm tired of **being lied to**. I want the truth.
   It's not easy **to be liked** when you're the boss.
   These pills need **to be taken** after meals.
2. He thanked them for **having helped** him.
   Having studied one language before makes it easier to learn another.
   How wonderful **to have finished** all our exams!
   By the time I'm 30, I hope **to have started** a family.
3. I would like **to have seen** your face when they told you you'd won the competition!
   We would rather **have stayed** in a more central hotel, but they were all full.
4. I'd like **to be lying** on the beach right now.
   She seems **to be coughing** a lot – do you think she's OK?

1. We use a passive gerund (*being done*) or a passive infinitive (*to be done*) to describe actions which are done to the subject.
2. We use a perfect gerund (*having done*) or a perfect infinitive (*to have done*) if we want to emphasize that an action is completed or in the past.
* Often there is no difference between using a simple gerund or infinitive and a perfect gerund or infinitive, e.g.
  He denied stealing / having stolen the money.
  It was our fault. We were silly not to lock / not to have locked the car.
3. We use the perfect infinitive after *would like, would love, would hate, would prefer*, and *would rather* to talk about an earlier action. Compare:
  I would like to see the Eiffel Tower. (= when I go to Paris in the future)
  I would like to have seen the Eiffel Tower. (= I was in Paris, but I didn't see it)
4. We use a continuous infinitive (*to be* + verb + *-ing*) to say that an action / event is in progress around the time we are talking about.

other uses of gerunds and infinitives

1. **It's no use worrying**. There's nothing you can do.
   Is there any point (in) asking Mark? He never has anything useful to say.
   It's no good talking to my sister, because she doesn't listen to me.
2. We had **an agreement to share** the costs.
   Our **plan is to leave** on Saturday.
3. You can't visit the Louvre in a day – there's **too much to see**.
   There wasn't **enough** snow **for us to ski**.
4. Is there **anything to eat**?
   There's **nowhere to go** at night.
5. I don't know **where to go** or **what to do**.
6. He's the **youngest** player ever **to play** for England.

1. We use the gerund after certain expressions with *it* or *there*, e.g. *It's no use, There's no point, It's no good,* etc.
We use the infinitive with *to*:
2. after nouns formed from verbs which take the infinitive, e.g. *agree, plan, hope,* etc.
3. after expressions with quantifiers, e.g. *enough, too much, a lot, plenty of,* etc.
When we want to refer to the subject of the infinitive verb we use *for* + person or object pronoun before the infinitive. This can be used before any infinitive structure, e.g. after adjectives: *It's very difficult **for me to decide**.*
4. after *something, anywhere,* etc.
5. after question words (except *why*).
6. after superlatives and *first, second, last,* etc., e.g. *Who was the first person to walk on the moon?*

> 🔍 *and + verb*
> We often use *and* + verb instead of *to* + infinitive after *try, wait, come,* and *go,* e.g. *Come and see me when you're next in New York.*
> *I'm not sure what's going to happen – we need to wait and see.*

a Complete the sentences with the correct gerund or infinitive form of the verb in brackets.

I don't like *being prescribed* sleeping pills, even if I'm having problems sleeping. (prescribe)
1. I was really stupid _____ my friend's advice. She was totally wrong. (follow)
2. I'd love _____ there when you told him you were leaving. (be)
3. If I had a serious illness, I would prefer _____ the truth by my doctor. (tell)
4. It's no use _____. We're already late. (run)
5. I'm not sure who _____ for help. (ask)
6. By the time I'm 55, I expect _____ enough to be able to just work part-time. (save)
7. The burglar denied _____ the jewellery. (take)
8. There will be plenty of time to have something _____ at the airport. (eat)
9. It's no good _____ him because he's bound to have switched his phone off. (call)
10. Who was the first woman _____ a Nobel Prize? (win)

b Complete the sentences using the **bold** word.

Don't get angry with the doctor. That won't help. **point**
There's no point getting angry with the doctor.
1. We haven't got much time so we can't do any more shopping. **enough**
   We _____ do any more shopping.
2. I hate it when someone wakes me up suddenly. **woken**
   I _____ suddenly.
3. Are you sorry you didn't study harder at school? **regret**
   _____ harder at school?
4. I love it when people help me in the kitchen even when I don't ask them. **without**
   I love it when people help me in the kitchen _____.
5. I really wish I'd been able to go to your birthday party. **love**
   I _____ your birthday party.
6. The children look as if they're having a good time, don't you think? **seem**
   _____, don't you think?
7. I'm hoping to have the operation as soon as possible. **hope**
   My _____ as soon as possible.

→ p.78

expressing future plans and arrangements

present and future forms

1 We**'re leaving** for the airport around 3.00.
I**'m meeting** Sam at the bus stop.
2 I**'m going to** have my hair cut tomorrow.
She**'s going to** get the last train home.
3 I**'ll be going** to the supermarket later – do you want anything?
Will we **be having** dinner at the usual time?
This time tomorrow I**'ll be flying** to Mexico.
4 The train **leaves** in five minutes. Our classes **start** next Tuesday.

1 The present continuous is the most common way to talk about arrangements, i.e. fixed plans for the future, when the time and place have been decided.
2 *be going to* is the most common way to express future plans and intentions and to imply that a decision has been made.
• When we talk about the future from the point of view of a time in the past, we use *was / were going to*, e.g. *We were a bit worried about what the weather* **was going to be** *like*.

> 🔍 *be going to* **or the present continuous?**
>
> In most cases we can use either *be going to* or the present continuous without much difference in meaning. However, the present continuous emphasizes that a time and place to do something has been decided, while *be going to* emphasizes the intention. Compare:
> *I'm seeing Sarah tomorrow.* (= it's our arrangement)
> *I'm going to give her a birthday present.* (= it's my intention)
> We do not use the present continuous when it is clear that something is only an intention, but no arrangements have been made, e.g. *I'm going to talk to Mike about it when I next see him.*
> **NOT** ~~*I'm talking to Mike about it…*~~

3 The future continuous can often be used instead of the present continuous to refer to future arrangements.
• We sometimes use the future continuous to emphasize that we are talking about something that will happen anyway rather than something we have arranged. Compare:
I'm seeing Sarah tomorrow. (= I have arranged it)
I'll be seeing Sarah at the party tomorrow. (= it will happen anyway, but I didn't arrange it)
• It is often used to make polite enquiries about arrangements, e.g. *Will you be meeting us at the airport?*
• We also use the future continuous to say that an action will be in progress at a certain time in the future.
4 We can use the present simple to talk about future events which are part of a timetable or a regular schedule.

other ways of expressing future arrangements

1 My sister **is due to** arrive at 7.30. Can you meet her at the station?
2 My daughter **is about to** have a baby, so I'm getting ready to go and stay with her.
3 It has been announced that the Prime Minister **is to visit** Malaysia next month.

1 *be due to* + infinitive can be used to say that something is arranged or expected at a certain time. This is a more formal style.
• We also use *due* on its own to mean 'expected', e.g. *The next train is due in five minutes.*
2 We use *be about to* + infinitive to say that something is going to happen very soon, but without giving a specific time.
• We can also use *be on the point of* + gerund with a similar meaning, but this is slightly more formal and implies something is more imminent, e.g. *It is believed that the Chancellor is on the point of resigning.*
3 We can use *be* + *to* + infinitive in a formal style to talk about official plans and arrangements.

a **Circle** the correct form. Tick (✓) if both are possible.
I see / *I'm seeing* some friends after class tonight.
1 Don't call me between 5.00 and 6.00 as I'll *be having / have* a massage.
2 **A** What are you going to do this evening?
   B I'm not sure. I'm probably *going to watch / watching* the match.
3 When I next see my brother I'm *going to ask / asking* him to pay me back the money I lent him.
4 My dad *is retiring / will be retiring* at the end of this year.
5 My flight *is due to arrive / arrives* at 6.00.
6 You'll easily recognize me when I arrive on Saturday. *I'll be wearing / I'm wearing* a white suit.
7 The new exhibition is *to open / going to open* next month.
8 *I'll be writing up / I'm writing up* my notes tomorrow, so I can check what we agreed then.
9 The train is *going to leave very soon / about to leave*.
10 The shop *closes / is about to close* at 8.00.

b Look at the sentences you ticked in **a**. Is there any difference in meaning or register between the two forms?

c Complete the sentences using the **bold** word.
   I'm meeting Myriam tonight. **going**
   I'm *going to meet* Myriam tonight.
   1 We're going to leave soon. Could you ring me back later? **about**

   _____.
   Could you ring me back later?
   2 Her new album is going to be released next month. **due**

   _____
   next month.
   3 Are you going to the canteen at lunchtime? If so, could you get me a sandwich? **will**

   _____?
   If so, could you get me a sandwich?
   4 The ministers are about to sign a new agreement. **point**

   _____
   a new agreement.
   5 The manager intends to respond to your complaint in the near future. **responding**

   _____
   in the near future.
   6 Will you be meeting us at the hotel? **going**

   _____
   at the hotel?

← p.82

9A

ellipsis

ellipsis after linkers

1 He fed the dog **and** (he) went to work.
She came to the meeting, **but** (she) **didn't say** anything.
We should phone him **or** (we should) **send** him an email.
We usually have dinner at 10.00 and **then** (we) **watch** TV.
2 They locked the doors and windows **before they left**.
We'll have a look at the photos **after we finish** dinner.
He's stressed **because he has** too much work.
She was horrified **when she saw** the mess he had left.
I met Sean **while he was working** in Italy.

1 After *and*, *but*, and *or* we often leave out a repeated subject or subject and auxiliary verb, especially when the clauses are short.
• After *then* we can also leave out a repeated subject pronoun.
2 We cannot leave out the subject pronoun after *before*, *after*, *because*, *when*, and *while*.

ellipsis after auxiliaries or with infinitives

1 Laura has never been to the States, but her sister **has**.
Gary thinks he's right, but he **isn't**.
They said I would love the film, but I don't think I **would**.
I didn't like the play, but Marcus **did**.
2 I thought I **would be able to** come tonight, but in fact I **can't**.
I know you**'ve** never **learnt** to drive, but I think you **should have**.
A You **must** read his latest book! **B** I already **have**.
3 I've never ridden a motorbike, but I**'d love to**.
The students cheated in the exam, even though I **told** them **not to**.

1 We often leave out a repeated verb phrase or adjective and just repeat the auxiliary or modal verb, or the verb *be*, e.g. *Laura has never been to the States, but her sister has ~~been there~~.*
• If the verb we don't want to repeat is the present or past simple, we use *do / does / did* in the ellipsis.
2 We can use a different auxiliary or modal verb from that used in the first part of the sentence.
3 We can also leave out a repeated verb phrase after the infinitive with *to*. This is called a reduced infinitive, e.g. *I've never ridden a motorbike, but I'd love to ~~ride one~~.*

ellipsis with *so* and *not*

1 I'll have finished the work by Friday, or at least I **hope so**.
A Will you be working on Saturday?
B I **suppose so**, unless we get everything done tomorrow.
A You do know it wasn't my fault, don't you?
B If you **say so**.
2 **A** Do you think it'll rain tonight? **B** I **hope not**.
A She's not very likely to pass, is she? **B** I**'m afraid not**.
The children may be back, but I **don't think so**.

1 With positive clauses, we often use *so* instead of repeating a whole ⊞ clause after verbs of thinking (*assume, believe, expect, guess, hope, imagine, presume, reckon, suppose, think*) and also after *be afraid, appear / seem*, and *say*.
• *I hope so.* = I hope I'll have finished the work by Friday.
2 With negative clauses, we can use a ⊞ verb + *not* or a ⊟ verb + *so*.
• We normally use a ⊞ verb + *not* with *be afraid, assume, guess, hope, presume*, and *suspect*, e.g. *I hope not*.
• We normally use a ⊟ verb + *so* with *think*, e.g. *I don't think so*.
• With other verbs (*appear, believe, expect, imagine, seem*, and *suppose*) we can use either form, e.g.
A *It's very late. I don't think they'll come now, do you?*
B *No, I **imagine not**. / I **don't imagine so**.*

a ~~Cross out~~ the words / phrases which could be left out.
They look happy, but they aren't really ~~happy~~.
1 Everyone else liked the hotel, but I didn't like it.
2 Nobody expects us to win, but we might win.
3 I didn't take the job in the end, but now I think I should have taken it.
4 I went to the gym every week and I played basketball when I was living in the USA.
5 **A** Would you like to come for dinner tomorrow?
B I'd love to come to dinner, but I can't come.
6 We don't go to the theatre very often, but we used to go before we had children.
7 I won't be able to go to the concert, but my wife will be able to go.
8 We didn't enjoy the film because we arrived late and we missed the beginning.

b Complete the sentences with the correct modal or auxiliary form.
I'd like to help you this week, but I *can't*.
1 I'm not vegetarian, but my wife _____.
2 I would love to fly a plane, but I know that I never _____.
3 Nobody believes me when I say that I'm going to resign, but I _____.
4 We thought that Karen would get the job, but she _____.
5 In the end they didn't come, even though they had promised that they _____.
6 If you haven't seen the film yet, you _____. It's absolutely fantastic!
7 If I could help you I would, but I'm afraid I _____.
8 I don't speak French, but my friend _____.

c Respond to the first sentence using the correct form of the verb in brackets and **either** a reduced infinitive **or** *so / not*.
A Would you like to come round for a coffee later?
B I*'d love to.* (love)
1 **A** The weather forecast said it would rain tomorrow.
B I _____. I want to do some gardening. (hope)
2 **A** Do you go to the gym?
B I _____, but I stopped going last month. (use)
3 **A** If you think she's coming down with flu, you shouldn't send her to school.
B I _____. She might give it to the other children. (suppose)
4 **A** Have you spoken to Martin yet?
B No, but I _____ after the meeting. (try)
5 **A** Do you think we should leave early to miss the traffic?
B I _____, though I'm really enjoying myself. (guess)
6 **A** Why are you going to do a parachute jump?
B I don't know. I _____. (always / want)
7 **A** Has James gone out again?
B Yes he has, even though I _____. (ask / not)
8 **A** The bank's closed on public holidays, isn't it?
B Yes, I _____. (imagine)

 p.88

nouns: compound and possessive forms

apostrophe *s*

> 1 The **company's** head office is in New York. I borrowed **Chris's** car.
>   It's my **friends'** wedding. That's the **children's** room.
> 2 The blonde girl is **Alex and Maria's** daughter.
> 3 We had dinner at **Tom's** last night. My mother is at the **hairdresser's**.
> 4 They played terribly in last **Saturday's** match.
>   She's got ten **years'** experience as a primary teacher.

* Possessive forms express the idea of 'having' (in a very general sense) which exists between two nouns.
1 We normally use a possessive noun (+ *'s*) when something belongs to or is a characteristic of a particular person (people) or thing (things).
2 If there are two people, we put the *'s* on the second name.
* If we are referring to things belonging to two separate people, we put the *'s* on both names, e.g. *John's and Kay's tastes in food are completely different.*
3 When *'s* refers to premises, e.g. 'the house of' or 'the shop of', we often omit, e.g. *house* or *shop*.
4 We often use *'s* or *s'* with time expressions, e.g. *yesterday's news, an hour's journey.*

using *of* (instead of apostrophe *s*)

> 1 Can you remember the name **of** the film?
>   My brother lives at the end **of** the road.
>   The problems **of** old age are many and varied.
> 2 Helen is the sister **of** my cousin in Rome I told you about.
> 3 Jack is a friend **of** my brother's.

1 We normally use an *of* phrase, not *'s*, with things or abstract nouns.
2 We tend to use *of* and not *'s* to express possession with a long phrase, e.g. **NOT** ~~my cousin in Rome I told you about's sister.~~
3 With *friend, colleague,* etc. we often say, e.g. *a friend of* + name / noun + *'s* (= one of my brother's friends).
* We also often use a possessive pronoun after *a friend of…*, e.g. *a friend of mine / hers.*

compound nouns

> 1 I need the **tin opener**. Do you know where it is?
>   I bought a huge **plant pot** in a **garden centre** near my house.
>   My brother is a **company director** and my sister is a **history teacher**.
>   I opened the **car door**, got in, and put on my **seat belt**.
> 2 I bought my son a new **story book**.
>   What does that **road sign** mean?
> 3 There was a **bottle of wine** on the table and two **wine glasses**.

1 We use compound nouns to express many common ideas in English. The first noun modifies or describes the second noun. *tin opener* = an opener for tins, *history teacher* = a teacher of history. The first noun is usually singular, unless it has no singular form, e.g. *clothes*, but the second noun can be singular or plural.

> 🔍 **One word, two words, or hyphenated?**
> Compound nouns are usually two separate words, but they are sometimes joined together as one word, e.g. *sunglasses, bathroom*, or occasionally hyphenated, e.g. *role-play.*

2 We use compound nouns to describe a common class of object or person. Compare:
* *a story book* **BUT** *a book about house decoration*
* *a road sign* **BUT** *a sign of the times*
3 With containers, a compound noun (e.g. *a wine bottle*) focuses on the container (usually empty), whereas the container + possessive noun (*a bottle of wine*) focuses on the contents.
* Other common examples are *a wine glass / a glass of wine, a jam jar / a jar of jam, a petrol can / a can of petrol, a coffee cup / a cup of coffee*, etc.

---

a (Circle) the correct possessive form. Tick (✓) if both are possible.

> Shall I make (chicken soup) / soup of chicken for dinner tonight?

1 I enjoy spending time with *my friend's children / my friends' children*.
2 Didn't I meet you at *Jenny's / Jenny's house* one night?
3 The hero dies at *the end of the story / the story's end*.
4 She's *the wife of my friend who lives in Australia / my friend who lives in Australia's wife*.
5 Sally wants to introduce you to Jake. He's a colleague of *her / hers*.
6 When you go to the supermarket, can you buy me *a milk bottle / a bottle of milk*?
7 The *photo of the house / house's photo* made me want to buy it.
8 I'm looking for a *stories book / story book* that would be right for an eight-year-old.
9 We found *an old photograph box / a box of old photographs* in the attic.
10 The Tower of London is one of *London's most popular tourist attractions / the most popular tourist attractions in London.*
11 There's *a wine glass / a glass of wine* on the table. Did you leave it there?

b Look at the sentences you have ticked in **a**. Is there any difference between the two phrases?

c Complete with a compound or possessive noun using a word from each list and *'s or '* where necessary.

| Alice and James | bottle | cats | ~~children~~ | garage |
| government | marketing | sea | today | |

| ~~bedroom~~ | bowls | door | manager |
| menu | opener | proposal | view | wedding |

> I always leave the light on in the
> <u>children's bedroom</u> – my youngest child is
> scared of the dark.

1 I can't find the _____. It's usually in this drawer, but it's not there now.
2 It's _____ next weekend and I don't have anything to wear yet.
3 There's shepherd's pie on _____.
4 Can I introduce you to Jess White, our _____?
5 Don't forget to lock the _____ when you take the car out.
6 We would like a room with a _____, if that's possible.
7 The _____ to freeze MPs' salaries has been met with criticism.
8 Make sure you fill the _____ with water every day – they get quite thirsty. ⟳ p.92

relative clauses

defining relative clauses

> 1 She's the woman **who / that won the marathon**.
> That's the stadium **which / that is going to be used** for the World Cup final.
> 2 That's the neighbour **whose dog never stops barking**.
> 3 James is the man **(who) I met at the party**.
> That's the shop **(which) I told you about**.
> 4 My sister's the only person **to whom I can talk**.
> My sister's the only person **(who) I can talk to**.
> This is the room **in which** I was born.
> This is the room **(that) I was born in**.
> 5 She told me **what she had seen**.
> **What I like best about London** is the parks.

- We use *who, which, whose, whom,* and *what* to introduce a defining relative clause, i.e. a clause which gives essential information about somebody or something.
1 We can use *that* instead of *who / which*. This is very common in conversation.
2 We use *whose* to mean 'of who' or 'of which'.
3 When *who* or *which* are the <u>object</u> of the verb in the relative clause, you can leave them out.
4 In formal English, after a preposition, use *whom* for a person and *which* for a thing. In informal English it is more common to leave out the relative pronoun and put the preposition after the verb.
5 We use *what* as a relative pronoun to mean 'the thing' or 'things which'.

See **Writing A review** *p.120* for the rules for reduced relative clauses.

non-defining relative clauses

> 1 My brother, **who doesn't like sport**, was given a tennis racket for Christmas!
> Buckingham Palace, **which was built in the 18th century**, is visited by thousands of tourists.
> 2 Adriana hasn't come to class for two weeks, **which is a bit worrying**.
> 3 They've got three children, **all of whom** are good at sport.
> My favourite foods are bread, biscuits, and cakes, **none of which** are very good for me.
> A lot of parents, **many of whose** children go to the local school, are protesting today about plans for the new road.

1 A non-defining relative clause gives extra, non essential information about a person or thing.
- In written English, this kind of clause is separated by commas, or between a comma and a full stop.
- You can't use *that* instead of *who / which*. **NOT** ~~My brother, that doesn't like sport,...~~
2 *which* can be used to refer to the whole of the preceding clause.
3 We sometimes use *of which / of whom / of whose* after *some, any, none, all, both, either, neither, several, enough, many,* and *few*.
- We can also use *of which / of whom / of whose* after expressions of quantity and superlatives.

a Right (✓) or wrong (✗)? Correct the mistakes in the highlighted phrases.

> She's the neighbour that her daughter has just had a baby. ✗
> *She's the neighbour whose daughter has just had a baby.*

1 This is the programme I was telling you about.
2 Is this the train that it goes to Birmingham?
3 She told her boss she'd overslept, that was absolutely true.
4 My son, that is very bright, is applying for a place at Oxford University.
5 The employee to who I spoke gave me some inaccurate information.
6 The woman whose suitcase didn't arrive never got it back.
7 The Canary Islands, which are situated off the coast of Africa, are a popular tourist destination.
8 Everyone in my family always eats that I cook.
9 That's the painting for which we paid over a thousand pounds.
10 The football club which fans sing the best is usually considered to be Liverpool.
11 That we love about living in Paris is the street cafés.
12 My doctor told me to go jogging, play tennis, or do Pilates, none of what I enjoy.

b Join the sentences using a relative pronoun and the correct punctuation. Sometimes more than one answer is possible.

> I've just failed my driving test. It's a pity.
> *I've just failed my driving test, which is a pity.*

1 They gave us a present. This was a complete surprise.
They…
2 My girlfriend is very intelligent. She's an architect.
My girlfriend…
3 It's too hot in my flat. This makes it impossible to sleep.
It's…
4 A car crashed into mine. It was a Mini.
The car…
5 I spoke to a police officer. She was working on the reception desk.
The police officer…
6 We only bought our computer two months ago. It keeps on crashing.
Our computer…
7 I left some things on the table. They aren't there any more.
The things…
8 That's the electrician. He did some work for my mother.
That's…
9 I've got two brothers. Neither of them can swim.
I've got two brothers…
10 The houses are still in very good condition. Many of them were built in 1870.
The houses…

 p.99

adding emphasis (2): cleft sentences

1 beginning with *What...* or *All...*

I need a coffee.	**What I need is** a coffee.
We don't like the weather here.	**What we don't like is** the weather here.
I just want to travel.	**All I want is** to travel.
I only touched it!	**All I did was** touch it!

2 beginning with *What happens is...* / *What happened was...*

You do a test and then you have an interview.	**What happens is (that)** you do a test and then you have an interview.
We left our passports at home.	**What happened was (that)** we left our passports at home.

3 beginning with *The person who / that..., The thing which / that..., The place where..., The first / last time..., The reason why...,* etc.

I spoke to the manager.	**The person (who / that)** I spoke to was the manager.
I was irritated by his attitude.	**The thing which / that irritated me was** his attitude.
We stayed in a five-star hotel.	**The place where we stayed was** a five-star hotel.
I last saw him on Saturday.	**The last time I saw him was** on Saturday.
I bought it because it was cheap.	**The reason (why) I bought it was** because / that it was cheap.

4 beginning with *It*

A boy in my class won the prize.	**It was a boy in my class who** won the prize.
We had the meeting last Friday.	**It was last Friday when** we had the meeting.
They charged us extra for the wine.	**It was the wine (that)** they charged us extra for.

- When we want to focus attention on or emphasize one part of a sentence, we can do this by adding certain words or phrases to the beginning of the sentence. This is sometimes called a 'cleft sentence'.
1 We can make some kinds of sentences more emphatic by beginning with *What* (= the thing) or *All* (= the only thing) + clause + *be* and then the part of the sentence we want to emphasize.
2 To emphasize an event or sequence of events, we can begin with *What happens is (that)... / What happened was (that)...*
3 We can make part of a sentence more emphatic by beginning with an expression like *The person who, The thing which, The place where, The first / last time, The reason why,* etc. + clause + *be*, with the emphasized part of the sentence at the end.
4 We can also use *It is / was* + the emphasized part of the sentence + a relative clause.

> 🔍 ***It was me who...* or *It was I who...*?**
> In informal spoken English, if the emphasized part is a pronoun, we normally use the object pronoun after *It is / was*, e.g. *I paid the bill. – It was me who paid the bill.*
> Compare: *It was I who paid the bill.* (= very formal)

a Complete the sentences with one word.

The *last* time I saw my brother was on his birthday.
1 _____ was my father who told me not to marry her.
2 _____ I hate about Sundays is knowing you have to work the next day.
3 The _____ why I want you to come early is so that we can have some time to chat.
4 After you've sent in your CV, what _____ next is that you get called for an interview.
5 It's not my fault you can't find the papers! _____ I did was tidy up your desk a bit.
6 The _____ where we're going to have lunch is a sort of artists' café near the theatre.
7 _____ happened was that I lost the piece of paper with her phone number on it.
8 It was _____ who told Angela about the party. I didn't realize it was a surprise.

b Complete the sentences using the **bold** word.

I only need a small piece of paper. **all**
All I need is a small piece of paper.
1 She left her husband because he cheated on her. **reason**
_____ because he cheated on her.
2 We stopped in an absolutely beautiful place for lunch. **place**
_____ absolutely beautiful.
3 We got stuck in an enormous traffic jam. **happened**
_____ we got stuck in an enormous traffic jam.
4 They didn't apologize for arriving late, which really annoyed me. **what**
_____ they didn't apologize for arriving late.
5 Your brother broke the laptop. **it**
_____ broke the laptop.
6 I only said that I didn't like her dress. **all**
_____ I didn't like her dress.
7 I like my Aunt Emily best of all my relatives. **person**
_____ is my Aunt Emily.
8 You pick up your tickets at the box office. **happens**
_____ you pick up your tickets at the box office.
9 Right now you need to sit down and put your feet up. **what**
_____ to sit down and put your feet up.
10 I first met Serena at a conference in Berlin. **time**
_____ at a conference in Berlin.

◀ p.101

Personality

1 ADJECTIVES

a Complete the sentences with an adjective from the list.

---
bright /braɪt/   conscientious /ˌkɒnʃiˈenʃəs/
determined /dɪˈtɜːmɪnd/   gentle /ˈdʒentl/
resourceful /rɪˈsɔːsfl/   sarcastic /sɑːˈkæstɪk/
self-sufficient /ˌself-səˈfɪʃnt/
spontaneous /spɒnˈteɪniəs/   steady /ˈstedi/
straightforward /ˌstreɪtˈfɔːwəd/
sympathetic /ˌsɪmpəˈθetɪk/   thorough /ˈθʌrə/
---

1 He's quite _resourceful_. He can usually work out how to solve a problem.
2 He's very _____. Whatever part of a job he's doing, he does it with great attention to detail.
3 My nieces are both really _____. They get very good marks at school in all their subjects.
4 She's such a _____ person. She's honest and open and says just what she thinks.
5 She's very _____. Once she's decided to do something, nothing will stop her.
6 He's very _____. He never needs anyone else's help.
7 He's not very _____. When I was ill last week, he didn't even phone me.
8 She is so _____! She worked all weekend to make sure she got everything done.
9 My sister's a very _____ person. She's calm and kind and she never gets angry.
10 Her boyfriend is a _____ kind of guy. He's sensible and she can really rely on him.
11 He's very _____. He can suddenly decide to go to Paris in the morning and in the evening he's there!
12 Our maths teacher used to be so _____. She loved making comments that made us feel small.

b 🔊 1.5 Listen and check.

> 🔎 **False friends**
> Be careful with *sympathetic*. Many languages have a similar adjective – *sympathique* (French), *simpatico* (Italian), *sympatyczny* (Polish), *sempatik* (Turkish) – which means *friendly, nice*. The same is true of *gentle*; this is not the same as, e.g. *gentil* (French), *gentile* (Italian), which mean *kind* or *polite*.

2 USEFUL PHRASES WHEN DESCRIBING PERSONALITY

a Complete the sentences with a phrase from the list.

---
a bit of a   a bit too   comes across   deep down   on the surface
on the whole   tends to
---

1 My father _tends to_ avoid conflict – he never argues with my mother, he just leaves the room.
2 _____ he seems self-confident, but _____ he's quite insecure.
3 I worry about my grandmother. She's _____ trusting, so it's easy for people to take advantage of her.
4 _____ he's pretty laid-back, though he can sometimes get very stressed about work.
5 She's _____ control freak – she always needs to organize everything and everybody.
6 He _____ as quite sarcastic, but in fact he's really friendly.

b 🔊 1.6 Listen and check.

3 IDIOMS

a Match the **bold** idioms 1–10 to their meanings A–J.

1 B My dad's got **a heart of gold**.
2 ☐ My brother-in-law is very **down to earth**.
3 ☐ My boss is a bit of **a cold fish**.
4 ☐ My brother's **a real pain in the neck**.
5 ☐ My mum's **a soft touch**.
6 ☐ My uncle has **a very quick temper**.
7 ☐ I know I shouldn't criticise your family, but your sister is really **full of herself**.
8 ☐ He comes across as aggressive, but in fact he **wouldn't hurt a fly**.
9 ☐ My brother never **lifts a finger** around the house.
10 ☐ My cousin's always **the life and soul of the party**.

A She's unfriendly and she never shows her emotions.
B He's incredibly kind to everyone he meets.
C He's so annoying – he's always taking my things.
D She's great at telling jokes and making people laugh.
E I can always persuade her to give me extra pocket money.
F He expects the rest of us to do everything.
G He's the gentlest person I know.
H He gets angry very easily.
I He's very sensible and practical.
J She thinks she's the most important member of the family.

b 🔊 1.7 Listen and check.

ACTIVATION Think of people you know for two adjectives from **1**, a phrase from **2**, and an idiom from **3**. Tell your partner about them and why they suit the description.
⬅ p.8

Work

1 ADJECTIVES

Committed
Helpful
Experienced
Adaptable
Passionate

FRAN

"So when it come to selecting STAFF these are the qualities I'm looking for."

a Match sentences 1–8 to A–H.

1 **C** My job as a divorce lawyer is very **challenging** /'tʃælɪndʒɪŋ/.
2 ___ Working as a checkout assistant can be a bit **monotonous** /mə'nɒtənəs/ and **repetitive** /rɪ'petətɪv/.
3 ___ I'm a primary school teacher. I find working with children very **rewarding** /rɪ'wɔːdɪŋ// (**fulfilling** /fʊl'fɪlɪŋ/).
4 ___ I work in a small design company and my job's really **motivating** /'məʊtɪveɪtɪŋ/.
5 ___ Being a surgeon is very **demanding** /dɪ'mɑːndɪŋ/.
6 ___ I always wanted an exciting job, but sadly, mine is incredibly **tedious** /'tiːdiəs/.
7 ___ He's in a **dead-end** /'ded end/ job in the local factory.
8 ___ She's got a very **high-powered** /ˌhaɪ 'paʊəd/ job in finance.

A I have to do exactly the same thing every day.
B I never mind having to work overtime.
C ~~It tests my abilities in a way that keeps me interested.~~
D It's important and comes with a lot of responsibility.
E It's really boring and it makes me feel impatient all the time.
F It makes me happy because it's useful and important.
G The wages are low and there's no hope of promotion.
H It's very high pressure and you have to work long hours.

b 🔊 1.10 Listen and check.

ACTIVATION Think of a job you could describe with each adjective in **1**.

2 COLLOCATIONS

a Complete the sentences with a word from **A** and a word from **B**.

A academic career (x2) civil events fast job work	B experience hunting ladder manager ~~move~~ qualifications servants track

1 I'm hoping it'll be a good *career move* to go from publishing to advertising.
2 I've been unemployed for six months now, so I spend most of my time _____-_____.
3 My brother works as an _____ _____, organizing conferences.
4 I left school at 15, so I had to look for a job that didn't require any _____ _____.
5 My problem is that all the jobs I want to apply for ask for some _____ _____, and as I've just finished university, I don't have any.
6 I'm a junior doctor, and if I want to move up the _____ _____, I need to work in several different hospitals and departments.
7 In Britain, people who work for government departments are called _____ _____.
8 In some careers, people with very good qualifications are put onto a _____ _____ so they get promoted more quickly.

b 🔊 1.11 Listen and check.

c Complete the two words which collocate with the groups below. What do the phrases mean?

maternity paternity sick compassionate unpaid	l_____	freelance permanent (*opp* temporary /fixed-term) full-time (*opp* part-time) zero-hours	c_____

3 THE SAME OR DIFFERENT?

a Look at the **bold** pairs of words or phrases. Write **S** if they have the same or a very similar meaning and **D** if they are different. If the meaning is different, what's the difference? If the meaning is the same, is there a difference in register?

1 **S** I get on very well with my **colleagues** / **co-workers**.
2 ___ I've had enough of my job. I think I'm going to **quit** / **resign**.
3 ___ Three-quarters of the **staff** / **workforce** are women.
4 ___ 400 workers have been **laid off** / **made redundant**.
5 ___ He's been **out of work** / **off work** for nearly six months.
6 ___ She **was sacked** / **was fired** for refusing to work on Sundays.
7 ___ Fantastic news! I'm going to **get promoted** / **get a pay rise**!
8 ___ What **skills** / **qualifications** do you have?
9 ___ We're too busy – we need to **hire** / **employ** more staff.
10 ___ The salary's a bit low, but we have some great **perks** / **benefits**.

b 🔊 1.12 Listen and check. ← p.10

 **Go online** to review the vocabulary for each lesson

Phrases with *get*

1 EXPRESSIONS WITH *GET*

a Complete the sentences with an expression from the list.

> hold of   into <u>trouble</u> with   out of the way
> (my / your, etc.) own back on   rid of   the chance   ~~the impression~~
> the joke   the wrong end of the stick   to know

1 I **get** *the impression* you're a bit annoyed with me.
2 When I told him to meet us at the station, he **got** _____ and went to the bus station, not the train station.
3 Since we stopped working together, we hardly ever **get** _____ to see each other.
4 Everyone else laughed, but I didn't **get** _____.
5 When you **get** _____ him, I think you'll really like him.
6 I need to speak to Martina urgently, but I just can't **get** _____ her.
7 I want to **get** _____ that awful painting, but I can't because it was a wedding present from my mother-in-law.
8 I'm going to **get** _____ my brother for telling our parents I got home late. Now I won't lend him my bike.
9 He's going to **get** _____ his boss if he's late again.
10 I tried to walk past him, but he wouldn't **get** _____.

b 🔊 **3.7** Listen and check. What do the expressions mean? Explain them in your own words.

2 IDIOMS WITH *GET*

a Match sentences 1–10 to A–J.

1 *I* **Get real!**
2 ▢ **Get a life!**
3 ▢ I'm **not getting anywhere** with this crossword.
4 ▢ She really **gets on my nerves**.
5 ▢ She really needs to **get her act together**.
6 ▢ They **get on like a house on fire**.
7 ▢ You should **get a move on**.
8 ▢ Your grandfather must be **getting on** a bit.
9 ▢ My boss just never **gets the message**.
10 ▢ She always **gets her own way**.

A It's just too difficult for me.
B Is he in his eighties now?
C They have exactly the same tastes and interests.
D Her exam is in two weeks and she hasn't even started studying.
E If you don't leave soon, you'll miss the train.
F Everything about her irritates me, her voice, her smile – everything!
G Everyone just does whatever she tells them to.
H I keep dropping hints about a pay rise, but he takes no notice.
I ~~There's no way you can afford that car!~~
J You're 40 and you're still living with your parents!

b 🔊 **3.8** Listen and check. What do the idioms mean? Explain them in your own words.

3 PHRASAL VERBS WITH *GET*

a Match the **bold** phrasal verbs to A–L.

1 *J* How did you and your boyfriend **get together**?
2 ▢ It can take a long time to **get over** a break-up.
3 ▢ I hate being interrupted when I'm trying to **get on with** my work.
4 ▢ We keep telling our teenage son how important it is to study hard, but it's impossible to **get through to** him.
5 ▢ She's studying economics at university, and then she wants to **get into** banking.
6 ▢ What's the best way to **get around** your city, on foot or by public transport?
7 ▢ Don't try to cheat in the exam, you'll never **get away with** it.
8 ▢ They have just enough money to **get by**, but they have to watch every penny.
9 ▢ I need to work this weekend because I **got behind** during the week.
10 ▢ The weather here is terrible in winter, it really **gets me down**.
11 ▢ I promised I'd help Matt move house, but I **got out of** it by saying I had a bad back.
12 ▢ Please leave a message and I'll **get back to** you as soon as I can.

A recover from
B start a career or profession
C move from place to place
D make sb understand
E manage with what you have
F fail to make enough progress
G make sb feel depressed
H respond to sb by speaking or writing
I avoid a responsibility or obligation
J ~~start a relationship~~
K continue doing
L do sth wrong without getting caught

b 🔊 **3.9** Listen and check.

ACTIVATION Look at A–L in **a** and remember the phrasal verbs.

↩ p.29

Conflict and warfare

1 PEOPLE AND EVENTS

a Match the people and definitions.

ally /'ælaɪ/   casualties /'kæʒuəltiz/
civilians /sə'vɪliənz/   commander /kə'mɑːndə/
forces /'fɔːsz/   refugees /ˌrefju'dʒiːz/
snipers /'snaɪpəz/   survivors /sə'vaɪvəz/
troops /truːpz/   the wounded /'wuːndɪd/

1 _casualties_ = people who have been killed or injured in a war
2 _____ = people who are forced to leave their country or home because there is a war, or for political or religious reasons
3 _____ = a group of people who have been trained to protect others, usually with weapons, e.g. *armed ~, security ~, peace-keeping ~*.
4 _____ = soldiers in large groups
5 _____ = an officer in charge of a military operation
6 _____ = people who have been injured by weapons
7 _____ = people who are not in the army, navy, or airforce
8 _____ = people who shoot at others from a hidden position
9 _____ = people who have managed to stay alive in a war
10 _____ = in time of war, a country that has agreed to help and support another country

b Match the events and definitions.

ceasefire /'siːsfaɪə/   civil war /ˌsɪvl 'wɔː/
coup /kuː/   rebellion /rɪ'beljən/
revolution /ˌrevə'luːʃn/   siege /siːdʒ/   treaty /'triːti/

1 _rebellion_ = an attempt by some of the people in a country to change their government, using violence
2 _____ = a sudden change of government that is illegal and often violent
3 _____ = when two armies agree to stop fighting temporarily
4 _____ = when an army tries to take a city or building by surrounding it and stopping the food supply
5 _____ = a war between groups of people in the same country
6 _____ = a formal agreement between two or more countries.
7 _____ = an attempt by a large number of people in a country to change their government

c ◖◗ **3.10** Listen and check your answers to **a** and **b**.

2 CONFLICT VERBS

a Complete the sentences with a verb from the list in the correct form.

blow up   break out   capture   declare   defeat   execute
loot   overthrow   release   retreat   shell   surrender

1 The rebels _overthrew_ the government. (= removed them from power using force)
2 Fighting _____ between the rebels and the army. (= started)
3 The army _____ the rebel positions. (= fired missiles at)
4 The rebels _____. (= moved back, away from the army)
5 Some of the rebels _____. (= admitted they had lost and wanted to stop fighting)
6 The rebels _____ the airport runway. (= made it explode)
7 The government _____ war on the rebels. (= announced their intention to go to war with them)
8 Some rebels _____ the city. (= stole things from shops and buildings)
9 The army _____ over 300 rebels. (= took them prisoner)
10 They finally _____ the rebels. (= beat them)
11 The army _____ most of the rebel prisoners. (= let them go)
12 They _____ the rebel leader. (= killed him as a punishment)

b ◖◗ **3.11** Listen and check.

3 METAPHORICAL USES OF 'CONFLICT VERBS'

a Complete the sentences with a verb from **2** in the correct form.

1 The fire _broke out_ at 3.00 in the morning.
2 The police have _____ details of the accident.
3 The new princess has _____ the imagination of the public.
4 I read the instructions three times, but they completely _____ me.
5 The minister was arrested and forced to _____ his passport.
6 A crisis has _____ over the new education policy.
7 He _____ that he was in love with her.
8 The flood water took a long time to _____ from the streets.

b ◖◗ **3.12** Listen and check.

↩ p.30

Sounds and the human voice

1 SOUNDS

a 🔊 **4.7** All the words from the list can be both nouns and regular verbs. Many of them are onomatopoeic (they sound like the sound they describe). Listen to the sounds and the words.

bang /bæŋ/   buzz /bʌz/   click /klɪk/   crash /kræʃ/
creak /kriːk/   crunch /krʌntʃ/   drip /drɪp/   hiss /hɪs/
hoot /huːt/   hum /hʌm/   rattle /ˈrætl/   roar /rɔː/   screech /skriːtʃ/
slam /slæm/   slurp /slɜːp/   sniff /snɪf/   snore /snɔː/   splash /splæʃ/
tap /tæp/   tick /tɪk/   whistle /ˈwɪsl/

b Complete the **Sounds** column with the words from the list in **a**.

		Sounds
1	This clock has a very loud ▢.	*tick*
2	Don't ▢! Get a tissue and blow your nose.	
3	To get the new software, just ▢ on the 'download' icon.	
4	There was a ▢ as he jumped into the swimming pool.	
5	Did you hear that ▢? It sounded like a gun.	
6	I heard a floorboard ▢ and I knew somebody had come into the room.	
7	I could hear the ▢ of a fly, but I couldn't see it anywhere.	
8	I hate people who ▢ at me when I slow down at an amber light.	
9	When I'm nervous, I often ▢ my fingers on the table.	
10	Don't ▢ your soup! Eat it quietly.	
11	The snake reared its head and gave an angry ▢.	
12	Please turn the tap off properly, otherwise it'll ▢.	
13	We could hear the ▢ of the crowd in the football stadium from our hotel.	
14	Some of the players carried on playing because they hadn't heard the ▢.	
15	I don't remember the words of the song, but I can ▢ the tune.	
16	Please don't ▢ the door. Close it gently.	
17	I heard the ▢ of their feet walking through the crisp snow.	
18	I can't share a room with you if you ▢ – I won't be able to sleep.	
19	Every time a bus or lorry goes by, the windows ▢.	
20	I heard the ▢ of brakes as the driver tried to stop and then a loud ▢.	

c 🔊 **4.8** Listen and check.

2 THE HUMAN VOICE

a Match the verbs and definitions.

giggle /ˈgɪgl/   groan /grəʊn/
mumble /ˈmʌmbl/   ~~scream~~ /skriːm/
sigh /saɪ/   sob /sɒb/   stammer /ˈstæmə/
whisper /ˈwɪspə/   yell /jel/

1 *scream* = to make a loud, high cry because you are hurt, frightened, or excited
2 _____ (*at sb*) = to shout loudly, e.g. because you are angry
3 _____ (*at sth*) = to laugh in a silly way
4 _____ (*to sb*) = to speak very quietly, so that other people can't hear what you're saying
5 _____ = to speak or say sth in a quiet voice in a way that is not clear
6 _____ = to make a long deep sound because you are in pain or annoyed
7 _____ = (or *stutter*) to speak with difficulty, often repeating sounds or words
8 _____ = to cry noisily, taking sudden sharp breaths
9 _____ = to let out a long deep breath, e.g. to show that you are disappointed or tired

b 🔊 **4.9** Listen and check.

c Answer the questions using one of the verbs in **a**.

What do people do…?
- when they are nervous
- when they are terrified
- when they lose their temper
- when they are not supposed to be making any noise
- when they are amused or embarrassed
- when they speak without opening their mouth enough
- when they are relieved
- when their team misses a penalty
- when they are very unhappy about something

ACTIVATION Choose five sounds from **1** and two verbs from **2**. Make the sounds for your partner to identify.

🔴 **p.40**

Expressions with *time*

1 VERBS

a Complete the sentences with a verb from the list.

give   have   kill   make up for   play for   run out of
save   spare   spend   take (x2)   take up   ~~waste~~

1 I _waste_ **a lot of time** playing games and messaging on my computer instead of studying.
2 If you take the motorway, you'll _____ time – it's much quicker than the local roads.
3 I had three hours to wait for my flight, so I sat there doing sudoku puzzles to _____ time.
4 There's no hurry, so _____ **your time**.
5 When my mother was young, she never had the chance to travel. Now she's retired and wants to _____ **lost time**, so she's booked a trip around the world.
6 The novel is 700 pages long and I'm a slow reader. It's going to _____ **me a long time** to finish it.
7 I'd better go home now. If I'm late again, Dad will _____ **me a hard time**.
8 I would like to go camping this weekend, but my final exams are next week, so I can't _____ **the time**.
9 My children _____ **all my time** – I never seem to get to read a book or watch a film!
10 New York's such a fantastic city! You're going to _____ **the time of your life** there.
11 Let's not _____ **too long** at the museum or we'll _____ time.
12 They want us to sign the contract today, but I'm not sure about it. I think we should _____ time.

b 🔊 **5.4** Listen and check.

2 PREPOSITIONAL PHRASES

a Complete the **Prepositions** column with the prepositions from the list.

at (x3)   before   behind   by   from (x2)   in (x2)   off
~~on~~   to (x2)

	Prepositions
1 I'm really punctual, so I hate it when other people aren't ▢ **time**.	_on_
2 I've never heard of that singer. He must have been ▢ **my time**.	_____
3 ▢ **the time** we got to our hotel, it was nearly midnight.	_____
4 I missed the birth of my first child. I was on a plane ▢ **the time**.	_____
5 She's been working too hard recently. She needs some **time** ▢.	

6 If we don't take a taxi, we won't get to the airport ▢ **time** for the flight.   _____
7 I don't eat out very often, but I do get a takeaway ▢ **time** ▢ **time**.   _____
8 He suffers from back pain and it makes him a little irritable ▢ **times**.   _____
9 You can come **any time** ▢ **10.00** ▢ **2.00**.   _____
10 My dad's a bit ▢ **the times** – he still thinks men should wear a suit and tie at work.   _____
11 Don't try to multitask. Just do **one thing** ▢ **a time**.   _____
12 I thought it would take ages, but in fact I finished it ▢ **no time**.   _____

b 🔊 **5.5** Listen and check.

3 EXPRESSIONS

a Match sentences 1–12 to A–L.

1 _I_ The referee's looking at his watch.
2 ▢ He hardly spoke to me at lunch.
3 ▢ I'm really looking forward to my holiday.
4 ▢ I'm sorry, I can't help you this week.
5 ▢ I can't afford a new car.
6 ▢ She's sure to find a job eventually.
7 ▢ I think I need to take up a hobby.
8 ▢ Stop writing, please.
9 ▢ I really thought I was going to be late.
10 ▢ Why not spend a morning at our spa?
11 ▢ I hate having to fill in my tax return.
12 ▢ You've had that computer for ages.

A But in the end I got to the airport **with time to spare**.
B He spent **the whole time** talking on his phone.
C **Time's up.** The exam is over.
D **I'm** a little **short of time**.
E **I've got time on my hands** since I retired.
F I'll have to carry on with this one **for the time being**.
G It's only **a matter of time**.
H It's very popular with people who want a bit of **me time**.
I ~~There isn't much time left.~~
J **This time next week** I'll be lying on the beach.
K **It's about time** you got a new one.
L It's incredibly tedious and **time-consuming**.

b 🔊 **5.6** Listen and check.

ACTIVATION Choose six of the **bold** time expressions and write a synonym or a phrase with the same meaning, e.g. *save time* = spend less time, *on time* = punctual. ⬅ p.48

Money

1 NOUNS

a Match the nouns and definitions.

~~budget~~ deposit donation fare fee fine grant instalment
loan lump sum quote will

1 _budget_ = the money that is available to a person or organization and a plan of how it will be spent over a period of time, *have a limited ~*
2 _____ = money that is given by the government or another organization for a particular purpose, e.g. education, *give / receive a ~*
3 _____ = money that a bank lends and sb borrows, *take out a ~*
4 _____ = an amount of money that you pay for professional advice or services, e.g. to a lawyer, *charge / pay a ~*
5 _____ = the money that you pay to travel by bus, plane, taxi, etc., *pay a ~*
6 _____ = a statement of how much money a particular piece of work will cost, *ask for a ~*
7 _____ = money that you give to an organization such as a charity in order to help them, *make a ~*
8 _____ = money paid as punishment for breaking a law or rule, *pay a ~*
9 _____ = one of a number of payments that are made regularly until sth has been paid for, *pay an ~*
10 _____ = the first part of a larger payment, *make / pay a ~*
11 _____ = a legal document that says what is to happen to sb's money and property after they die, *make a ~*
12 _____ = an amount of money that is paid at one time and not on separate occasions, *pay a ~*

b 🔊 5.9 Listen and check.

2 MONEY IN TODAY'S SOCIETY

a 🔊 5.10 Listen to the sentences. With a partner, say what you think the **bold** phrases mean.

1 We live in a **consumer society**, which is dominated by spending money on material possessions.
2 The **standard of living** in many European countries is lower than it was ten years ago.
3 People's **income** has gone up, but **inflation** is high, so the **cost of living** has also risen.
4 House prices are rising and people **can't afford** to buy a home.
5 Online banking allows people to **manage their accounts**, e.g. check their **balance** and make **transfers** and **payments**.
6 People who have loans have to pay high **interest rates**.
7 A lot of people are **in debt** and have problems getting a **mortgage** to buy their first home.
8 Some people make money by buying and selling **shares** on the **stock market**.
9 Our **currency** is unstable and **exchange rates** fluctuate a lot.
10 A lot of small businesses **went bankrupt** during **the recession**.

b Which aspects of the sentences above are true in your country?

3 ADJECTIVES

a Look at the *Oxford Learner's Thesaurus* entries for *rich* and *poor*. Match the synonyms and definitions.

rich *adj.* rich, affluent, loaded, wealthy, well-off
[1] *rich* / *wealthy* having a lot of money, property, or valuable possessions
[2] _____ (rather formal) rich and with a good standard of living: The ~ Western countries are better equipped to face the problems of global warming.
[3] _____ (often used in negative sentences) rich: His parents are not very ~ .
[4] _____ [*not before noun*] (very informal) very rich: Let her pay. She's ~ .

poor *adj.* poor, broke, hard up, penniless
[5] _____ having very little money; not having enough money for basic needs
[6] _____ (literary) having no money, very poor: She arrived in 1978 as a virtually ~ refugee.
[7] _____ [*not before noun*] (informal) having no money: I'm always ~ by the end of the month.
[8] _____ (informal) having very little money, especially for a short period of time: After he lost his job, he was so ~ he couldn't afford to eat out at all.

b 🔊 5.11 Listen and check.

4 COLLOQUIAL LANGUAGE

🔊 5.12 Read and listen to the conversations. What do you think the **bold** slang words mean?

1 A Nice car! How much are you going to ask for it?
  B **Five grand**. What do you think?
2 A I need **five bucks** for the subway.
  B Sure, here you are.
3 A Great hat! Was it expensive?
  B No, only **five quid**. I got it in a charity shop.
4 A What's the building work going to cost you?
  B About **50K**. We're redoing the kitchen as well.
5 A Can I borrow twenty pounds?
  B Sorry, I've only got a **fiver** (OR **tenner**).

ACTIVATION Make sentences about your country or people from your country with two words from each section **1**, **2**, and **3**.

← p.50

Prefixes

1 NEGATIVE PREFIXES

a Write the words from the list in the correct column to make negatives.

~~agree~~ appropriate attractive capable coherent competent continue do
embark helpful honest hospitable legitimate literate logical mobile moral
official personal practical rational regular relevant replaceable

im-	il-	ir-	in-	un-	dis-
					disagree

b 🔊 7.4 Listen and check. What letters do the words begin with after *im-*, *il-*, and *ir-*?

2 PREFIXES WHICH ADD OTHER MEANINGS

a Read the sentences carefully and match the **bold** prefixes to their meanings A–U.

1 D My daughter has **out**grown most of her clothes – she needs a bigger size.
2   A lot of common English verbs are **mono**syllabic, like *get, have, give*, etc.
3   The whole town was **re**built after the earthquake.
4   After the operation, I'll have to go to the hospital once a week as an **out**patient.
5   My dog was **ill**-treated* as a puppy, but he's much happier now.
6   I haven't been feeling very well recently. The doctor told me to take **multi**vitamins.
7   I must have **mis**understood you. I thought you said you didn't want to come tonight.
8   I need to install a new **anti**virus on my computer.
9   I was incredibly lucky on my flight to Mexico – I was **up**graded to business class!
10   High consumption of meat is leading to **de**forestation of the planet.
11   My brother did a **post**graduate course in translation and interpreting.
12   A ceasefire is an essential **pre**condition for any negotiation.
13   Even though I set my alarm clock, I **over**slept this morning and was late for work.
14   The committee has **bi**annual meetings in October and March.
15   Several different species now **co**exist peacefully side by side.
16   This work is totally **sub**standard. It's just not acceptable.
17   There will be an **inter**governmental conference to look at climate change.
18   They're really **under**staffed at the moment because a lot of their workers are off sick.
19   With a **super**human effort, he managed to lift the car and save the injured man.
20   I'm not very good with my camera. I almost always use the **auto**focus setting.
21   Bacteria are **micro**organisms which often cause disease.
    *The prefix *ill* is always followed by a hyphen.

A not enough
B too much
C more than one, many
~~D more than, better than,~~
   ~~bigger than, etc.~~
E wrongly
F below
G two, twice
H against
I one
J by yourself, by itself
K after
L outside, not inside
M before
N remove or reduce
O higher, towards the top
P together
Q badly
R between
S above average
T extremely small
U again

b 🔊 7.5 Listen and check.

🔍 **Prefixes with more than one meaning**
Some prefixes have more than one meaning, e.g. *out-, de-*. Compare:
- *out-* + verb usually means *more than, better than*, etc., e.g. *Boys outnumber girls in this class* (= there are more boys than girls)
- *out-* + noun / adjective means *outside*, e.g. *He lives on the outskirts of the city*
- *de-* often means *remove or take away sth*, e.g. *demystify* = remove the mystery
- *de-* can also mean *reduce*, e.g. *devalue* = reduce the value of sth

ACTIVATION Which prefixes from **2** could you use before each of these words?

-cook (*verb*)   -lingual   -war
-national   -place (*verb*)

◀ p.67

 **Go online** to review the vocabulary for each lesson

Travel and tourism

1 DESCRIBING PLACES

a Complete the sentences with a word or a phrase from the lists.

> [+] ~~breathtaking~~ /ˈbreθteɪkɪŋ/   iconic /aɪˈkɒnɪk/
> imposing /ɪmˈpəʊzɪŋ/   lively /ˈlaɪvli/
> off the beaten track /ˌɒf ðə ˌbiːtn ˈtræk/   picturesque /ˌpɪktʃəˈresk/
> remote /rɪˈməʊt/   unspoilt /ʌnˈspɔɪlt/

1 The view is absolutely _breathtaking_. (= impressive, spectacular)
2 It's a really _____ area at night. (= full of life and energy)
3 We found a tiny café in the back streets of Venice, right _____. (= away from where people normally go)
4 We went to a very _____ little fishing village yesterday. (= pretty, especially in a way that looks old-fashioned)
5 It's a lovely city, almost completely _____ by tourism. (= beautiful because it has not been changed)
6 The site of the temple is extremely _____ – you can only get there on foot and it takes four hours. (= far away from places where other people live)
7 The enormous statue at the entrance to the palace is very _____. (= large and impressive to look at)
8 The Leaning Tower of Pisa is one of Italy's most _____ sights. (= acting as a symbol of the place)

> [–] dull /dʌl/   overcrowded /ˌəʊvəˈkraʊdɪd/   overrated /ˌəʊvəˈreɪtɪd/
> pricey /ˈpraɪsi/   run-down /ˌrʌn ˈdaʊn/   soulless /ˈsəʊlləs/
> spoilt /spɔɪlt/   tacky /ˈtæki/   touristy /ˈtʊəristi/
> unimposing /ˌʌnɪmˈpəʊzɪŋ/

9 I think that restaurant's _____. (= with a better reputation than it really deserves)
10 The museum's pretty _____, but the café's good. (= boring)
11 The shops are quite _____, but we bought some nice things. (= designed to attract a lot of tourists)
12 The seafront has been _____ by all the new hotels. (= changed for the worse)
13 The hotel pool is always _____. (= with too many people)
14 The souvenirs were all plastic Eiffel Towers and key rings, really _____ stuff. (= cheap, badly made, and / or lacking in taste)
15 The main square is quite smart. But the buildings behind are very _____. (= in bad condition)
16 The old town has a lot of character, but the modern part of the city is mainly _____ office blocks. (= with no attractive or interesting qualities)
17 The hotel breakfast was a bit _____, but it was worth it. (= expensive)
18 The hotel entrance is _____, but the lobby inside is spectacular. (= unimpressive)

b ● 8.8 Listen and check.

"We would like an unspoilt paradise, but with lots of shops."

2 VERB PHRASES

a Complete the phrases with a verb from the list.

> chill out   extend   get away   go   go on
> hit   postpone /pəˈspəʊn/   recharge
> sample /ˈsɑːmpl/   ~~set off~~   soak up
> wander round /ˈwɒndə raʊnd/

1 _set off_ (SYN set out) on a journey / early / late
2 _____ a trip / a visit (= finish later than planned)
3 _____ camping / backpacking / sightseeing / for a stroll
4 _____ holiday / an outing / a trip / a safari / a trek / a cruise / a journey
5 _____ (SYN put off) a trip / a visit (= reschedule it for a later time)
6 _____ the old town (= explore in a leisurely way)
7 _____ (SYN unwind) (informal) after a tiring day
8 _____ (SYN immerse yourself in) the atmosphere / the culture
9 _____ the local cuisine
10 _____ the shops IDM
11 _____ from it all IDM
12 _____ your batteries IDM

b ● 8.9 Listen and check. What do you think the three idioms mean?

ACTIVATION Think of a place in your country that you could describe with each of the adjectives in **1**.

Talk about your last holiday using some of the verb phrases in **2**.

← p.81

Animal matters

1 ANIMALS, BIRDS, AND INSECTS
Young ones

a Match the animals and their young.

calf (plural *calves*) /kɑːf/   chick /tʃɪk/   cub /kʌb/
foal /fəʊl/   kid /ˈkɪd/   puppy /ˈpʌpi/

1 dog	*puppy*	4 cow	_____
2 goat	_____	5 hen	_____
3 horse	_____	6 lion	_____

b ◑ **9.1** Listen and check. Which word from the list would you use for: a baby bear / whale / fox / elephant / donkey?

Where they live

c Match the animals, birds, and insects and the places where they live.

bee   blackbird   canary   dog
goldfish   horse

1 a hive /haɪv/   *bee*
2 a stable /ˈsteɪbl/   _____
3 a cage /keɪdʒ/   _____
4 a kennel /ˈkenl/   _____
5 a tank /tæŋk/   _____
6 a nest /nest/   _____

d ◑ **9.2** Listen and check.

The noises they make

e Match the animals and the noises they make.

bird   cat   dog   horse   lion   mouse   pig

1 squeak /skwiːk/   *mouse*
2 bark /bɑːk/   _____
3 neigh /neɪ/   _____
4 meow /miˈaʊ/   _____
5 roar /rɔː/   _____
6 grunt /grʌnt/   _____
7 twitter /ˈtwɪtə/   _____

f ◑ **9.3** Listen and check.

Animal parts

g Match the words and pictures.

☐ a beak /biːk/   ☐ horns /hɔːnz/
1 claws /klɔːz/   ☐ paws /pɔːz/
☐ a fin /fɪn/   ☐ a shell /ʃel/
☐ fur /fɜː/   ☐ a tail /teɪl/
☐ hooves (sing. *hoof*) /huːvz/   ☐ wings /wɪŋz/

h ◑ **9.4** Listen and check.

ACTIVATION Make mind maps for the animals below.

dog   bird   cat   horse

← p.87

bark (v, n)
dog — puppy (n)
kennel (n)

2 ANIMAL ISSUES

◑ **9.10** Listen to the questions below and focus on the meaning and pronunciation of the **bold** words and phrases. With a partner, say what they mean.

In your country, are there any…?
1 organizations that **protect** animals and their **environment**, or **animal charities**
2 **animal rights activists** who organize protests against the use of animals for entertainment, product testing, or medical research
3 local or regional festivals where animals are **treated cruelly**
4 national parks or conservation areas where animals **live in the wild**
5 **endangered species** /ɪnˌdeɪndʒəd ˈspiːʃiːz/
6 animals that are **hunted for sport**
7 zoos or centres where animals are being **bred in captivity** in order to reintroduce them into the wild
8 animals that are kept or transported in **inhumane conditions**, e.g. veal calves

ACTIVATION Answer the questions above. Give examples.

← p.89

Go online to review the vocabulary for each lesson

Preparing food

1 HOW FOOD IS PREPARED

a Match the words and pictures.

- [ ] baked figs
- [ ] <u>bar</u>becued pork ribs
- [ ] boiled rice
- [1] chopped <u>par</u>sley
- [ ] deep-fried <u>on</u>ion rings
- [ ] <u>gra</u>ted cheese
- [ ] grilled <u>fill</u>et of fish
- [ ] mashed po<u>ta</u>toes
- [ ] <u>mel</u>ted <u>cho</u>colate
- [ ] minced beef
- [ ] peeled prawns
- [ ] poached egg
- [ ] roast lamb
- [ ] <u>scram</u>bled eggs
- [ ] sliced bread
- [ ] steamed <u>mus</u>sels
- [ ] stewed plums
- [ ] stuffed <u>chi</u>cken breast
- [ ] a <u>toas</u>ted <u>sand</u>wich
- [ ] whipped cream

b 🔊 **9.12** Listen and check.

2 UTENSILS

a Match the words and pictures.

- [ ] a <u>bak</u>ing tray /ˈbeɪkɪŋ treɪ/
- [ ] a <u>chop</u>ping board /ˈtʃɒpɪŋ bɔːd/
- [1] a <u>col</u>ander /ˈkʌləndə/
- [ ] a <u>food</u> processor /ˈfuːd prəʊsesə/
- [ ] a <u>fry</u>ing pan /ˈfraɪɪŋ pæn/
- [ ] a (<u>mix</u>ing) bowl /bəʊl/
- [ ] a <u>sauce</u>pan /ˈsɔːspən/ (or pan) /pæn/
- [ ] scales /skeɪlz/
- [ ] a sieve /sɪv/
- [ ] a <u>spa</u>tula /ˈspætʃələ/
- [ ] a whisk /wɪsk/

b 🔊 **9.13** Listen and check.

ACTIVATION Have you had any food recently that was prepared in any of the ways in **1**?

Which of the utensils in **2** might you need to make…?

   an omelette   spaghetti   biscuits

◀ p.90

Appendix

adjective + preposition

A lot of young people are **addicted to** social media.

I can't eat prawns because I'm **allergic to** seafood.

He always seems to be **angry about** something.

There's no need to get **angry with** me.

We weren't **aware of** the problem with our ticket until we got to the airport.

The film, which is set in Sweden, is **based on** a best-selling novel.

She may be old, but she's quite **capable of** looking after herself.

Albert Einstein was very **close to** his sister.

Many 30-year-olds are still **dependent on** their parents.

The architecture is very **different from** my city.

We're very **dissatisfied with** the service we received at the hotel.

I'm very **excited about** his new film.

Are you **familiar with** the computer software we use?

The city is **famous for** its university.

I'm **fed up with** waiting for the electrician to come. I'm going out.

Are you **frightened of** insects?

I get very **frustrated with** waiting for my brother.

My children are all **good at** sport.

They say taking half an hour's exercise a day can be very **good for** you.

People are usually very **helpful to** foreign tourists.

We're **hooked on** that new TV series – we never miss it.

Her daughter isn't **interested in** music.

My wife isn't very **keen on** moving to London.

She was very **kind to** me when I was going through a bad time.

A lot of people are **obsessed with** celebrities and their lifestyles.

Older people aren't always as **open to** big changes as younger people are.

I was very **pleased with** my presentation. I thought it went very well.

As a nation, we are very **proud of** our sporting achievements.

As Marketing Manager, I am **responsible for** all our publicity campaigns.

I'm **sick of** listening to her complain about how many hours she has to work.

The staff felt very **sorry for** us and gave us a free cup of tea.

I'm **tired of** being told what to do all the time.

verb + preposition

The police have **accused** her **of** stealing from her employer.

I think the film is definitely **aimed at** people under 25. I didn't enjoy it at all.

We're still waiting for Laura to **apologize for** her awful behaviour last night.

I've **applied for** more than ten jobs since graduating.

Everyone **blamed** me **for** the mistake, even though it wasn't my fault.

I'm so hard up I'm going to have to **borrow** some money **from** my sister.

I'm going to **complain** to the manager **about** this.

I can't **concentrate on** what I'm doing with all that noise outside.

The exam **consists of** speaking, writing, listening, reading, and use of English papers.

I'm getting much better at **coping with** stress than I used to be.

The government was heavily **criticized for** not acting faster.

My children have had to **deal with** a number of challenges.

I was **faced with** a huge pile of work when I got to the office this morning.

I want to **focus on** my work for the next few weeks.

Which historical figure do you most **identify with**?

When I visit a country, I like to **immerse** myself **in** the local culture.

Simon **insisted on** paying for everything when we went out.

It's rarely a good idea to **lend** money **to** a friend.

I was **named after** my grandmother, who died before I was born.

Eating tomatoes are said to **protect** the body **against** certain diseases.

I know I can **rely on** you to keep a secret.

My brother is a lawyer who **specializes in** criminal law.

His ex-wife **took revenge on** him by cutting up all his suits.

I need to **translate** this document **into** German. Can you help me?

I was **vaccinated against** yellow fever before visiting Ecuador.

noun + preposition

I worry about my great-aunt. She's so trusting that it would be easy for people to take **advantage of** her.

We don't have the same **attitude to / towards** animals.

The sea always has a calming **effect on** me.

He doesn't have enough **faith in** his own ability.

The police have reported a sharp **increase in** crimes involving identity theft.

I have absolutely no **intention of** resigning.

The **lack of** water is becoming a very serious problem in some countries.

There is an urgent **need for** qualified teachers to work in developing nations.

They've organized a **protest against** the new law.

The **reason for** the delay was the late arrival of the incoming flight.

My boss has asked me to write a **report on / about** the new computer system.

The new Managing Director has a **reputation for** being completely ruthless.

Jack has a lot of **respect for** his grandfather's achievements.

There doesn't seem to be an easy **solution to** the problem.

Vowel sounds

	usual spelling	! but also
fish	**i** kill drip risk idiom stick quit	message rewarding repetitive business building synonym
tree	**ee** screech fee **ea** creak treaty **e** even tedious	routine suite siege key receipt people
cat	**a** bang crash slam tap balance salary	
car	**ar** bark smart sarcastic **a** chance grant staff advantage	calf calm laugh draught heart
clock	**o** occupation obviously shock sob contract deposit	squash sausages cough knowledge
horse	**(o)or** forces snore outdoor **al (+l, +ll)** although instalment call **aw** paw claws **au** long-haul cautious	caught fought war roar pour
bull	**u** bullet pushed **oo** cooking goodness stood wood	should would woman
boot	**oo** loot troops **u*** due flu **ew** view blew	moving coup wounded through bruise suit beauty queue shoe
computer	Many different spellings – always unstressed. assertive relative practical challenging member opinion profession stubborn successful	
bird	**er** herbs nerves **ir** circuit birth **ur** slurp fur	earth learner world worse journey
egg	**e** gentle debt neck tense benefit temporary surrender	wealthy breathtaking steady friendly many said says

	usual spelling	! but also
up	**u** hum hunt gun gut stuck mussels discuss **o** above oven	blood flood tough enough couple trouble
train	**a*** wages hatred **ai** tail training **ay** away tray	great steak neighbour weight survey obey
phone	**o*** totally joke bonus post **oa** groan loaded **ow** arrow below	soulmate doughnut aubergine
bike	**i*** sniper wild wi-fi **y** deny ally **igh** sigh bright	eye neither aisle guy
owl	**ou** around amount profoundly **ow** powerful overcrowded meow	plough drought
boy	**oi** point spoilt voice choice **oy** loyal employer	
ear	**eer** career beer **ere** adhere atmosphere **ear** fear spear	period ideal weird
chair	**air** aircraft fair repair **are** fare spare	scary bear wherever there their
tourist	**ur (+r)** curious during plural **ure** mature endure secure **eur (+r)** Euro Europe	
/i/	A sound between /ɪ/ and /iː/. Consonant + y at the end of words is pronounced /i/. happy angry thirsty	
/u/	An unusual sound between /ʊ/ and /uː/. education usually situation	

* especially before consonant + **e**

☐ short vowels   ☐ long vowels   ☐ diphthongs

Consonant sounds

		usual spelling		! but also
	parrot	p	perks poached recipe deep	
		pp	apparently gripping	
	bag	b	breed bite tablet grab	
		bb	scribble bubble	
	key	c	screen economic	chorus chiropractic technician accurate
		k	skill bankrupt	
		ck	click tick	
		qu	quick picturesque	
	girl	g	grunt guided arguably drug	ghost colleague
		gg	giggle aggressive	
	flower	f	fire refugee	laugh rough
		ph	photography metaphor	
		ff	affluent sniff	
	vase	v	vast voicemail survive review government hive	of
	tie	t	track touristy strength retreat	mashed chopped debt doubt receipt
		tt	rattle settings	
	dog	d	defeat declare update crowd	steamed bored
		dd	add middle	
	snake	s	stranger responsible	scenery psychoanalyst fancy
		ss	hiss across	
		c (+ e, i)	ceasefire civilians	
	zebra	z	zip zone	dessert
		zz	buzz dizzy drizzle	
		s	misery refuses trousers avoids	
	shower	sh	shocked sheet shellfish rash	sugar sure chef cliché anxious pressure
		ti (+ vowel)	addiction operation	
		ci (+ vowel)	species crucial	
	television	An unusual sound. invasion conclusion pleasure casualties massage		

		usual spelling		! but also
	thumb	th	thorough thriller thick sympathetic breath death	
	mother	th	though therefore either nevertheless smooth	
	chess	ch	charge crunch	
		tch	switched match	
		t (+ ure)	capture sculpture	
	jazz	j	juggle enjoyable	soldier suggest
		g	cage besiege	
		dge	edgy gadget	
	leg	l	legal lively landline deal	
		ll	colleague scroll	
	right	r	revolution ribs grand scrambled	wrist wrinkled
		rr	surrender overrated	
	witch	w	wings waist willing towards	one once
		wh	whistle whisper	
	yacht	y	yell yoga yogurt yourselves	
		before u	mule consumer	
	monkey	m	mumble motivated temper consumer	limb dumb
		mm	stammer recommend	
	nose	n	nightmare internet monotonous	knowledge knight design foreigner
		nn	penniless cannon	
	singer	ng	length strong wing sting	
		before k	ankle blink	
	house	h	heat horns history inherit behave unhelpful	whoever whom whole

☐ voiced   ☐ unvoiced

Go online to watch the Sound Bank videos

OXFORD
UNIVERSITY PRESS

Great Clarendon Street, Oxford, OX2 6DP,
United Kingdom

Oxford University Press is a department of the
University of Oxford. It furthers the University's
objective of excellence in research, scholarship,
and education by publishing worldwide. Oxford
is a registered trade mark of Oxford University
Press in the UK and in certain other countries

© Oxford University Press 2020

The moral rights of the author have been asserted

First published in 2020

2024 2023

10 9 8 7 6

No unauthorized photocopying

ISBN: 978 0 19 403836 2

Printed in China

This book is printed on paper from certified
and well-managed sources.

ACKNOWLEDGEMENTS

Back cover photograph: Oxford University Press building/David Fisher

The authors would like to thank all the teachers and students round the world whose feedback has helped us to shape English File.

The authors would also like to thank: all those at Oxford University Press (both in Oxford and around the world) and the design team who have contributed their skills and ideas to producing this course.

Finally very special thanks from Clive to Maria Angeles, Lucia, and Eric, and from Christina to Cristina, for all their support and encouragement. Christina would also like to thank her children Joaquin, Marco, and Krysia for their constant inspiration.

The publisher and authors would also like to thank the following for their invaluable feedback on the materials: Paz Alonso, László Aradi, Elif Barbaros, Zahra Bilides, Brian Brennan, Philip Drury, Jane Hudson, Rosa María Iglesias Traviesas, Polina Kukharenko, Dagmara Łata, Kenny McDonnell, Magdalena Muszyńska , Lesley Poulaud, Célia Regina Bolognesi

The Publisher and Authors are very grateful to the following who have provided information, personal stories, and/or photographs: Emma Rosen p.11, Eliza Carthy p.14–15 Anna Johnstone p.28, Mary Beard p.34–35, Adrian Hodges p.32, Beverly Johnson p.38, Alessandro Savelli of Pasta Evangelists p.53, Jordan Friedman p.54–55, Jon Turner p.72–3, Quentin Blake p.74–75, George McGavin p.94–95, Olly Hogben p.98–99, David and Emma Illsley p.100–101, and the Conversation participants: Duncan Laing, Joanne Bowlt, Alice Dillon, Sean Gibson, Emma Green, Ida Berglöw Kenneway, John Bowlt, Josie Thornton, Debbie Bird, Christian Vaccaro, and Lucy Cowdery

The authors and publisher are grateful to those who have given permission to reproduce the following extracts and adaptations of copyright material: p.9 Adapted extracts from the Myers Briggs Test included in the BBC programme 'What's your personality type?'. Reproduced courtesy of Mentorn Media. p.10 Adapted from 'The radical sabbatical – this woman did 25 jobs before she turned 25' by Hilary Rose, www.thetimes. co.uk, 10.12.2018, copyright The Times/News Licensing. Reproduced by permission. p.12 Adapted text and illustration from 'What I'm really thinking: the female boxer' 30.01.2016, www.theguardian. com. Copyright Guardian News & Media Ltd 2019. Reproduced by permission. p.12 Adapted text and illustration from 'What I'm really thinking: the night receptionist' 19.11.2016, www.theguardian.com. Copyright Guardian News & Media Ltd 2019. Reproduced by permission. p.12 Adapted text and illustration from 'What I'm really thinking: the orchestral musician' 09.04.2016, www.theguardian.com. Copyright Guardian News & Media Ltd 2019. Reproduced by permission. p.16 Extract from 'Chocolates' from *Boy – Tales of Childhood* by Roald Dahl, Jonathan Cape Ltd & Penguin Books Ltd. © The Roald Dahl Story Company Limited. Used by permission of Puffin, an imprint of Penguin Young Readers Group, a division of Penguin Random House LLC and David Higham Associates. All rights reserved. p.20 Adapted text, logo and banner from 'English Spelling is broken. Let's fix it.' www.spellingsociety. org, © The English Spelling Society 2020. Reproduced by permission. p.23 Adapted from '10 words that don't mean what they used to: when meerkats were monkeys and bimbos were boys' by Paul Anthony Jones, 26.10.2016,www.theguardian.com. Copyright Guardian News & Media

Ltd 2019. Reproduced by permission. p.25 Adapted from 'How children learn language – what every parent should know' by William O'Grady, https://linguistlist.org. Reproduced by permission. p.26 Adapted from 'If you want to be a good lover, be a great hater' by Giles Coren, www. thetimes.co.uk, 10.02.2017, copyright The Times/News Licensing. Reproduced by permission. p.27 Adapted from 'Share the hate, ruin the date' by Victoria Coren Mitchell, 12.02.2017, www.theguardian. com. Copyright Guardian News & Media Ltd 2019. Reproduced by permission. p.28 Adapted from 'I swapped apps for dating in real life – this is what happened' by Anna Johnstone, www.bbc.co.uk/bbcthree/. Reproduced by permission. p.37 Adapted from 'Spoilers actually enhance your enjoyment' by Alison Flood, 17.08.2011, www.theguardian.com. Copyright Guardian News & Media Ltd 2019. Reproduced by permission. p.39 Adapted from 'Untranslatable words into English: the ultimate list' (Nov 2014), https://global-lingo.com/untranslatable-words-ultimate-list/. Reproduced with permission of the rights holder, Global Lingo. p.42 Adapted from 'Ssshhh! How the cult of quiet can change your life' by Lara Williams, 23.10.2016, www.theguardian.com. Copyright Guardian News & Media Ltd 2019. Reproduced by permission. p.45 Adapted from 'Experience: We fell in love without speaking' by Faith Ristic, 07.12.2018, www.theguardian.com. Copyright Guardian News & Media Ltd 2019. Reproduced by permission. p.46 Adapted from 'Are YOU addicted to being busy?' by Michelle Cheng, www.dailymail.com, MailOnline, 19.03.2018. Reproduced by permission. p.47 Adapted from 'Forget relaxing. What keeps you healthy is being busy, busy, busy! Wealth of research shows having plenty to do helps us live longer and may keep dementia at bay' by John Naish MailOnline,22.08.2017. Reproduced by permission. p.47 'The Chocolate Meditation' by Dr. Danny Penman and Professor Mark Williams from http://franticworld.com/. © 2015 Danny Penman. Reproduced by permission. p.48 Fictitious interview with Sam Greenspan was adapted from his book 11 Points Guide to Hooking up by permission of Skyhorse Publishing, Inc. p.51 Adapted from 'From freecycling to Fairphones: 24 ways to lead an anti-capitalist life in a capitalist world' by John Harris, 10.12.2018, www.theguardian.com. Copyright Guardian News & Media Ltd 2019. Reproduced by permission. p.52 Adapted from 'Six reasons to shop small and local' by Elaine Pritchard, 12 December 2017, www.wireuk.org. Reproduced by permission of the author. p.53 Interview with Alessandro Savelli, logo and banner from https:// pastaevangelists.com. Reproduced by permission. p.58 From Why Small Pleasures Are a Big Deal from The School of Life, 5 December 2016. © The School of Life. Reproduced by permission. p.60 Adapted from 'How to quit your tech: a beginner's guide to divorcing your phone' by Martha Hayes, 13.01.2018, www.theguardian.com. Copyright Guardian News & Media Ltd 2019. Reproduced by permission. p.65 Adapted from '7 self-care apps that will help make your life a little easier' by Tolani Shoneye, https:// inews.co.uk. Reproduced by permission. p.66 '1,342 QI facts to leave you flabbergasted' by John Lloyd, John Mitchinson & James Harkin, Faber and Faber Limited. Reproduced by permission. p.66 '2,024 QI facts to stop you in your tracks' by John Lloyd, Faber and Faber Limited. Reproduced by permission. p.68 Adapted from In the Interests of Safety by Tracey Brown and Michael Hanlon published by Little, Brown Book Group. Reproduced by permission. p.77 Adapted from 'What doctors won't do' 19.01.2013, www.theguardian.com. Copyright Guardian News & Media Ltd 2019. Reproduced by permission. p.78 Adapted from 'Forget the pills – tennis, dancing and chess are better for your health' by Peta Bee, www.thetimes. co.uk, 06.10.2018, copyright The Times/News Licensing. Reproduced by permission. p.80 Adapted from 'You can't see the Empire State Building for the top': readers on overrated tourist sights' by Guardian Readers and Rachel Obordo, 15.12.2017, www.theguardian.com. Copyright Guardian News & Media Ltd 2019. Reproduced by permission. p.85 Adapted from 'Why you always get ill on holiday and how to fight it when you do' by Caroline Jones, 19 June 2014 www.mirror.co.uk/news. Reproduced by permission of Reach Publishing Services Limited. p.86 Adapted extract from 'In defence of not liking animals' by Tim Lott, www.theguardian.com, 03.05.2013. Copyright Guardian News & Media Ltd 2019. Reproduced by permission. p.90 Adapted from The Food Lab: Better Home Cooking Through Science by J. Kenji López-Alt. Copyright © 2015 by J. Kenji López-Alt. Used by permission of W. W. Norton & Company, Inc. This selection may not be reproduced, stored in a retrieval system, or transmitted in any form or by any means without the prior written permission of the publisher. p.93 Adapted extracts from How to Eat Out: Lessons from a Life Lived Mostly in Restaurants by Giles Coren, (Hodder & Stoughton, 2012). Reproduced by permission of Hodder & Stoughton and Curtis Brown Group Ltd, London, on behalf of Giles Coren Copyright © Giles Coren 2013. p.96 Adapted from 'Battle of the workouts' by Peta Bee, 06.03.2007, www.thetimes.co.uk. Copyright Guardian News & Media Ltd 2019. Reproduced by permission. p.100 Adapted from 'Las Chimeneas' by David and Emma Illsely, www.laschimeneas. com. Reproduced by permission. p.102 Adapted from 'Go home Polish' graffiti prompts photographer's 1,200-mile walk' by Michal Iwanowski, www.bbc.co.uk. Reproduced by permission of the author. p.109 Adapted from 'Living with your parents as an adult – a survival guide' by Tom Meltzer, 21.01.2014, www.theguardian.com. Copyright Guardian News & Media Ltd 2019. Reproduced by permission. p.112 Lamb to the Slaughter and Other Stories by Roald Dahl, Jonathan Cape Ltd & Penguin Books Ltd. © The Roald Dahl Story Company Limited, 1953. Reproduced by permission. p.114 Adapted from 'The secret to... living with adult children by Camilla Palmer, 10.02.2018, www.theguardian.com. Copyright Guardian News & Media Ltd 2019. Reproduced by permission.

Sources: www.bbc.co.uk/programmes; www.datingscount.com; www.theguardian.com. courtesy of Guardian News & Media Ltd; http:// news.bbc.co.uk; http://timexgroup.com; The Speckled Band from The Adventures of Sherlock Holmes by Arthur Conan Doyle.

Although every effort has been made to trace and contact copyright holders before publication, this has not been possible in some cases. We apologize for any apparent infringement of copyright and if notified, the publisher will be pleased to rectify any errors or omissions at the earliest opportunity.

The publisher would like to thank the following for their kind permission to reproduce photographs: Advertising Archives p.16 (Cadburys advert); Alamy pp.6 (wall/Ekwisit saysuwan), 14 (Eliza and parents/Lebrecht Music & Arts), 18 (baby in pram/KGPA Ltd), 31 (The Darkest Hour/Landmark Media), 33 (The Favourite/Landmark Media), (Victoria and Abdul/ Sportsphoto), (Mary Queen of Scots/AF archive), (The Crown/Landmark Media), 34 (Roman fresco/The Print Collector), 43 (quiet zone/Trevor Mogg), 58 (Uffizi Gallery/David Burton), 70 (Lamassu/Shakeyjon), (Nelson's Ship in a Bottle/Adrian p. Chinery), 81 (Outback/Genevieve Vallee), (Mona Lisa/Iain Masterton), (Times Square/Richard Levine), 88 (B Christopher), 89 (orcas/imageBroker), 96 (running outside/MediaWorldImages), 96 (gym/ Photopat), 98 (boxing/Zoonar GmbH), (swimming/PCN Photography), 118 (hopscotch/Heritage Image Partnership Ltd), 126 (Sasha Stowe), 165 (Zoonar GmbH), 166 (tap/Witold Krasowski), 171 (hooves/Image Source); Helen Audley Photography p.100 (panorama view); Sarah Bench p.21 (Laura, Anita); Quentin Blake illustration of The BFG by permission of A P Watt at United Agents on behalf of Quentin Blake and also by permission of the Roald Dahl Estate via David Higham Associates; Bridgeman Images pp.6 (Tolstoy), (Kennedy/CSU Archives/Everett Collection), (Picasso/Private Collection), (Gandhi/Dinodia), (Tsar's daughters), (Einstein/Universal History Archive/UIG), 8 (Dali/© Gordon

Roberton Photography Archive), 110 Van Gogh, Bedroom at Arles, 1889. Musée d'Orsay, Paris; Sarah Brown Photography Ltd. pp.10–11 (all photos of Emma Rosen); CartoonStock.com pp.163 (cartoon by Fran), 170 (cartoon by Dave Carpenter); © The Roald Dahl Story Company Limited, p.16 (Roald Dahl as a teenager from Roald Dahl, Boy – Tales of Childhood, Jonathan Cape Ltd & Penguin Books Ltd) By permission of David Higham Associates; Salvador Dali Suburbs of a Paranoiac-Critical Town: Afternoon on the Outskirts of European History, 1936. © Salvador Dali, Fundació Gala-Salvador Dalí, DACS 2019. Museum Boymans van Beuningen, Rotterdam/Bridgeman Images © Gordon Roberton Photography Archive p.8; © Michael Elmgreen and Ingar Dragset, Powerless Structures, Fig 101, 2012 © DACS 2019. p.70. Photo Shutterstock/Kiev.Victor; Courtesy of The English Spelling Society p.20; Eyevine p.61 (Anisah Osman Britton and Clive Myrie/both © David Vintiner/Guardian); Getty Images pp.15 (Eliza performing/Caitlin Mogridge), 19 (girl/Hoxton/David Bradbury), 19 (brothers/Created by Lauriann Wakefield), 26 (Giles Coren/Dan Burn-Forti), 32 (Adrian Hodges/ Frederick M. Brown), 38 (sobremesa/Molly Aaker), 39 (baby/JGI/Jamie Grill), 40 (snow/SrdjanPav), 41 (chimp/Kyodo News), 42 (LeoPatrizi), 48 (FG Trade), 54 (train/Don Emmert/AFP), 56 (PhotoAlto/Ale Ventura), 58 (marriage/George Shelley), (old photos/catscandotcom), 72 (Fiona Bruce and Philip Mould/Neale Haynes), 80 (Little Mermaid/Michael Runkel), (Waikiki/M Swiet Productions), (Mount Rushmore/ RiverNorthPhotography), (Isla del Sol/Photography by Gene Wahrlich), 89 (birds/Mara Brandl), (fur coat/Yevgen Romanenko), 93 (flying tray/Mike Powell), 98 (ice-skating/David Madison), (gymnast/Kyodo News), (golf/ David Cannon), (basketball/Tom Pennington), (judo/Bruna Prado), (athletics/Paul Burns), 99 (Stig-André Berge/Valery Sharifulin), 108 & 113 (Berlin/Travis P Ball), 118 (watching ipad/Stephen Simpson), 124 (Tim Robberts), 167 (Westend61); Courtesy of Haterdater.com p.26; By permission of Hodder & Stoughton p.93 How to Eat Out by Giles Coran, 2013, Hodder Paperbacks; Courtesy of Olly Hogben p.98; iStockphoto p.22 (DrAfter123), 107 (scrambled eggs/SeanZeroThree), 111 (pgcata), 128 (bonchan); Courtesy of Mat and Kat at www.iteracy.com p.100 (Las Chimeneas logo); © Michal Iwanowski p.102; Christina Latham-Koenig p.72 (Jon Turner); Lostandtaken.com p.72 (painted background); Jaya Miceli p.90 (cover of The Food Lab by J Kenji Lopez-Alt, W. W. Norton & Company2015); Magnus Naddermier www.studionaddermier.com p.100 (David and Emma Illsley); Cover Design Orionbooks, Image © Bernd Ott/Gallerystock p.120 Gone Girl by Gillian Flynn, 2014; Oxford University Press\Shutterstock p.58 (hang-gliding/Alexandra Lande); Courtesy of Pasta Evangelists pp.52 (Alessandro Savelli), 53 (pasta box, Sfoglina); By permission of Penguin Random House front covers of Roald Dahl, Boy – Tales of Childhood and Charlie and the Chocolate Factory both illustrated by Quentin Blake pp.16–17; © Michael Rakowitz, Lamassu, 2018, part of The Invisible Enemy Should Not Exist project, by permission of the artist. Photo Alamy/Shakeyjon p.70; Courtesy of The School of Life p.58 (logo and icons); © Yinka Shonibare CBE, Nelson's Ship in a Bottle, 2010. All Rights Reserved, © DACS 2019. Photo Alamy/Adrian p. Chinery p.70; Shutterstock p.6 (frames/Peshkova), 7 (family icon/ ankudi), 20 (girl/Olivia4567), 30 (canon/Aayam 4D), 36 (Eliane Haykal), 40 (fire/ksamurkas), (bubble wrap/Maddas), (nail filing/Markus272), 41 (soup/HiCam), (motorbike/Vladimir Konstantinov), 49 (Bruce Rolff), 52 (Wayhome studio), 54 (beach/Filip Fuxa), 58 (sandwich/Vavstyle), (beach/NadyaEugene), (violinist/Artem Furman), (fig/alicja neumiler), (caviar/Africa Studio), (lily of the valley/vnlit), 65 (yoga & apple icon/ krissikunterbunt), (sleep icon/Iyikon), 70 (PowerlessStructures/Kiev. Victor), 75 (quill/Galushko Sergey), (nib/koosen), 76 (bandage/Early Spring), (red plaster/Picsfive), (doctor/Dmitriy Podlipayev), 77 (plasters/ Abramova Elena), (pills/AngieYeoh), 78 (dancing/Halfpoint), (cycling/ Sergey Mironov), (yoga/GoncharovArtem), (golf/Dragon Images), (gardening/Tretyakov Viktor), (pet/PhotoCreo Michal Bednarek), (knitting/ Fotos593), 79 (mule/Claudia Otte), (secateurs/Mitand73), (trowel/ Nakornthai), 80 (Empire State Building/GagliardiPhotography), (Machu Picchu/Seumas Christie-Johnston), 81 (Sphinx/cornfield), (Stonehenge/ David Cardinez), 86 (tabby kitten/Olhastock), (whiteish kitten/Tony Campbell), (dog facing/Sergio Schnitzler), (lamb/Eric Isselee), (rabbit/ Djem), (grey kitten and profile dog/Ermolaev Alexander), (tortoise/ fivespots), 87 (dog/Eric Isselee), (kitten/Tony Campbell), 89 (panda/ clkraus), 90 (egg shells top/goir), (egg shells bottom/xpixel), 91 (hard boiled eggs/Sommai), 92 (salad/Jakov Filimonov), (lamb/Atsushi Hirao), (tart/gurmevegan), (herb butter/joanna wnuk), (onion rings/atajetamon), (sorbet/Alexey Savchuk), 94 (ant/Andrey Pavlov), (shield bug/Eric Isselee), (plant hopper/Mr. Suttipon Yakham), (cockroach/7th Son Studio), (bee/ Allocricetulus), (wasp/irin-k), (mealworm/Michiel de Wit), (cricket/Eric Isselee), 95 (moth/Anton Starikov), (flea/Cosmin Manci), 96 (volleyball/ Ververidis Vasilis), (cycling/Ian Melvin), 103 (stick man/Janis Abolins), 105 (football/pling), 116 (Flamingo Images), 122 (Monkey Business Images), 129 (Andy Dean Photography), 166 (droplets/Claudio Divizia), (splash/Serg64), 168 (rzarek), 171 (calf/Eric Isselee), (chick/yevgeniy11), (lion cub/Eric Isselee), foal/Eric Isselee), (kid/cynoclub), (puppy/Nikolai Tsvetkov), (canary/xpixel), (bee/Allocricetulus), (goldfish/Gunnar Pippel), (blackbird/xpixel), (beak/holbox), (claws/NomadSoul), (fur/Kondor83), (fur/ inter reality), (horns/Chris Gardiner), (paws/tim elliott), shell/Pearl Media), (tail/schankz), (wings/Erni), 172 (figs/Ekaterina Kondratova), (pork ribs/ Everything), (rice/highviews), (sieve/Africa Studio), (parsley/Elena Elisseeva), (onion rings/Brent Hofacker), (whisk/Jiri Hera), (cheese/ GayvoronskayaYana), (grilled fish/svry), (mash/Dmitrii Ivanov), (chocolate/ kaband), (mince/Elena Elisseeva), (prawns/Bildagentur Zoonar GmbH), (poached egg/sengerg), (leg of lamb/Joe Gough), (scrambled eggs/Robyn Mackenzie), (bread/graham oakes), (mussels/Nadezda Cruzova), (plums/ bjphotographs), (stuffed chicken breast/Robyn Mackenzie), (toasted sandwich/Alexander Bark), (cream/Tamara Kulikova), (baking tray/Elena Elisseeva), (chopping board/Evlakhov Valeriy), (colander/Gavran333), (food processor/Sean van Tonder), (frying pan/Evgeny Karandaev), (bowl/ Andrey Starostin), (saucepan/goutam kr. sen), (spatula/Zelenskaya), (scales/Africa Studio); Shutterstock Editorial pp.23 (treadmill/Universal History Archive/UIG), 27 (Victoria Coren Mitchell/Guy Levy/BAFTA), 31 (Gladiator/Dreamworks/Universal/Kobal), 32 (Braveheart/Icon/Ladd Co/ Paramount/Kobal), 34 (Gladiator/Jaap Buitendijk/Dreamworks/Universal/ Kobal), 108 & 113 (tree/Lisi Niesner/EPA-EFE); Photo by Adam Żądło (www.adamzadlo.com)

Pronunciation chart artwork: by Ellis Nadler

Illustrations by: Agnes Biocchi/Eye Candy p.47; Lo Cole/licensed via The Guardian p.12; Mark Duffin p.96–97; John Haslam pp.144, 146, 148, 151, 162; Martin Hargreaves/IllustrationX p.115; Maguma/IllustrationX pp.46, 66–67; Klaus Meinhardt/IllustrationX pp.50, 51, 68–69

Commissioned photography by: Gareth Boden pp.28, 38 ('Ta'arof'; MM Studios pp.16 & 17 (book covers), 90 (book cover); Oxford University Press video stills pp.14 (Eliza Carthy portrait), 15 (The Conversation), 21 (Diarmuid, Jerry, Andrea, Lily, Paul, Mairi), 23 (Shakespeare), 34 (Mary Beard), 35, 38 (Beverly Johnson), 42 (Evelyn Glennie), 54 (Jordan Friedman, massage), 55, 63 (Dr Graham and phone users), 74 (Quentin Blake portrait, at desk, close-up of hands), 75 (The Conversation), 82 (Clive Oxenden), 83, 94 (George McGavin), 95 (The Conversation), 103

We would like to thank the following for their kind permission for use of locations (p.28); The Alchemist Restaurant, Westgate Oxford; Blackwell's Bookshop Westgate Oxford; Junk Yard Golf Club, Westgate Oxford.